ENCOURAGING ENCOUNTERS

Reframing time by dialogue in
the intergenerational pastoral process

Nel van Doorn

Text translated and adapted by Daniël Louw

Copyright © 2020 Biblecor
Biblecor is a division of Bible-Media
Private Bag X5, Wellington 7654
Orders: 0860 26 33 42
www.biblemedia.co.za

Design by Marthie Steenkamp
Set in Minion Pro in 12 pt on 15 pt by Marthie Steenkamp
Cover design by Natascha Olivier

Painting on cover page: *Joseph and his amazing technicolour
dreamcoat* by Daniël Louw, used with permission

First edition, first print 2020

ISBN 978 1 77616 058 7

We believe the right product at the right time
in the right hands can make all the difference.

Our aim is to provide young believers,
congregation members and leaders of our country
with a wide variety of affordable products.

Become part of our team by sponsoring products,
giving donations or supporting us financially.

Bible Media Team

Contact us at: 021 864 8268 or info@bmedia.co.za
Banking details: Bible Media, Absa, Wellington | Cheque account: 405 118 1699 | Reference: Surname and cell number

Dedicated to all my children and grandchildren

Encountering you is encouraging me!
I am grateful and privileged.

My gratitude for the financial support by the
Hans Gerlach Fonds and KerkinActie (The Netherlands).

Contents

Foreword   13

Chapter 1. Dialogue   19

1.1   **The characteristics of pastoral care: Dialogue**   19
     Genuine dialogue   20
     A counter partner   21
     The human person as object   22
     The importance of subjectivity in Nagy's thinking   24
     Dialogue: The changing and stirring of images   25
1.2   **True dialogue: John 2:1-11**   28
     The narrative: Jesus changes water into wine   28
     Different sequences of the dialogue   29
1.3   **What precedes the dialogue?**   34
1.4   **The Other/other as 'neighbour' – the quest for compassionate caregiving**   35
1.5   **Nagy: From dialectics to dialogue**   37
     Dialectics in the thinking of Nagy   37
     The ethical and relational dimension in therapeutic endeavours   39
1.6   **Dialogue in the thinking of Martin Buber – The word pair *I/Thou/it***   40
     Meeting as the acknowledgement of being   42
     The immanency of God in human encounters (Buber)   43
1.7   **Dialogue in Levinas' thinking**   44
     The ethical dimension between *I* and the *Other/other*   45
     Transcendence: The surplus of the *Other/other*   46
     The exteriority of 'God': Transcendence in the mode of infinite becoming   47
1.8   **About distance and proximity between one another**   47
     Re-positioning and habitus in caregiving (four positions)   48
     From dialogue to 'Here I am'   53

Chapter 2. The art of commitment: The availability of 'Here I am' (*Hinéni*)   55

2.1   **The calling and the answer**   55
2.2   **The hermeneutics of dialogical interpretation in biblical exegesis**   59
     The *Other/other* as text   59

Towards a Jewish reading and instruction 62

2.3 **The calling of Abraham: Genesis 22:1-19** 63

'Now-it-came-to-pass' (*way-hî* and *egeneto*) 65

The test case: A remarkable aftermath 67

A fundamental repositioning: *Hinéni* – here I am 70

The grace of answering: On becoming a subject 73

The command: Go and take! 75

Hinéni: The brief interlude between father and son 77

Moriah: Mountain of many vistas – on seeing the unseen 79

2.4 **Odysseus and Abraham** 83

The multiplicity of many different calling voices 83

Chapter 3. Loyalty 85

3.1 **Context: Inter-relationality and ethical entanglement** 86

Context: The paradigmatic optic of four lenses 88

The first dimension of facticity: Facts 89

The second dimension of psychology: Psychological consciousness and experiences 90

The third dimension of relational dynamics and interactive networking: Transactions 91

The fourth dimension of relational ethics: Care and responsibility (ethical entanglement) 93

The ethical paradigm: Core concepts 94

3.2 **An exemplification of loyalty and trustworthiness: 2 Samuel 9:1-13** 95

Chēsēd (*ḥēsēd*): Faithfulness, loyalty 96

Covenantal faithfulness: The crippled and vulnerable Mephibosheth 97

Disequilibrium in the triade: Ziba, David, Mephibosheth 99

The discomfort of David 100

The *ḥēsēd* of Rizpah: The first 'foolish mother'! 101

3.3 **Loyalty: The fibre of relational ethics** 103

Horizontal and vertical loyalty 109

The dilemma of conflicting loyalties 112

Split loyalty 113

Group loyalty 115

Loyalty in Wuppertal 116

The very powerful but also vulnerable edge of loyalty 117

Chapter 4. Giving and receiving   118

4.1   The dynamic of balancing: The movement of reciprocity   118
4.2   The significance of relational ethics   120
4.3   Genesis 38: The balance of giving and taking   122
      Judah and Tamar: An undignified, inhumane encounter (Genesis 38)   123
4.4   The balance of giving and receiving   128
      The right to give   131
      Constructive and destructive entitlement   133
      The burning question: What is meant by an appropriate mode of giving?   136
      The ledger of merit and indebtedness   138
      Parentification   139
      Different forms of parentification   142
      The sexually abused child: Violating the borders   145
4.5   The healing space of fairness   146
      Towards authentic subjectivity   147

Chapter 5. Towards mature dialoguing: The basic aspects of
timing and asymmetry   148

5.1   On becoming mature: Growing into adulthood   148
5.2   Dialoguing time: The diachronic dimension   150
      Fair memory   150
      Qualification of time: The diachronic dimension   151
      On dealing with a twofold future   153
5.3   Three aspects of dialogue in the thinking of Nagy and Krasner 153
      The first aspect: Polarisation and differentiation   154
      The second aspect: The advantage of symmetry and asymmetry   161
      The third aspect: Multi-directed partiality   164
5.4   2 Samuel 13:1-22: The case of disturbed asymmetry   165
      Violated asymmetry (sexual seduction): Amnon – Tamar   165
      Asymmetry between parent and child   171
      Exodus 20:14: The plea for loyal partnership in congeniality and kinship   171

Chapter 6. Multi-directed partiality: The quest for inclusiveness 174

6.1   The crucial role of multi-partiality: Towards a core strategy of
      inclusivity in dialoguing   175
      The pastor and helper as caregivers: The decisive role of attitude (habitus)   176

6.2	Luke 15:11-31: A father had got two sons	177
	The preceding events: The muttering of Pharisees and teachers	179
	The parable: The fair father with two sons	180
6.3	**Multi-directed partiality: A framework for inclusivity**	**184**
	The multilateral dimension in the parable	186
	Loyalty in diverse settings: The father with two different sons	187
6.4	**Siblings: The mutual interaction between brothers and sisters**	**188**
6.5	**Some basic skills contributing to a professional stance**	**192**
	Connecting listening and speech	195
	Suspension of judgement	197
	Patience: Ethics in action!	200
	Moratorium: The necessary luxury of compassionate pausing	201
	Liturgy and multi-directed partiality	202

Chapter 7. Relational ethics in "Honour your father and your mother" 204

7.1	**To honour: Obedience, obligation or ethical concern?**	**204**
	Towards the interpretation of the command	206
	The astonishing exclamation: Pastor, it cannot be true!	207
7.2	**Exodus 20:1-17**	**211**
	The words of the Decalogue: Ten wording directives for meaningful living	212
	The imperative tone	212
	Arranging and grouping the ten words	214
	Differences between the Exodus account and the Deuteronomy text	215
	Explaining the significance of the different words in the texts	217
7.3	**The dilemma of decision-making (the choice)**	**228**
	The sequence of alignments: From the fourth to the fifth to the sixth wording	229

Chapter 8. Legacy: The ethical imperative in multi-directed partiality 231

8.1	**Receiving and the passing on of legacies: The intergenerational thoroughfare passage**	**231**
	Intergenerational patterns	232
	Like a mandate	233
	Delegate: When legacies become compellable and enforceable	233
	Multi-directed partiality in the passing on of legacies in decision-making: On being partial for coming generations	234
	Transgenerational solidarity	235
	The intriguing triadic position: The intergenerational thoroughfare	238

8.2	**The impact of loyalty**	**239**
	Loyalty as stumbling block	239
	The dilemma of decision-making: The making of hard choices	241
	Legacies within diverse cultural settings: The dilemma and tension of conflicting loyalty	242
	The quest for new modes of loyalty	245
8.3	**The purification of legacies: Judges 6:25-32**	**246**
	The calling of Gideon	247
	Judges 6:25-32	248
	Conjugation of verbs: The reframing and narrating of time – 'a time as new'	249
	Space for justice: On the top of a stronghold	249
	The way through the night until dawn: The next morning	250
8.4	**The revolving slate**	**251**
	What about guilt accompanying the legacy?	254
8.5	**'Sins of the Fathers': Exodus 34:4-7**	**254**
	On evil, guilt and forgiveness	256

Chapter 9. Injustice and evil: The interplay between perpetrator and victim   **257**

9.1	**Relating to the Other/others: The art of caring and helping**	**258**
	The realm of presencing in pastoral caregiving: *Coram Deo*	258
	Basic vital existential questions	259
	Towards a dialectical attitude	260
	The ethical predicament: If we can only name 'evil'!	261
9.2	**Martin Buber: The middle position between good and evil**	**262**
	Reaching out wholeheartedly	263
	Withdrawal: The selfish monologue within the guilt of missed opportunities	264
	Connecting to evil by doing good	265
	Indecision: A whirlpool next to an abyss	266
	Tendency to do good and tendency to do evil	267
9.3	**Karl Barth: The speechlessness of naming evil (*Das Nichtige* – sheer nothingness)**	**268**
9.4	**On being human: The interplay man-woman within the framework of the knowledge of good and evil (Genesis 2–3)**	**270**
	The tree of life: The knowing of good and evil	271
	The narrow ledge of discomfort	272
9.5	**God within the realm of human coexistence: Human beings living together (the God-Cain-Abel triadic)**	**273**
	Genesis 4:1-17	273

Eve gives birth twice   275
The gift of bread and the gift of flesh   276
The shattering of visage: 'Cain's face fell to the earth'   276
A challenging gap in the text   278
And so, it happened   278
A sign of life for Cain!   279
God and Cain after the murder   280
9.6   Our vocation to the earth (*adama*)   **282**
A plea for justice   283

Chapter 10. Reframing time: Guilt, forgiveness, exoneration   285

10.1 Guilt and forgiveness within the confines of a judicial process   **285**
Guilt and forgiveness: A recurring theme   287
10.2 The place of guilt in processes of healing and human well-being   **288**
The dehumanisation of guilt   289
Guilt: An existential and relational phenomenon   291
Neglected guilt   293
10.3 Guilt and forgiveness in the thinking of Martin Buber   **295**
The turning point: Repentance   296
Our conscience   297
10.4 Joseph among his brothers   **300**
Joseph in Egypt   301
All together back in Egypt   303
The moving plea for forgiveness: Genesis 50:15-21   304
Forgiveness: Weakness under cowardice   304
10.5 Existential guilt and guilt feelings within the framework of
exoneration: More than generosity (Nagy)   **308**
Nagy's stance on forgiveness   310
Exoneration in the thinking of Nagy and Krasner   311
Right to retaliation   313
Retributive and distributive justice   315
Hope on the renewal of time   319
Towards a hopeful approach   319
10.6 Encouraged to encounter: Job invites guests at the table!   **320**

Bibliography   324

Foreword

This is what I first learned from Martin Buber: In the event of a real meeting between me and the other, we no longer experience colour, hair and skin. Details disappear. What really matters in this moment of encounter, is the mutual focus on the interaction between the *I* and the *Other/other/others*. As soon as this moment of reciprocity has passed away, we return to the happenstances of life, to sheer empirical experiences and daily observations. However, what lingers, and echoes back is the quality of the encounter. A real meeting adjusts images that people create of each other in the movement of time, hither and thither. In this way, mutual justice is established. Eventually, what remains are sparks of confidence which enkindle hope. Hope for establishing a new kind of union and companionship, other than before, founded by sincere trusting. When we are faithful to new bonds of trust, we can no longer go behind adjusted images.

This is what I have learned from Aat van Rhijn: Time after a real meeting is as *new*. In fact, time is reshaped into new forms of being and coexistence. New, not in the sense of restoration, but new in the sense of a qualitative reshaping of our being human. It is new, due to shared trust. In this way, the quality of time is readjusted in terms of a re-assessment of the now and the anticipation of the time to become. Both present and future are now being reframed with a view to justice.

True encountering is encouraging. It touches the very fibre of human existence.

The sad reality of life and relational interaction is that, often, they damage mutual trust; they even contribute to terminating bonds of trust, and, thus, discourage *hope for new timing* wherein justice is being done to one another. To put it in Buber's words: By focusing merely on the colour of hair and skin, the opinions and judgments, we become stuck in remnants of the visible, and will be hindering, and eventually preventing a real meeting. The authenticity of being-there with the Other/other, true subjectivity within intersubjectivity, is damaged and harmed. Present becomes a turnabout into regression, living merely back into the past while hope for a benevolent, humane and meaningful future becomes obstructed. Relationships stagnate, *me voici* (Levinas: I'm adressed and here I am) is silenced; what human beings can contribute to the enrichment of life and mutual well-being is hampered.

Fortunately, life can be different as well. New timing and healing are possible if people can speak openly and in confidence, based on mutual trusting. And this is where pastoral care comes into play. Those who work in caregiving constantly meet people in all dimensions and spheres of life. They encounter people in their vulnerability and woundedness due to loss of trust and hurtful relationships. They become engaged with people searching for new modes of justice. People who are desperately in need of encouragement by significant encounters that encompass everyone involved!

Encountering implies becoming involved in the networking space of interacting human beings. This space is delicate and frail indeed. Entering this space requires humility and a professional stance. However, knowledge and skills do not suffice. They are merely means in order to establish meaningful conversations. To establish trust, more than knowledgeability is required.

The basic intention of this book is to establish genuine dialogue as a kind of helping communication-structure, thereby fostering human well-being in caregiving. It will be argued that genuine dialogue brings about flexibility in human encounters, and by doing so, new perspectives are opened. A dialogue contributes to, what one may call the dignifying of the unique being of the other by means of the unique humane being-for and being-with the other.

This book seeks to contribute to the knowledge and skills of those who work in pastoral care and counseling, either professionally or as volunteers. The approach focuses on encounters between different generations as well as encounters between contemporaries. It is oriented on the 'dialogical perspective', rendered from the Hungarian psychiatrist and family therapist Boszormenyi-Nagy. His scholarly insight is most valuable for expanding the theory and vision of pastoral care. Therefore, several times in this book we will come across his name.

In addition, I wish to promote awe for Bible stories, and how narrating of human beings in their interaction with one another within the background of the echoing voice of God sheds new light on the actuality and relevance of interactional encounters. In this sense, the stories on the complexity of life but also on the healing of life underline anew the actuality of Biblical storytelling. In each chapter, I have connected exegesis with examples of encouraging encounters and dialogues in the Bible. My endeavour is to connect them with paradigmatic frameworks (patterns of thinking and conceptualisations), as well as with insightful concepts as discussed and related to significant modes of caregiving. However, I must admit that these exegeses are never complete. The encounter with the text, like any encounter with any human being, has a temporary character. But none-the-less, sometimes surprisingly, beyond rational conceptualisations, they encourage people on their journey through life, opening new perspectives on dialogue and justice.

While writing, students of the DIPP master's degree programme (DIPP is the MTh Dialogical Intergenerational Pastoral Process at the Faculty of Theology, Stellenbosch University, South Africa) surrounded my working table, despite being 10 000 km away. The DIPP is especially focused on inter-generational family pastoral care. I recall how they have challenged me several times with their critical questions about connections to their South African environment and cultural heritage. The results of their questions run through this book.

It is to be noted that the scope of the book is not strictly limited to families. The outline is also applicable to the individual, as well as to communities operating within the public sphere of life. Furthermore, the book is also of great significance for resolving conflict and facilitating greater understanding between people and cultures in general within the context of diversity.

The MTh was realised after years of collaboration between Prof Christo Thesnaar (Practical theology, pastoral care and counselling, Faculty of Theology, Stellenbosch University), Dr Hanneke Meulink-Korf, and myself. We have been working together for fifteen years in the establishing of 'contextual pastoral care'. Prof Thesnaar has been interested in this dialogical approach from the beginning, partly because of his involvement with processes of reconciliation in South Africa.

Since the 1980s in the Netherlands, Dr Hanneke Meulink-Korf, together with Aat van Rhijn, developed the *contextual pastoral care approach*. They developed it as an alternative approach to the already existing (person or family oriented) pastoral care models. Originally, this contextual approach was inspired by Boszormenyi-Nagy (from now on referred to as 'Nagy'). Scholars, such as Martin Buber, in turn inspired Nagy. Several times in this book we shall come across his 'I -thou thinking' and his contribution to reflection on the notions of guilt and guilt feelings.

Hanneke and Aat generated a relational ethical approach for pastoral care, inspired by the perspectives of Martin Buber, as well as by the philosophical reflections of Emanuel Levinas. The thinking of these scholars weaves the paradigmatic framework into the basic articulation of my thinking throughout many of my writings.

The reference to *contextual* needs to be explained, because the concept 'contextual' was too confusing in South Africa. Mostly it was interpreted as referring to the realm of situational settings and not necessarily to relational networking. Thus, the decision to subsequently rename 'the contextual pastoral care approach' to: *The Dialogical Intergenerational Pastoral Process (DIPP).*

To provide some background information, a brief introduction to the life and work of Ivan Boszormenyi-Nagy, as the founding father of the contextual therapy, is important.

Ivan Boszormenyi-Nagy was born in 1920 in Hungary. He died in 2007 in Philadelphia, USA. Nagy began studying medical psychiatry and was very interested in the biological causes for serious suffering of psychiatric-based impairments and disorders. In 1948, when he was 28 years of age, as a medical doctor and psychiatrist, he had to flee to Austria because of the rise of communism in Hungary. After two years he received permission to immigrate to the USA. After completing the required American examinations, he worked as a psychiatrist and university professor in Chicago. Later he became involved in the slums of Philadelphia engaging with people who experienced the hurtful consequences of racism on a daily basis. In his approach, he started to meet with the different generations of families exposed to serious interpretational problems. In order to address relational obstacles, Nagy searched for resources to support them by applying their own relational support systems. He recognised the deep existential connection between family members and realised the healing power residing in these existential forms of interconnectedness. It proved to be the case that these interactional connections were sometimes stronger than all the misery they were exposed to.

His attention became focused on the irrevocable interconnectedness of mutual interactions. In recognising their healing potential, he coined this interconnectedness of familial bonds as *Loyalty*. In this regard, loyalty can be rendered as the undergirding fabric of humane coexistence which (especially in times of suffering and mistrust) stimulates family members to step in on behalf of the other (substitutional), standing in for each other, even amongst young children. In working with families, he applied the principal of multi-directed partiality in order to establish fairness in his approach to all family members. As a psychiatrist he became aware of the importance of intergenerational family systems. This approach helped him to focus not only on the client suffering from illness or hurt trust, but also on family members as co-sufferers. In this regard, Nagy was one of the first researchers who emphasised relational ethics in caring and helping, and its fundamental impact on familial intersubjectivity and the balance sheet of giving and receiving. It is then, in this context, that the notions of fairness, trustworthiness, trust and loyalty play a decisive role in healing and human well-being.

In a quick overview, it is possible to detect the concepts rendered from Nagy. However, they should not be read and assessed separately. In order to become engaged in the paradigmatic framework of this publication, they should be dealt with comprehensively, as integrated with the core argument regarding encouraging encounters, and the meaning thereof for appropriate and significant forms of pastoral caregiving. I, therefore, heartily recommend to start reading from the beginning and to persist reading the publication as a whole.

On the shoulders of …

It would only have been possible for me to write this book due to the support, contribution and inspiration of so many others. I can, therefore, stand and lean on the shoulders of many people who assist me to develop a wider perspective and range of conceptualisations, especially for being sensitised to develop a fine eye for detail. It is impossible to thank everyone personally. At the same time, I will not fail to mention a few.

I want to thank my parents, children and grandchildren for their enduring trust and support.

I thank Hanneke and Aat wholeheartedly. They taught me the richness of relational ethics within all dimensions of human existence. I thank Aat for his perspective on 'time as new'. I thank Hanneke because I have journeyed with someone in my life and in South Africa. To be frank, I have never met a person who exhibited the principle of multi-directed partiality in such a convincing and consequent way.

I wish to thank Christo Thesnaar for his faithful commitment to the underprivileged, to those who struggle with poverty and injustice; his quest for justice in a post-apartheid South Africa; for the space he offered us all, and especially, for the recognition he offered me.

I thank Daniël Louw for the reciprocal playfulness in paradigmatic articulation and expressive language; for his professional approach and multi-coloured touch.

My sincere gratitude to Henry Mbaya who took me by hand to introduce me to the amazing world of African cultures.

I thank Johan de Koning for his critical eye, his most valued friendship and persistent inspiration.

Nel (Neeltje) van Doorn
Middelburg
The Netherlands
26 May 2020

CHAPTER 1

Dialogue

1.1   The characteristics of pastoral care: Dialogue

The very heart of pastoral care could be captured by the notion *coram Deo*':
To appear before God; being in the presence of the living God. Literally, to
stand before God as unique subject: Facing divine countenance within an
intimate communion.

This being in the presence of God implies that we never stand alone;
we never appear as a sole individual. Standing before God means that we
stand over against God as unique subject together with all others. It means
furthermore: Living in his presence standing hand-in-hand with the other,
and simultaneously, the other with me. Due to the mutuality in human encounters, the other is immediately implied in this interconnectedness. We
are connected to one another, to friends, to strangers within a networking
dynamic of relationality. We discover the *other* as a kind of co-partner,
coexisting mutually and cooperatively. One can, therefore, conclude that
pastoral care seeks to care for people within the humane networking of
multiple relationships: The reaching out to others in the presence of God's
compassionate being-with.

For the establishment of a relationship, mutual trust is fundamental. One
can therefore posit that dialogue is primarily the most essential characteristic
of pastoral care.

In this regard, the research done by Dr Hanneke Meulink-Korf and Dr Aat
van Rhijn is most helpful in detecting the character and hallmark of pastoral
care. They helped to develop both a relational and ethical perspective to
processes of counselling and pastoral caregiving. In a more extensive way,
they broadened the approach of the Hungarian-American psychiatrist and
family therapist Ivan Boszormenyi-Nagy (*Nagy*). They studied intensively
the relational and ethical meaning of dialogue and made use of the 'I-Thou

thinking' of Martin Buber's dialogical thinking and Emmanuel Levinas' emphasis on justice and trustworthiness as moral and ethical framework for the legitimacy of human encounters. Later in this chapter, I will return to this relational and ethical meaning of dialoguing within the framework of meaningful human encounters.

Genuine dialogue

Dialogue has become a kind of buzzword in global thinking. The mass media encourages people to participate in processes of dialoguing. However, to dialogue just for the sake of dialoguing does not necessarily guarantee true and authentic modes of human interaction. Therefore, the invitation for dialogue is not necessarily a guarantee for authentic dialoguing.

Dialogue is in fact a unique event between human beings. For example, within group dynamics and interaction between family members, dialogue establishes something new between participating individuals. To promote authentic modes of interaction, dialogue presupposes trust. It even summons participating partners to trust one another. *'Encouraging encounters' are therefore based on mutual trust.* This kind of trust cannot be established artificially. *Trust comes into being when people are willing to take responsibility for one another and to be available for the well-being of the other.* One should be devoted to the other in terms of service and diaconal outreach.

The focus on the well-being of the other cannot be manipulated or forecasted automatically. Most of times, authentic dialoguing is the outcome of significant encounters and not the starting point.

> Every year, on the first of July, the abolition of slavery is celebrated as a day of freedom in Suriname, a former Dutch colony. The heritage of slavery is also commemorated in the Netherlands because our country has had a large share of it. For example, in one of the cities in the Netherlands, the inhabitants were invited to participate in a dialoguing roundtable on slavery. The invitation stressed that the dialogue would take place on the following conditions: The dialogue will be strictly structured and take place under professional guidance and control.

This formal structuring of dialoguing and conversing cannot automatically guarantee authentic modes of insight and understanding. Only afterwards can one assess the quality of the process. The core question will be whether the process has established such a kind of trust that participating members are prepared to open towards one another and at the same time are willing to take risks.

When an authentic mode of dialogue has been established between partners, this experience of trustworthiness challenges them to proceed with ongoing encounters. It even challenges and encourages them to take risks and to become prepared to take up relationships with many other people, irrespective of possible hampering factors, whether on the side of the other person or oneself. Trustworthiness enhances a more inclusive approach in human encounters and intersubjective communication.

A counter partner

In terms of a more spiritual assessment of human encounters, trustworthiness helps one to discover the truth embedded in Genesis 2:18 where the Lord God said: "It is not good for the man to be alone. I will make a helper suitable for him." As in verse 20 'suitable' refers to the Hebrew word *nēgēd* which means a counter partner. This helper is in fact distinct of the other and operates over against the *I* of the first subject. The implication is that the other as helper is not a duplication of the speaker. On the contrary, the other is always a unique entity and a separate individual. In their interrelatedness, the two address one another in terms of their 'otherness'.

In a dialogical perspective, trustworthiness promotes and enriches the otherness of the other. It even surpasses the often scientific presupposition that one cannot penetrate the subjectivity of the other and know the other as person fully. In fact, trustworthiness nurtures the notion that in encountering, one must reckon with the fact that despite first impressions, the other is a container of many other possible dimensions. Knowing the other is to a certain extent the surprise of 'identity-discovery'. It tends to unmask the fixation of first impressions and helps the viewer to get behind the so-called personal perception; it helps one to proceed towards a more balanced and objective approach in mutual dialoguing. Rather than to fall into the trap of fixed objectifications, dialogue becomes more authentic when the encounter is guided by trust and the ethical framework of justice and fairness. It creates space for the dynamics of hope, a mode of hope for the otherness of the other. Authentic dialoguing even penetrates the fixation of perceptions that eventually could become barriers in human encounters.

This brings us to the basic intention of the book, namely, to establish genuine dialogue as a kind of helping communication-structure that fosters human well-being in caregiving. It will be argued that genuine dialoguing brings about flexibility in human encounters and contributes to what one can call the dignifying of the other by means of constructive hoping; that is, a kind of hope that focuses on the unique humane being-for the other.

The human person as object

Two world wars in the twentieth century revealed what could happen to our being human when a human being is exposed to shear objectification, that is, to be treated as a 'thing' and 'object' of inhumane manipulation, violent suppression and unjust discrimination. Over a period of five years, more than six million people were killed in concentration camps. They were ostracised to the level of becoming non-beings; they were labelled as 'Jews' in anti-Semitism or as 'homos' in homophobia.

The twentieth century was also a period wherein the impact of previous European power-expansion (imperialism) was experienced, particularly in Africa and the Americas. Colonialism robbed human beings of land and dignity due to materialistic and imperialistic exploitation. Local people were treated as 'uncivilised beasts' and as 'second-class' citizens. Due to prejudice, mostly based on skin and colour distinctions (pigmentocracy), racism classified people and robbed them of their dignity. Social life was structured according to cruel 'apartheid policies' wherein unjust systems were developed to classify people according to race, class and cultural diffe-rences. In this way, stigmatisation and racial prejudice contributed to the dehumanisation of human beings. The so-called Western civilisation became brutal constellations of inhumane exploitation leaving behind a legacy of imperialistic suppression and collective guilt.

After World War II, the international and global perspectives on our being human started to change. The notion of 'liberalism', freedom for all, and the emphasis on human rights fuelled a kind of 'new humanism' with the emphasis on basic, fundamental human rights for every human being. Hopefully, the lessons learnt regarding the paramount importance of 'human rights for all', and its implication for meaningful human existence should be maintained at all costs. Unfortunately, it seems as if the new dictators of our time act in total ignorance of the irrevocable implications of these historical lessons.

In the previous century, the holocaust in Europe stirred new philosophical reflection on human freedom and human rights. Very specifically from Jewish thinkers, as a reaction to the crisis periods inflicted by two world wars, attention was given to the question of how the brutal and inexpressible objectification of human beings could be addressed anew in order to restore justice. They all began to express the paramount importance of the interconnectedness in human relationships, the importance of a basic humane sense of belongingness, and the prominence of trust in the fostering of authentic subjectivity. In this regard, thinkers like Martin Buber, Eugen Rosenstock-Huessy and Emmanuel Levinas played a decisive role. They all tried in their own unique ways to illuminate the significance of our being a unique subject, and how impossible it is to degrade subjectivity into a dehumanised objectification.

In a very profound way, their Jewish cultural background and spiritual insight in the Talmud moulded their thinking. In the Talmud Schools, they learnt the importance of a dialectical and dialogical approach to the text of the *Thenach* (the Jewish Bible). Among teachers, scholars and students a very vivid mode of dialoguing was established. It was emphasised that the meaning of the text is never fixed. They discovered the value of a dialogical hermeneutics and the advantage of mutual discussion between teachers and scholars.

To continue with dialogue helps one to deal with different perspectives. In this dialectical way of conversing, new and different insights emerge continuously. One discovers that in the mutuality of dialoguing, truth and the significance of a text are never determined by one interpretation or the viewpoint of merely an individual. A text is a living entity and a vivid organism. The interpreting subject also adds to the meaning and unique life of the text. In a dialoguing hermeneutics, the Descartesian thesis that 'I think, therefore I am *(cogito ergo sum)*', is unmasked as a kind of irrational delusion, namely that the thinking human being and the rational analyses of the human mind detect meaning in isolation, as if the human mind with its analytical capacity is the centrum of the whole world. In a dialogical approach, the fundamental thesis is rather: *I am relating and dialoguing, therefore I am.*

In this regard, the intergenerational approach of Nagy has deeply been influenced by Martin Buber's I-thou thinking. In their research on a more contextual and relational approach to healing and therapy in caregiving, Meulink-Korf and Van Rhijn (1997) made use of both Buber's relational approach to human encounters and Levinas' ethical approach to the I-thou dynamics. Thus, their emphasis is on a more humane approach to the application of the biblical narratives in pastoral care. Their hermeneutics contributes to a better understanding of the dynamics of interrelational networking, and the necessity for a more humane approach to the founding of a biblical anthropology. Such a humane approach in pastoral caregiving should be grounded in, and directed by, biblical reasoning. It is within this context that authentic and genuine dialogue should be viewed as decisive in processes of caregiving that intend to contribute to a qualitative and more pastoral approach to human well-being.

> During the First World War it became clear to me that a process was going on which before then I had surmised. This was the growing difficulty of genuine dialogue, and most especially of genuine dialogue between men of different kind and convictions. Direct, frank dialogue is becoming ever more difficult and rarer; the abysses between man and man threaten ever more pitilessly to become unbridgeable. I began to understand at that time, more than thirty years ago, that this is the central question for the fate of mankind. Since then I have continually pointed out that the future of man as man depends upon the rebirth of dialogue (Buber, *Hope for this hour*).

The importance of subjectivity in Nagy's thinking

For Nagy, acknowledgement of subjectivity is a kind of fundamental a priori within these relationships where more than two persons are relationally involved because they are indissolubly connected to one another. His concern is to emphasise that in all connections the person is in the centrum and how he/she is connected to a third – the other.

It is quite remarkable, that for Boszormenyi-Nagy and Krasner (1986:73), the first aspect of dialogue is about polarisation/differentiation. When differences between people are acknowledged and articulated, it is possible for human beings to start trusting the trustworthiness of the other. To trust the otherness of the other is indeed a risk. One can accept the presupposition that every human being puts a kind of reserve on trusting the integrity of the other. Trusting is indeed a challenge for human souls. Trusting is a hazardous undertaking because one must be prepared to sacrifice something. The pitfall in relationships is often the attempt to defend oneself. This mode of self-defence needs to be rejected. One needs to be prepared to acknowledge one's own vulnerability. The challenge in processes of dialoguing is not to start objectifying oneself. This challenge is also applicable in processes of connecting to the other, namely, not to objectify the other and to establish the subjectivity of the other.

Dialogue: The changing and stirring of images

The important point Nagy wants to make, is that individuation does not mean static self-maintenance. The process of individuation implies change. Both the I, as well as the image of the other, are exposed to change and transformation. Dialoguing changes images and perspectives.

True dialogue is subjected to surprise and unpredictability. It is indeed a surprise when one discovers within dialoguing that the outcome is never the same as the starting point. The discovery that the previous image of the other has changed, and that one cannot anymore maintain the 'older image', is part of the dynamics of relational encounters. To maintain the previous fixed image can be rendered as a breach in mutual trust.

The point is: Within the dynamics of the dialoguing processes, new ideas, perceptions and perspectives are being created anew. Dialoguing is primarily about space and place. It encompasses timing as well. All these facets contribute to the surprise of changing images, whether expected or unexpected. Even the shock of new impressions contributes to the renewal of time and space and the quality of life. Our self-image and self-understanding are constantly being affected. The value of our being human and need for acknowledgement become subjected to the dynamics of dialoguing so that one can categorically make the following statement: The value of humane existence, how we behave towards others, is not solely dependent on individual qualities, but evolved within the dynamics of intersubjective encounters; it emerges from the movement between my-self and the countenance of the other.

The act of dialoguing is in principle about the dynamics of interaction within the networking of relationality. After a genuine dialogue, a relationship is never the same as before. Something new comes into being. To discover in the other more than what can be observed, is to start justifying the subjectivity of the other; sparks of justice become visible within the mutuality of human encounters. Genuine dialogue qualifies the meaning of life and contributes to the humanisation of our being human. It even transforms time and our daily orientation within the different happenstances of life. Dialogue in this sense, can be described as a feature of our daily existence. It supersedes the narrow boundaries of 'now' (present tense) and stretches back into the past as well as forward into the future. That shows the importance to reckon with the fact that to live life meaningfully is not merely a generational challenge. *Meaningful existence is intergenerational; it exceeds the limitations of time and probes into the dimension of the not-yet.* It underlines the reason why dialoguing is an expression of the future tense of meaningful living and the fostering of a vivid hope.

One can conclude and say that processes of dialoguing cannot be fixed or structured according to static principles; it cannot be encapsulated by the parameters of merely time and space; it is not a commodity that can be used to exploit the other. Dialogue is about the ontic feature of creative hope and the outcome of trustworthy intersubjectivity. Authentic dialogue overcomes barriers and prevents stumbling blocks like distrust and the separation of human beings due to stigmatisation, unfair prejudice, social discrimination and cultural schisms. It exemplifies the nurturing of our being human by means of trust and friendship. Authentic dialogue fosters true relationship. This existential truth, which is the core focus of this chapter, is delicately illustrated in the story of *The Little Prince*.

The *Little Prince* (French: *Le Petit Prince*) is a novella by French aristocrat, writer, and aviator Antoine de Saint-Exupéry. During World War II, he landed by accident in the desert and thought his life was over. Reflecting on the events, he wrote the small book: *The Little Prince*. This literary jewel could be called a brief philosophy on meaningful existence and life on our planet. It captures the true meaning of interconnectedness and a sense of belonging. He has to learn through the experience of a little fox, what bonding means and implies.

The little fox remarked and said: "If you need a friend, then you will have to tame me." The prince asked: "What does it mean to be tamed?" The fox replied: "That is a quite forgotten concept. To be tamed means to be connected, it is about a kind of bonding." "Bonding?" asked the prince. "Yes, indeed," said the fox. "For me you are just a small youngster as all the other young foxes. And I don't need you. For you, I am merely a fox as all other foxes. But if you start taming me, we will desperately need one another. Then you will become unique to me in this world, and, inversely, I will become unique for you in this world as well"... "If you really need a friend, please tame me!" said the fox. "Well then, what must I do?" said the prince. "You need to display more patience," replied the fox. "Well, in the first place, please remove yourself from me and sit on the grass over there. I am going to observe you stealthily and please keep quiet. Words only create misunderstanding. However, you can come and sit nearer and nearer to me each day ... Taming each other implies trusting." Eventually one grows into befriending. At the end of the story, the fox captured the gist of the narrative and discourse: Taming the other implies the continuity and trustworthiness of responsibility. It fosters genuine dialogue.

In the encounter between the prince and the fox, the novel illustrates what genuine bonding is about. The fox explained his desire to be tamed and, thus, taught the prince to tame him. Taming implies to move from the ordinary to the small unacknowledged experiences wherein one is treated as very special and unique. The acknowledgement of being unique gives trust in trusting the trust of the other. So, we come closer in establishing a fair distance and safe proximity.

> One only understands the things that one tames ... Men have no more time to understand anything. They buy things already made at the shops. But there is no shop anywhere where one can buy friendship, and so men have no friends anymore.[1]

1   From *The Little Prince*. Online: https://www.shmoop.com/study-guides/literature/little-prince/ fox. Accessed on 3 January 2020, p 35.

The previous outline helps one to understand what dialogue and trust are about. Dialogue and trust penetrate time and change temporality into the exciting venture of something new; time as not merely renewal in the sense of repetition (sameness) but time as 'bright new'. Dialogue and trust establish moments of hope and justice. They address the obstacles that resist trust and hamper the fostering of true dialogue. And this is what my first chapter is about. Insight into the significance of dialogue is the key to understanding the dilemma of broken relationships between persons, generations, cultural and ethnic groups, and desperate attempts to restore relationships by exploring new avenues to start with a fresh beginning. The value of the novel (*The Little Prince*) resides in the fact that the fox very aptly remarked that friendship is not a commodity to be bought 'for sale' in a shop. People think they can buy everything. But by emphasising that trust is not a commodity, the little prince must learn that it cannot be bought and is unenforceable. Trust comes into being where somebody dares to start speaking. This starting point is often frail and unsure, but eventually it can envelop into a significant conversation.

1.2   True dialogue: John 2:1-11

The enduring value of an authentic encounter is illustrated in a very profound way in the Gospel of John (John 2:1-11, NIV). In this pericope we have Jesus' first dialogue which has been started by Mary. Jesus, his mother and disciples have been invited to a wedding. Therefore we are going to focus on the dynamic of this unique dialogue. Noteworthy is the fact that the whole conversation in the text is structured in a dialogical way.

The narrative: Jesus changes water into wine

> [1]On the third day a wedding took place at Cana in Galilee. Jesus' mother was there, [2]and Jesus and his disciples had also been invited to the wedding. [3]When the wine was gone, Jesus' mother said to him, "They have no more wine."
>
> [4]"Woman, why do you involve me?" Jesus replied. "My hour has not yet come."
>
> [5]His mother said to the servants, "Do whatever he tells you."
>
> [6]Nearby stood six stone water jars, the kind used by the Jews for ceremonial washing, each holding from twenty to thirty gallons.

[7]Jesus said to the servants, "Fill the jars with water"; so they filled them to the brim. [8]Then he told them, "Now draw some out and take it to the master of the banquet." They did so, [9]and the master of the banquet tasted the water that had been turned into wine. He did not realize where it had come from, though the servants who had drawn the water knew. Then he called the bridegroom aside [10]and said, "Everyone brings out the choice wine first and then the cheaper wine after the guests have had too much to drink; but you have saved the best till now."

[11]What Jesus did here in Cana of Galilee was the first of the signs through which he revealed his glory; and his disciples believed in him.

[12]After this he went down to Capernaum with his mother and brothers and his disciples. There they stayed for a few days.

Different sequences of the dialogue

The apostle John describes a wedding that is taking place. However, quite amazingly, there is no bride. Furthermore, there is no water ready and available for the purification ritual, and, if we take what Maria said literally, it is stated that 'there is no wine'. No bride, no wine but indeed a bridegroom. His only function is to receive credit for the more excellent wine. In the rest of the sequences, he plays no further role than merely to be present.

On the third day a wedding took place at Cana in Galilee. Cana was a very small village just above Nazareth. The third day resonates with the third Genesis day of the creation narrative. This is the day when God separated the water (sea) from the dry ground. It was about the greening of the earth and the production of vegetation. The earth became a living space for human beings. One can trace this remarkable event and exposure to a living space back in many cases where the third day in the Bible indicates a kind of timing, indicating a radical change. Time is reframed as a qualitative, quite different entity. The events in Cana are therefore quite remarkable in the sense that something very unique is going to take place.

In terms of the experience of the evangelist John, in this third day lurks an existential moment in his personal life, namely the ending or fulfilment of his gospel, pointing in this sense to the third day of the resurrection of Christ. This kind of hour and *Kairos*-moment is, in terms of the current very peculiar wedding, still not-yet. This metaphorical reference to the resurrection day does not imply that the current wedding is not genuine. Twice John referred to the reality of this wedding.

At the wedding, the mother of Jesus is present while his disciples are summoned to a calling. Quite remarkable, in these first words between Jesus and his mother, he never addressed her as Mary. When she starts to speak, she conveys the predicament that there is a shortage of wine. She turned to Jesus and said: "They have no more wine." In this translation extra words are added, namely 'no more' wine. However, that is not written in the original text. The mother shared the factuality of the shortage of wine without insinuating that there was wine available beforehand. She was merely describing the desperate situation and predicament concerning the fact that it was a wedding festivity. She asks nothing from Jesus. She does not ask him to do something. It is only an open appeal. The account does not compel the other publicly. It is indeed an open question what motivated this mother to approach her son. What then is indeed her responsibility in this case? Could it be perhaps for the guests, the bridegroom, or the absent bride? On behalf of whom did she act and become a spokesperson? My hunch is not to answer this question, because any attempt to suggest an answer robs this kind of questioning of its awe and open-endedness.

Jesus then responded to the request of his mother in a very strange way. It caused a lot of confusion and controversies in exegetical circles. Literally it is written: "What's up to me and you woman?" (What have we in common?) (What have you to do with me?)

This very peculiar sentence is often interpreted as if Jesus is rebuking or even reprimanding his mother. It seems as if he is disclaiming any connection with her. However, what Jesus' answer entails is captured by a Hebrew expression with two possible exegetical options (Brown 1966:99).

a)   When one party obstructs another and it points to injustice,
     the wronged party could respond by saying: "What have I done
     inappropriately to deserve such a treatment; what exactly is the bone
     of contention?"

b)   The second possibility comes into play when somebody is asked to
     become involved and is not sure whether the issue at stake corresponds
     with the intention of the other. It is then possible that one can respond

as follows and say: "What's up to me and you?" This response opens the possibility to refuse of becoming involved in an improper way.

The implication of Jesus' response to his mother is not that he rebuked her but that he reframed the issue, namely, that they should respond in an appropriate way; that is, if the issue at stake is actually not their concern and responsibility, they should rather not become involved.

What needs our attention is the reference to *woman* in Jesus' answer: "Woman, why do you involve me?" Commentaries interpret this rather strange remark as an indication of detachment. However, in terms of Hebrew custom and tradition, it is rather a mode of courtesy and a title given to a woman who gave birth to a son (Mt 15:28; Jn 4:21; 8:10). For a second time Jesus called Mary 'woman' at the cross: "Woman see/behold your son" (Jn 19:26). Jesus did not reduce his mother to the level of becoming merely a woman in relationship with her dying son. He transposed her to the dimension of a unique identity, distinguished from him as her son. They are not absorbed into a kind of simplified 'sameness' or familial loyalty. Both are unique in terms of their position towards one another: She is mother, and he is son. They do not overlap in a kind of sameness; each one of them is acknowledged in his and her otherness.

Jesus responded and made a profound statement: "My hour has not yet come." The reference to 'my hour' is indeed intriguing. Which hour? Is Jesus trying to soothe and console his mother? Or is Jesus asking patience? Does Jesus refer to merely an event or to time as an indication of eschatology and the fulfilment of God's messianic promises: Kairos-time? Does 'hour' indicate his death or resurrection or the completion of his mission? Does John in his writing connect these words with the hour of Jesus' dying, or is he trying to alert the reader/hearer with this first appearance of Jesus, that the hour of his imminent resurrection is in becoming; that remarkable hour, namely, that surpasses the impression of the cross as being the disastrous ending of Jesus' mission?

The reference to 'my hour' sounds more like a foreboding. Perhaps as a sign; as an indication of an inclusive mode of hope, as a promise that is not restricted to one specific day but operates as a blessing that sets in with this hour; a time that transcends the desperate and bleak prospective of this very strange wedding festivity.

It is indeed interesting that, after these words of her son, Jesus' mother proceeds in a very calm and convincing way. Just as if she knows about something that is going to be disclosed. *His mother said to the servants, do whatever he tells you.* It is as if she just knows something is going to happen and that her son is going to take action. Her remark becomes a gesture of trust and indication of trustworthiness. Her summoning represents a kind of authority, an imperative that does not reside in her own capacity. It is witness of an authority that resides in the authority of Jesus. It exemplifies a spirituality of trust that emanates in courageous hoping, superseding the factuality of merely seeing and observing. The imperative is about a not-yet that will definitely be realised. Therefore: Just do it!

Hereafter followed three imperatives from Jesus: "Fill the six (empty) jars; fill them to the brim." Converted into litres, it was approximately 400/500 litres of water. Then followed the second and third imperatives: "Now draw some out and take it to the master of the banquet." The rather unobtrusive 'some' provides a very terse but exciting perspective. Nowhere is written that a miracle has been performed when 100 litres of water start to flow as wine. The reference is merely to the act of drawing, perhaps a container, a sudden gulp and mouthful of liquor and the possible surprise that water has become wine. In a very strange way, the 'unobtrusive some' sounds like the eucharist, a real wedding fest!

The wine that has been drawn from the jar must be carried from Jesus … but to whom? Not in the first place to the bridegroom but to an unexpected third: The *arché* of the table, the master of the banquet. He will be the first to discover that the drawn water proved to be indeed wine. But very important, excellent wine, the very best! But who is this person? Very interesting, John left the question open-ended. And now, at this moment there is gesture to the bridegroom who remainded invisible until this moment. Surprisingly, he received the acknowledgment for presenting such excellent wine at this very late stage. "Everyone brings out the choice wine first and then the cheaper wine after the guests have had too much to drink; but you have saved the best till now." And now very suddenly, both the *arché* and bridegroom disappeared from the scene. It is now only the servants who realised who the one was that could make water taste like wine. Surprisingly, not even the disciples.

In his account, it seems as if John is suddenly making a very abrupt end to his description of the wedding: *What Jesus did here in Cana of Galilee was the first of the signs through which he revealed his glory; and his disciples believed in him.* One starts to wonder whether the festivities proceeded after the miracle. What happened to the bride? These questions are perhaps, in terms of the account of the Gospel, not that important. What John wanted to narrate, was achieved. In fact, he started his Gospel regarding Jesus with: *En arché.* The becoming reality of this Word was, from the beginning, the main issue on his agenda. In this way his Gospel is connected to the *arché* of the beginning; that is, the very beginning as in Genesis 1. This *en arché* of the Word became herewith visible at Cana in Galilee; it was revealed in a sign. He thus proceeds with the Gospel while making an important addition: The disciples put their faith in Jesus. After the excitement of the wedding, they started going down to Capernaum, that is, Jesus with his mother, his brothers and disciples, to stay there for a few days.

What still remains afterwards, are the words spoken between Jesus and his mother; words that serve as a transition to change, a change that could be rendered as fruitful and indeed good. The account and answer took place within the respectful realisation of being different. It was done within an acknowledgement of each one's otherness, as if their roles fit this kind of fundamental differentiation. The dialogue between Jesus and Mary underlines the asymmetry of their subjectivity. It illustrates the dynamic movement of intersubjectivity. It reveals the importance of what had to be done in order to display the doksa of love that evokes the festivity of life.

It is quite remarkable that in the encounter between Jesus and his mother, the guests at the wedding were present indeed but stayed in fact inaudible. They appear as a kind of 'third party' – the so-called other. They are the so-called 'silent audience'. The whole narrative and conversation took place on their behalf.

According to Eugen Rosenstock-Huessy, this kind of dialoguing is bearer of fruitful discussions and humane encounters. It contains the seed of completion, renewal and new beginning. One can call this kind of speech, eschatological verbalisation; it creates future. In a very clear and illuminated way this is exactly what John wanted to demonstrate.

1.3   What precedes the dialogue?

The fundamental preceding factor for the establishment of authenticity in dialoguing and human encounters is a calling. It is about a calling away from becoming encapsulated in self-absorption into the open space of other-acknowledgement and responsible co-humanity. Calling and summoning function as indicators for change; they challenge human beings to move from exclusivity into inclusivity. Summoning to change is a vital element in the establishment of a genuine dialogue. Rosenstock-Huessy (1996:28) refers to this calling as *respondeo etsi mutabor*: "I respond, although I will be changed." In this sense, the calling summons one into a mode of *respond*-able *responsibility*.

At stake, in the summoning, is the question: Who or what is the authoritative entity that is making an appeal to the *I* to respond? Who or what is the key summoning factor in relationality and intersubjective networking?

Within the dynamics of intersubjectivity, the imperative comes from the *Other/other*. Although subjectivity is the fundamental a priori for authentic being and individuation, it is the *Other/other* that summons me to become a subject.

According to Emmanuel Levinas, it is the *Other/other* that summons me into true humanity. Due to this calling, it is virtually impossible that the *I* becomes the centre of authentic being. On the contrary, calling implies that the *I* is under the domain of the *Other/other*. Calling is about being invited to move away from my-*self*; I am enthroned and become subjected to the authority of the *Other/other*. As subject my new status is *subjectus*. Subjectivity is, therefore, about the very strange ontic paradox: I am both free but immediately unfree; I am dominated by the *Other/other* due to an ethical imperative, namely the *demand* and *command* of becoming a humane and trustworthy being. Therefore, the relationship between *I* and the *Other/other* is basically ethically structured.

The ethical imperative is a strange mystery. In terms of Emmanuel Levinas' understanding of dialogue, humane encounters are about transcending. Encountering the other is the shocking discovery: *I am there*, with, and, *for* the other. That is then the ethical character of genuine dialoguing.

Eventually, to identify and trace back the calling factor, the who within the demand and command, is very difficult indeed. Most of times, the who is detected afterwards. However, in many cases, the who tends to be unidentifiable. What one detects is merely a trace or sign. Even the content of my answer, is difficult to detect.

The point is, even though the 'what' of my answer is difficult to pinpoint, the fact that I answered is of paramount importance. What really counts is that in my answer I discover that, in my wording, gaze and gesture, I have become a human being for somebody else; in fact, *I* have become an *other* for the other. What resonates in me is a trace of the *Other/other* that has been captured and acknowledged by me. The advantage of being called by the *Other/other* is that I myself has been acknowledged and been recognised in time and space. Both the *I* and the *other* have been justified, and, in this sense, life has gained the quality of trustworthiness.

What is of paramount importance is the quality of my response while encountering the face of the other, because in this moment I am challenged by the ethical imperative emanating from the presence of the *Other/other*. In the parable of the caring Samaritan, one discovers that not every human being will respond to the woundedness of the other (Lk 10).

1.4 The Other/other as 'neighbour' – the quest for compassionate caregiving

The narrative describes a human being on his way from Jerusalem to Jericho. The person was attacked by robbers and stripped of clothes, beaten and left as dead. It so happened that a priest and a Levite passed by. One can say that the *official church* passed the *dead man*. After their important official meetings, their minds were full of memories regarding the performed religiosity and many rituals in the temple. They deliberately turned a blind eye. It so happened that a Samaritan passed by as well. He was indeed a stranger. But when he saw the man, he took pity and was moved by an intensified feeling of sincere compassion.

Pity describes a very deep and sincere movement of the entrails. The word to describe this inner movement is *splanchnizomai*. This word is used several times in the Gospels when the need and predicament of suffering human beings are at stake. It also describes the deep-seated pity and compassion of God (*ta splanchna*; the verb *splanchnizomai*). *Splanchnizomai* refers to the movement of the entrails and encompasses a form of existential pain – the ontic movement of compassionate being-with. In the Hebrew context, *splanchnizomai* is closely related to *rachamim* – the nurturing space of the uterus and the contracting movement though which our being human comes into existence.

The bowel categories of pity moved this Samaritan even though there was a huge racial and social schism between the Jews and the Samaritans. According to Luke 10:34-35, the Samaritan transcends all forms of social and cultural prejudice by means of pity. "He went to him and bandaged his wounds, pouring on oil and wine. Then he put the man on his own donkey, brought him to an inn and took care of him. The next day he took out two denarii and gave them to the innkeeper. 'Look after him,' he said, 'and when I return, I will reimburse you for any extra expense you may have.'"

In terms of Luke 10:25-29, the parable is an answer and exposition on the question of the biblical expert in the law. He asked and put a test case before Jesus: "Teacher," he asked, "what must I do to inherit eternal life?" The painful answer: The sacrificial challenge of becoming a neighbour to the suffering other. The suffering other, the human being in need mirrors back the question in the form of a 'new command': The *I* should become an *other* to the other.

The dialectics are not about becoming equal partners in a 'compassionate business'. The dialectics are not between equals but due to asymmetry, between unequal entities; between two people who, to a large extent are foreigners to one another, and thus always unknown strangers to one another. Due to disproportionality, encounters are therefore always open to surprise and awe. Between two human beings, encounter is embedded in a mysterious space even before the spoken word. In the encounter the gaze between human beings probes into a void space as if one stares into the abyss of being, hearing the cry of a desperate soul.

This desperate call for becoming a neighbour and compassionate carer is aptly captured by Psalm 42:6-7 (NIV). "My soul is downcast within me; therefore, I will remember you from the land of the Jordan, the heights of Hermon – from Mount Mizar. Deep calls to deep in the roar of your waterfalls; all your waves and breakers have swept over me." This calling resonates to a large extent with the very prompt and rather abrupt remark of Jesus' mother: They do have no wine.

When the recalling of this Psalm is merely a recitation in the head and not a vibration in the heart, when the Psalm is merely used to maintain oneself and not to focus on the depth of the call, and not a wake-up call for compassionate engagement, the hearer becomes stone deaf like the Levite and the priest in the parable. It is then that piety becomes merely the recitation of a text within one's head in order to turn the head away from the reality that is making an appeal to one's heart. It is then that one does not recognise the deep void abyss in one's own existence. The hearer becomes stone deaf indeed. One does not respond and answer; one avoids the challenge of becoming a neighbour to the other.

Only then neighbouring becomes a compassionate outreach like an exodus towards the need of the suffering other (Van Rhijn & Meulink-Korf 1997:282; 2019:279). It is then that dialogue becomes authentic because the hearer is called to move from a self-maintaining monologue to a co-existing prologue wherein reciprocity (Martin Buber) is transformed into co-humanity. Hearing the voice of the other is to be summoned into the responsibility of compassionate being-with.

> The voice must not only be listened to, it must be answered and led out of the lonely monologue into the awakening of dialogue between peoples. Peoples must become engaged in the art of talking to one another if 'the great peace' is to appear and the devastated life of the earth renews itself. The great peace is some-thing essentially different from the absence of war (Buber, *Hope for this hour*).

1.5   Nagy: From dialectics to dialogue

The connection between dialogue and dialectics is quite complicated. Even the notion of reciprocity as linked to mutuality and intersubjectivity differs from the formalised schematisation of the traditional understanding of dialectics. Thus, it remains a challenge to get clarity on how authentic dialoguing is related to both dialectics and reciprocity.

Dialectics in the thinking of Nagy

The dialogical perspective in Nagy's intergenerational dynamics made use of the I-thou dynamics in Martin Buber's interpretation of reciprocity (Bos-zormenyi-Nagy & Krasner 1986:33). In this regard, Nagy refers to Maurice Friedman's research on Buber's thinking: Martin Buber: *Life of Dialogue* (1995).

According to Nagy (Nagy and Spark 1973:19), "… the dialectical approach defines the individual as partner to a dialogue, that is, in a dynamic exchange with his/her counterpart: the other or non-self." In this context, the interplay between dialectics and dialogue comes into play again.

For the further discussion, it is important to get clarity on the question of how Nagy interprets dialectics. Dialectics is in principle a relational issue and not an automatic structure of dialoguing. The dynamics of dialoguing is embedded in asymmetry. The mutual dynamics of giving and receiving is, therefore, not self-evident. It is also not structured in a formal logic construction of theses, antitheses and syntheses as in the Hegelian triad. Reciprocity is definitely not about the psychology of behavioural responses. For Nagy, dialectics is an ethical endeavour.

Dialectics is embedded in an ethical framework of reciprocity as determined by the notions of care and responsibility. Exchange is not automatic but a qualitative category dependent on the ethos of calling and responsive 'hearing'; on sensitive 'seeing' and compassionate 'engaging'. Reciprocity and mutuality cannot be calculated and manipulated as a tit for tat business. It can only be evaluated in terms of an ethics of caring responsibility.

With reference to a case study, the dynamics within a very strict and pious family explains the impact of dialectics amongst siblings and the parent-child interaction. Jan was part of a very religious family system with too many children. It was difficult for Jan's parents to spread their attention evenly and in a fair manner. Each child that believed differently and deviated from their parents' religious convictions became excluded from important family events, sessions and moments. In this way, various children received special treatment while others not – the so-called favourite child. So, it happened that when Jan, as the eldest son who met a girl who did not belong to any church or religious affiliation, came home, every weekend unfortunately ended in destructive quarrels. Jan then decided to leave his family for keeps and departed for a foreign country. Many years later, he conveyed that his decision to leave was an attempt to make things within the family system easier for his parents, so that they could deal with the complex family dynamics. However, when reflecting, he realised that he missed his brothers and sisters desperately. It also dawned on him that this kind of loss, and the cost attached to the leaving of the sibling system, was too high. But now it was too late to turn back the clock.

The case illustrates the dynamics of dialectics and loyalty. In his exposition of dialectics, Nagy was convinced that in the mutual dynamics between people who are interconnected, dialectics forms a kind of pushing power-pressure within the dialectic of yes and no, of being connected (attachment) and disconnection (detachment). But dialectics is never a mechanistic system. It also does not operate autonomously. It is not about the exchange of commodities, and, very precisely, not about the logic of causality and fixed predictions. Dialectics is about a vital process of interconnectedness. "The dialectical resolution is never a bland, grey compromise between black and white, it is living with live opposites" (Nagy & Spark 1973:19).

The ethical and relational dimension in therapeutic endeavours

The implication of Nagy's attempt to reframe dialectics within the parameters of ethics and genuine dialoguing is that theories regarding the individual and personality become more relational and open to the realm of trust and responsibility.

A relational and ethical approach also has implications for the notion of autonomy. Autonomy is not attained through merely self-assertiveness, but by means of heteronomy. Networking in an intergenerational approach becomes linked to a trans-generational ledger and mandate that opens up new options for freedom and responsibility. It even reframes care in the sense that the concern for the well-being of the other is not only focused on past events and the happenstances of the present but also on the future of coming generations. A more mature approach to autonomy implies that one must reckon with advantages for multiple partners over a longer period. It includes appropriate structures that benefit coming generations as well (Van Rhijn & Meulink-Korf 1997:116; 2019:110).

For Nagy, dialogue is dependent of a very specific understanding of reciprocity, namely, that the partners are unequal. In the reckoning with the other, the notion of balance and the exchange between giving and taking are always exposed to the dynamics between fairness and unfairness. The texture of the balance oscillates between different forms of gradation; that is, between what is fair and what not. Symmetry is never without the factuality of asymmetry. Therefore, the process of becoming a person and individual is always embedded in the asymmetry of reciprocity. The further implication is that identity cannot be structured without the other/others. It is totally dependent from the dynamics of giving and receiving and open for both the possibilities of fairness and unfairness.

The advantage of a dialogical point of departure is that it describes subjectivity within the multiple dynamics of two selves, interacting mutually with one another. This interaction between selves should be studied from a multiple subjective vantage point and not from the helicopter position of an outsider. This is exactly what Nagy had in mind when he started to wrestle with the question of how to structure caregiving and helping so that the subjectivity and individuality of the two selves stay intact and do not become objectified from an 'above-position' (a helicopter view).

To return to the notion of authentic dialoguing, the argument thus far is that, in order to become a reliable and trustworthy person, one is totally dependent on the other. Dialogue is the most authentic and original mode of human existence. Together with many 'selves', one is absorbed in the dynamics of an I-thou relationship. In this regard Martin Buber's reciprocity-structure for authentic dialoguing is most valid.

The texts of the German philosopher Martin Buber played a notable role in Nagy's paradigmatic reinterpretation of psychotherapy and its very narrow focus on the intra-psychic processes of the human person. In this regard, Buber's enigmatic publication, I-Thou' (Ich und Du), made a huge impact on Nagy's application of systems theory, especially the application of the 'familial between' within intergenerational interaction (Van Rhijn & Meulink-Korf 1997:157).

1.6   Dialogue in the thinking of Martin Buber – The word pair I/Thou/it

One must understand that intersubjectivity is about the complexity of many different layers of interrelatedness, operating within different contexts. Contexts are multiple-structured and multi-dimensional. In this regard, it is noteworthy to take cognisance of different philosophical models explaining the complexity of authentic dialoguing.

The value of the research of Van Rhijn and Meulink-Korf (1997) resides in the fact that they recognised that, despite mutual differences, Martin Buber, Franz Rosenzweig, Eugen Rosenstock-Huessy and Ernst Simon formed a new pact regarding the interpretation of existential life problems. They called their thinking and methodology a new thinking and a paradigmatic renewal. The new paradigm was to view intersubjectivity as the beginning and origin of authentic human existence. Nagy's new approach to therapy should be understood against this philosophical background.

The basis for dialogue in Buber's thinking is the subject-subject relationship, that is, the dynamics of intersubjectivity. The attitude of human beings is determined by the word pair: *I/Thou* and *I/it*. The *two I's* are not the same and oscillate indefinitely between *I/Thou* and *I/it*.

In the introduction to *I-Thou*, Buber therefore distinguishes between two basic modes of being. One mode is about the word pair: *I-Thou*. The other mode is about the word pair: *I-it*. In the *I-Thou* relationship the subject-subject dynamics are at stake. The *I* orientation takes place in close connection with another subject. In the *I-it* relationship, the *I*-object dynamics (subject-object) are at stake. The *I* orientation takes place in close connection with an object, things and events.

Thou can also become *you*. *It* can also become *he/she*. The pronouns are therefore many layered (Buber 1988). Without *thou* or *it*, the posing of *I* becomes impossible.

For Buber, the word pair *I/Thou* can only be pronounced with the dedication of the whole of one's heart (Deut 6:5). However, the relationship cannot be established by merely the contribution of *I*. But, the relationship cannot be maintained without *me*. *I* becomes *me* due to the connection and direct pronunciation with *you*. This kind of pronunciation can also take place within the articulation of a gesture.

Another important feature of the *I-Thou* dynamics is that the *I* in the *I-Thou* relationship cannot speak about the *Thou* as in the case of general objectifications. 'To speak about' resides within the *I-it* dynamics. Everything that becomes, for the reflecting and feeling *I*, a kind of 'content', resides within the *I-it* dynamics, that is, processes of objectifying things (Van Rhijn & Meulink-Korf 1997:157; 2019:146).

I-Thou takes place in the mode of an actuating dynamics; actuality as pure present tense – the actuality of 'now'. The relationship between *I* and *Thou* occurs as a happenstance in the actuality of now, surrounded by the silence of being. The dialogue between *I* and *Thou* is about pure silence; nothing exists, only the two selves of being within the reciprocity of the in-between moment (Friedman 1995:36-38). The event takes place without a specific mindfulness, because, when the *I* starts to observe, when the *I* becomes aware of things and starts to signify things, the encounter already belongs to the past and becomes part of history, sinking back into the completion of time.

The becoming of *I* (the developmental and growing person) is intrinsically interconnected with the *Thou* – whether you like it or not. Immediately, when the other is addressed by me as *Thou* or *you*, a relationship is established. The person addressed becomes a *Thou* or *you* for me. *And this pronouncement is what Buber calls encounter.* In his later works, he calls this engagement in relationships a genuine dialogue (the authentication of subjectivity). The latter can only be performed *wholeheartedly* – with the whole of your very being. In this way, *he/she* establishes the existence of the other and vice versa. To reframe this statement, encounter is about confirming and affirming, approving and acknowledging, and in this event of substantiation, healing comes to pass, and trust is established.

Meeting as the acknowledgement of being

For the legitimacy and the ongoing fostering of authentic dialogue, as well as the establishment of a legitimate encounter, a total commitment is necessary. The dialogue and encounter must take place wholeheartedly in order to acknowledge and confirm the existence of the other. This acknowledgement and confirmation are mutually structured. Within this mutuality of confirmation and ontic acknowledgement, two important aspects of caregiving occur, namely healing and trust.

In his article *Hope for this hour*, Buber elaborates further on the notion of acknowledgement (Buber 1952). Acknowledgement does not occur within a brute collectivity. Acknowledgement belongs to the unique identity of our being human. As structure of our being human, acknowledgement can be rendered as a kind of structure of being. It can only be pronounced within an '*I-Thou* relationship'. For the pronouncement of authentic being, trust in the legitimacy of the event is a prerequisite. When one cannot entrust oneself to the happenstance of the word-event wherein the '*I-thou*' is pronounced, authentic dialoguing becomes questionable. One can even say: The dialogical perspective becomes absent without a trustworthy commitment.

The further implication is that even time (as renewal of existence and of the *I-thou* dynamics) cannot take place. Engagement with the other and to be exposed to identity-differentiation can only occur within the framework of trust and responsibility. Without the word pair *I-Thou*, the dialogical perspective in encounters becomes absent. In order to be prepared to become engaged in the *I-Thou* relationship and to enter the space of human encounters with trust, one has to be willing to face the differences between myself and the other. Differentiation and asymmetry are part and parcel of the whole event. Otherwise, it becomes virtually impossible to say: I trust you even when I cannot understand you fully. Within commitment and trust, the *I-thou* encounter becomes the key to detect the meaning of human existence. According to Buber, *all real living is meeting*, because in the encounter, new time for significant living comes into being. *Time does not create meeting; it is meeting that creates time.*

Meeting (as framed and structured by commitment, trust and I-acknowledgement) implies even more than merely pronouncing one another and the reciprocity of an *I-thou* dynamic. Meeting and encountering implies the 'more' of transcendence and divine presence – the immanency of God.

The immanency of God in human encounters (Buber)

Within the *I-Thou* encounter, the realm of transcendence, the realm of the Thou is immanent as well. This realm has been articulated by Buber as divine presence. This is what Buber means that God is immanently present in the whole of creation, even within human beings. In this capacity, God is wholly present – always being *there* (Friedman 1995:34).

The relationship with God is indicated with a capital: *I-Thou*. The capital is an indication of differentiation between God and human beings. The fact is that human beings can never possess God. There is always distance which cannot be bridged by human attempts. The encounter between God and human beings is fundamentally asymmetric; dialogue takes place on the level of interaction between unequal entities. To meet with God within the asymmetric of a fundamental relationship implies that God can never become one's friend in a social and public sense. General truths cannot capture God.

Furthermore, human beings and God can never coincide or be synchronised. However, despite the mystical element in transcendence, the relationship between God and human beings is always 'bright' and distinct. The *I-Thou* encounter within the happenstances of 'now' contributes to what one can signify afterwards as spiritual experiences.

In the Old Testament, the presence of God is closely related to the notions of countenance (facing God) and communion (intimate relationship and communication with God). In a very poignant way, the paradox between absence (invisibility) and presence (experience) is described in Exodus 33:12-23 (NIV). Moses displays a moving plea that God should accompany them through the desert. He founds his plea on the fact that the name of God is closely related to God's pity, grace and compassion. In his plea, he builds his argument on verse 16: "How will anyone know that you are pleased with me and with your people unless you go with us? What else will distinguish me and your people from all the other people on the face of the earth?" Thereafter, he asked: "Now show me your glory" (verse 18). The Lord then said: "I will cause all my goodness to pass in front of you, and I will proclaim my name, the Lord, in your presence." But still the differentiation between God and human beings should be maintained. "You cannot see my face, for no one may see me and live" (verse 20).

God then puts Moses on a rock beside him so that Moses can see God's doxa. Verse 21: "There is a place near me where you may stand on the rock." God also puts his palm on Moses as a covering so that God can pass by. The implication is that Moses can only observe God from the back, so to speak – only afterwards. God's appearance is like tracking a footprint afterwards, backwards. *Acharee* can also indicate: The Other! God is only to be seen as the Other, but then afterwards.

What a remarkable text indeed!

1.7   *Dialogue in Levinas' thinking*

The research of Meulink-Korf and Van Rhijn (1997) was quite aware of the possible contribution of Emmanuel Levinas' thinking to the meaning of dialogue in pastoral caregiving. This is the reason why it was necessary to expand Nagy's insight on healing and human well-being, with the perspectives of Emmanuel Levinas on the interplay between ethics, responsibility, divine countenance and the surprise (awe) of dealing with the Other.

The basic supposition in Van Rhijn and Meulink-Korf's research (Van Rhijn & Meulink-Korf 1997) is that Buber's 'between' (the realm and space of the between) differs from Nagy's interactional between. In fact, according to them, Buber's *I-Thou* space is empty. It is filled with a silence, void of any mindfulness. That explains the critical stance of Levinas.

The ethical dimension between *I* and the *Other/other*

For Levinas, it is important not to maintain that the terms in the *I-Thou* relationship are symmetrical. The unique quality of subjectivity should be defended because each human being differs from the other. When the differences are not acknowledged, the question should be posed: Can one still claim that an ethical relationship is still intact; a relationship that is more than merely an abstract system? This is the very intriguing question posed by Meulink-Korf and Van Rhijn in their extensive research on dialogue and human encounters (Van Rhijn & Meulink-Korf 1997:166; 2019:156).

In Levinas' approach, the *Other/other* is always demarcated by difference and asymmetry. The *Other/other* is always 'more' and 'higher', even 'lower' and 'poorer'. This otherness of the other is the decisive factor that appeals to the *I* in the mode of a *command* and demand. Therefore, it is an appeal that puts my own being into question. This question becomes a call: With ethical and existential implications: "Where are you?" Immediately this call resembles the calling voice in Genesis 3:9: "Adam, where are you?"

With this call, Levinas emphasises the responsibility of the subject. The responsibility does not emanate from the relationship; it is not determined by causality and cannot be forecasted or achieved. In Levinas' thinking, my being a subject precedes the process. It starts with the *Other/other*, and is therefore totally dependent on the *Other/other* as precondition for authentic subjectivity. The *Other/other* determines in this sense my ontic fate: Freedom as a calling because the *Other/other* predestined my freedom. I am chosen by the *Other/other* and thus become a 'self'. Therefore, the reason why subjectivity is defined by passivity: Being touched and summoned by the *Other/other*.

Furthermore, my becoming an *I* does not start with a nominative (the first case) but with the fourth, the accusative: *Me voici*, here I am, or in the language of Thenach: *hinéni*. Within the vivid moment of *me voice* (here am I), the *I* is moulded into subjectivity, and at the same time endowed with responsibility for the *Other/other*; the *I* becomes *respond*-able within the total zest of my being; with body and soul despite often painful stumbling blocks. It is precisely in corporeality and human embodiment that the human being is moulded into becoming a brother or a sister. That kind of formation should come into being with the whole of my being; with the whole of my soul and with all my abilities; abilities not as abstract entities but very concrete in terms of bedding, washing and sharing of bread. This is the reason why the space between *I* and *Thou* is not vacant and void, but ethically structured with an appeal to compassion and diaconal outreach. It is indeed an ethical in-between.

> Transcendence seems to be connected in all circumstances with the riddle regarding the proximity of the other. This is how Reneé van Riessen explains the interplay between transcendence and proximity (the nearness of the other) in her book: *Van zichzelf bevrijd: Levinas over transcendentie en nabijheid (On becoming free from oneself: Levinas on transcendence and proximity,* 2019).

Transcendence: The surplus of the *Other/other*

Levinas' thinking brought about a paradigmatic change in existentialism. In Levinas' thinking, the *Other/other* precedes the responsibility of the *I.* Being is no longer encapsulated in itself, for itself. Being is embedded in the dynamics of responsibility wherein the exteriority of intersubjectivity, and the transcendence of the *Other/other* determine the qualitative value of subjectivity. Levinas' point of departure is transcendence, an exteriority that encompasses *the more* of subjectivity. It refers to the surplus of the *Other/other.* This surplus is much more comprehensive than the totality of all that can be observed, perceived and reflected upon.

The *Other/other* as exterior to the 'me', comes into play as the surprise of being: I am shaped by 'the more' of the *Other/other* that appears as phantom, concealed in the language and grammar of the future. In this sense, the *Other/other* is in becoming. As a surprise, the *Other/other* is concealed but also in envelopment. The *Other/other* is, in this sense, expected within the hopeful mode of anticipation and refers to the *not-yet* of time and being. In the language of Levinas, this *not-yet* could be viewed as a kind of eschatology (Van Rhijn & Meulink-Korf 1997:194; 2019:182). One can therefore conclude that dialogue is geared towards the future (eschatology as the future of dialogue). It is about a dialogue that sets hope free. This kind of hope is not about wishful thinking and the satisfaction of emotional desires. Hope is structured by a desire for significant being as related to transcendence. The desire for transcendence surpasses the fixation of objectification; it exceeds any form of stagnation and massified totalisation by means of reflecting on actions of care, compassion, justice, kindness and fairness.

Within the structuredness of being there lurk traces of 'remaining trust' (deposits of trustworthiness) that eventually lead to true commitments; commitments that can set being free (Michielsen et al., 1998:51-80).

The exteriority of 'God': Transcendence in the mode of infinite becoming

In pastoral care we must acknowledge that we are connected to God as exterior to our being human. God is the infinite factor in our lives; our soul cannot grasp the Other by means of comprehensive categories. God as the Other can only be met in dialoguing. God as subject is constantly looking for me. He approaches me as subject despite overlooked experiences. He is searching and penetrating me in order to promote responsible actions.

The Exterior comforts but at the same time disturbs my being a subject. In this way our existence takes place *coram Deo*. However, we face not merely the countenance of God (Visage) but we are also summoned to face and serve the *Other/other* as the Other.

> In the master's programme at Stellenbosch University on *Dialogical Intergenerational Pastoral Process*, a student once posed the following question: But why Emmanuel Levinas in our reflection on theory formation for pastoral caregiving? Very aptly Hanneke Meulink-Korf answered: Because Levinas framed and described the stranger by means of biblical terminology. The other who is intrinsically strange to me, transforms my own very being into becoming a stranger. In this sense, the *Other/other* addresses 'me' and makes an appeal to both my re-*spond*-ability and responsibility. According to Levinas, my becoming a stranger founds all forms of accountability.

1.8 About distance and proximity between one another

Meulink-Korf and Van Rhijn (1997:283) desperately wanted to enhance the quality of the pastoral ministry. The emphasis should be on the responsibility of the caregiver/pastor. Responsibility should be linked to trustworthiness. Without any doubt, the ethical framework for authentic dialoguing in caregiving has implications for the subjectivity of the caregiver/pastor.

In their research, Meulink-Korf and Van Rhijn also wanted to reinterpret the role of relational dynamics in caregiving, healing and helping. That explains their attempt to reinterpret the thinking of Nagy regarding the dynamics of relationships.

As said, Meulink-Korf and Van Rhijn want to enhance the caring capacity of pastors and helpers in ministry. Caregiving is embedded in the relational context of several modes of interaction. Fundamental, however, is the emphasis on fairness in the positioning and habitus of the caregiver. Fairness should safeguard the ethical quality of dialogical relationships and enhance sound, humane interaction. In order to promote fairness in the defining of interpersonal positioning, two prerequisites are required, namely due consideration for the other, as well as a kind of appropriate self-delineation. For the effectivity and legitimation of the pastoral ministry, the caregiver must become aware of the impact of his/her position on interpersonal encounters and intersubjectivity. In fact, positioning and the quality of habitus should be viewed as kind of 'pastoral hygiene' that precedes the pastoral conversation. The quality of everyone's subjectivity and attitude (*habitus*) in dialogical encounters and relationships determines whether the relationship will be fair or not.

The pastoral caregiver should, thus, become aware of different positions in approaching the *Other/others*. It is in this regard that one can speak of a kind of 'pastoral hygiene'. The latter refers to both the subjective status of the *I* and the differentiated status of the *Other/other* (identity formation). The position and habitus of the pastoral caregiver are therefore decisive for the ethical quality and trustworthiness of dialoguing in human encounters and pastoral counselling. One can say that the ethical quality of pastoral care is, to a large extent, a case of re-*positioning* and habitus: How am I, when I am there?

Re-positioning and habitus in caregiving (four positions)

Meulink-Korf and Van Rhijn describe four positions in interrelational dynamics which are decisive for every individual engaged in helping, healing and caring. Noteworthy is the fact that position is not a fixed entity or prescribed function. Position describes a dynamic invitation for continuous re-orientation within the bipolar tension of proximity (nearness) and safe distance (detachment) (1997:283; 2019:280).

Positions are part of the networking dynamics within the framework of ethical entanglements. Whether the positions are trustworthy (positive) or not (negative: distrustful) is based on the principle of justice and fairness. An inappropriate position is directly linked to the immaturity (unfinished business) of the caregiver and his/her capacity to deal with own vulnerability (woundedness). The latter is the reason why one cannot hear the yearning of the *Other/other*. When the counsellor or pastor is more involved in own shortcomings, it hampers the process of dialoguing and becomes a stumbling block in giving thorough attention to the need of the other.

Furthermore, inability to deal with own shortcomings can easily lead to the danger of a static objectification of the *Other/other*. The further disadvantage is that it contributes to stigmatisation, labelling, asocial behaviour and negative perceptions. Inappropriate attitudes can lead to artificial gestures and inappropriate wording that eventually contribute to manipulative techniques in counselling procedures. Inappropriate approaches are often only disguised attempts to hide personal anxiety for loss and possible failure. They create fences that disturb authentic dialoguing and the promotion of legitimate subjectivity and intersubjective reciprocity.

Due to personal and practical experiences of the researcher, it is paramount to different modi of habitual responses. That is the reason why thorough knowledge of the four different positions enhances the quality of authentic dialoguing. It helps to detect why dialogue in some cases is constructive but in other cases leads to greater confusion and even failure. The description of the four modi illuminates why appropriate attitudes contribute to helping, caring and healing within ethical entanglements. It also enhances the professional character of dialoguing. Dialogue and pastoral conversations entail much more than conversing in a counselling room or private space of one's home. The interplay between positioning, dialoguing and thorough knowledge (knowledge regarding their character and different functions) helps to understand why some encounters are fruitful while others fail.

1. *The I – Other/other dynamics.* Significant reciprocity between the *I* and the *Other/others* in pastoral encounters is characterised by mutual trust. It entails more than merely operating on the level of the affective in terms of empathy. It is asymmetric and operates fundamentally

according to justice, fairness and trustworthiness as determined by ethical entanglements. According to Nagy, in this *I-Other/other* dynamics, the other is inclusively and immediately at stake and present. The *Other/other* constellation exercises a strong appeal and demand for fairness and responsible treatment. The *I* is challenged to be available and become engaged in dialoguing. This challenge is, most of times, even without words and embedded in the daily happenstances of life. The claim occurs without force (*sans force*) or violent manipulation. It does not come into being due to mere obedience to the *Other/other*. Obedience is intrinsically part of the identity and ethical awareness of the self (Van Rhijn & Meulink-Korf 1997:284). The unique character of trust and respect in authentic dialoguing is reflected in the preparedness to even become an object of service as part of the autonomy of the self.

"I believe, despite all, that the people in this hour can enter into dialogue, into a genuine dialogue with one another. In a genuine dialogue each of the partners, even when he stands in opposition to the other, heeds, affirms and confirms his opponent as an existing other. Only in such a way can conflict certainly not be eliminated from the world but be humanly arbitrated and lead to overcoming" (Buber 1952:238).

2. *Intersubjectivity: The subject-subject dynamics.* Intersubjectivity requires differentiation between subjects (individuation) in order to establish authentic dialoguing. Even when the two bipolar entities are in opposition to one another, the other is affirmed and confirmed in his/her otherness. Even differences make subjectivity possible. The intersubjective space is always an invitation towards dialogue. Even though the dialogue is heteronomous, both the *I* and the *Other/other* are present as autonomous entities. Due to the immanent presence of the *Other/other*, the therapist always probes into this invisible realm of the *Other/other* and has to deal with the question of how the client as unique subject is interacting and dialoguing with the *Other/other*. Trust is, therefore, not merely personal and subjective but also related to the *Other/other* so that one needs to trust the trustworthiness of the *Other/other* in order to exceed fixed perceptions and unhealthy stigmatisations.

For Buber, the between (*das Zwischen*) in the space of dialoguing encounters encompasses a mode of 'timing' (temporality). It is about the newness of time wherein all forms of discrimination (colour or race or pigment) become irrelevant (see also Buber 1988).

A very poignant question surfaces in this regard: Where does God fit into these intersubjective dynamics of relational interaction?

This question was posed by a student in pastoral care and pastoral theology. According to the researcher it is indeed difficult to detect the position of God in different kinds of dialoguing. Within the context of various biblical narratives, it seems that God is always, in one way or another as subject, present in human encounters. God's subjectivity operates based on a covenantal partnership that summons human beings into the ethos of responsibility and *respond*-ability regarding neighbour and stranger. God calls us into subjectivity. We are, therefore, addressed by God to display care and service to all others whether neighbour or stranger. The student suddenly kept quiet while staring in front of him. Then he responded: "This is quite amazing, 4 000 years of theologising in a nutshell; God summons me into subjectivity! Now it is my turn!"

3. *The subject-object relationship*. The subject-object relationship is not triadic but dyadic. Both the self, as well as the other, can become subject and object for one another, and vice versa. Relational self-demarcation/delineation takes place not in the 'internal dialogue', or within fusion, but in the authentic dialogue (between subject and subject) wherein both can become subject or object for one another; in other words, context for 'self-delineation' of the other.

    The problem with dyadic relationships is that the client could become isolated and objectified. In a dyadic relationship, the notion of multi-partiality is most of times absent and threatens the voice of the third party. From the perspective of the client as subject, a subject-object relationship is about the threat that I start to view the other in his/her participation as object (a collusion). Due to a desire for significance, objectification sets in. This desire can become acute in the other ('evidence of their worth', Nagy 1987:93). The point is that the ability (passive) of the other could become exploited. Unfortunately, this is a very subtle expression of sheer affective violence, even of altruistic exploitation. This is what Levinas calls intersubjective violence, because the other is degraded to the position of an object due to selfish gain.

The danger of objectification is always present in many projects of helping and diaconal outreaches. A good example is the many 'soup kitchens' in South Africa that provide soup to many displaced people living under poor conditions. Due to the danger of objectification, Prof Christo Thesnaar (Professor in Pastoral Theology and Caregiving at the Faculty of Theology, Stellenbosch University, South Africa) posed the intriguing question: "Did we ever ask the people what their real needs are, and if they so desperately need soup at all?"

Sometimes objectification is necessary and unavoidable, for example in case of medical procedures. This kind of objectification is not about power and exploitation but it is embedded in an ethos of service and ethical entanglement. However, it does not exonerate one from the responsibility to act in all circumstances with respect for the integrity of the other, including the maintenance of 'relational integrity'.

In the contact with students, the question arises of whether the minister still has a role to play due to ritualisation and formalisation in many churches. The threat of objectification is indeed a danger in many kinds of ministerial engagements and the function of ecclesial offices. Many churches focus on the artificiality of clerical rituals. The implication is that even the office of ministry becomes objectified and estranged from the vividness of real life events. The minister then negates the basic feature of authentic dialoguing, namely, to establish intersubjectivity in responsible modes of reaching out to others.

4. *The threat of fusion in object-object relationship.* Fusion is about the inability to differentiate and understand the value of ethical cognition, recognition and acknowledgement. The danger in object-object relationships is unhealthy dependency and confusion about demarcation and the borders of one own's position. Eventually there is only proximity with a lack of sound distance (detachment). Furthermore, fusion threatens the necessity of differentiation and sound individuation. Fusion also leads to fear for loss and the disintegration of intersubjectivity; it negates distance and the space

of the between. The further danger is that negative behaviour and destructive responses are copied and projected onto the other. Subjects are then easily degraded to the status of nameless entities (one-we-subject) and it becomes virtually impossible to hear the appealing voice of the *Other/other*; the accusative of *Hinéni* (Here I am) loses its subjective impact. Levinas calls this condition the decline of ethical individuation.

The eventual impact of fusion is that when a person is not prepared to take responsibility for his/her own behaviour, relationships become entangled. In the therapeutic relation, fusion is about improper transference. It is about transference that has not been corrected. This will be confirmed by inappropriate modes of contra-transference. The real danger lurks that the therapist takes control over the being of the other. In this respect, the therapist fails and commits a kind of subtle therapeutic violence to the patient. The effect on the patient is most of times an upheaval of guilt due to apparent disloyalty towards the real others in his/her environment (parents, partners, children). In these cases, the therapist inflicts further violence to others as related to the client's social networking environment. Every form of 'partiality' is then lacking and absent.

During a lecture over the subject-object dynamics, a student shared the following incident: A fourteen-year-old son entered the house and told his parents that he had fallen in love with a girl. Immediately his father responded with a question: "But is she white or black?" The son replied: "No, I haven't seen, but give me a moment I will go back and have a look!" What an excellent example of fair impartiality.

From dialogue to 'Here I am'

The hallmark of pastoral care is dialogue. Dialogue implies more than merely conversing with one another. Many general conversations can indeed develop into dialogue. Even without dialogue, conversing has its place in human encounters.

It should be stated categorically that dialogue comes into being when a subject-subject relationship has been established. In order to enter into the legitimacy of intersubjectivity, trust and trustworthiness within the dynamics of distance and proximity are required. Genuine dialogue moves between being called, the art of hearing and the responsibility of appropriate answering. In fact, this is how Jesus understood his mother, and provided a unique answer. Jesus thus set an example of how humane dialoguing should take place. What is most needed is a habitus of availability as a kind of starting point towards temporality as the *Kairos*-moment of something totally new. In order to experience timing as openness to the new of the not-yet, the quality and character of a calling and an appropriate answer are becoming paramount. We therefore proceed to the dynamics of 'Here am I' in inter-subjective encounters.

CHAPTER 2

The art of commitment:
The availability of
'Here I am' (*Hinéni*)

The argument thus far is founded on the basic assumption that a human being is a relational creature and being. Subjectivity is shaped and determined by intersubjectivity. Our daily existence within the happenstances of life is embedded in a networking dynamic of interconnectedness and inter-relationality. Individuality is shaped within close communion with the other and many others. In this sense, dialogue is embedded by the dynamics between the *I* and the *Other/other*. Many others shape individuation. In fact, they make an appeal to our existence. We must and should respond: the ethical imperative. Their calling summons the *I* into responsibility. In this sense, dialogue is bracketed by 'calling' and 'answering'.

2.1 The calling and the answer

One can say that *respondeo ergo sum* is supplemented by the notion: I am interrelated and interconnected, therefore I am. With this reframing of *cogito ergo sum*, our understanding of dialogue is very close to what we can call 'an African interpretation' of the significance of life and the meaning of our being human. *Umuntu ungumuntu ngabantu/motho ke motho ka batho* – approximately translated as: "A person is a person through other people" (Mtetwa 1996:24).

It is quite remarkable that many cultural traditions in Africa do not even have a concept that refers to the individuality of personhood – the human being as a psychic entity. Traditional, African anthropology functions according to what can be called a kind of 'communal spirit' influenced by cosmic forces. *The human 'I' is shaped by tradition and the community (kinship, local, tribal customs) since one exists within the communality of an 'inclusive we'*. The *I* cannot be isolated from the community. The *I* as an isolated entity is not possible in an African view on life; it can only exist within the interconnectedness – the communal *we*. Without the other, personal existence is virtually impossible. Furthermore, the human person becomes an *I* because the community makes an appeal on my being there for them. The community calls my being into significant existence. The calling of the other functions like an event of being named, of being summoned into identity. The *I* finds its unique identity within this call and demands to respond with responsibility. If that is not the case, the *I* becomes insignificant, without any function and meaning. One could even say there would have been no need to exist and to be at all (see Buber 1964:14).

In authentic dialoguing, the only one who can respond and answer is the *I*. I am so to speak taken into hostage, entitled to answer and to say: *Here I am!* In fact, I cannot refuse to answer.

It sounds like an unavoidable fiat; it makes me liable, whether I want it or not. To answer and to make a commitment to be there for the other, establishes the relationship. In this calling, that is, to be pronounced as *I*, to experience oneself as an addressed *me*, encompasses much more than being named and approached as is often the case in social conversations and mass communication. In authentic dialogue, the calling of the name is ontic; it is directly focused on the 'I-identity' (the event of becoming *me*). The vocative is orientating me in the multitude of many others but, at the same time, it is directly addressing me in my unique subjectivity. The calling is in fact a claim that entitled the *I* to respond in a re-*spond*-able and *responsible way*. Within the mutuality of being questioned but, simultaneously, being summoned to answer, lurks the significance of becoming a humane human being.

To answer in such a way that the *me*-response is indeed an expression of an ontic event, and an indication of becoming humane, is to discover: *I am endowed and clothed with responsibility*, even if the answer does not indicate a specific need to be satisfied. The point is, as an ontic event, my answer is captured by a mode of sincerity and care that does not indicate in the first place a '*what*' (substance), but a '*how*' (*habitus*).

To be summoned and to respond are about a dynamic movement in coexistence. The art of living together is bracketed by both the risk of trusting, as well as the failure of a breach. The dynamic movement oscillates between fall and rise, breaking down and rebuilding, distance and proximity. In many cases, it is merely impossible to answer wholeheartedly. The call and command are therefore still unanswered. In other cases, it is indeed possible to answer. However, despite the answer, the outcome is not necessarily the establishment of a new kind of trust within the relational dynamics.

Responsibility for the other is, in terms of a re-*spond*-able habitus, about an entitlement that implies a *possible sacrifice*, the risk of failure, the exposure to exploitation but also the challenge to act as a moral being, to respond within an ethos of trustworthiness. It becomes clear that the giving of an answer does have limitations. It does not imply that one must stretch oneself beyond any form of personal limitation so that one puts one's own life, or the life of the other, at risk with destructive consequences.

Appropriate answers do not imply a total mode of self-denial (self-sacrifice). In *Breaking the waves*, a 1996 drama film directed and co-written by the Danish producer Lars von Triers, the notion of *sacrifice* is explored in such a way that the pathological side of selflessness is revealed in a very painful drama wherein duty (loyalty) and physical abuse lead to deadly self-destruction. However, despite the very strange interpretation of the call, wavering between the uncertainty of whether one should answer or not, in one way or another an answer has been formulated: *Here I am*. It points to a moment that appears like an unexpected flash of responsibility. When one assesses this moment afterwards, it seems to point indeed to a mode of trust and trustworthiness.

> Bess, a devoted believer and churchgoer married Jab Nyman (a non-churchgoer). He worked on an oil platform and was away from home for long periods. Bess prayed for his return. The next day, after her plea to God, Jan was severely injured in an industrial accident. Bess believed that her prayer and selfish needs were the reason why the accident occurred. Her skewed piety convinced her that God punished her for the selfish plea that Jan must neglect his job and return to her. Jan was paralysed and asked Bess to find a lover. She was also convinced by her sister-in-law to explore this insane avenue and started to interpret this very strange summoning as the will of God. She started to pick up

men from the street. Even to have sex with barbarous sailors who violently raped her and caused her death. Due to her 'immorality', the church refused to hold a funeral for her. She was totally excommunicated. Her notion of self-sacrifice and pathological God-image destroyed her life and robbed her from all dignity.

Breaking the waves illustrates that the habitus of re-*spond*-ability is in many real scenarios of responses to the challenges within the happenstances of life, complex, even precarious. It often implies (despite even resistance) to leave the safe comfort zone of personal need-satisfaction and to be exposed to the cruelty of life. The entitlement of *Here I am!* penetrates the private zone of being an *I*. This private zone is often the confused realm of many nuances of being an *I*. These many nuances are often hiding places and difficult to leave. However, the call-and-response dynamic reveals these hiding places; it uncovers the many 'folders' or 'wrinkles' of the *I* (Dirk de Wachter, a Belgian psychiatrist).

The entitlement of *Here I am* is called *Hinéni* in the Bible. Important to note is that *Hinéni* does not merely refer to a social or behavioural entity. It is also a spiritual phenomenon and appears in many of the calling narratives in the Bible. For example, in Exodus 3:4 Moses responded to the revelation of God in the narrative on the 'burning bush' as follows: "God called Moses from within the bush, 'Moses! Moses!' And Moses said, 'Here I am'" (NIV). In 1 Samuel 3:2-8 Samuel responded several times with the phrase 'Here I am'. *Hinéni* can be rendered as a refrain in many of the prophecies. It is even an indication of God's caring love: "I myself will search for my sheep and look after them" (Ezek 34:11) (NIV). In Genesis 3, Abraham responded three times with the phrase 'Here I am'.

In order to detect the spiritual depth of calling and answering within the Genesis narrative, it is necessary to understand the underpinning theory in the hermeneutics of dialogical interpretation, and how this methodology can be applied to biblical texts.

2.2 The hermeneutics of dialogical interpretation in biblical exegesis

Narratives are not about fixed facts. Rather, they articulate the vividness of the happenstances of life and thus represent history. Narratives are history within the rhythm of daily life events. In this regard, narratives direct contemporary historic events and create opportunities for new decisions. In a nutshell, narratives create options for the display of something new; for the making of *new history* (Den Dulk 1998:57). One can even go so far as to say, stories are indications of *living history*, *contemporary history* and *new history*. They form a triadic dynamic which represents the diachronic movement bringing the so-called 'archaic texts' to life. Stories take events further into future speech and the writing of tomorrow's new narratives.

According to Den Dulk (1998), and due to these triadic dynamics of interconnectedness, the message of the biblical text is not merely linked to individuals but fundamentally to the community as well. And it is right here, where the pastoral conversation comes into play. The latter tries to capitalise on this dynamic character of narratives and explore their significance for the human quest for meaning and direction. It is the same with preaching. Every sermon is at the same time a mode of pastoral care and an attempt to link the meaning of the text to the present context. In this sense, both preaching and pastoral caregiving can be seen as modes of authentic dialoguing and narrating attempts to delineate a kind of intersubjectivity wherein the text in itself reveals the *Other/other* and, at the same time, becomes an *Other/other* to others as well. The implication is that one should always approach the biblical text from the viewpoint of a dialogical approach that reckons with different contexts, directives and connections.

The *Other/other* as text

With reference to our argument thus far, in authentic dialoguing, the text should not be regarded as an object and be treated as a series of objectified facts. Even the text itself is subjected to the unpredictability and the realm of the unknown. Because, in the text the unfamiliar *Other/other* speaks with a unique articulation and own voice. This is the reason why acquired knowledge, commentaries, doctrinal truths, dogmatic formulations and logic reasoning in terms of cause and effect hamper the dynamic dialectics between reader and text.

It is unfortunately a fact that the sanctification of fixed opinions, 'holy confessions' and favourite commentaries create an own life that eventually blocks the free flow of meaning between text and reader. In this way, the text as the subject disappears behind the objectified text – the *Other/other* as object. A heuristic approach, rather, challenges one to bracket fixed guarantees and static truths, irrespective of the status or skilfulness of the reader. When the text is not an object but a kind of 'commandment' that approaches one as subject, to be addressed by the text as *Other/other* and to respond appropriately becomes complicated. A dialogical approach is not easy because one has to leave previous comfort zones behind. In a milder formulation, one has to bracket these acquired guarantees first. And this bracketing requires a mode of patience irrespective of the amount of experience of the interpreter.

This open and free space of authenticity between text and reader is the same as the space of dynamic encounters in a counselling room. The open space of encounter is always surrounded by the mystery of not-knowing. Even the counsellor and caregiver are incorporated in this mystery of the unknown. In every encounter, both counsellor and counselee are subjected to change and are never the same, even if one reads the Biblical text regularly. Reading and encountering occur within the dynamics of contexts and the variable of different observations. In fact, one cannot negate this dynamic of irregularity. To treat the text merely as a past remembrance of learnt truths, the mutuality between text and interpreter is reduced to a kind of insignificant parroting. In this way the surprise of new insight becomes hijacked.

> Every interpretation of a text is unpredictable and, thus, a temporarily penetration of longstanding 'sacred' truths. This kind of risk within the act of reading and hearing determines the dynamics of a sermon and the processes of interaction in a traditional worship. Very specifically, are hearers exposed to the surprise of unpredictability and the uncertainty that results when new layers of meaning emerge? Even the preacher should be prepared to view the congregation as the *Other/other* and help them to make the crossing into the discovery of new horizons of meaning. That is the reason why preaching as well as pastoral conversations are in fact unrepeatable. It is therefore indeed difficult to preach a

sermon a second time. In this sense, a pastoral encounter is every time irrevocable and cannot be repeated.

The insight of Levinas that the text is an *Other/other* is indeed helpful and illuminating. The subjectivity of the *Other/other* is in this sense a mystery and lurks *invisibly* behind the level of mere observation (*visibility*). Behind the visible face (the encounter with visage) lurks *the more* of a meta-physical realm. Encounters, thus, attain the value of 'holy ground' so that one starts to 'get rid of one's shoes' (Moses in Gen 3:5). It is in this sense that Emmanuel Levinas' *metaphysical mystique* contributes to the insight that authentic dialoguing in humane encounters is fundamentally about transcending – the mystical, even meta-physical superseding of human transience. It actually cuts one down to size in order to discover humility.

Listening to the unique voice of the text requires the art of patience and waiting; the skilfulness of waiting until ... It is then that we realise we are subjected to the mystical transcendence of the text that can break into the reality and experience of healing and reading like a flash of lightning. We then become subjected to the authority of the text and rediscover our relationship to the *Other/other*. We can even rediscover traces of care, pity, grace and trustworthiness – all traces of God's faithfulness. In this rediscovery and re-connectedness, one is overwhelmed by a magnificent surprise, namely, how one can trace down in the biblical narratives significant, rhythmic signs that expose one to the penetrating transcendence of God (the exteriority of God). It is about God's condescending otherness wherein the *Other/other* is revealed as exterior to our very limited experiences. The *Other/other* breaks into our existence as the invisible and unpredictable factor that disturbs our pretended presuppositions regarding the significance of the text. In the encounter with this *Exteriority* (God as the Other) the interpretation of the text changes, it disturbs. Presuppositions can become so pretentious that they become totalitarian and should indeed become disturbed.

In terms of Levinas, the totalitarianism of our human mind and thinking should be penetrated by the otherness of the *Other/other*. This otherness is timeless, and, in this sense, endless, infinite. In the same way, the interpretation of the biblical text is 'infinite'. Therefore, it is necessary to explore different readings of the biblical text in order to discover the many layers of significance and infinite surprises.

Towards a Jewish reading and instruction

The Old (First) Testament is intrinsically linked to a Hebrew paradigm. It functions as framework of reference in a biblical hermeneutical approach to authentic dialoguing. In the Jewish culture and religious instruction, the many Talmud schools teach students that each generation should read and learn texts within their own unique context. Each generation is taught how to interpret the text in a unique way. One generation's interpretation will differ from the previous. In this way, a vivid, ongoing chain of intergenerational dialoguing is established.

In *La lecture infinie: Les voies de l'interprétation midrachique* (Banon 1987:50), David Banon wrote extensively about this multi-generational mode of dialoguing. In a Jewish reading and daily mode of living in terms of the Hebrew tradition of wisdom, the repetition of keywords (*Leitwörter*) and central motives (*Leitmotiven*) are decisive for the significant articulation of the message of the text.

For example, when the authors of the Bible use the notion of 'the third day', the meaning is embedded within the rhythm of recurrent sequences. Many forms of direct speech in the text confirm the dialogical character of the text. The narratives convey reflections about one person or character in mutual exchange with other characters. For example, if a narrative starts with '*and David thinks and says*', the implication for the book is that texts are divided in terms of colometry. The further implication is that parts in the direct speech are rendered as prior to the second part, namely, the indirect speech.

This Jewish mode of reading and instruction within the paradigmatic background of Hebrew wisdom thinking, is clearly illustrated in the life and teachings of Jesus the Messiah. This is quite understandable because he was brought up and instructed in terms of the Jewish culture and Hebrew paradigm. When he was twelve years of age, one can already trace down this cultural background in his discussions with the teachers in the temple courts (Lk 2:46). Jesus connected his thoughts and actions with texts from the *Tenach* (*Tanakh*)[1]. Surprisingly, in his interpretation of texts, he connects the significance of the message to the context and situation of the people he encountered. For example, one Sabbath Jesus was wandering through the cornfields while his disciples began to pick some ears of corn, rub them in their hands and ate the grain (Lk 6:1-2). He, thus, responded to the context.

1   The Jewish Scriptures comprising the books of law, the prophets, and collected writings.

On the Sabbath, Jesus also healed the man with the shrivelled hand. In a very provocative way, Jesus challenged the Pharisees with a question that revealed new levels of meaning and understanding of the Jewish tradition: "I ask you, which is lawful on the Sabbath: to do good or to do evil, to save life or to destroy it?" (Lk 6:9). In the centre of his interpretation stood not a legal principle but the desperate need of a sick and vulnerable human being.

In terms of the *ḥēsēd* of Yahweh, the availability of living *coram Deo* (in the presence of the Lord) requires obedience to the meaning of the text as expression of God's vivid intervention in the predicament of suffering human beings. This kind of obedience can be radical, even requiring a sacrifice, as in the test case of Abraham and the offering of his son Isaac.

2.3 *The calling of Abraham: Genesis 22:1-19*

As argued, authentic dialoguing is bracketed by both a calling (listening to the voice of the *Other/other*) and a response – the realm of listening, seeing and responsibility. Genesis 22:1-19 starts with the calling of Abraham. He answered with *Hinéni*. Within this calling and answer, Abraham shows a readiness to present Isaac as an uplifting heaving and wavering to the Lord. When he arrived at Moriah, Isaac approached his father and for the first time called him 'father'. Abraham answered with the very poignant answer: "Here I am" (*Hinéni*). When Abraham reached out his hand to kill his son, the angel intervened and called from heaven. For the third time Abraham responded with: "Here I am" (*Hinéni*).

It is of paramount importance to read the whole narrative within the parameters of the "Here-I-am" – response (*Hinéni*). Noteworthy is the fact that it was repeated three times. In the repetition, the response gained the spiritual value of a total commitment and sign of unconditional, absolute obedience.

The narrative unfolded in the following texts (Gen 22:1-19). The account of the events functions as a kind of test case probing the authenticity and legitimacy of Abraham's response: "Here-I-am" (*Hinéni*).

> [1]After these things God tested Abraham. He said to him,
>   "Abraham!"
> And he said,
>   "Here I am."

[2]He said,

> "Take your son, your only son Isaac, whom you love, and
> go to the land of Moriah, and offer him there as a burnt
> offering on one of the mountains that I shall show you."

[3]So Abraham rose early in the morning, saddled his donkey, and took two of his young men with him, and his son Isaac; he cut the wood for the burnt offering, and set out and went to the place in the distance that God had shown him. [4]On the third day Abraham looked up and saw the place far away. [5]Then Abraham said to his young men,

> "Stay here with the donkey; the boy and I will go over there;
> we will worship, and then we will come back to you."

[6]Abraham took the wood of the burnt offering and laid it on his son Isaac, and he himself carried the fire and the knife. So, the two of them walked on together. [7]Isaac said to his father Abraham,

> "Father!"

And he said,

> "Here I am, my son."

He said,

> "The fire and the wood are here, but where is the lamb for
> a burnt offering?"

[8]Abraham said,

> "God himself will provide the lamb for a burnt offering,
> my son."

So, the two of them walked on together. [9]When they came to the place that God had shown him, Abraham built an altar there and laid the wood in order. He bound his son Isaac, and laid him on the altar, on top of the wood. [10]Then Abraham reached out his hand and took the knife to kill his son. [11]But the angel of the LORD called to him from heaven, and said,

> "Abraham, Abraham!"

And he said,

> "Here I am."

[12]He said,

"Do not lay your hand on the boy or do anything to him; for now I know that you fear God, since you have not withheld your son, your only son, from me."

[13]And Abraham looked up and saw a ram, caught in a thicket by its horns. Abraham went and took the ram and offered it up as a burnt offering instead of his son. [14]So Abraham called that place

"The LORD will provide";

as it is said to this day,

"On the mount of the LORD it shall be provided."

[15]The angel of the LORD called to Abraham a second time from heaven, [16]and said,

"By myself I have sworn, says the LORD: Because you have done this, and have not withheld your son, your only son, [17]I will indeed bless you, and I will make your offspring as numerous as the stars of heaven and as the sand that is on the seashore. And your offspring shall possess the gate of their enemies, [18]and by your offspring shall all the nations of the earth gain blessing for themselves, because you have obeyed my voice."

[19]So Abraham returned to his young men, and they arose and went together to Beer-sheba; and Abraham lived at Beer-Sheba.

'Now-it-came-to-pass' (*way-hî* and *egeneto*)

As in so many accounts regarding the sequences of events in storytelling, Genesis 22:1 starts with the following introductory remark: "After these things God tested Abraham." And it happened, 'Now-it-came-to-pass' – (*way-hî*). This moment is quite remarkable; it indicates a significant change. It is often an indication that the story can take a different direction from the one expected.

In life, one is exposed to many such radical moments of change. It is typical of many narratives in life that the sequences are narrated chronologically. Important transitions are then described in a very dramatic tone, namely, *And it so happened that …; and then …* With this phrase *(way-hî and egeneto)* the narrator wants to emphasise something that is over and gone. The event is now engulfed by the past tense. Something with great importance, a happenstance which impacted decisively on one's life, has become past tense. In this way we recall the sequences of life.

It is quite remarkable that in the Hebrew grammar of the Biblical language (in the old Testament *way-hî*; in the New Testament *egeneto*) the narrative is not rehearsed in the past tense by means of a cyclic movement, but every time in the *imperfectum*; that is, in the language of the present tense as an indication that the now is open and incomplete. In this way, the discontinuity within the continuity of the Biblical narrative sets in anew (*way-hî*; in the New Testament *egeneto*). The discontinuity partakes in the drama of the new episode. It seems as if the *way-hî* wants to bypass the strict causalities of logical reasoning. It is as if the *way-hî* resists the rapid sequences of logical reasoning; as if the narrator wants to breathe deeply and needs a pause before the next, unexpected step sets in as a kind of bolt from the blue.

The reference that a decisive sequence in time came into pass implies that the happenstance does have an origin. But, at the same time, it fosters an anticipation of that which is still going to take place. In this way, time is directed forwards and becomes a bearer of hopeful expectations. Temporality is therefore no longer clock time that sets in between sunrise and sunset. In the announcement, the momentarily dynamic as captured by *way-hî*, narrates about the quality of life amongst human beings; it points to the ethical entanglements of our responses in time, namely, about the interplay between justice and injustice, good and evil, peace and disputes, between birth and death, and between power and powerlessness.

Way-hî represents an ethical qualification of time, that is, time as qualified by the mode in which people can promote and enrich one another but, at the same time, can harm one another. It is about time that is not fulfilled yet, and, in this sense points to the not-yet of subjectivity. Being is thus anchored in the reality of happenstances in the now. It also implies that our subjectivity and time are relational and mutually intertwined.

It is quite remarkable that a rather brief and unobtrusive phrase at the beginning of a sentence and text signifies the dialogical space of intersubjectivity. The telic question is: To whom and for what purpose is this ethical and fulfilled time designated? To whom and on account of whom does it take place? To whom does the voice belong that summons one to go ahead or to merely mark time, to rise or not, to answer or to keep quiet, to make a choice regarding life or death? Is it the voice of God, a neighbour or just anybody? What is the instance that summons me so that I am prepared to say *Hinéni*, or, in terms of Emmanuel Levinas, respond to *me voici*? Subjectivity then as an identity, articulated from the start as an accusative: This is me, and here I am (*me voici*). And the peculiarity of this answer is that it is pronounced without knowing exactly which route to take and in which direction to proceed.

In the Genesis 22 text it so happened that God (*Elohim* – the naming of God as in the Garden of Eden) said: "Abram!" The previous time when God summoned Abraham, he was still addressed as Abram. In fact, it was JHWH who uttered the name Abram (Gen 12:1). When Abraham is going to stretch out his hand in order to take the knife, it will be again JHWH; the One and Only who revealed the significance of his name to Moses; the One who is revealed in verbing terminology as a promise, namely, *I am who I am, and will always be there where you are*. However, what all these different names of God separately designate is very difficult to unravel for a human being. Could it be that God on the top of the mountain is entering into a very personal relationship with Abraham and personal encounters require different names? For now, we leave that answer open as an unknown mystery.

The test case: A remarkable aftermath

It so happened that, after these events and words, God tested Abram. The intriguing question arises: Which words? Do these words refer to everything that happened in Abraham's life, or do they refer merely to the immediately preceding events? Or do 'these words' refer to the promises in Genesis 12:2-3 that the Lord will make him into a great nation and will bless him? It could even refer to Genesis 15:4-5 regarding a possible son and many offspring? Or is the calling generated because of the existence of the son Isaac after the long barrenness of Sarah?

The profound question now at stake is: How did Abram interpret and respond to the promise that the Lord will make him into a great nation through a son of Sarai?

The promise that the Lord will make him into a great nation (Gen 12:2) seems initially to be fulfilled in Ishmael, the son of Hagar. However, after quite a long period of time, Isaac the son of Abraham and Sarah was born. If the words in Genesis 22 refer back to the period between the different events, the summoning to take his son Isaac to mount Moriah and to sacrifice his only son (as heaving-offering), the one he loved, seems bizarre indeed. The summoning and test are indeed strange as if there exists only one son, and as if Abraham loved only this one. Furthermore, to specifically offer this son Isaac seems to be totally irrational. Therefore, the question: Why this summoning and why did God want to test Abraham? What will God want to prove by this test to Abraham?

After the promise regarding an offspring and becoming a great nation, due to a severe famine, Abram moved swiftly in the direction of Egypt (Gen 12:10). Events enfolded in a strange way. Sarai was beautiful and Abram feared that the Egyptians would recognise her, and he would have to give her away. He, therefore, proposed that she must say she is his sister so that he could be treated well for her sake and his life be spared because of her. In this way their relationship will not cause confusion and eventually lead to any form of trouble. And so it happened that, when Abram came to Egypt, the Egyptians saw that she was a very beautiful woman. When the officials of Pharaoh saw her, they praised her to Pharaoh. The story becomes quite tense when she was taken into his palace. What will happen when Pharaoh takes her as his wife and has intercourse with her? It could then happen that a pregnancy occurs without the protection of the covenantal promise of JHWH.

The Lord then inflicted serious diseases on Pharaoh and his household because of Sarai. So, Pharaoh was up in arms and summoned Abram: "What have you done to me? … Why did you say, 'She is my sister,' so that I took her to be my wife?" Pharaoh then gave order about Abram to his men, and they sent him on his way, with his wife and everything he had received form Pharaoh 'because of her' – all the cattle, servants, donkeys and camels (Gen 12:16).

After a period, Sarai took the initiative to fulfil the promise regarding a son by means of her own intervention. She could not wait any longer and so decided to misuse Hagar, an Egyptian maidservant. According to Genesis 16:2, Sarai said to Abram: "The Lord has kept me from having children. Go, sleep with my maidservant; perhaps I can build a family through her." The command was more or less in line with Hebrew custom that when the wife was barren, a maidservant could opt as a kind of replacement and carrier of a child in order to safeguard the generational claims of the clan. With this act Sarai tried to sidestep the covenantal promise. And Abram supported her. He slept with Hagar (literally he came into her) and she conceived. Knowing that she carried Abram's offspring, she started to despise Sarai. In return, Sarai now blamed Abram for the predicament. She could not bear the presence of Hagar anymore and started to ill-treat her. Eventually Abram delivered Hagar into Sarai's hands. So, Hagar fled from her into the desert. Near a spring, the angel of the Lord found her and announced that she is with child. She must call the child Ishmael which means 'for the Lord has heard of your misery.' Hagar then appealed to the very specific name of the Lord that has spoken to her, namely, El Roï: "You are the God who sees me." She also called the well *Beer Lachai-Roi*. Afterwards she returned to her place, serving under the hand of Sarai.

The waiting period for the promise to become fulfilled continued until Abram was ninety-nine years old. God then confirmed a new covenant with Abram and promised to greatly increase the number of his descendants. Abram will become the father of many nations indeed. Even the name of Abram should be changed. "No longer you will be called Abram; your name will be Abraham, for I have made you a father of many nations" (Gen 17:5). Even the name of Sarai should be changed. She will therefore no longer be called 'my queen' but Sarah, the queen, blessed by God. She will be blessed by many nations; kings will rise from her (Gen 17:6).

When Abraham heard all these words, he fell face down and laughed. It seemed quite impossible for him that a son will be born to a man of hundred years. That Sarah will bear a child at the age of ninety, sounded like a ridicule. Later on, when they camped at Mamre, God appeared in the form of three angels, three unexpected guests, at the tent of Abraham and Sarah. According to Hebrew hospitality, bread and meat had been served. Within this very kind and hospitable space, the angels made the announcement that within one year they will have a son. Sarah was listening at the entrance of the tent and when she heard the news, she laughed to herself, thinking that she was worn out and Abraham was already too old.

Ironically, laughing became a response of both Abraham and Sarah due to the irrationality of the promise and the very long period of waiting that seemed to be insane. In the account of the events, the long period of a year became stretched out. So many things happened. For example, there was the account of the possible wiping out of Sodom and Gomorrah, and Abraham's plea to spare the cities. It seems as if the promise is postponed indefinitely. But for how long? Is it perhaps because destruction and promise are often interrelated?

In the meantime, Abraham settled in the desert of Negev. As a kind of guest and stranger he must become a wanderer. And it seems amazing for the outsider, but for a second time he lied and told a different king, Abimelech, king of Gerar, that Sarah is his sister (Gen 20:2). Even Sarah acknowledged the lie by confirming that Abraham is indeed her brother. Luckily, God intervened, and in a dream warned Abimelech, revealing that Sarah is indeed a married woman.

Even though the two spouses played a very risky game, the event had a happy ending. They were mutually honoured in a very friendly way (*chēsēd*). Eventually, it seemed as if everybody involved in the drama saved his/her face. So, Abraham departed anew with sheep and cattle. In fact, he gained from the events. He even received a thousand shekels of silver due to his pretence to be called Sarah's 'brother'.

Eventually Sarah became pregnant and bore a son to Abraham in his old age. He gave him the name Isaac which means 'they laugh'. Another advantage for Abraham was that now he had in fact two sons: Ishmael and Isaac. The setting was very difficult for Sarah to deal with. Due to pressure from Sarah's side, Abraham sent Hagar and her son away. Surprisingly, for a second time, Abraham listened to Sarah.

Furthermore, it seems as if Abraham is not much concerned about his two sons. However, the matter distressed Abraham because the sending away indeed concerned his son. But God consoled him and promised to care for Ishmael as well. God also promised to make Ishmael into a nation because Ishmael is still Abraham's offspring.

After the treaty at Beersheba between Abraham, Abimelech and Phicol (the commander) the story continued and unfolded in a very dramatic way. We are now back to the second son of Sarah and Abraham. It is quite clear that God is not yet finished with Abraham. After all these events and words, God approached Abraham with a very peculiar test. He is going to test him in his son Isaac, the very one he loved.

A fundamental repositioning: *Hinéni* – here I am

After these words and events, it came to pass that God put Abraham to the test. He called him personally by his name. Abraham responded with the very poignant phrase: *Here I am* (הִנֵּנִי). The latter is a combination between 'seeing' (the event of gazing) and the addition of an *I* (an indicative pronoun – indicating the being-there of the I). With this response, and very indicative answer: *See me, here I am*, one positions oneself within the concreteness of time and place. One pronounces oneself as being wholeheartedly available with body and soul to the one who called one by his/her name and made an urgent appeal on one's being there.

Buber and Rozenzweig translated הנני consequently with *Da bin ich* (*Here I am*) (Buber & Rozenzweig 1981). *Hinéni* carries a deeper meaning than merely to say literally 'it is me'. It even implies more than a pure yes as a kind of confirmation. In fact, what happens is that one writes a kind of account: The answering *I* is within this event indeed *me*. Within this very acute mode of an accusative, a very poignant mode of availability is implied, namely I am ready, irrespective of what needs to be done (Levinas 1997:35-49). This mode of answering (*here-I-am*) is an intentional explication of that kind of availability wherein the *I* is willing to be endowed with responsibility. In this very moment of being called, one revealed that one is wholeheartedly prepared to take up the very 'spiritual position' of becoming that kind of *adama* (the Hebrew for earth and red soil) that is implied in our creatureliness. One can even say: "One is summoned into the mode of a vulnerable creature" – the embodiment of being within the concreteness of earthliness.

The point is: Somebody is calling. It sounds like an urgent appeal. In reality, what happens is that a subject is summoned and, in this summoning, the *I* presents him/herself to the Other in a very precarious asymmetry: The difference between the Other and me. The Other puts my very being and freedom into discussion. Even to the point where the positioning between the calling instance and the answering human being implies operating on two different levels. In this way, the calling delineates time and transposes it from chronological time into qualitative time. Since I am challenged by a Thou/thou, and thus have to answer, this response of answering qualifies time. Time is transposed into diachronic time, that is, into relational time. The dynamics of reciprocity that is created within intersubjectivity has a very specific feature. It does not reserve the in-between for a private business between two isolated *I*'s; it is not about performing a *pas de deux* – a kind of duet and two-step movement. This mutuality is rather a movement towards an unknown third one: The challenging Other/other. In fact, we are never ever merely twofold partners (Meulink-Korf & Van Rhijn 2016:41). We exist simultaneously within the bigger, interrelational framework of a coexisting whole.

The relationship between me and the Other/other can never be detached from my neighbour. And the alarming fact is that even the neighbour, who is suppressed and victimised by my presence, can turn up in the we-space of coexistence. The unknown third person, the unidentified stranger, becomes – in this very precarious encounter in a very profound way – my neighbour. That provides the reason why fairness and justice are necessities for creating appealing spaces of genuine dialoguing.

According to Genesis 12:1, God said: Abram. This vocative and personal pronouncement is the starting point to move away from the anonymity of brute massification into the humane space of trustworthy responsibility. One cannot ignore the urgent character of this personal address. One is invited to partake, because not to respond implies that even the name 'Abram' becomes insignificant. In reality, an ethical relationship has been established. The imperative mode of the summoning implies that our being human is now directed by a sense of destiny and meaning.

Imperative speech is often used in the Bible as a mode of being called personally by name. This is exactly what is illustrated in Genesis 12 in the calling of Abram: You go! The personal appeal implies that nobody can respond on your behalf. One is faced by a kind of inconvenience. According to Levinas, a kind of *divine discomfort*.

Eugen Rosenstock-Huessy captures this kind of existential predicament with the following phrase: *Respondeo etsi mutabor* (I respond, although I will be changed) (Rosenstock-Huessy 2003, chapter 3). Answers imply a mandate and are accompanied by the endeavour of taking a risk. The strange irony is that I am prepared to answer despite the pre-knowledge that the change implies the leaving of comfort zones and all forms of material gain. It could even result in sacrificing convictions, long-lasting customs, and habits very dear to one's daily orientation in life. To leave all these behind due to the vocative mode of speech, and imperative mode of addressing a human being to start anew, is quite radical. One needs to release every form of control and become prepared to forsake all forms of neat planning regarding orientation in life. To be called personally by your name is to be reminded of the fact that one is indeed a wanderer (*homo viator*); one is merely a kind of guest on this planet; nothing belongs to you permanently; one sojourns within a vast, desolate landscape. One, therefore, needs to continuously leave behind what has been achieved and proceed with life; it is about disorientation and reorientation and the meeting of new challenges; always being en route.

The rhythm of life envelops according to the different seasons of life. According to Ecclesiastes 3:1-2, there is a time for everything: A time to be born and a time to die; a time to plant and a time to uproot. Despite all these uprooting experiences, the significant calling and summoning are signals of reorientation in space and place and time. The entitlement into authentic being is in fact an appeal to move from anonymity into the uncharted landscape of a new destiny, and even reframed identity. Abraham, thus, gained a surprising I-awareness that reshaped his whole being. His unique existence is about a renaming framed by freedom and accountability. He is furthermore challenged to respond in a rather prophetic mode of answering that encompasses the other, as well as the next becoming generation. Abraham's availability follows the traces of the other; he is responding to a mandate that forces him to move from subjectivity into intersubjectivity (Meulink-Korf & Van Rhijn 2016, chapter 4).

The grace of answering: On becoming a subject

To be summoned into responsibility indeed causes a kind of existential discomfort. Without any doubt, responsibility implies accountability, and in this sense can become a heavy burden, especially when one takes the calling seriously. On the other hand, the discomfort is also a privilege and blessing. The privilege of answering is caused by grace and therefore an expression of *titre gratuit*: What one receives is totally free, free from charge because it is determined by grace alone. One is, so to speak, entitled to answer because the answering shapes the *I* into an accountable subject.

The sad thing in life is that within many inter-human relationships, there is no space for this kind of free expression of subjectivity. Many human beings are robbed of the opportunity and privilege to answer gracefully in freedom and in authenticity. In many forms of communication and interconnectedness, it seems that the real person does not count at all and is ignored without even the expectation of answering – the subject becomes voiceless, powerless and negated. In fact, the subject is treated as a non-entity without a name.

> The anonymity of namelessness can be viewed as a mode of blatant objectification, that is, our being human is reduced to the status

of a 'thing'. There are many very pungent examples of this kind of dehumanisation in history. The displacement of migrants and the xenophobic treatment of refugees in many refugee camps in Italy and Greece are witness of this kind of crime against humanity. Other examples are the spiral of violence in many townships in South Africa, the Uyghurs in China, sex workers and sex slaves, domestic workers. The degradation into becoming merely an object creates the anonymity of speech. The answers are no longer expressions of identity and subjectivity but abstractions of speech. One is merely allowed to say, 'yes sir' or 'no madam'. The responses do not emanate from the depths of authentic subjectivity.

The degradation of a human being into an object robs one of the opportunity of answering with 'Here I am.' One is thus excluded from the dynamics of reciprocity and the privilege of partaking in the grace of being human and the aesthetics of co-humanity – the grace of becoming a fellow human being. And this is exactly what happens to many people mentioned in the Bible.

The Bible often refers to 'the poor'. In Hebrew they are literally called the *anaviem*, from the core *anah*. In this sense, the poor are in fact the suppressed people robbed of their dignity. Within the dynamics of relationships, they are the victims of the abuse of power and many forms of discriminating malpractices such as racism, pigmentocracy, sexual orientation (homophobia), psychological or physical disabilities, religious fanaticism, ethnic hypocrisy and poverty exploitation. In many totalitarian social systems and regimes, human beings are tortured to the extent that they become victims of power abuse without any form of free expression or opportunity to pronounce: 'Here I am.' Thus, the reason why one needs to be most grateful for the privilege to make your choice of even becoming discomforted and disturbed, because in this kind of disorientation lurks the grace of subjectivity! In fact, this kind of discovery of the significance of true subjectivity qualifies the quality of our very being human, that is, to be summoned into accountability.

It is quite remarkable that the meaning of the Biblical understanding of 'soul' (Hebrew *nēfēsh*, Greek *psychē*) accentuates the quality of life. We often associate soul with non-human immortal images. That underlines the importance of taking care of the human soul. In terms of etymology, *nēfēsh* stems from throttle or throat as associated with processes of breathing and the movement of air. In connection with life (*chaja*), *nēfēsh* links ensoulment with the vitality of life. Life becomes endangered when the throat is put under pressure and breathing becomes hampered. Without a voice, life becomes threatened. When food and water cannot pass through, the quality of life is directly impacted.

Due to this etymological background of the concept *nēfēsh*, 'soul' cannot refer to an abstract entity or an unembodied spiritual manifestation of an unqualified entity. 'Soul' is essentially embedded in the intersubjectivity of a 'we-reality'. This 'we' is always located in place and space and anchored in concrete reality. The soul as a we-dynamic is, thus, a relational entity and always exposed to the possibility of being reduced to the level of merely becoming a sheer object, a brute kind of anonymity without a voice.

One should maintain the concreteness of 'soul'. Soul is endowed with the free spirit of graceful subjectivity and the capacity to decide. Proverbs 25:25 describes this vibrating, breathing and energetic soulfulness (the urge for life) in very poignant terminology: "Like cold water to a weary soul, is good news from a distant land."

With reference to the previous exposition, one can say that God tested Abraham's quality of being, his soulfulness as established by graceful subjectivity. Thus, the energetic response and auditive answer: "Here I am!"

The command: Go and take!

The command is very direct and clear: "Take your son, your only son Isaac, whom you love, and go to the land of Moriah, and offer him there as a burnt offering on one of the mountains that I shall show you." God made it very clear that the person implied in the command is Isaac and not Ismael. It is his only son, which makes the triad between this father and two sons complicated. For the second time, the words *lech lecha* (go or leave; literally: "Go for you" – Genesis 12:1) are used to address Abraham. Here in Genesis 22:2 the command is very abrupt: "Take and go!" One will find this kind of repetition 'to go' not elsewhere in the Bible. The command sounds like an invitation, but in fact it is very straight forward. It is about a very urgent commandment. He should depart immediately and go to the spot indicated by God. In Abraham's sight and immediate scope is now Mount Moriah (the mountain seen by Yahweh).

It has already been pointed out that the response 'Here I am' plays a pivotal role in the whole account. After this 'Here I am', seven times the imperative to go resonated. Despite several changes in terms of direction and place (so typical of Abraham's life journey), the change is now not merely affecting Abraham but very specifically his son. Isaac should go with him, moving upwards to the mountain as a kind of elevation. The momentum proceeds as a kind of 'raising up'. It becomes a gesture by which the offering is presented as a kind of gift by means of an uplifting gesture (Buber & Rosenzweig 1981:58 – "und höhe ihn dort zur Darhöhung"). The Hebrew word olah means that which goes up (in smoke). Besides the meaning of raising up or going up, it can also indicate growth (hifil). In order to keep track of the basic text, it becomes clear that in this 'moving up', the event does not refer to the sacrificial burnt offering (kind of sacrificial murder) as in many translations but to an act of responsible commitment and sheer trusting of heaving towards JHVH.

A quick glimpse over the text seems as if we encounter one of the sacrificial offerings of the first-born son as in many Canaanite rituals and religious practices. The translation of an uplifting gesture as an indication of dedication and accountable dutifulness (devotion) is nearer to the basic meaning of the account; it helps to prevent several moralistic interpretations or even psychological references as if we encounter in this ritual an example of an Oedipus complex or perhaps even an indication of a rivalry problem within the parent-child interaction. It should however be quite clear that God does not demand the offering of a child. The summoning is about a very urgent bidding to uplift his son by means of an elevating ritual around an altar, presenting the son as a gift.

It is quite remarkable how Abraham immediately began to prepare everything for the trip. Early the next morning he got up and saddled his donkey. He took two servants and his son Isaac with him. After he had cut enough wood, he set out for the place God had told him about. On the third day, Abraham looked up and saw the place in the distance. He told the servants to stay with the donkey while he and the boy will go further to the indicated place. Very specifically, he declared that they are going to worship and said: "We will come back to you." Noteworthy in this regard is the using of 'we'. Abraham then took the wood and placed it on his son Isaac. He himself carried the fire and the knife. So, the two of them went together.

Hinéni: The brief interlude between father and son

On the third day, Isaac spoke up and said to his father: "Father?" In his reply "Yes, my son?" Abraham responded for a second time with *Hinnéni*. Noteworthy is the fact that *Hinnéni* has now an extra dot before the duplication of *noen* (a double n). Now follows a very short conversation between father and son. In a very direct manner Isaac enquired about the lamb for the offering. In the context of the whole journey together with his son, this very brief exchange of a few words is quite remarkable. It is an indication of the value of a genuine dialogue. *The son acknowledged the father when he addressed Abraham. Vice versa, the father acknowledged his son in his response.* This brief conversation can be rendered as an excellent example of what authentic dialoguing is about: An exemplification of true reciprocity as based on mutual trusting. In this togetherness and mutual interconnectedness, the dynamics of attachment and detachment comes to the fore: Together, but still totally different. This moment becomes a kind of learning curve regarding the dynamics of intergenerational interaction. The son questions the father: "Father?" The father heard the son. In this kind of reciprocity, the true meaning of intimacy is captured. Intimacy therefore does not imply sameness. Even the experience of proximity does not become a kind of smothering nearness that changes the intimate space into a demanding authoritarian command. What is maintained in this intimate space of authentic dialoguing is the establishment of an ethically qualified distance (detachment) that creates the trustworthy character of true proximity. Both father and son maintain their specific role function within the dynamics of intergenerational interaction. The moment of encounter exemplifies what true asymmetry is about.

Asymmetry in dialoguing establishes both a qualified position and intergenerational differentiation: My father – my son. The established intersubjectivity in this relational mutuality exemplifies how equality and differentiation, as directed by justice, qualify the value of relational ethics (Meulink-Korff & Van Rhijn 2016:96). In this encounter the name Abraham was not echoed as a kind of vocative followed by an imperative as in other parts of the narrative. Here he is addressed as father (*ab*) and thus, the very meaningful presentation of his being there for *all, everyone, everybody* (even for offspring and coming generations): *Hinnéni*. Seeing me, deserves in this context indeed some extra dots.

The account regarding the different sequences of the narrative becomes excited and tense. Suddenly the son enquired: "Where is the lamb for the burnt offering?" This question does not refer to a kind of rivalry from the side of Abraham. Isaac responded quite respectfully by asking and posing an obvious question. If there is fire and wood, there should obviously be a lamb as well, otherwise the uplifting of a wave-and-heave-offering (gift of dedication and commitment) becomes insignificant. The answer of Abraham reveals true reciprocity and trustworthiness. He took the question seriously and pointed to the providence of God that opens new perspectives of seeing and the vista of the unseen. The response of the father is an indication that he learned from his son. At the same time, he helped his child to look further than the totality of what can be observed on the level of the senses – *the more* within finiteness. He spoke about a seeing that probes into transcendence; something external to the senses; a seeing that penetrates the unknown and the realm of the infinite: "God himself will provide, my son." With this remark, it is fascinating to discover how Abraham is in fact both teacher and scholar. One can even toy with the idea that Abraham is now entering the core of a personal affliction; he is facing the consequences of the trial, namely the affliction of becoming the father of a great nation.

> It has been narrated that when St Augustine was baptised at the same event with his son Adeodatus, he wrestled on his way to the baptismal fond with the burning question of how he, already as an aging person, could partake in the future of his son. He immediately realised that his position as clergy, his status and knowledge are no guarantee for being part of the future upbringing of his child. Being part of the future of his son is only possible and feasible by being alternately both teacher and scholar.

When Abraham looked up, he saw the mountain from a distance (Moriah as mountain of vision and seeing). We are again facing the notion of seeing. The same as in the incident with Hagar and her son Ishmael, El Roï and Lacha Roï, and now in the case of Abraham approaching this mountain of seeing, specifically in the seeing and facing of God who recognises (seeing as countenance) and provides. In both the cases of Hagar and Abraham, the parents must learn how to manage the limitations of time and space, and at the same time, how to learn to 'see' the more within visible perceptions; that is, how to deal with dialogical time as a more pure and true mode of looking behind mere factuality. They have to learn how to face moments of trustworthiness. One can even go so far as to toy with the idea that *noen* in *Hinnéni* received an extra dot due to the movement and reciprocity between father and son. It is as if, within this duplication, the availability of Abraham received an extra accent (Van Rhijn & Meulink-Korf 1997:370).

At this point in time, it seems that the conversation between father and son has reached its peak. This only dialogue is, so to speak, 'saturated', once in a lifetime! And so, they proceed together, upwards to the top of the mountain.

> One can conclude and say that this account of a very brief dialogue can help one to become more sensitive to insignificant details in pastoral counselling and conversing. Is it indeed possible that a fairly insignificant dialogical moment between a parent and a child from a very ancient story confirms the fact that even nowadays a sequence of moments can generate anew that kind of trust that establishes a mode of interconnectedness and experience of partaking in one another's existence. It is about a kind of mutual trust that can foster an intergenerational sense of belonging that surpasses even death. If the latter is indeed the case, pastoral caregivers should learn how to probe into the delicate texture and fabric of relational ethics and the impact of trustworthy moments of human encounters on the quality of dialoguing.

Moriah: Mountain of many vistas – on seeing the unseen

Eventually the two of them reached the place God has told them about. For the fourth time Abraham built an altar. However, this time it was quite different from the others. In the other occasions the altar was built for the Lord. This time there is no specific reference to whom. Abraham proceeded to bind his son Isaac and laid him on the altar. Surprisingly, here is no resistance from the side of Isaac. There is even no question about the lamb to be offered.

The sequence of unquestioning actions is indeed remarkable. It brings into discussion the notion of trust, specifically, the trusting of Isaac. Does his passive acceptance of the ritual point to trust in the promises and providence of the God of his father? Is his reaction an aftermath upon the *Hinnéni* (Here I am, my son) of his father? Albeit, the surrender of Isaac is twofold: It evokes awe as well as dreadful shuddering. What is indeed amazing is the very calm expression of trust as an act of confidence in the trustworthiness of the other whether the other is God or his father. The binding suddenly becomes an act of mutual trusting.

Is this trusting perhaps a sign or metaphor of the existential trust in the Jewish tradition and their religious heritage? Perhaps the reason why this event on the mountain is known in Israel as the *bounding of Isaac* and, even up to now, plays a decisive role in Hebrew thinking? This emphasis on the trust of Isaac stands in strong contrast to how traditional Christianity often tried to interpret the event as an example of Abraham's willingness to sacrifice his son (Jagersma 1995:253).

It is quite extraordinary how Isaac, later in his life, was tested when he became blind. In his blindness he has to discover that God foresees even if blindness implies to probe into the unforeseen realm of life by trusting God. A trusting that served as an exemplification of faith by starting to see the unseen realm of life!

Despite the response that God will provide, it seems that Abraham indeed reached for the knife. He reached out his hand and took the knife to slay his son. Suddenly, it seems as if it is no longer about a heave-offering as the lifting up of a gift (gesture of dedication) but indeed a kind of slaughtering. In fact, the text refers to *sjachat* from the verb which means to slay (in the case of killing a sheep). It is quite remarkable that God did not use the word *sjachat* himself. It is merely mentioned in the account of the narrative. And then, very suddenly, there is the voice of an angel of the Lord (now mentioned as JHWH) that called out from heaven: "Abraham! Abraham!" Here the doubled vocative is used that appears seven times in the Bible (see also Jacob in Gen 26:2; Moses in Ex 3:4; Samuel in 1 Sam 3:4; Martha in Lk 10:41; Simon Peter in Lk 22:31; Saul in Acts 9:45). In these examples, the doubled vocative is used within an imperative mode. Time and again it came as an appeal to reorient oneself, to develop a different perspective and to change radically. All of these originated on account of a voice from the outside, from facing the Other. At stake is the so-called 'third factor' reaching into the space of human existence from above (the transcendent realm).

The intriguing question right now is what motivated the authors of the Bible to no longer refer to the heaving-offering but to transgress to a more sacrificial stance in referring to the slaying of his son. Why the movement from heaving to slaying? Was the test really not to spare his son and to withhold him from God? Did he fear God so much that he will sacrifice and slay this son who God has entrusted him with? Even be prepared to 'kill' his son? However, the latter is totally not asked by God. God merely asked Abraham to take his son and to abide him within the ritual of heaving a gift to God. The summoning is not about a physical offering of a child. The summoning is to heave the child towards God within the ritual of thankfulness around an altar.

One can indeed pose the intriguing question: Why did Abraham initially change from heaving to slaughtering? What could be the reason behind this change? What happened to his faith that God will provide and will see them through? How thin the ledge of children or whatever is fabricated as being appropriate by virtue of one's own faith, personal ideas and fabricated ideologies? Instead of heaving and waivering one's own life in its dedication to one's destiny in life and calling, one can easily become a victim of self-fabricated shortcuts.

For Abraham, this intervention was costly but timely. In his overeagerness to direct his own life, and in his voracity to do more than what was expected from God, he objectified his son. It is as if he totally forgot how he instructed the two servants to wait and stay with the donkeys while they are going to worship. He was very adamant in the instruction and promise that they will return and come back to them.

To return to the question regarding Abraham's sudden change, one must admit that it is not quite clear why Abraham decided to change his mind. The reader should therefore keep the question open and unanswered. It is perhaps beneficial to keep the question open so that one can critically turn to one's own children in order to wrestle with the painful question of whether we really rendered our own children as precious gifts heaving them to life rather than pressurising them into ways and modes of living, foreseen by our own selfish convictions and short-sighted stubbornness. It is perhaps most appropriate not to force the text into too many possible explanations that serve different personal presuppositions. We should rather allow the text to speak in its own voice to the happenstances in our life, and how it impacts on the lives of so many people who cross our path in pastoral caregiving.

The remarkable intervention of the voice deletes the mythical and speculative interpretation of child-offering. The point is that Abraham heard the voice of the messenger of God and so echoed the third time his *Hinéni* in this text. But now not with a double *noen*. There is now no longer any mentioning of an intimate relationship between father and son. No reference whatsoever of a brief conversation and any dialoguing between the two of them. The only outstanding issue is another imperative: "Do not lay a hand on the boy." Very clear came the message: "Do not do anything to him." In fact, please Abraham, realise that he is not 'your son', your only begotten son. From now on you will side with your son in terms of a *bar mitswa*; he is now a son in terms of his own identity developing into personal and unique adulthood. He is indeed a *youngster* and young man within his own capacity.

Suddenly, when Abraham looked up, he saw the ram. There in a thicket was already the provision for the destined burnt offering. The scenario is now exactly as Abraham has described it: God will provide. But not the name 'God' in the very general meaning of *Elohim*, but as designated by *JHVH*; a name that cannot be pronounced in human language; a name indicating the promise of a continuous mode of presence: *I will be there where you are*. Abraham is now talking about that very specific Lord who will step in as a foreseeing factor on this mountain of never-ending vistas.

Thereafter, Abraham has been blessed by the angel of the Lord. In the narrative, there is no form of blame accusing Abraham for initially withholding his only begotten son from the 'God who will provide'. The point is that Abraham listened to the voice and did not perform the act of slaughtering when he took the knife. Abraham became blessed, but not because he was prepared to offer his son. Any form of moralistic causality in the interpretation should be abandoned. The blessing is connected to the fact that he heard and listened to the voice. Thus, the content of the blessing: All nations on earth will be blessed because Abraham responded to the voice of the Lord.

Then Abraham returned to his servants and they set off together for Beersheba. From now on there is no account of any spoken words between Isaac and Abraham. Not even between God and Abraham. The name Abraham is not pronounced any more by God. The test to obtain an offspring by means of Abraham's own efforts and interventions is now completed. So, the narrative reached its peak in the portrayal of God's gracious provision.

2.4   Odysseus and Abraham

In a recent publication of Reneé van Riessen, in the introduction she refers to Emmanuel Levinas' position and his connection to other philosophers (Van Riessen 2019:10-14). She did the description according to an image used by Levinas, namely the connection between Abraham and Odysseus.

The name Odysseus has become a symbol for the longing and desire to return to the island of Ithaka. Odysseus wanted to return to the place and space from where he originally departed. After twenty years of wandering and the exposure to many hardships, he eventually returned to Ithaka. But now, however, as a beggar hardly recognisable by anybody. Only his very old dog Argos recognised him.

Abraham became a symbol of a courage to be, namely, the courage to leave his home country and fatherland. He embarked on a journey not knowing whether he will come back. To wander about without any specific address, and to start searching every time for a new place, presupposed courage and a zest for life. The difference between Odysseus and Abraham was that Odysseus was not free from his own human limitations. In the case of Abraham, it was different because he listened to a voice reaching him from a transcendent realm.

Levinas used the symbol of Odysseus in a very critical way. According to Levinas, philosophy always tends to think in terms of circularity wherein one returns to what is in fact merely the same. This kind of circular movement eventually leads to the danger of a kind of neglect and disparagement of the other. Within Abraham's response, the voice answers so that the journey proceeds from the known environment towards the realm of the unknown. This kind of journey becomes a sign of courage. It displays a movement towards the Other/other (otherness within the realm of the unknown). The movement is not merely about a journey, but according to Levinas, a lifework. One is always exposed, time and again, to the challenge of making choices, life choices.

The multiplicity of many different calling voices

One is indeed confronted in life with many voices making an appeal on one's being. Unfortunately, it is impossible to respond to all of them simultaneously. One cannot respond to all of them with the answer: *Here I am!* One is always challenged to make a fundamental choice. That proves the awareness of an unavoidable existential discomfort. Because after I have made my decision to respond in one setting with *here-I-am*, it seems as if I have a kind of preference for one over another. It could leave the impression that the other option is of less value or that I am just stubborn and totally ignorant. Is it just about unwillingness? Why is it that one is willing to move in one direction without any logical reason and clear mindfulness? According to Nagy, it is about an irrevocable sense of belonging that steers one, even against one's own will, into the priority of one's family. This is what one can call loyalty – intergenerational, familial loyalty.

CHAPTER 3

Loyalty

The answer: 'Here I am', is the most basic stance in true dialogue. But immediately, this ontic stance implies many others – a whole network of intersubjectivity. One is therefore absorbed by a system of others stretching into the chain of becoming generations. In this chain of intergenerational interconnectedness, the most intimate circle is about familial connections.

In one way or another, family ties and familial interconnectedness contribute to an irrevocable sense of belongingness. Whether we acknowledge that or not, this kind of connectivity enjoys preference to many other forms of intersubjectivity. Nagy is one of the first researchers to recognise this peculiar pull and affinity between family members. He calls this connectivity an expression of *familial loyalty*. In his theory regarding family care, loyalty plays a fundamental and decisive role in his thinking about healing and human well-being (Boszormenyi-Nagy & Spark 1973:37).

Due to Nagy's work in the slums of Philadelphia, he was challenged by the intriguing question, namely, why interdependency develops between different generations and seems to form real bounding ties and lasting connections. For him, the only logical reason was that this sense of intergenerational interconnectedness, as well as a deep sense of belonging, could only be explained as an ethical entanglement based upon the phenomenon of loyalty. Nagy's research also pointed out that even during family crises and conflict situations, a mutual sense of healing power suddenly envelops amongst family members. Against all odds and all logic, family members start to defend one another and tend to be willing to take care of one another. He observed that this kind of behaviour even develops amongst very young children. Suddenly a sense of belonging is established that wants to set things right. It is especially discernible when family members must make important decisions regarding heavy burdens affecting relationships between family members and non-family members. Family connections are, for them, irrevocable and based on a deep sense of mutual obligation.

This observation of Nagy leads, in his theory formation, to the basic assumption that human beings live within the dynamics of relationships. *Nagy called this relational networking context.* And in every person's context, loyalty is the fundamental source for a sense of belonging and the cohesive factor of interconnectedness.

3.1   *Context: Inter-relationality and ethical entanglement*

With *context* is not meant a kind of networking activity that is quite normal in the world of business, economic scheming and industrial practices of negotiations where networking often implies the obligation to take advantage for own productive concerns. For Nagy, networking is radically different. Networking is about the ethical entanglements of interrelationality. A network is, thus, a relational entity. He calls the network of a human person a *loyalty fabric.* When a person is involved in networking entanglements, this relational interconnectivity implies that this person becomes immediately woven into the fabric of a huge embroidery of interconnected modes of loyalty. The threads of interconnectivity are like a tapestry of interwoven connections (Van Rhijn & Meulink-Korf 1997:65; 2019:71). In contextual therapy, context is therefore not an indication of a concrete situation referring to merely *local issues on grass roots level.*

For Nagy, context represents *the relational reality of every person.* Every human being is an offspring of a father and mother. We are therefore all existentially connected to more than one person. *This interconnectedness is like an organic cohesion, woven into the dynamic of a mutual sense of togetherness.* Within a more vertical perspective and approach (vertical line), one can say that every human being is intergenerationally connected. Intergenerationality creates an inclusivity with the still-to-be-born generation – the upcoming generations of the future. Therefore, loyalty brings about an interconnectedness irrespective of whether you have died or are still alive, whether you are present or not. In this way context and loyalty are comprehensive entities, they are all-inclusive. Within a horizontal perspective and approach (horizontal line), every human being is simultaneously generationally connected with both the vertical dimension and the immediate established relationships as well, namely, with partners, friends, colleagues, teachers and all other people irrespective of age.

The connections between relationships within a networking whole are not neutral. They are characterised by the 'how' of mutual caregiving. In fact, they display responsibility, namely, how responsibility is exercised as well as how it is received. In this respect, mutual caregiving and responsibility display context, and, very specifically, the character of *relational ethics*. The context reveals in this sense the multi-dimensionality of life stories; it points to layers of motivation, the exercising of options, the promotion of rights, the maintaining of obligations and the concern for indebtedness. That is the reason why everybody's context is unique. Context always refers to the unique space and place wherein a human being exists in terms of the mutuality of relational sense of belonging. *Context can even be viewed as an account on the mutuality of give and take.* Furthermore, in context, one can also detect whether this kind of exchange between giving and taking is directed by fairness or not. "The embroidered threads, woven by loyalty, create a kind of safety net (catcher) that prevents us to fall back into a kind of anonymity deprived of vital relationships, in the same way a safety net catches acrobats when they run the danger of losing their balance and tend to fall down" (Ducommun-Nagy 2008:25).

The following case study refers to a young man phoning his sister while in a state of total confusion. He shared that he and his wife are experiencing a severe marriage crisis after a short period of two years. The detachment started shortly after the marriage due to unexpected foreign travels of his wife which again and again presented him with an accomplished fact. He immediately realised he had to start coping with the situation, namely, how to arrange everything with work, friends, two dogs, housekeeping, all things that were not directly her business. However, it was as if he did not really cope with the challenges. "I completely lost myself," said the man. "Completely?" asked his sister. "Is that indeed the case with your connections with me and our mother? Do these connections confuse you as well?" "No," said the brother, "not really." She then asked: "Is that the same scenario with your friends?" "Neither," said the brother. "Hey, then I haven't completely lost myself, at least I'm still in one way or another connected to you both!"

Context: The paradigmatic optic of four lenses

The argument thus far is that context refers to a dynamic network of relationships that embeds every human being. In fact, context is woven into many stories and narratives. People talk about issues, namely, who really counts, who would be missed, who is truly reliable, who needs care, who helps to cheer up others. For pastoral caregivers and helpers, it is important to obtain a general view regarding personal narratives and the undergirding realities in these networking relationships. It is important to probe into possible sources that contribute to a sense of relational embeddedness.

Nagy and Krasner describe four dimensions of contextual networking that can help to detect a kind of order (regularity) in the dynamics of contextual networking (Boszormenyi-Nagy & Krasner 1994:60). The ordering is not about an attempt to systematise the dynamics into fixed categories. It is more designed to be used as a kind of mapping in order to reckon with everyone's needs and concerns simultaneously. For this mapping, Nagy and Krasner use four lenses, namely, facts, needs, patterns within the dynamics between power and powerlessness, and the interplay between care and responsibility. These four lenses function as paradigms that exist strictly independently but, at the same time, are closely connected.

The differentiation between the separate dimensions helps to develop a more comprehensive understanding of someone's intergenerational, relational reality. Noteworthy is the fact that this network is in principle intergenerational. The dimensions provide first impressions of how a person is interconnected and who are all the role players at stake within a very specific context.

In order to get clarity on the character of the ordering in terms of four lenses, one should understand that the attempt to classify refers merely to perspectives and is not meant to identify ontic stratifications. To be clear, the ordering therefore presents *views* (perspectivism), not *modes of being* (ontic).

The four lenses provide a framework of reference:

1. The dimension of possible objectification of facts (facticity).
2. The dimension of individual psychology (psychological realm).
3. The dimension of transactional patterns and systems (relational dynamics).
4. The dimension of relational ethics concerning appropriate attention, deserved trust, care and responsibility (ethical entanglements) (Meulink-Korf & Van Rhijn 2016:9-15).

The first dimension of facticity: Facts

The first dimension is about gathering facts from the social and economic background and historical setting. Important information detects decisive facts like the year of birth, place of birth, school years and education, general well-being, religious affiliation, church connection, disasters, war and conflict, political ideology like apartheid, colour of skin, marriage connection and divorce, and so on. These kinds of information reside under the category of semi-objectifiable facts. They are exposed to many variables. They are connected to often unprovoked or even irrevocable differences between family members and siblings, between friends and researchers, between inhabitants living together in the same street or neighbourhood. The point is that no-one has asked to be born with a brown, white or black skin. The colour of our skin is a sheer given. However, these kinds of facts belong to our heritage. One can even say, I inherited them, and they are part of my existential baggage. For example, in South Africa it is indeed a question whether your parents were removed from District Six in a brutal and violent way to eventually be forced to settle down in the barren outskirts of Cape Town. And fifty years later, the conditions have not improved much so that many are still exposed to severe poverty. This kind of situational factuality indeed has consequences that become transferred to a next generation. The same argument is valid in cases where one's parents owned, through many generations, a prosperous wine farm so that wealth has become an obvious advantage.

Facts are not neutral and without any implications for the quality of one's living conditions. As argued, they also imply ethical consequences as well. For example, it makes a huge difference whether one has been born in a stable marriage environment where both parents had the time and financial means to take care for one's upbringing, or, whether one has grown up in a single parent setting with an absent father wherein the mother has been forced to struggle daily just to survive, knowing that she could hardly cope. Even though facts belong eventually to our past, they always determine processes of decision-making, and in this sense, the quality of our present and even future living conditions. This does not mean that facts are per se absolutely the last, final determinants for the significance of being and direction of our lives. The point is that one has to deal with the consequences for personal behaviour and responses, specifically in terms of the impact of facts on one's relational networking and how data and information impact on the different dimensions of our daily existence. Facts are not indicators for a fatalistic outlook on life as if one is determined by fate. Even against all negative factual indicators, one can still respond with trustworthiness and experience a kind of trust. But the opposite is true as well. Despite all positive indicators and facts, one can still respond in a destructive manner.

For caregivers, pastors and helpers, facts are indeed very important. They are decisive for the quality of caregiving. It is therefore important to attend to important facts because they prevent caregivers from too easily jumping to conclusions and formulating presuppositions based on intuition and the so-called 'professional pre-knowledge'. Not to attend to facts and to be informed by prejudice, plays a decisive role in the formation of skewed impressions and incomplete images of the other. To ignore facts is in fact unethical because it can rob the other of his/her dignity and unique subjectivity. It can even make the other a captive of his/her own individual limitations; it detaches human beings from being interconnected with history and their unique family legacy. Facts are intrinsically related to the narratives of generations and familial traditions. They demarcate and narrate how loyalty colours kinship and congeniality; they even render a more intensive and broader perspective on interconnectivity.

The second dimension of psychology: Psychological consciousness and experiences

According to Nagy, individual psychology belongs to the second dimension. How a person responds to the factuality of historical events and interprets them; how a person responds to needs, behaviour, emotional urges and observes the impact of life events on human existence, all these phenomena determine individual behaviour. That explains why Nagy developed his psychotherapeutic knowledge on clinical observation as well as on insights and developments in individual psychology by peer researchers (Meulink-Korf & Van Rhijn 2016:10; Van Rhijn & Meulink-Korf 1997, chapter II.2; 2019, chapter 2).

Nagy emphasised the importance of individual directed psychology. For him it is not to the advantage of theoretical simplicity when the significance of human drives, psychological development and subjective experiences are ignored (Nagy 2000:22). It is in this regard that theory formation for Nagy should always serve the purpose of sound practice. Without insight in the psychological make-up of a person, it is virtually impossible to support a person in how to cope with his/her personal discomfort and confusion in life. In his theoretical reflection, Nagy links with many different schools and researchers in psychology and therapy. He made use of their concepts and incorporated them in his therapeutic approaches. He even enriched different theories with his view on *relational ethics* and its impact on intersubjectivity.

Furthermore, for Nagy an individual approach and treatment should always be about a *multi-directed partiality*. Multi-directed partiality is one of the keystones in a contextual approach. Its aim is to focus not merely on the client, but also to simultaneously deal with many other people who are directly or indirectly always present, and thus involved in therapeutic sessions (Nagy 2000, chapter 6). Nagy very aptly pointed out how this multi-directed partiality safeguards one and offers protection against possible harming consequences of transference and contra-transference between client and therapist as well between clients and their existing relationships with other people. Noteworthy is the fact that Nagy's approach provided new perspective and insight on the disturbed balance of give-and-take within the mutual interaction between parent and child. This new insight was most helpful in the explanation of the phenomenon of parentification (rendering a child as if he/she is already a parent; see chapter 4, Nagy 2000).

The third dimension of relational dynamics and interactive networking: Transactions

This third lens is about information regarding the organisational structure of systemic interaction (transaction) and how transactions impact on the texture of intersubjectivity and reciprocity. It describes the mutual dynamics in terms of a more diagrammatic design and informative sketch. It depicts the relational reality of families and familial interaction and portrays how group interaction is structured. It helps one to 'see' how a group of people, sharing mutually with one another, functions. It helps one to understand that people who do have something in common with one another are more than the sum of the different parts that constitute the whole. A group is compiled by more than the addition-sum of all the individual psychological entities together (Meulink-Korf & Van Rhijn 2016:11).

This dimension of organic structuredness regarding the dynamic ordering of relational interaction helps one to make visible how interactions and transactions develop mutually. The depiction portrays how people influence one another; how interchange can make people free or bind them; how power and powerlessness can be decisive for self-understanding. Transactions help to indicate possible collusions or coalitions; they reveal how conflict originates and by who conflict is established or not. The further advantage is that transactions help to detect patterns of interaction between partners, family members and the linkages in group dynamics. These patterns operate like regulative directives or rules. The regulative directives (see *loi*, the French for *law*) are decisive for the how and quality of human interaction. The ordering summons one to display fairness and loyalty within all these processes of interaction.

The dynamic transactions that regulate patterns of behaviour function like self-regulating mechanisms. They operate even when one is not aware of their impact on interactional patterns (Boszormenyi-Nagy & Krasner 1994:71). When a system is closed, it robs human behaviour from authentic freedom and individual expression. It is therefore to the advantage of researchers that, in the therapeutic field of operations, many creative forms and portrayals have been developed in order to describe and detect these mechanisms.

During the time when Nagy started to develop his family therapy, it was still presented in the more linear paradigm. However, gradually it developed into a more circular approach which Nagy used to emphasise the value of *subjectivity and intersubjectivity* within the space of human interaction. His basic starting point is the notion of *multi-partiality* which helps to build more confidence in intersubjective communication despite the existence of even many destructive systems. Confidence and trust invite individuals to respond with constructive responsibility. They even promote a sensitivity and concern to focus more on the vulnerable link in the family or group system.

The advantage of transactional systems is that they contribute to more clarity on how mutual communication envelops, and how one becomes aware of the ethical structuredness of relationships within mutual interaction. Listening to everybody's story helps one to discover how the ethical structure renders significance to human encounters. Also, how interactions can promote or even hamper sustainable trust. Without a deep concern and attention, the sensitivity for relational ethics can become lost.

The dimension of transactional analysis helps to illuminate the depth of human interaction within all three dimensions. In a very poignant way, it highlights the value of the fourth dimension of relational ethics. It helps to identify dysfunctional forms of reciprocity in family systems or between colleagues. It also reveals how responsibility is dealt with or even neglected; how dysfunctional power struggles envelop in family systems; how social systems within communities can boycott the display of civil and public loyalty and eventually contribute to social disloyalty.

The fourth dimension of relational ethics: Care and responsibility (ethical entanglement)

Within the realm of caring, helping and human well-being, Nagy's largest contribution is his emphasis on the link between ethics and relational networking. That explains the emphatic promotion of the relational and ethical dimension as lens for understanding the value of intersubjectivity in human interaction and encounters. In order to listen very accurately to how people develop and expand their coexistence, how they harm the quality of interaction and often obscure the dynamics of intersubjectivity, it is necessary to attend to the core issues and basic concepts at stake concerning an ethical approach to relational connections. This focus will also help to assess to which extent processes of human interaction are fair or not. In order to maintain fairness and dignity, to establish trust and probe into distrust, to foster trustworthiness and to deal with harmed trustworthiness, to promote the quality of mutuality and to identify hampering factors, a discussion of basic concepts and words are imperative.

The second and third dimensions help to understand individuals within their relational settings. They provide insight regarding mutual human behaviour on the level of intersubjectivity. The value of the third dimension is that it reveals what exactly motivates people to care for themselves and other people. It is in this fourth dimension that Nagy's contribution to healing and helping becomes evident. It also indicates why this dimension is fundamental to all the other three dimensions. Since this dimension is for many quite an eye opener, it is necessary to repeat: *This dimension reveals the fact that human behaviour and mutual interaction are shaped by an ethical dynamic.* The latter helps to focus on what is fair or not, who is responsible and how people should behave. It operates like a source for new modes of trusting and the instalment of justice. This dimension also sheds light on how one observes and listens to what takes place between people and how it impacts on human freedom, on human obligations and indebtedness. In order to establish constructive modes of being, and to maintain the quality of all such relationships, one needs to understand that the quality of relationships boils down to justice, trustworthiness and fairness. These concepts are indeed heavy but decisive in order to learn how destructive modes of interaction can be stopped or prevented and how harmful transactions can be steered into more constructive movements and behaviour.

In his work with families, Nagy observed that there is always 'a more' existent in systemic dynamics. This more exceeds the parameters of mere objectified observation. One can even say that this more emerges within awe and the expression of different kinds of hoping. This hope expands in the in-between space amongst people as a very unique thread of caring and trusting; it contributes to the establishment of new modes of trusting.

The ethical paradigm: Core concepts

The specific concepts described by Nagy in this fourth dimension are ethical because they demarcate a sound consciousness of responsibility. They refer to a kind of ethics that is embedded in the a priori of existential happenstances and therefore not bounded to abstract logic and external, legal prescriptions.

In this publication, core concepts such as giving and taking, parentification, revolving slate, multi-directed partiality, exoneration and aspects of genuine dialogue, will be discussed. A most basic concept within an ethical paradigm is loyalty. Loyalty is fundamental because it can be traced back to a basic frame of reference within all of these dimensions; it functions as a kind of cohesive factor. It is self-evident why loyalty is decisive for the fourth lens of relational ethics.

The exposition will start with the book of Samuel. The text is about King David who illustrates how in a very reliable way, trustworthiness should be exemplified in human relationships. The story is quite impressive. It illustrates that loyalty is not easy and implies a kind of discomfort because in the making of choices, one wavers between the difficulty to whom one should bestow more loyalty and to whom one should be less loyal.

3.2 An exemplification of loyalty and trustworthiness: 2 Samuel 9:1-13

[1]David asked,

> "Is there still anyone left of the house of Saul to whom I may show kindness for Jonathan's sake?"

[2]Now there was a servant of the house of Saul whose name was Ziba, and he was summoned to David. The king said to him,

> "Are you Ziba?"

And he said,

> "At your service!"

[3]The king said,

> "Is there anyone remaining of the house of Saul to whom I may show the kindness of God?"

Ziba said to the king,

> "There remains a son of Jonathan; he is crippled in his feet."

[4]The king said to him,

> "Where is he?"

Ziba said to the king,

> "He is in the house of Machir son of Ammiel, at Lo-debar."

[5]Then King David sent and brought him from the house of Machir son of Ammiel, at Lo-debar. [6]Mephiboshet, son of Jonathan son of Saul, came to David, and fell on his face and did obeisance. David said,

> "Mephibosheth!"

He answered,

> "I am your servant."

[7]David said to him,

> "Do not be afraid, for I will show you kindness for the sake of your father Jonathan; I will restore to you all the land of your grandfather Saul, and you yourself shall eat at my table always."

[8]He did obeisance and said,

> "What is your servant, that you should look upon a dead dog such as I?"

[9]Then the king summoned Saul's servant Ziba, and said to him,

"All that belonged to Saul and to all his house I have given to your master's grandson. [10]You and your sons and your servants shall till the land for him, and shall bring in the produce, so that your master's grandson may have food to eat; but your master's grandson Mephibosheth shall always eat at my table."

Now Ziba had fifteen sons and twenty servants. [11]Then Ziba said to the king,

"According to all that my lord the king commands his servant, so your servant will do."

Mephibosheth ate at the table, like one of the king's sons. [12]Mephibosheth had a young son whose name was Mica. And all who lived in Ziba's house became Mephibosheth's servants. [13]Mephibosheth lived in Jerusalem, for he always ate at the king's table. Now he was lame in both his feet.

Chēsēd (ḥēsēd): Faithfulness, loyalty

Mephibosheth was the only son of Jonathan, the very close friend of David. He was also the grandchild of Saul. Many years after the death of Jonathan and Saul, David took Mephibosheth into his household. At that time, David was king, settled in his palace in Jerusalem. Motivation for David's decision is the ḥēsēd as established by a covenant of faithfulness between David and Jonathan (1 Sam 20:12-17). In this text, ḥēsēd is used four times during the confirmation of the covenant. In fact, ḥēsēd is a keyword in the Bible and appears regularly. The most appropriate way to explain ḥēsēd is with the concept faithfulness as indication of an indissoluble connectedness and devotion as displayed in just care and responsibility. It could be thus rendered as a relational concept in the same way that all biblical concepts are in fact relational.

In German ḥēsēd is translated as *Zugehörigkeit*, that is, a sense of belonging that expresses connection and relationship as well. Buber and Rozenzweig translate ḥēsēd consequently with grace (graciousness) and the bestowing of a kind of preference (favouritism) or partiality that displays a choice. In the New Revised Standard Version, the English translation of ḥēsēd is kindness. In De Naarden's translation, ḥēsēd is translated as friendship.

However, the translation into kindness or friendship seems to be too vague and without any obligation or engagement. The concept *ḥēsēd* is not optional but summons one to an obligation. The Greek translation of *ḥēsēd* is *eleos* and implies a relational and ethical character as being displayed in compassion and pity. In Genesis 24:27, *ḥēsēd* refers to an obligation that is related to a marriage contract and covenant of faithfulness and commitment as in the case of Isaac, the son of Abraham. In the treaty at Beersheba between Abraham and king Abimelech, they bestowed *ḥēsēd* towards one another (Gen 24:27). One can, therefore, conclude and say that *ḥēsēd* is characterised by covenantal acts of obligation, displaying justice and compassion. The latter display of deep concern is indeed valid for the quality of establishing trustworthy ties with family, friends, guests and strangers. Jonathan Sacks writes that *ḥēsēd* originates from a sentence in the second chapter of Genesis, namely "It is not good for the man to be alone" (Gen 2:18). He then points out that *ḥēsēd* refers to love that represents loyalty, and, vice versa, to a kind of loyalty that represents love (Sacks on *ḥēsēd*: 2016:61-63; 2005:47-48). Therefore, whenever one uses the concept of *ḥēsēd*, it is of paramount importance to connect it with loyalty.

Covenantal faithfulness: The crippled and vulnerable Mephibosheth

Mephibosheth was five years old when the news about the death of Saul and Jonathan came from Jezreel. Immediately the future of Mephibosheth was in jeopardy. Due to the news of a coming war, his nurse picked him up and fled, but as she hurried to leave, he fell and became crippled (2 Sam 4:4).

Many years later, David asked whether there is anyone still left of the house of Saul to whom he can show kindness for Jonathan's sake (2 Sam 9:1). It seems as if the question came as a bolt from the blue without any connection to the chronology of the facts. For David, his question is connected to *his covenant of faithfulness with Jonathan*. So, it happened to be that there was a servant of Saul in the household with the name of Ziba. They called him to appear before David. When the king asked him whether he is Ziba, he replied: "Your servant." He answered that he knows about Jonathan's son who was crippled in both feet. He also informed David that this son is at the house of

Makir in *Lo Debar*. Literally the name means *without any word or deed*. It is a place where no word is spoken, and no action is performed. In Lo Debar there is nothing and nothing happens there. It is as if this place weaves within a silent space interlocked between past and future without chronology. It is about a place and space without any perspective on time, not even a movement into something new.

> This place seems like Lesbos, an island near Greece where refugees landed after surviving the trip over the Mediterranean see. They are totally displaced and captured into a state of timelessness and hopelessness. Without affiliation to any state, they could not even appeal to the Universal Declaration of Human Rights, article 6 that reads that everybody, wherever you are, does have the right to be recognised as a person before the law.

David then sent messengers to bring Mephibosheth from Lo Debar. The dynamic between very short and unobtrusive words is decisive indeed. It demarcates the difference between life and death. Mephibosheth was brought to Jerusalem and ushered into the palace of King David sitting upon his throne.

It is quite remarkable that during the ceremony where Mephibosheth was presented to David, Ziba was absent. When Mephibosheth bowed down to pay David honour, he answered with the same phrase used by Ziba: "Your servant" (2 Sam 9:6). David responded and told him not to be afraid for he will surely show him kindness (*ḥēsēd*) for the sake of his father Jonathan. The concept *ḥēsēd* is used twice in the Hebrew text to underline the trustworthiness of him being faithful to his covenantal promise to Jonathan. Furthermore, David promised that he will restore all the land that belonged to his grandfather Saul. David also gave Mephibosheth the guarantee that he will always eat at his table. In this way Mephibosheth received back his fair position within the generational family tree.

Mephibosheth was humbled by these words of David so that he bowed down and said: "*What is your servant, that you should notice a dead dog like me?*" (2 Sam 9:8). David was however deeply committed to what he said. He ordered Ziba, with his fifteen sons and twenty servants to farm the land for Mephibosheth and to provide him with the crop. It is indeed very interesting that David maintained the division between Ziba and Mephibosheth. Ziba and his whole entourage of servants will henceforth serve Mephibosheth.

The intriguing question right now is: How will this difference between Ziba and Mephibosheth determines the relationship David-Ziba-Mephibosheth?

In Jerusalem Mephibosheth grew up. He flourished and it is even mentioned that Mephibosheth had a young son Mica. Nothing is further mentioned about the whereabouts of Mephibosheth. However, the important point to grasp is that just the mentioning of his name connected Mephibosheth intergenerationally. He became part of the fourth generation from the household of Saul, now hosted in the household of David. In this way, the familial tie is sustained and prolonged into the future. And all of this happened due to David's faithfulness to his friend Jonathan. Loyalty is indeed durably. Catherine Ducommun-Nagy wrote as follows about loyalty: "Loyal is also somebody who respects his different engagements, acts in a trustworthy way and not commit any fraud or any betrayal" (Ducommun-Nagy 2008:82).

Mephibosheth, thus, stayed in Jerusalem. He was still crippled in both feet. This is how the translation referred to Mephibosheth. However, this is not completely true. Something changed indeed: He jumped and skipped. Instead of the word for *cripple*, a word is used from the root *pèsach*. What is implied is that Mephibosheth was more than being an invalid (crippled). *Pèsach* is the stem which is used for the angel passing by the evening before the exodus of Israel from Egypt. The angel passed by the houses and the people of Israel, skipping and jumping on their way to freedom. Mephibosheth departed from *Lo Dabar*. Now it is suddenly *pèsach* for Mephibosheth. Suddenly he is skipping and jumping in Jerusalem like the angels in a miraculous exodus!

Disequilibrium in the triade: Ziba, David, Mephibosheth

The relationship between David, Ziba and Mephibosheth was not without any complication. It was not easy to maintain fairness and equilibrium in this triadic dynamic. Later, it became clear that Ziba's behaviour is going to cause some disequilibrium and discomfort in the relationship.

David had to face the conspiracy of Absalom and left Jerusalem to attend to urgent matters. In 2 Samuel 16:1 Ziba approached David. With him he had a string of donkeys saddled and loaded with two hundred loaves of bread, a hundred cakes of raisins, cakes of figs and a skin of wine. He revealed to David that Mephibosheth is also busy in Jerusalem to overthrow the throne of David. According to Ziba, Mephibosheth stayed in Jerusalem because he thought that on this very day the house of Israel will give him back his grandfather's kingdom. David believed Ziba and said to him: "All that belonged to Mephibosheth is now yours." In this way the whole inheritance shifted towards Ziba. It is therefore quite understandable why Ziba humbly bowed and said: "*May I find favour in your eyes, my lord the king*" (2 Sam 16:4).

After a long absence, David returned to Jerusalem. On his way to the city, Mephibosheth went down to meet the king. He approached David like a person in mourning. He had not taken care of his feet or trimmed his moustache or washed his clothes *from the day the king left until this hour of his return* (2 Sam 19:25). With this gesture he wanted to prove his loyalty to David due to David's kindness (*ḥēsēd*) to him. Mephibosheth then revealed Ziba's deceit and how he betrayed him. Actually, Ziba slandered him. Mephibosheth also affirmed his devotion to David and called him David's servant. To him, David is like an *angel (messenger) of God*. He also acknowledges that all Saul's descendants deserve nothing but death from David. "So, do whatever pleases you" (2 Sam 19:27). In his response, David ordered Mephibosheth not to speak to him in this way anymore. David now must face the dilemma of conflicting loyalties and experiences a huge discomfort. Knowing that he has to face different kinds of conflicting loyalties, and that he is facing a Catch-22 situation (Naastepad 2004:267). On the one hand, there is the *ḥēsēd* to Mephibosheth, on the other hand, there is the promise (pledge) he made to Ziba which he could not break. While facing this dilemma, David summons Mephibosheth and Ziba to divide the fields. With this very wise decision, Ziba thus also would partake in the heritage of his master Saul. Even Mephibosheth gained because there was enough to provide in his basic needs.

However, the complexity of the triad Ziba-David-Mephibosheth is not resolved by this very fair deal. David's loyalty will be tested again in the book of Samuel.

The discomfort of David

The account about David's *ḥēsēd* turns out to become a never-ending story. The trouble to decide which of the two forms of loyalty deserves preference just continued. According to 2 Samuel 21:1 there was a famine during the reign of David. When David sought the face of the Lord, the Lord said that it was on account of Saul and his blood-stained house. Due to the grim law of causality, the famine should be linked to the fact that Saul put the Gibeonites to death. Here David has to face the inevitable fact of a revolving slate.

The king, thus, summoned the Gibeonites and asked them: "What shall I do for you: How shall I make amends so that you will bless the Lord's inheritance?" (2 Sam 21:4). The Gibeonites answered him: "We have no right to demand silver or gold from Saul or his family." They also do have no right to put anyone in Israel to death. But because they were decimated and have no place anywhere in Israel, they will be satisfied if seven of the male descendants be given to them to be killed. David responded immediately. He spared Mephibosheth, this very special son of Jonathan because of the oath between David and Jonathan (ḥēsēd) before the Lord. He maintained his oath even if it will cost him seven men from the descendants of Saul. In this way David was challenged by the divine discomfort of ḥēsēd. It was impossible for David to reject the request of the Gibeonites. He has to maintain the oath even at the disadvantage of others. In this way David saved the life of Mephibosheth at the cost of two of the sons of Rizpah (concubine of Saul) and the five sons of Merab, the daughter of Saul.

The whole account illustrates how the challenge and decision to install justice and to stay loyal can put one in distressing situations. An oath (ḥēsēd) can sometimes become devastating, even deadly.

The ḥēsēd of Rizpah: The first 'foolish mother'!

All seven men were put to death during the first days of the harvest. The Gibeonites killed them and exposed them high on a hill. They became, so to speak, the prey of wild animals and birds of the fields. When she heard the news, Rizpah took sackcloth and spread it out before her on the rock. Very much in the same way that Jacob put on a cloth when he received the news of the death of his beloved son Joseph (Gen 37:34). She continued from the beginning of the harvest until the rain poured down on the bodies. She did not let the birds of the air touch them by the day or the wild animals by night.

This account is quite remarkable. Amongst all the heroic tales of men in the Bible, this mother and woman made the significant meaning of ḥēsēd visible as an impressive illustration of what loyalty entails (2 Sam 21:10). Rizpah became a symbol of what justice entails. She demonstrated loyalty and resisted the very cruel act of hanging. When David was told what Rizpah did, he went and took the bones of Saul and his son Jonathan from the citizens of Jabesh Gilead. Together with the bones of those who had been killed and exposed, they buried all of them in the tomb of Saul's father Kish, at Zela in Benjamin.

Rizpah can be called a symbol of loyalty, demonstrated by a woman. In this way she could be called the first 'foolish mother'! Wisdom enacted in the disguise of sheer foolishness.

> She can be compared to what is known as the *Mothers of the Plaza de Mayo* (Spanish: *Asociación Madres de Plaza de Mayo*). The latter is about a movement of Argentine mothers who campaigned for their children who 'disappeared' during the military dictatorship (military junta who reigned from 1976 to 1983). When they pursued the government for answers, they were not received. However, statistics revealed that at least 13 000 people had been killed. They began to gather for remembering this event every Thursday, from 1977, in front of the presidential palace (Casa Rosada) at the Plaza de Mayo in Buenos Aires (Argentine). They did it in public defiance of the government's law against mass assembly. Wearing white head scarves, they thus symbolise the diapers (nappies) of their lost children, embroidered with the names and dates of birth of their offspring. The mothers marched in pairs in solidarity to protest the denials of their children's existence and their mistreatment by the military regime. Despite personal risks, they wanted to hold the government accountable for the violation of human rights, committed during the 'Dirty War'. Every week, for thirty years they continued to perform this demonstration against injustice done by the military regime.

In his writings, Levinas refers to Rizpah. He wrestles with the question of how to respond to this very bleak vision on our being human (*condition humaine*) and the quest for justice. What is that *more* that surpasses the cruelty of the rational order of our being human? To Levinas the image of this mother, this woman, protecting the victims of this cruel onslaught against the birds of prey and the wild animals, should become a symbol of courage and loyalty. For six months she kept watch over the dead bodies of her sons, hanging there in the bleak outskirts amongst others who were not her sons (Levinas 1990:51-52). This mother understood that justice had to be done to the Gibeonites. She did not question this deed of justice, albeit that her loyalty (*ḥēsēd*) is an expression of *justice blended with the grace of kindness*. According to Levinas, this blending is about an exemplification of pity and compassion.

It is most remarkable to take cognisance of the fact that in the Tanakh the word *rachamim* is used for pity. Up to now, in Arabic, it refers to the womb (uterus). It is within this context that the deed of Rizpah can be rendered as an expression of both kindness and pity. Her action is an example and expression of durable loyalty. Hopefully, her act should inspire others as well, namely, to stand steadfast in the exemplification of trustworthiness and the establishment of true justice.

3.3   Loyalty: The fibre of relational ethics

It is important to emphasise that loyalty belongs to the fourth dimension of relational ethics. For Nagy, this is a core issue. Within contextual therapy, loyalty refers to the dynamic of that kind of care where one family member is obliged to take care of the other family member. This mutuality of caregiving is linked to previous modes of care within the family system. Care becomes an investment in bestowing compassion to the other; it is about a gratuitous response for benefits previously received (Boszormenyi-Nagy & Krasner 1994:223). In this sense, loyalty is an expression of faithfulness to a multiple number of people with whom one has relationships. It demonstrates entitlement and priority when it is about the maintenance of precious, previous connections with the other. Loyalty links one existentially with intergenerational modes of interconnectedness; it links one to people to whom the *I* belongs and vice versa. This multi-partiality puts a lot of pressure on attempts to stay loyal to somebody because this prior position is also difficult (sometimes even quite awkward). Co-existence is most of times only between two persons, that is, between the *I* and the *other*. If that were indeed always the case, decision-making would not have been that necessary. It would have been easy to decide who needs care and to whom justice should be done. However, loyalty is complex because there is always the possibility of the unexpected third person (other/others) also making an appeal on our sensitivity. Therefore, our context always puts us before a choice, whether we like it or not.

Facts, psychology and systems – transactional patterns of interaction and interrelatedness – influence different modes and levels of loyalty. Vice versa, loyalty influences all the different dimensions mentioned; it colours the lens of human observation. When caregivers or helpers really want to be engaged in dialogical relationships and familial connections, it is paramount to identify the functioning of loyalty. It is not that easy because loyalty is often concealed. To detect the different forms of loyalty, and to understand that loyalty is embedded in ethical entanglements, it is, therefore, necessary to inform clients. From the side of caregivers, much patience is needed.

Nagy views the significance of loyalty in the first place as a relational and ethical power. This is the reason why he describes it as a category belonging to the fourth dimension. In all the other dimensions, loyalty is present but not necessarily as ethical power. Loyalty is not a pure fact. It is not even an object. And despite the saying that *loyalty is thicker than blood*, it does not reside in human blood or physicality. One cannot trace loyalty back by observing it under a microscope. Neither does it belong to our DNA (the second dimension). It also entails more than merely acknowledging an intra-psychological event of a feeling (the second dimension) or insight about a self-regulating system (third dimension).

Loyalty is existential. It is about *preferential faithfulness* oscillating and waving between different generations. For Nagy, it is quite interesting how different generations can step in on behalf of one another and display loyalty. Sometimes, one can even observe how family members, even against all odds and logic, try to maintain interdependent modes of interconnectedness. It is inevitably the case that loyalty puts human beings before intriguing choices. Loyalty is, therefore, about a preferential connection; it functions as a triadic, relational configuration. It thus demonstrates a commitment to the other and others, and precedes even the freedom of making independent decisions (Van Rhijn & Meulink-Korf 1997:259). Although it is true that loyalty precedes decision-making, however, when a decision has to be taken, it always resonates and influences the whole process. That is indeed the case when choices must be made concerning preference for one relationship over against displaying concern for another. And, it is exactly here, where the triadic discomfort comes into play. The fact is that one always has to reckon with a third factor – the other as invisible third person. It could happen that in one setting loyalty is audible and/or visible for the caregiver. Another time, loyalty must remain underground because there is a reason not to show it openly.

The character of loyalty is determined by ethics. *Loyalty is essentially ethically structured.* The ethical notion of goodness, that is, to do good to others and to promote human well-being, frames acts of loyalty. This ethical endeavour delineates the differences between people whereby someone makes different considerations than somebody else. Each preference for a very specific kind of care or need or responsibility does not necessarily point to a qualitative difference. Loyalty is in itself the source for responsibility. It is about a motivational and pulling force that impels one to take care of one another. It is also to do justice to one another within the dynamics of a safe environment and reliable network. The real instigator to act in a loyal and just way, in the same way how David cared for Mephibosheth in the exemplification of his oath of kindness (*ḥēsēd*), is faithfulness. Faithfulness is durable and a guarantee for the sustainability of loyalty. The fact is that when faithfulness is maintained and one has displayed loyal kindness to the other, these gestures could be denied, but not become undone.

Loyalty infiltrates life as an indication of how discontinuity penetrates continuity. Therefore, loyalty and faithfulness are diachronic. They perforate time. Unexpectedly, they could become involved again and be employed as source for how to proceed with life in a significant way. The only condition is that one needs to be fair and accountable enough to continue recognising and acknowledging these costly moments in time and space.

> I often ask people to do the following exercise. They were asked to draw a long straight line on a clear and unwritten page. The line symbolises the time between birth and the present. One is then asked to identify three moments or events where somebody has been faithful to this person. One is then asked to describe the event. Thereafter, the person is asked to pose the reversed question, namely, to identify three moments or events where he/she acted in a reliable way towards somebody else and then to share these experiences with the counsellor. The sharing of stories reveals loyalty as an ethical reality; it delineates how responsibility demonstrates that people can take care for one another.

Loyalty cannot be resisted and be kept at bay by the limitations of age or any other hampering factor. This is indeed the case concerning geographic, political, social, economic and religious borders, very specifically the limitation and threat of death. Family will always be family, irrespective of culture or race or the fact of being distanced from one another in time and space.

> There is the case of a mother who was totally surprised when visiting the gravesite of her daughter. Every time when she came there, the name of her daughter was written in the sand. The mother thought she was the only one visiting the grave. However, it seemed that it was not the case. She became very curious wondering who wrote her daughter's name every time. She shared to one of her children her astonishment. Then came the answer: "Did you spot the stick in one of the shrubs?" On it was written: "Please do the same. You can write her name as often as you like." This message came like a spark of justice. It creates the opportunity for everyone to express his/her loyalty in a very unique way.

In his own life, Nagy knew thoroughly what loyalty is about. He was born in Hungary in 1920. In 1948 he had to fly to Austria. From there he emigrated to the United States of America where he died in 2007. After his departure from Hungary, he has never seen his father again. He wrote about loyalty between him and his father: "My father will always remain my father, even though he is dead, and his burial ground is thousands of miles away. He and I are two consecutive links in a genetic chain with a life span of millions of years. My existence is unthinkable without his. [...] He was obligated to me, his son, and subsequently, I have become existentially indebted to him" (Boszormenyi-Nagy & Spark 1973:3).

In the Western part of the world, contextual therapy focuses more on loyalty within the intergenerational familial context. In non-Western cultures, the borders of loyalty are less demarcated. It is often the case that all people belonging to a clan are rendered as family. The connectedness to the clan must sponsor the upholding of a mutual, indissoluble display of loyalty. This kind of guarantee is quite inclusive stretching back to ancestors even into the seventh generation (Gathogo 2008). Every member of the clan is rendered as a brother or sister. Furthermore, a child is always rendered as being connected to a father or mother even when the biological parents are absent. A daughter-in-law, even if she belongs to another clan, is also rendered as 'daughter' due to ties of loyalty. She can even carry the name of the clan and claim, in an inclusive way, basic rights and obligations. Loyalty is general and could be traced back in all cultures. However, the mode in which loyalty becomes visible is dependent on the local feature of that specific culture. In the same way, a family has its own forms and ties of displaying loyalty.

South Africa is a very diverse country consisting of many different cultures who are challenged to live peacefully together. This unique cultural and social setting needs a kind of coexistence founded on trust. One has therefore to acknowledge and reckon with the fact that South Africans are challenged to discover different presentations of loyalty.

> In most African cultures, loyalty to ancestors is one of the pillars of spirituality. When important decisions must be taken, it is custom to consult first with ancestors and the elderly. This web of generational ties plays a decisive role and should be consulted in decision-making. Specifically, when decisions must be made regarding ethical considerations with practical implications. This praxis precedes all forms of logic. This route is clearly illustrated with a case where a patient in the hospital suffered from a brain tumour. The surgeon informed the family that an operation is urgent. Therefore, an immediate decision must be taken. However, the patient declined the operation. He was convinced that the brain tumour was a signal pointing to the disturbance of the balance with the ancestors. He then asked the sangoma to step in on behalf of the sufferer. In African spirituality, sangomas operate like an intercessor that is summoned to contact ancestors. The task of the sangoma in this case was to consult regarding the appropriate ritual that could contribute to the restoration of the imbalance and would be decisive for healing of the breach.

Loyalty consists of two sides. On one side, there is the realisation that there are indeed others who hear me and put an *obligation* on the mutuality of hearing and responding. The other side is the realisation that the *I* hears the other and is shaped by this hearing. Due to this dependency, the *I* becomes *indebted*.

Furthermore, loyalty starts with the engagement of our parents and the fact that they feel obliged to be available for us. This is specifically the case in the prenatal and infant stage. Our loyalty to parents resides in a kind of original indebtedness. These two aspects – obligation and indebtedness – play a decisive role in the whole of life and all connections with the other (our neighbour). They demarcate an ambivalent role because they serve the purpose to maintain a mutual balance in the search for fairness in our being accountable for one another. At the same time, lurks in the ambivalence a movement of hope. This wavering of hope is not mainly because somebody cares and takes on responsibility for us when we are desperately in need of attention but also because we ourselves could be reliable and are able to make our loyalty visible.

Despite many differences between human beings and the threat of estrangement and distance, it is loyalty that displays the ethical movement within different relationships. This happens every time when people decide deliberately or by force to be trustworthy to one another and to promote the other's interests. Even to be prepared to step in on behalf of the other is firmly based on loyalty.

Loyalty is encompassed by two forms, namely, a *visible* and *invisible* side. It seems that every form of existential connectedness can indeed become invisible. However, it is never absent. That was also the reason for the title of the first publication of Nagy: *Invisible Loyalties*. Invisible loyalties are not immobilised but are merely concealed. They still operate and appear often unexpectedly. If one makes a negative statement regarding one's parents, this kind of expression of free speech does not necessarily imply disloyalty. However, very surprisingly, when somebody else makes such a negative re- mark, it is met by a wavering resistance. Deep within there is a feeling of uneasiness and disgust. It is as if something is making an appeal on our loyalty and one is forced to step in on behalf of the other (the criticised father or mother). It is as if one wants to settle any dispute between one's mother and the other due to her being exposed to a form of disrespect. In fact, *she is my mother!* It is then as if I should be the one who should take care to honour her legacy, even many years after she had passed away. This loyalty emerges as a kind of defence: *Do not discredit my mother whatsoever!*

The following case study refers to the impact of cultural settings on loyalty. This is the viewpoint of a victim of the apartheid ideology: My father was not flawless during the time of apartheid. Due to him, many blacks and coloured people became disadvantaged. I even know that due to his intervention, people died. But still, the burning question for me was how to still maintain that he was for me a trustworthy farther. Why? I often asked myself the question if I, on the other hand, indeed tried to become a trustworthy and loyal son. Or am I merely trying to repay a part of my father's account? It is as if I need to set something right on his behalf in order to cope with the future. And very amazingly, you will not believe it, I am doing it quite often.

Horizontal and vertical loyalty

Nagy makes a distinction between horizontal and vertical loyalty. The first refers to the social and generational dimension and the second to the intergenerational dimension.

On the vertical level the connections are about a given. One does not choose one's parents or grandparents in the same way that parents cannot choose a child or a grandchild. These kinds of relationships are irrevocable and indivisible. They cannot be abandoned or be given up. They could neither be denied. One can negate them but not delete them. With horizontal loyalty it is different. Partners and friends can be gathered. The loyalty towards them resides to a great extent in choices one can make. One can abandon these relationships if you prefer to. Horizontal loyalty offers the opportunity to let all these connections and engagements go.

The relationships between siblings are, however, more complex. The relationships between brothers and sisters consist of both the horizontal and the vertical dimension. In the relationship with absent parents there is indeed an intergenerational indebtedness at stake. With brothers and sisters, it is not about intergenerationality alone but also about qualitative issues.

Familial relationships are triadic. For example, there are brothers, sisters and parents. It can thus happen that different forms of loyalty take place within the mutuality of familial interaction. Due to power struggles, rival, competition and conflicting issues, relationships are not intact. It can indeed be the case that my father is more concerned about the whereabouts of the other than displaying any understanding for mine. Furthermore, there could be the constant complaint that one of the other siblings does not care so much for their mother as I do.

> It so happened that a mother had four children. She developed a quite peculiar approach, namely, to switch between the four alternatively regarding who will enjoy her preference for a certain period. The children felt very uncertain because they never knew how long one period will take. For example, she proceeded for many years with spoiling one of her children. But then, suddenly, she will switch to one of the others depending on a very specific service required by her. This uncertainty created a lot of distrust, suspicion and mutual rivalry amongst the brothers and sisters. The uncertainty continued after her death.

Intergenerational relationships are never equal. That is very specifically the case when it is about different concerns and interests. For example, when the concerns of the younger generation are at stake, differentiation is inevitable. Due to the vulnerable stage of puberty and adolescence they are much more exposed to conflicting interests.

In the case of parents, loyalty towards children is compulsory. To be honest, besides the so-called joys of parenthood, the responsibility of parenting could sometimes become quite a burden. Responsible parenting is without any doubt a challenge. "Even before a child discovers his/her unique individuality, there is the realisation that one needs to opt in a responsible manner. This obligation is not always easy. It is often a painful burden. It is not true that every pregnancy is necessarily about a joyous expectation. It is also not true that every pregnancy ends with the birth of a healthy child" (Meulink-Korf & Van Rhijn 2016:80).

To take care of a handicapped child for example, or an infant suffering from a chronic disease, can indeed become a huge challenge. It is also true that teenage pregnancies can become extremely complicated. In all these cases a whole circle of reliable supporters is needed so that parents can cope with the difficult challenges and have the opportunity to relate to the child in a constructive manner. "The concept of a multi-personal loyalty fabric implies on the other hand the existence of structured group expectations to which all members are committed" (Boszormenyi-Nagy & Spark 1973:17).

When vertical loyalty and horizontal loyalty intersect, new expectations, obligations and indebtedness come into being. It even entails mourning in cases of loss of engagement. In these intersections, one is challenged to weigh the value of several choices against one another. It can even imply a shifting of connections in loyalty. New triadic intersections evoke inevitable new different dilemmas. A change in context can contribute to a shifting of concerns and interests.

For example, there is always the jeopardy of interests when different families are involved. After the death of a father, there is the burning question amongst siblings: How are we going to deal with mother the next Christmas Eve? In this way, every birth, death, divorce, parting creates a crisis of loyalty. To whom must I stay loyal? The unwritten concerns of parents and grandparents can become quite confusing. That is the case when concerns for a partner, friends, brothers and sisters intersect at the same time. It is even impossible to differentiate between all the concerns and still detect exactly what is now my responsibility! The reason for that is because it is impossible to fulfil everyone's wishes at the same time. There is always the possibility of loss and shortcomings, even of missed opportunities to have done justice to previous forms of indebtedness. This kind of confusion is even more complicated when relationships of different cultures are at stake. One must reckon with the fact that loyalty to parents or a clan should deal with other traditions simultaneously. Conflicting intergenerational loyalties render therefore authentic dialoguing.

Marc Colpaert refers to the appropriateness of Nagy's thinking concerning the different needs and problematic complexities of migrants and refugees. This was specifically the case in Belgium in the encounter with the other/others. (But also in the Netherlands!) The advantage of Nagy's approach is that one needs to understand that people always operate from their own familial embeddedness. It became crystal clear that an intercultural dialogue is in fact meaningless and impossible without an intergenerational dialogue. And an intergenerational dialogue is always ethically based. Relational ethics, and the attempt to promote the other, to do justice to the other, but at the same time to experience that the *I* is also being justified, are therefore a lifelong process (Colpaert 2007:46).

The dilemma of conflicting loyalties

As said, loyalty consists of a triadic structure. Coexistence with the other is never about only one other person but always simultaneously about many others. They all partake in the networking dynamics of interacting encounters and the mutuality of dialoguing. And the challenging issue is that everyone's networking constellation and vibrant context are different. To exist within the network of relationships implies at least three persons. The difficulty is that it becomes virtually impossible to be loyal to everyone simultaneously. Coexistence presupposes the challenge to live with differences within diversity. That is the reason why one has to make choices regarding emerging *differences* in the attempt to live a meaningful life.

The real dilemma therefore in coexistence is how to make choices when confronted with different concerns, needs, desires and expectations. This dilemma brings about the discomfort of staying loyal to one another because when I make space for the concerns and wishes of one person, it could leave the impression that I negate the concerns and wishes of the other. It becomes indeed a very tricky game to realise that a second choice is not right now at stake, but that the ethics of putting the concern of the other first is now on my agenda. The point is that one cannot say *Hinéni* to two or more persons simultaneously. It is therefore quite interesting in general communication and dialoguing how people manoeuvre in order to find ways to deal with this dilemma.

> The mother of a Xhosa man fell ill. She lived 500 kilometres away on the land of the clan they belonged to. She was desperately in need of care. In terms of their tradition it was the expectation that his wife should step in, in order to take care of her sick mother-in-law. Due to her marriage, she is rendered as belonging to the clan. This relationship was more fundamental than the fact that she was married to her husband. This woman possessed, at that stage of her life, a very important professional position. At the same time, she was preparing for an examination in order to get a promotion that will benefit her future career. Suddenly, the husband has to deal with the following dilemma: Must he stay loyal to his wife and support her in the development of her future career (something which he dearly wanted and wished to promote), or must he pay

loyalty to his mother and his community? He decided to sacrifice his own job in order to care for his mother all by himself. He therefore left his job and carried the burden of the consequences of his decision with dignity and in silence.

Split loyalty

Within the triad of parents and children, differences and conflicting arguments often disturb the rhythm of interaction and communication. These kinds of quarrels could become painful indeed. Nagy calls these painful experiences *split loyalty*. For children it is very disturbing and alarming to discover distrust between parents and to be exposed to parental conflicts. Necessarily, they become confused and entangled. They start to oscillate between visible and invisible modes of loyalty.

From a very early stage in their life, children can develop a deep concern for the well-being of their parents. Often, the situation is that if they need to decide, the most obvious choice is to side with the more vulnerable partner. The child will then show his/her loyalty in a very visible way. The other parent can immediately experience and interpret this siding as an act of treason. The further implication is that this hurt parent will start trying to find a balance between the conflicting interests. These attempts could be visible or invisible. When the parents do not realise the impact of their quarrel on the child, the child becomes a victim of parental conflict. When the child is pressured to survive in this dilemma of loyalty, his/her confusion could develop into pathology, namely the delusion in adulthood that he or she was never good enough and failed to meet the expectations of the parents. It could even contribute to the idea that he or she is intrinsically a failure. Obviously, such a delusion can lead to many guilt feelings that hamper further development into maturity (Boszormenyi-Nagy & Krasner 1986:194).

Loss of trustworthiness and safety in the living space of a child often surpasses the coping mechanisms of a child. The intriguing question is then how to free a child from the burden of conflicting, split loyalty. One can reason and say well that is, in the first place, the responsibility of the parents. However, in many cases the parents do not have the ability to understand the complexity of split loyalty. The dilemma is that they are often totally blindfolded by their own pain and not in the position to act on behalf of the child. In these cases, it becomes paramount that others such as grandparents or friends should become very sensitive in their communication, that is, not to put the parents in a negative light or to speak ill of one of the parents.

> During a vacation, the author swam every day in the swimming pool. I had just arrived when a very young child stood at the side of the pool. He was staring at me and was so impressed how I managed to swim underneath the surface of the water. He immediately thought it would be nice to do the same. He wants to learn as well. He asked if I could help him to learn the skill. I directed him in the direction of his parents nearby. In a very vague way, he referred to his father but said that he does not know the woman with his father. She was quite new. The day when he returned to his house, he sat in the back seat with his sister. The father with the new partner sat in front. Theo opened the window to give me a hand. I thanked him for swimming together and wished him luck for a safe return to his home. Softly he whispered: "Do you know my mother is a nurse!"

Afterwards, there were many confusing issues in my mind: Divorced parents, confusing vacations, new partners, triadic issues, invisible loyalties? Must Theo wrestle with them all simultaneously? And then there is still his sister sitting next to him. What about her? Each of them was captured in his/her own triadic connection with the father and mother. From an ethical point of view each one of them was wrestling with his/her own unique split loyalty. In their struggle, they weave between different experiences of self-evaluation. Am I good enough or indeed merely bad and a culprit? How destructive or constructive has my behaviour been? They are each challenged by so many decisive moments that involved so many intriguing ethical entanglements. And still there was the painful question of how to make loyalty visible or not. However, the main point to grasp is that children do have the right that their expression of loyalty should be heard and recognised.

This is also the case with adopted children or children in foster-care. One must understand that existentially they feel themselves connected to their biological parents who brought them into life. They feel themselves indebted towards them while at the same time they missed the presence and care of their real parents. One should realise that their loyalty to their biological parents is always a reality irrespective of whether the foster-parents are fine or not. The further dilemma is that they can also experience a duty towards the new parents. Loyalty can therefore become very confusing indeed. Due to split loyalty, children are captured between many different forms of opting in a trustworthy way, that is, they should pay respect to both the biological and the foster parents simultaneously.

Group loyalty

The fabric of loyalty within multiplicity creates expectations that put a lot of obligations on family members. One needs to accept that a family system functions according to specific agreements and delimitations regarding appropriate and inappropriate behaviour, habits, rituals and many unwritten regulations pertaining to general human well-being. When engagement is regulated by strict moral values, it becomes difficult for individuals to deviate from established expectations. In cases where a family member acts differently, one can expect that family members will react while the long-term consequences will be very difficult to control. And reactions are woven within a complex whole that is connected to conservative religiosity, racism, sexual issues and intriguing political convictions. Moral values can even exceed relational ethics. Choices that deviate from the customs of the family can leave the impression that they are in fact signs of disloyalty, even indications of betrayal with the risk of becoming excluded from the clan or family system.

Group loyalty has an impact on individual decision-making. For example, it reveals the dilemma of conflicting interests. Group loyalty within the parameters of a family system can become a severe hampering factor when choices must be made that fit personal needs or that impact on the future of the next generation. Nagy, therefore, often refers to the very vital impact of loyalty on a next generation, that is, the invisible third factor that partakes in family relationships. He calls this third factor *transgenerational solidarity* (Boszormenyi-Nagy 2000, chapter 4).

Due to transgenerational solidarity, this kind of networking loyalty always plays a role when one is involved with caring and important decisions, namely, how to deal with the heritage of the past and the accomplishments of the current generation. Because one must keep in mind that what has been received and achieved should, in a very just way, be handed over to the not-yet of the coming generation. For Nagy, this kind of transgenerational solidarity functions like an *inner tribunal*. Solidarity, therefore, implies a burden because in exercising the ethics of solidarity, one becomes indebted to people belonging to the future generation. It sounds a little bit moralistic, but one should assess this kind of solidarity in terms of the many layers of motivations (the conative dimension of life). It is within these layers that hope resides; a hope "for repairing the hurt human justice" (Boszormenyi-Nagy & Krasner 1973:53).

Loyalty in Wuppertal

Wuppertal is a small village in the Western Cape of South Africa with approximately 4 000 inhabitants. It is located in a quite desolate and remote area within the Cedarberg mountain area. It seems as if time came to a standstill. Characteristic of this village are the small thatched-roof cottages.

The village was founded in 1800 by the *German Rhenish Missionary Society*. It is quite remarkable that the village was not well planned along streets. Houses were scattered all over the place. In 2018 most of the inhabitants were pensioners. Most of them were born in Wuppertal. In December of that year a huge fire destroyed the old centre and *45 thatched cottages* were irreparably damaged. It is quite understandable why the community wanted to build new houses without thatched roofs due to the risk of future fire damage. They also wanted proper streets so that in future it would be easier to combat possible risks and provide emergency services.

This planning fuelled severe protest. One of the elderly reacted as follows: "Sorry, but this is my property and my house. It belonged to my father. You have no right to confiscate the heritage of my father." One of the members of the church council told me that *the protest is in fact about identity*. However, it entails more than mere identity. It is indeed possible to change identity and to reposition yourself within new circumstances. What is at stake is loyalty. Loyalty cannot be deleted. The loyalty is linked to an intergenerational chain, to a family safety net. The proposed change will be, for him, a loss in terms of safety and roots; he will feel not merely robbed of land but stripped of his existential rootedness.

What is most needed in this very desperate case is a pastor who can acknowledge his deep-seated sense for familial embeddedness. He should be assisted to discover new avenues of how to express his sense of loyalty. These new routes should be sensitive to his strong feelings about heritage so that, in any form of change, his father could journey with him. The point is his family story should be continued. He does not need the full stop of a dot; he needs an open-ended comma.

The very powerful but also vulnerable edge of loyalty

When the concept 'human' is pronounced, loyalty is immediately implied. We all exist within a network of relationships. We are embedded in context. The power of loyalty resides in caring and the exercising of sound responsibility.

The vulnerable edge in loyalty is that it cannot be spread simultaneously in an equal manner to all. Loyalty urges one to make choices. When David was confronted to make a choice that gave preference to Mephibosheth, his loyalty to Jonathan brought him in direct contact with a divine discomfort.

Loyalty is a very strong tie between different generations. Loyalty can be invisible. We can even be quite ignorant about its consequences, as in the Wuppertal case. To stay loyal is about a concrete action. The act reveals the people who are connected to us. It contributes to the relational balance that rotates amongst people. It functions within the mutuality of give-and-take. Nagy refers to this dynamic of give-and-take when he calls it a fundamental right of our being human. It is also about the right of being recognised for all the material and immaterial care which we render to one another. The balance of give-and-take reveals anew that this approach is not focused on merely an individual, although it is true that two people are involved. However, many other people are simultaneously implied as well. This dynamic of give-and-take impacts on the well-being of the other. Without any doubt, relational ethics is embedded in a multilateral network.

CHAPTER 4

Giving and receiving

The basic assumption of this chapter is that every relationship is intrinsically dependent on what is mutually given to one another, and what each one receives within the dynamics of reciprocity. With the latter is meant the practice of exchanging things with others for mutual benefit, promoting the humane quality of daily living. Within dialogue and human encounters, the link with mutuality explains the reciprocal movement between interdependent entities.

With reference to the dynamic of balancing, the reciprocity indicates that which is given to one another and, in return, which is received from one another. This zigzag determines the uniqueness of each relationship and the quality of intersubjectivity. It creates a vivid space for mutual interaction and exchange wherein giving and receiving can take place. Due to this space, human encounters are not about merely talking with one another; reciprocity is not about a neutral field of mutual exchange. Giving and receiving is embedded within the fourth lens of networking: the ethical entanglement of multi-directed partiality. At stake in this networking process is the quest for fairness in relationships and the establishment of relational justice.

4.1   The dynamic of balancing: The movement of reciprocity

Between giving and receiving exists a kind of fictional balance. One can compare this dynamic movement with the needle of a scale within the moment of balancing. It operates in the same way as an old-fashioned scale tries to balance two sides, so that one could assess what is everyone's contribution to the relationship, and what each one has received from the relationship. The process of balancing is always in flux due to the dynamic of reciprocity, that is, the mutuality of an unpredictable movement between giving and receiving.

Therefore, relational ethics operates like a wavering between the question regarding how just/fair or unjust/unfair relationships are.

With reference to the four lenses discussed in the previous chapter, we now turn to the value of this dimension, namely, to probe the balance of giving and receiving. This probing, as a kind of assessment of the quality of balancing, is only possible when one is prepared to listen to the stories that people are prepared to share with one another.

Concepts like justice, fairness and righteousness do not refer to the *what*-question, namely, *what* someone has contributed, and how it should be returned with equal currency (quantification). For example, when I buy flowers for my sick friend, the implication is not that he/she should do the same when I am sick. It could be that he/she brings me soup. It should therefore be crystal clear that in the process of balancing between giving and receiving, the question at stake is not *what* has been given but the *act,* namely, *the fact that something has been given as well as the how* (qualification). One must grasp this point in order to understand the dynamic of relational ethics. At stake is the readiness and willingness of a person to be prepared to contribute to the relationship with the other. The act is then determined by one's abilities and assets, so that the act is never prescriptive in character. The dynamic of this balancing is, therefore, determined within that very moment when someone contributes to the weighing process, or takes something away. In this weighing process, the needle, indicating the position of the balance, is seldom set exactly in the middle. When everyone contributes according to need and asset of the other and vice versa, the outcome is determined by trust. *Over the long term, it is the ability to trust one another and, therefore, the quality of trustworthiness, that eventually determines the quality of this dynamic of balancing and not the 'what' of the content.* That explains why this dynamic movement between giving and receiving does not develop in terms of a straight line, but rather in terms of a zigzag that oscillates between the different bipolarities.

The advantage of a contextual approach is that it helps to provide insight in terms of everyone's contribution as well as one's own contribution to balance. This is also applicable to what has been received or not. To develop a sensitivity for the fairness and quality of accountability in mutual caring implies, obviously, disturbances in this quest for balance. This could happen where trust in reasonableness and fairness is damaged or denounced. In order to probe into the sources of broken trust, multi-directed partiality is required so that new avenues for dialoguing, as well as new modes of trusting, could be explored.

In this text I mainly use the term *'give and receive'*, although in the literature it was initially about *'give and take'*, partly due to the title of the book *Between give and take* by Nagy and Krasner. Despite the general assumption that giving implies taking, the argument will be that giving presupposes the art and grace of receiving. Over a period of time, Nagy started to doubt the appropriateness of this title: *Between give and take*. The impression could be that the coupling *give-and-take* is static. This impression would be wrong because *give-and-take* describes the dynamics between two selves. The notion of taking also contributes to the meaning of improper appropriation, while receiving happens to you, such as in the case of true gratitude. Taking, however, leaves the impression of usurping something, while receiving is in the passive: It overwhelms one and carries the hallmark of *gratuitous thankfulness*. In terms of the ethics of relationality, it is not appropriate to take unasked, as if one can just grasp what is handed over. That is the reason why Nagy started to ask attention for *the art of giving* (the how and mode), as well as the *art of receiving* (the how and mode).

With reference to the four lenses in contextual networking, giving-and-receiving is classified within the fourth dimension of relational ethics. What Nagy means with ethics needs further clarification.

4.2   *The significance of relational ethics*

For Nagy, the category of relational ethics does not reside within the general prescriptions for morality. Relational ethics is therefore not determined by prescribed regulations issued by social institutions such as government, church, culture or civil society. Ethics is anchored in being and is therefore an ontic issue.

An ontic and existential approach refers to ethics as part of the qualitative character of being within the dynamic of relationships, interactions and all human encounters with the other/others. This is the reason why Nagy prefers to speak of *ethics within relationships*. The latter forms the basic orientation network for our being human and the establishment of all forms of humanness. "Ethics focus on the unique human process of achieving a fair balance of equity between people" (Boszormenyi-Nagy 2000:22). For Nagy, ethics is therefore not focused on ideas regarding good and evil as based upon principles established by institutions from the past. It is not to be derived from fixed regulations. The most basic concept to describe the focus of ethics is *'justice in relationships'* and its endeavour to promote the perspective of fair relationships. Relational ethics is thus not about a prescribed specification, as in the discipline of medical ethics or occupational ethics for professionals.

All human reality is in fact relational. Relational ethics is a given that corresponds with our being human. It is not a kind of aftermath or extra, a posteriori. It presents itself quite visibly within the long chain of previous generations reaching into the relational dynamics of present generations. It narrates about all people who contributed to the quality of life. But, at the same time, it is prepared to deal with the disturbed and harmed values of life as well.

For Nagy, ethics is deeply situated and anchored in the being of humans, and in this sense, an authentic characteristic of human orientation and existential engagements. Ethics does not determine human behaviour and actions from a prescribed moral order but instigates and instils, within our very being, a sense of responsibility, a will and motivation to act appropriately and a passion for caring. *Ethics is existential indeed!*

In Nagy's mind, relational ethics functions as the common denominator that founds the dynamics between generations and families. This provides the reason why the dynamics is steered by a deep sense of intrinsic justice and righteousness. It is intrinsic and not derived from an external source. It emanates from a very original and authentic structure of our being human and subjectivity (Meulink-Korf & Van Rhijn 2002:137; 2016:92). How the ethical movement becomes visible is dependent on the situation and the people involved. It all hinges on the how of human being and, in this sense, is never prescriptive.

Whether relational ethics is fair or unfair is revealed within the quest for balance within the give-and-receive dynamic. The point is that justice and injustice permeate the networking of next generations. They determine qualities like equality and trustworthiness. One has thus to understand that relational ethics aims to make a fair contribution to human well-being; it impacts on the quality of being and has therefore even a rippling effect on the well-being of future generations. One finds more or less a comparison in Exodus 20:5-6, with the reference that God will punish the children for the injustice of the fathers to the third and fourth generation of those who hate him, but showing *chēsēd* (trustworthiness) to a thousand generations of those who love him and keep his commandments.

There is a text in the Bible where the movement of giving and receiving becomes quite evident. It shows that the balance can be disturbed and even extinguished in cases where unfairness and inequality dictate the dynamics. In Genesis 38, the relationship between Judah and his daughter-in-law is described. Judah is the fourth son of Jacob. He had three children by his wife, the daughter of Shua. Due to tradition, Judah got a wife for Er, his firstborn. Her name was Tamar. The further development of relationships between Tamar and his sons is described in terms of the repetition and mutual deployment of 'giving' and 'taking'. At the end of the whole story, the concept of *righteousness* suddenly turns up (Gen 38:26).

In the following discussion, the concept of 'taking' will be used, in order to be in line with the Biblical translation.

4.3   *Genesis 38: The balance of giving and taking*

This chapter seems to be out of step with the other chapters when compared to the bigger picture of the Joseph narratives that has just started (Genesis 37-50). The information in the account deals with Joseph, the eleventh child of Jacob. Joseph had been favoured by his father. Joseph's ten brothers were not amused at all about how Joseph wandered amongst them with his richly ornamented robe. In fact, they hated him. Eventually they threw Joseph into one of the cisterns in the desert and decide to sell him for twenty shekels to Midianite merchants who took him to Egypt. But now suddenly, after the Midianites sold Joseph to Potiphar, one of Pharaoh's officials, the chapter on Judah and Tamar turns up. This chapter does not deal with Joseph at all. On the contrary, the chapter is about 'lessons learnt' from Judah! It seems as if Genesis 38 is delaying the major account on events regarding what happened to Joseph in Egypt. It is interesting to remember that Judah's descendants are later mentioned in the account on the direct generational line of King David. But before attention could be given to this intergenerational connection, Judah has first to learn a lesson of what righteousness implies.

We now turn to the Biblical texts. In the explanation of the text and the version of the account, it has been decided by the author to put giving and taking into brackets and italics when the Hebrew text is at stake. The reason is that the account is translated freely so that the real meaning is not always captured appropriately.

Judah and Tamar: An undignified, inhumane encounter (Genesis 38)

¹It happened (*wajehie*) at that time that Judah went down from his brothers and settled near a certain Adullamite whose name was Hirah. ²There Judah saw the daughter of a certain Canaanite whose name was Shua; he married (*took*) her and went in to her. ³She conceived and bore a son; and he named him:

"Er".

⁴Again she conceived and bore a son whom she named

"Onan".

⁵Yet again she bore a son, and she named him

"Shelah".

She was in Chezib when she bore him. ⁶Judah took (*take*) a wife for Er his firstborn; her name was Tamar. ⁷But (*wajehie*) Er, Judah's firstborn, was wicked in the sight of the Lord, and the Lord put him to death. ⁸Then Judah said to Onan,

"Go in to your brother's wife and perform the duty of a brother-in-law to her; raise up offspring for your brother."

⁹But since Onan knew that the offspring would not be his, he spilled his semen on the ground whenever he went in to his brother's wife, so that he would not give (*give*) offspring to his brother. ¹⁰What he did was displeasing in the sight of the Lord, and he put him to death also. ¹¹Then Judah said to his daughter-in-law Tamar,

"Remain a widow in your father's house until my son Shelah grows up" –

for he feared that he too would die, like his brothers. So, Tamar went to live in her father's house.

¹²In course of time the wife of Judah, Shua's daughter, died; when Judah's time of mourning was over, he went up to Timnah to his sheepshearers, he and his friend Hirah the Adullamite. ¹³When Tamar was told,

"Your father-in-law is going up to Timnah to shear his sheep."

¹⁴She put off her widow's garments, put on a veil, wrapped herself up, and sat down at the entrance to Enaim, which is on the road to Timnah. She saw that Shelah was grown up, yet she had not been given (*not given*) to him in marriage. ¹⁵When Judah saw her, he thought her to be a prostitute, for she had covered her face. ¹⁶He went over to her at the roadside, and said,

"Come, let me come in to you,"

for he did not know that she was his daughter-in-law. She said,

"What will you give (*give*) me, that you may come in to me?"

¹⁷He answered,

"I will send you a kid from the flock."

And she said,

"Only if you give (*give*) me a pledge, until you send it."

¹⁸He said,

"What pledge shall I give (*give*) you?"

She replied,

"Your signet and your cord, and the staff that is in your hand."

So he gave (*give*) them to her, and went in to her, and she conceived by him. ¹⁹Then she got up and went away, and taking off her veil she put on the garments of her widowhood. ²⁰When Judah sent the kid by his friend the Adullamite, to recover (*take*) the pledge from the woman, he could not find her. ²¹He asked the townspeople,

"Where is the temple prostitute who was at Enaim by the wayside?"

But they said,

"No prostitute has been here."

²²So he returned to Judah, and said,

"I have not found her; moreover, the townspeople said, 'No prostitute has been here.'"

²³Judah replied,

"Let her keep the things as her own (*what she took*), otherwise we will be laughed at; you see, I sent this kid, and you could not find her."

[24]About (*and it happens*) three months later Judah was told,

> "Your daughter-in-law Tamar has played the whore; moreover she is pregnant as a result of whoredom."

And Judah said,

> "Bring her out and let her be burned."

[25]As she was being brought out, she sent word to her father-in-law,

> "It was the owner of these who made me pregnant."

And she said,

> "Take note, please, whose these are, the signet and the cord and the staff."

[26]Then Judah acknowledged them and said,

> "She is more in the right than I, since I did not give (*give not*) her to my son Shelah."

And he did not lie with her again.

[27]When (*and it happens*) the time of her delivery came, there were twins in her womb. [28]While she was in labour, one put out a hand (*gives a hand*); and the midwife took (*take*) and bound on his hand a crimson thread, saying,

> "This one came out first."

[29]But just then he drew back his hand, and out came his brother; and she said,

> "What a breach you have made for yourself!"

Therefore, he was named Perez. [30]Afterward his brother came out with the crimson thread on his hand; and he was named Zerah.

The whole event followed the account of the deep mourning and grief of Joseph's father, Jacob. The brothers told their father that some ferocious animal has devoured him. This was in fact a blatant lie. But the lie and grief of Jacob was the point in the events when Judah turned away from his brothers. He left his brothers and went down to stay with a man of Adullam, named Hirah. There Judah met the daughter of a Canaanite man named Shua.

He married her and she gave him birth to three sons. He named the first son Er. Later on, Judah got a wife for Er with the name Tamar. However, Er was wicked (*ra*) in the Lord's sight; so the Lord put him to death. Now suddenly the custom of the Levirate marriage should be applied. The latter means that the second son, Onan, should have intercourse with Tamar so that he can fulfil his duty to her as a brother-in-law to produce offspring for her (according to the laws in Israel). Tamar was at this stage without children. In this way Onan could function as a substitute for his dead brother Er. But Onan knew that the offspring would not be his. So, whenever he lay with his brother's wife, he spilled his semen on the ground to keep from producing offspring for his brother. This was also a wicked act (*ra*) in the sight of the Lord; so the Lord put him to death. Judah then told his daughter-in-law to wait in her father's house until the youngest son, Shelah, is a grown up. In the meantime, he wrestled with his fear that Shelah may die too just like his brothers.

After a long time, Judah's wife died. When Judah had recovered from his grief, he went up to Timnah, to the men who were shearing his sheep. When Tamar received the news that Judah was in Timnah, she took off her widow's clothes, covered herself with a veil to disguise herself, and then sat down at the entrance to Enaim (the opening of an eye), which is on the road to Timnah. She deliberately did that, for she saw that, though Shelah had grown up, she had not been given to him as his wife. She thus reasoned that she could claim her right for an offspring through Judah.

When Judah saw her, he thought she was a prostitute, perhaps a shrine prostitute (*qadosja*). He went over to her by the roadside and asked to sleep (come to) with her. But Tamar started to negotiate with Judah and asked what he will give to her when she is willing to sleep with him. Their agreement was a young goat which was the normal reward to be paid to a whore. But that could not be paid immediately because Judah did not have the goat with him. So, Tamar asked whether he would give something to her as a pledge until he could send for the goat. Judah asked her what pledge he should give to her. She answered: "Your seal and its cord, and the staff in your hand" (Gen 38:18). What she asked was his royal attributes. So, he gave them to her and slept with her. Eventually she became pregnant with him.

Meanwhile Judah sent the young goat by his friend the Adullimite in order to get his pledge back from Tamar. He asked the men who lived there about the shrine prostitute (*qadosja*). However, he could not find Tamar. Judah felt quite uncomfortable with the outcome and said that she should keep what she has, otherwise they will become a laughingstock.

About three months later Judah was told that Tamar (now addressed as his daughter-in-law) was guilty of prostitution, and as a result she is now pregnant. Judah reacted with rage and said she had to be brought out and should be burned to death. As she was being brought out, she sent a message to her father-in-law that she was pregnant. As proof that Judah was the father, she showed his pledge, namely, the seal, cord and staff. Judah was indeed the owner. Judah recognised them and made a huge confession: "She is more righteous (*tsaddiqa*) than I, since I wouldn't give her to my son Shelah" (Gen 38:26). And he did not sleep with her again. Sleep then, in terms of the real meaning of intercourse, as an event of personal acknowledgement in bestowing *hēsēd* and fostering righteousness.

When the time came for her to give birth, there were twin boys in her womb. After the two dead sons of Judah, Er and Onan, there were suddenly two living boys! As she was giving birth, one of them put out his hand. So, the midwife took a scarlet thread and tied it on his wrist and said: "This one came out first" (Gen 38:28). But suddenly he drew back his hand and his brother came out first. The midwife then said: "So this is how you have broken out!" (Gen 38:29). So, he was called Perez (breakthrough). Then his brother with the scarlet band on his wrist came out. He was given the name Zerach (it can mean scarlet or brightness like the early morning sunrise).

At the end of chapter 38, the rotating theme arises anew, namely, that the first born is not necessarily the real firstling (*bechor*) who should appear in a messianic way as the decisive one directing the future of his clan. Zerach is not the firstling, but against all odds, it is Peres. And, very noteworthy, Peres, the son of Judah, was the ancestor of Boaz, the father of Obed, the father of David. And so, it happened that the names of Judah and Tamar, Peres and Zerach, were mentioned in the genealogy by the Gospel of Matthew. In a very peculiar way, they all became connected to Jesus who was called the Christ (Mt 1:1-16).

It is perhaps now possible to grasp why this text (chapter 38) had been included at the very beginning of the great account on the life of Joseph. Despite the merit of Joseph in his acts of saving his family during the famine, the genealogy of Jesus was not set forth by Joseph the son of Jacob. However, in the genealogy by Matthew, very surprisingly, the name 'Joseph' did turn up. From Jacob there is suddenly an offspring with the name of Joseph, the husband of Mary, the mother of Jesus. Indeed, a magnificent surprise.

It seems as if in Genesis 38, the disturbance between the fairness of giving and taking is reaching a breaking point in this abrupt account regarding the genealogy of Judah. Five times, the concepts of giving (as verb) and taking arise. It looks like a kind of fair balance. But three times there is the indication of not-giving. Without any verbal remark, Judah acknowledged his guilt over against Tamar when he took back his royal attributes which he gave as pledge.

When one starts to reflect on the deeper spiritual meaning of the text, one discovers that it is actually Tamar who carried the pledge. In this way, she became the pledge herself due to Judah's guilt for not giving Selah his son as should have been the case when he had fulfilled his obligation regarding the Levirate marriage stipulation. Without her peculiar intervention, the genealogy of Judah would have come to an end. However, Tamar stepped in, and thus became a kind of embodied pledge even by means of the intimacy of her body. In verses 25 and 26, the Hebrew word *jada* (to acknowledge) is used for sexual intercourse. And this is indeed challenging and very fascinating. Tamar now acted as a kind of embodied substitute for the nation of Israel on behalf of Judah. In this way, she is incorporated into the inter-communion of genealogy, and thus she is mentioned as one of the five women in Matthew's account on Jesus' genealogy (Rozenzweig 1987).

The acknowledgement of Judah is quite remarkable: "She is more righteous (*tsaddiqa*) than I." This is indeed a very dignified and royal acknowledgement. He did not have to sleep with her again. The irony is that later in his life, Judah had to act as guarantor when Joseph demanded to see Benjamin and insisted that one of his brothers will have to be a pledge (Gen 43:8-9).

4.4   The balance of giving and receiving

The balance between Judah and Tamar was disturbed due to the not-giving of Judah. It is a very clear indication that the dynamic movement in balancing can become stagnant. It can even fall apart. One needs to understand that the dynamic of balancing is frail and, therefore, always temporary. The point is that human beings and situations differ from time to time. Life is to a large extent relative. Therefore, to display responsibility and trustworthiness is never constant. But it is exactly because nothing is stable and always constant, that giving-and-receiving is exposed to uncertainty, unpredictability and precariousness. But at the same time, this discontinuity in balancing creates space for reciprocity. It is in any case a fact that not every act of giving could or should be answered immediately with an appropriate response. There is always a flexibility existent that grants an opening for change as well as an opportunity for the other to respond. Balancing is not about *do ut es*: I give because you give to me. Neither is it about the pressure that I give so that you can in return, give something back to me. Giving is not an incentive to barter.

Giving and receiving are framed by intersubjectivity. When the balance between people is merely fair, giving and receiving take place according to everyone's sense of personal subjectivity and fairness within the realm of intersubjectivity. I give because I orient myself according to the relationship. I, thus, invest according to my ability and capacity within that relationship. The same is valid for the other person. The movement is therefore dialectical. The other receives from me. Simultaneously this receiving creates the opportunity for giving. When the balance oscillates in terms of the dialectical interplay between giving and receiving, one can assume that a form of justice could be instilled. The dialectic and the non-simultaneity create space for the phenomenon of unpredictability. One is then challenged by questions like: What happens to me? What happens to the other person? Because these questions are beyond my personal expectation; I cannot know them precisely; they are difficult to grasp in rational terminology. It takes confidence not to determine and calculate those personal expectations of myself. How the other eventually will respond is always difficult to detect or to forecast.

What is indeed difficult and even uncomfortable, is when giving is demanded in a very subtle way as a hidden requirement or obligation. It is then very difficult to promote authentic intersubjectivity. Immediately the danger of objectification lurks. The other then runs the risk of becoming manipulated and abused due to the selfishness of the I in his/her focus on personal need-satisfaction. I then make the other a captive of *me*-interests. This kind of absorption of the other puts justice under huge pressure.

When people talk about their coexistence, we hear the murmur of what is just and what is not: The credits and shortages, the interests and needs of everyone, motivations, disappointment and obstacles. All those relational ethical movements in relationships depict an ethical texture in which imperfections and settled possibilities between people become aligned. What they themselves repeat and retell reveals a suspicion regarding how fair or not the relationship was. It also gives an indication about the current quality of the relationship and how it will envelop in future. This process of conjecture is called ethical *imagination*. It is, as it were, a preliminary description of the functioning and non-functioning of a (family) system. It points to aspects that tell about reliability (trustworthiness) and infidelity, about right and wrong, about profit and loss, about detachments and new attachments.

Within the balance between giving and receiving, the strange preference of family connections always plays a pivotal role in the making of fundamental choices. This is specifically true in choices in which loyalty calls for priority, namely, to whom and how connectedness becomes visible and to whom not?

It requires professionalism from the pastor and counsellor to approach everyone within an attitude of multi-partiality but, at the same time, to maintain fairness. It is indeed a challenge to assess everyone's giving and receiving, and still to simultaneously deal with unique differences. The caregiver is only an observer and must see and hear, in the different dimensions, how fairness has been dealt with. In helping interventions, one has also to detect who is the most vulnerable link in the dynamics of the family system. Within a professional approach, the assessment must be made of whether the balance is hampered and who has been most affected and exposed to severe forms of vulnerability. What is most needed is patience. Patience helps one to detect and explore sources of new confidence.

The contextual dialogical approach to pastoral care is unthinkable without this balance of giving and receiving. "Ensuring relational balance is key to keeping close relationships viable and is the cornerstone of contextual work" (Boszormenyi-Nagy & Krasner 1986:58; 1994:75). The basic assumption is that good and healthy relationships are in a dynamic balance of giving and receiving, which involves the fair weighing of tangible and intangible gifts. In a reliable relationship, recognition for what is given is just as important as giving itself. Nagy calls this ethical response of fair recognition *entitlement*, that is, one is entitled to receive recognition regarding merit. Everyone's contribution to justice in any way deserves to be seen and named, in language or gesture. When the balance of giving and receiving is moving reciprocally and without too many shocks, new confidence is created. In the contextual approach, trust is the key concept, the key to renewed justice. Nagy's therapy aims to be a trust-based therapy.

The right to give

For Nagy, it is existentially evident: Every child has the right to give and to be seen and recognised. In fact, for a child it is hardly impossible not to give. The unborn baby already gives joy and creates a significant network of meaningful experiences. Toddlers already contribute by placing a blanket over the father who comes home tired and exhausted after a hard day's work. When the attempts of a child to give are seen and recognised, even in difficult situations, also in the dramas that happen in every family interaction, the child develops resilience and gains *constructive entitlement*. The giving that a child displays requires to be seen and recognised.

In the beginning of everyone's life, the balance of giving and receiving is asymmetrical. Parent(s) (grandparents) put countless more weight on the scale because the small child needs more care, is dependent on it, and, thus, motivates them to do so. The child responds to gestures of care and concern with acknowledgement in the form of a first smile, turning the head when the name is recognised as a first orientation in modes of expressing sincere trust.

Nagy repeatedly asks attention for the availability and preparedness of parents to respond appropriately in their caring to the receiving child. The question could be posed: But why? Because the child is entitled to give, to profit from the ethical balance even before he/she is able to make their own choice. This means that a contribution cannot be limited to a mere psychological development within the spur of a moment. Giving originates from an existential source; it is embedded in the quality of being, intersubjectivity and temporality. The child is unconsciously aware that his/her giving changes something in the quality of time. The child even experiences that he/she perforates the obvious naturalness of time.

Due to the asymmetry in giving and receiving between parents and child, there is always an indebtedness present that is never refundable. Sometimes, the grown-up child is given the opportunity to take care of the aging and more dependent parent. This opportunity points to a kind of care that cannot be demanded by parents. After all, giving can only be done from within a sense of being free (an authentic expression of subjectivity).

Among parents who tend to enforce equal payback, we see that children (including adult children) develop a destructive attitude that is tragic for all parties. However, adult children do try to comply (existentially) with their parental indebtedness. It could, thus, happen that they take up their obligation to life as a whole and express it in other places, for example, by working on justice for the next generation. This indebtedness (sense of owing) translates constructively into a multitude of choices: Commitment to never make war again; involvement in processes of reconciliation; commitment to the climate; a choice to live as a vegetarian, a choice to travel less around the world at the cost of polluting our environment. And most challenging, a commitment to promote human well-being and health, as in the case of the current, global corona-crisis. These contributions tell everyone about a desire to pass on quality of life to the next generation. The expression of justice within those contributions often only becomes apparent over more than one generation because the networking of giving and receiving between generations could extend over a longer period.

Wilhelm Verwoerd (1968 – Stellenbosch) works as a political activist for reconciliation. He wrote a book with the challenging title: *Bloedbande, 'n donker tuiskoms* (2018) (Freely translated: *Ties of blood – a bleak and dark homecoming*). In this book he talks about his struggle with the dilemma of split loyalty in the choice between grandfather Hendrik Verwoerd who gave him the bottle as a baby while sitting on his lap, and grandfather Hendrik Verwoerd who, as a politician, played a decisive role in the design of the apartheid ideology. The very painful but burning question is the following: How can Wilhelm be entitled to fully commit himself to reconciling regarding what has been suffered as a result of his grandfather's politics, while, on the other hand, trying to remain loyal to this grandfather? The fact is Hendrik Verwoerd will always be his grandfather. He cannot deny the fact that he saw and even experienced how his grandfather loved his wife, their children and grandchildren too.

The burning question remains: How to explore a quite different route without feeling that he is now betraying his whole generational heritage and familial connectivity? Even his intergenerational sense of loyalty? It is indeed fascinating to read how Wilhelm made new choices for the sake of a future generation. It moves one to discover how he is struggling to pay back wrongdoings as related to deficiencies from the family past in order to promote human well-being and to, thus, foster a humane future. Wilhelm's legacy is indeed a life devoted to giving …

Constructive and destructive entitlement

Everyone's right to give deserves recognition, implying one or another form of entitlement. However, it is not that easy because giving recognition is different from giving compliments. For Nagy, giving recognition means openly expressing the ethical merit of making someone available to the relationship, that is, to make space for their commitment to the relationship and the quality of intersubjective communication.

The acknowledgment of giving indicates a right to be there; to exist as human being within the dynamics of relationships. One's contribution to processes of giving justifies being on an ontic level. Giving and acknowledgment could be rendered as modes of justification (Boszormenyi-Nagy & Krasner 1986:57; 1994:74). What is at stake on this deep level of human existence is an exemplification of care as result and indication of loyalty. It is about care that comes from being mutually reliable. At the same time, recognition is also a giving, namely a gratuitous investment to self-esteem and future self-confidence. It motivates new initiatives to give and encourages one to act in a responsible, viable and accountable manner. Nagy calls this recognition *a constructively entitled claim that grants inner freedom and security*. At the same time, this recognition is an invitation to proceed with further expressions of giving.

Dialogically oriented pastoral care seeks to pay attention to everyone's visible and invisible merit, and modes of fairness. For a child, the input of his/her contribution should be appropriate to his/her age and/or development. When a child gets recognition, he/she knows him/herself entitled to increasingly seek constructive ways of how to express one's own unique sense of imaginative creativity. In this way, confidence in the other person, and confidence in one's own value, is learned. Both aspects are important in order to grow towards adulthood, unique individuation and equitable autonomy. When children rarely, if ever, receive an acknowledging response for their contribution, they will want to continue to exert themselves to the extreme. Never being able to do enough is a form of exploitation and comes at the expense of oneself. The child is left with a sense of guilt which can be another motivation to give even more. And with that, a right to distrust the other person is established. The child then becomes *entitled destructively*.

In adulthood this impression of '*never enough*' (lack of achievement) can have an unhealthy effect in a person's individual development. It can create a continuous delusion, namely, an inability to cease to be responsible (form of hyper-responsibility) with all the complications that arise from this. "If a person cannot expect a profit from continuous investment in his/her relationship, then abandonment of that relationship becomes a reasonable alternative" (Boszormenyi-Nagy & Krasner 1986:58; 1994:75).

> Years ago, Prof Elna Mouton (Emerita Professor of New Testament at the University of Stellenbosch) and I discussed the not so visible contribution of women to theology. Nevertheless, women engaged in theology sometimes exert themselves to the extent of *doing well* (*the quest for excellency*), especially in the eyes of everyone and other professionals. This emphasis on excellency (*I-must-achieve*) does not always translate into theological contributions but more into giving endless care within the congregation rather than being acknowledged in academic and professional circles as skilled theologians. Delineation is extra difficult for women under that pressure. Prof Mouton called this the *Woltemade syndrome*. You continue to prove yourself in a very courageous way, but in the meantime, you are in fact drowning yourself. Wolraad Woltemade was a farmer who emigrated from Germany to South Africa. In 1773, he made a name for himself by attempting to rescue Dutch castaways on the West Coast after their ship broke in two. His son was a coast guard and quickly started to help his father because bystanders were more interested in rescuing some of the jetsam released by the sinking ship than in saving people. Wolraad entered the water with his horse and urged sailors to grab the tail of the horse. In this way, he started to rescue and drag them ashore. He took sailors out of the water, seven times. The eighth time, too many desperate drowning sailors held unto the tail of the exhausted horse. The horse disappeared under the water and all of them drowned, including Wolraad Woltemade. He had saved fourteen men, however, it cost him his life. For a long time, the *Woltemade Cross* was awarded in the Western Cape as a medal for brave deeds.

Destructivity grows when a person is not recognised for given merit and does not receive what he or she is entitled to. If acts of responsibility are not seen and recognised, for whatever good reason, it becomes a deficit on the balance of give and take. A kind of unsettled account is then opened, and the deficit is continued, even transferred to other members within the family system. The deficit is then deposited elsewhere. Usually it is transferred to the so-called unguilty third person. This is what Nagy called the *revolving slate*. In intergenerational terminology, the 'revolving slate' implies that the children inherit an outstanding account about something that was unsettled between the parents and their ancestors. The outstanding guilt of pre-generations becomes the responsibility of possible 'innocent children'.

The problem in this revolving slate is that consciously or unconsciously, third parties are required to compensate the account. Within intersubjectivity and intergenerational connections, a very strange kind of right is created: Shortfall as an 'inherited right' but transferred to an unguilty party. The further problem is that this deficit can no longer be collected from the person(s) who failed to pay. Van Rhijn and Meulink-Korf call this destructively entitled claim a permissive indifference, namely, closing one's eyes, in becoming insensitive to the consequences of third parties (Van Rhijn & Meulink-Korf 2019:242). This destructive tendency can also be aimed at the Self, an aspect that should be considered when dealing with complicated life disorders such as depression, addiction, eating disorders and suicidal tendencies.

It requires insight to recognise how people and groups can try to take advantage of this destructive right (*destructive entitlement*). The revolving slate has a snowball effect. The bill that rotates always leads to new debts. Initial recognition is then claimed from those who did not cause the injustice, and the unpaid bill rolls through affecting others, even including a next generation. When phenomena like the spiral of violence, extreme forms of disrespect, even racial discrimination are critically analysed, it often points to a basis of previously built up destructively entitled claims.

The positive outcome of the revolving slate is, that because people have a strong sense to continue with life and often develop the ability to survive, they can profit from it. This will happen when, in new relationships, trust is discovered and people are permitted to receive it. The impact is that the receiving party is challenged to relate more constructively and is willing to take risks that always lurk in the dynamics of intergenerational networking. This cannot undo the earlier deficit, but it makes the ethical injury less disturbing. It can even help to prevent developing improper forms of motivation which eventually can lead to more destructive actions.

It is indeed not easy to deal with the revolving slate in counselling and pastoral caregiving. From the side of the pastor and counsellor is required a delicate professional skill, namely, to develop a sensitivity for the impact of credits and shortages on different members within the family system and familial genealogy. But when caregiving operates from the perspective of multi-partiality, and an attitude of multi-sensitivity, there is indeed hope that one can probe for pointers and compassionate directives that contribute to the finding of appropriate sources for the establishment of new confidence.

The burning question: What is meant by an appropriate mode of giving?

There is no objective measure of what is fair and appropriate when it comes to our giving to others. Giving is appropriate (*fair giving*) when the contribution is good for both the giver and the recipient. The norm to measure whether giving is appropriate or not is fairness and how it impacts on loyalty and the establishment of justice. We learn what is fair by recognising the needs of the other person as valuable, and at the same time considering our own needs. Nagy calls giving fair and just when the balance continues over a long period of time without too many disturbances. He calls it unjust when giving and receiving over a longer period of time comes to a halt or exceeds the existing capacity of the networking system due to overload or shortage.

With major life events such as birth, illness, death, marriage and divorce, the balance of what is appropriate can temporarily exceed limitations. When there is enough confidence, this should not cause a problem. However, it becomes more difficult with an accumulation of negative and/or long-life facts that continue endlessly. When, due to circumstances, care for the relationship has become one-sided, the question of inappropriate giving surfaces. The latter is indeed complex because a disturbed expression of giving does not necessarily imply that this kind of giving must be unjust. When the balance goes far to one side due to extra demands, a great reliance is placed on trust. What really counts is the development of a mature self-esteem. Within this context, one should understand the value and advantage of the delicate art of defining the self. Reckoning with own unique abilities, acknowledging differences in individuation and facing inevitable shortcomings are decisive for maintaining appropriate modes of balancing (more on this in chapter 5). However, paramount is how confidence is achieved during all the stages of self-development. At stake is how to promote the dialogical character of the relationship.

It can indeed become confusing when someone is no longer able to give, for whatever reason. How staggering it can become when one suddenly discovers that, for example, during a huge medical and health crisis (such as the current corona epidemic) your mother was in intensive care and you realise there is a high probability that she will die, but unfortunately, you cannot give her your presence and personal assistance. This can be experienced as an amputation of part of the self. After the death of a loved one, the giving also seems to stop.

In any case, reciprocity in its connection to the dynamic of the balance sheet, comes to a standstill in severe cases like death and dying. Suddenly it becomes a search and quest to discover new forms for giving and receiving. One is challenged anew to, thus, give meaning in processes of mourning that could do justice to the deceased person and ourselves. Albeit, what should be realised is that the uniqueness of mourning of all who are associated with the loss should not be forgotten (Boszormenyi-Nagy & Krasner 1986:282). Grief could become a startling process and eventually pathological (retarded grieving) when it is approached as merely a monological process. However, the inability to give to those who have died can become a new challenge to contribute to the well-being of the life of others. In terms of Nagy's approach to the promotion of human health, he will continue to insist on paying special attention to young people in a family during processes of grieving because they tend to efface themselves for the sake of older (grand) parents.

"Everyone's grief is too big, Mommy," said a 12-year-old girl after her older brother was killed in an accident. "I can no longer cope with the painful loss." The mother offered to create a kind of symbolic 'parking garage' where everyone's grief could be parked for a while. She made the garage from a pen box and put into it a bed, complete with small pieces of cloth. The girl wrote small notes with the names of everyone who was sad about her brother's death on them and put the names one by one in the box. Two days later she came from school and took her own name from the box. She said: "I think I can now cope with my grief all on my own."

In dialogical counselling in pastoral care, one seeks to gain an overview regarding the impact of an ethical balance on the different nuances within interacting transactions. Nagy uses a metaphor for that overview, stemming from accounting terminology: *The ledger of merits and credits.* This ledger is about a kind of bookkeeping system regarding the balance between merit and indebtedness of people interrelated. The hypothetical ledger functions as kind of referential framework of 'merit-positions' reflecting the interplay between 'merit', 'trust' and 'reward'.

The ledger of merit and indebtedness

This ledger of relational ethics stores the intergenerational files of concrete acquired earnings, obligations, credits and merits between family members and relatives. The ledger provides insight into the accumulation of what is earned, what is reimbursed and what is still outstanding. It refers to both sides of the relational dynamic. So, it is better to speak of a plurality of ledgers because we always target more than one person (multi-partiality). At the same time, everyone's ledger functions as a family memory in which the economics of relational ethical debt are preserved. Assessment of *fairness* partly depends on the symmetry and asymmetry in a relationship. This notion of 'partly' determines the degree of fairness of a relationship. After all, the giving of a parent to a child can never be repaid to the same extent by the child. Moreover, one person's guilt cannot simply be offset over against another's guilt. After all, guilt (debt) is always very personal and remains with the person who caused it. What happens with guilt depends on many factors (see on guilt, chapter 10).

Nagy argues that a ledger works as an inner tribunal, as a forum for sound judgment regarding the functioning of conscience. Where a person is no longer challenged by that inner intergenerational tribunal, one loses responsibility for justice in the present and for the next coming generation. Nobody can give up this responsibility although it is indeed possible to ignore and deny that responsibility.

While browsing through the demands of relational ethics, it becomes visible that it is often the case that someone is pressurised beyond existing capacities to exercise care for a long time. Sometimes one has been excessively involved and responsible. It could then happen that the effort and what it cost had not been seen or could not be recognised. The balance sheets are then seriously disturbed. Nagy calls a child's excessive concern for a parent parentification. In parentification, the giving of the child is no longer in proportion.

Parentification

With reference to what happens in the fourth dimension (ethical entanglement), parentification resides in this fourth lens on the dynamics of relational networking. Parentification should be read and understood in connection with the art of giving. The notion of *parentification* in the process of guiding children into adulthood is not per se about a destructive process (a pathological mode of parenthood) but could also become a constructive investment in the developmental growth into maturity. However, in this process of becoming a parent and the challenge to guide children into the responsibility of being an adult, Nagy also warned against the possible dangers of destructive modes of parenting. He refers to 'destructive idealising'; that is, the danger that parents work with inappropriate images (distorted perceptions) that do not fit the reality and personality of the child. The child becomes pressurised into a role function that is not appropriate for that particular age. The asymmetry is reversed. The parent leans on the child and he/she becomes like a parent to the parent. Nagy sees this unfair relationship in the reciprocity of give and take as a possible disturbance of balance because it has everything to do with disturbed justice and trust in that relationship. His starting point is the giving child, who, out of his/her existential loyalty, wants to take care of his/her parent(s) (Michielsen, et al., 1998:84). In parentification, a parent makes use of the availability of a child, with the parent claiming more (however subtle sometimes) than is fair to the child. When this claimed care does not last too long, but is seen and recognised timely, parentification is also an opportunity to contribute constructively to the balance of giving and receiving.

For a child who is expected to fill in the parent's deficits, exploitation is always a lurking threat. Parentification becomes destructive when a child has no choice but feels obliged to meet an inappropriate requirement for expressing responsibility. For Nagy, it is rather important that the interests of a child in principle take precedence over the interests of a parent. When this is harmed, asymmetry is exceeded, and it is no longer clear that the interests of the child should take precedence over the interests of a parent. A concern for the safety of the child is then at stake. When a parent seeks in the child that which is a kind of self-deficiency in him/herself (or is still deficient), it manoeuvres a child into a substitute, functional parent (or partner). It is sometimes difficult for parents and the environment to recognise that due to the unfairness in parentification, that is, the child is contributing above his/her burden.

See the following case study on the relationship between Jimmy (14 years old) and his mother who suffered from substance abuse.

Jimmy's mother was periodically alcohol addicted, during one period more than the other. The father was not in the picture. When his mother was less addicted, she would cook a nice meal so that there was something to eat when Jimmy came home from school. Then she helped with homework and even enjoyed it. However, due to her habitual and periodic drinking problem, it would so happen that she was often more addicted and half sick, lying on the couch when he got home. Such a period could continue for a couple of weeks. In such a time, Jimmy will get himself something to eat and force his mother to eat as well. He will then usher her into bed. Afterwards he will clean up the kitchen and empty bottles. Sometimes she would cry and say, "Sorry Jimmy, I feel so sorry." He took special care of his homework because he did not want to disappoint his mother. Years later, he could not bear someone saying something negative about his mom because, when the phrase "sorry Jimmy" echoed in him, it revived quite good memories. For him, it meant that she has recognised, despite her addiction, what it cost him to take care of her. That was enough for him.

In psychology, this inappropriate attitude of a child to take care due to external pressure has long been known as parentification. For Nagy, however, psychological insights about parentification are not enough to deal with this phenomenon within the dynamics of the family system. Parentification should be understood within the larger framework and comprehensive paradigm of what he called *relational ethics*. Within merely a psychological hermeneutics this relational and ethical character becomes underplayed. Another problem is that if parentification is merely an individual and psychological issue, it seems as if the problem only resides within the child and is not seen as a disturbance of the balance between parent and child. Where this is not understood and fully recognised, it becomes virtually impossible to work towards fairness and to establish new modes of reliability for the child in relation to the parent. For Nagy, there is hope for restoration of parentification and its consequences, especially when it is reframed by new insights as linked to the fourth lens, namely, the ethically relational dimension. The implication is that one must reckon with the fact that loyalty plays a major and decisive role in giving and caring for a child, as illustrated in the case of Jimmy.

Within the paradigmatic idiom of Martin Buber's relational thinking, the danger in processes of parentification is that the child remains trapped in an I-It relationship and becomes, thus, an object of parental deficit. In a dialogical, and therefore asymmetrical, relationship between parent and child, the child is recognised for his/her contribution to the I-Thou relationship. In the intersubjectivity of I-Thou, justice comes into play as a decisive and optional factor in reciprocity. What is the reason? It happens because both parent and child are repositioned as subject within the mutual dynamics of intersubjective reciprocity.

Even if a parent needs long-term care, it should not cause a problem so long as the parent acknowledges what the child does, and he/she gets recognition for his/her contribution. But even when care and concern go unnoticed, it can so happen that the child continues in an attitude of giving abundantly; the child is constantly focused on the well-being of the parent(s). This can develop into one of the most destructive tendencies in attempts to stay loyal, namely, a *servile mode of obedience*. This means to please the other just for the sake and impression of pleasing others. It is easier to please than to risk an open discussion on what is needed in the recognition of one's own needs, because what should have been done is to set boundaries. It should therefore be made very clear that giving too much does not originate from a sound wish to do so; it does not necessarily emanate from an attitude of compassionate reaching out. The alarming fact is that rather, it results most of times from an impossibility to refuse the unfair demands. Eventually it coincides with the inability to openly enter a frank discussion on how to address the real issue at stake.

It is difficult for one who is engaged in excessive modes of giving (the danger of *over-giving*) to receive care and attention from third parties. Unfortunately, when an appeal is made to give, this appeal can stir new guilt feelings that leave the impression that one must give even more than before. The problem is that in a pathological mode of parentification, the child has become a captive of disturbing patterns of giving. These patterns hamper development into adulthood. The further hampering factor is that the developing adolescent becomes dependent of approval from a third factor in an unhealthy way. If this is not recognised and dealt with, it is likely that the consequences will establish a revolving slate that will determine future generations and contaminate them with an unhealthy sense of indebtedness.

Helpers and caregivers – including pastors and all kinds of workers in the church – soon develop the tendency to be responsible beyond the limits of one's own abilities. Therefore, a concern of how to deal with parentification and how to grow towards a more equitable giving, deserves thorough attention!

It is inevitable that all caregivers should learn how to plan and cater, in a mature manner, for coping with the distress and need of the other. But then immediately, helpers and caregivers will have to learn how to delineate in a very fair way their own needs. Simultaneously, there is the challenge of how to attend to personal distress.

It is not always obvious for parents how to recognise that, in becoming a parent, one has to care for oneself and recognise the urgent necessity of 'parenting caring'. In parentification this mode of self-care is inevitable. There-fore, in parentification we can broadly recognise active and passive forms of helping and caring. Some of them are recognisable, others less so. That explains the attempt to explain some of the most obvious occurrences.

Different forms of parentification

Within active reactions, we mainly see the caring child who is always busy contributing to the relationship between that specific parent and the child. Sometimes, the focus is on the relationship between both parents and even between parents and grandparents. The passive form is recognisable by the child who tries to help the parents by *remaining a child*, and who then allows this kind of childlike behaviour that even seems to become quite infantile.

In many cases, the actively caring child eventually responds by taking some other kind of action. For example, there is the case where a couple with two children, who regularly has an argument during the evening meal, creates such a tension that one of the children suddenly throws his plate of spaghetti across the room to deflect the heat of the argument. In this way, the child draws the tension away from the parents and focuses attention on him/herself. The other child quietly crawls from the chair and disappears between the curtains so as not to bother the parents. In this example, both children unconsciously take responsibility for the parents' relationship: One by choosing an active form and becoming angry, the other by becoming actively *invisible*. In both settings the children are mildly contributing to giving. Within a very quick instant evaluation it does not seem as if they are contributing to giving. However, the problematic side comes to the fore when these forms of giving develop into established modes and fixed patterns of trying to be loyal. These forms of toxic giving eventually hamper children from developing into maturity. It can even obscure their ability to assess what is fair or not, as well as attempts to delineate what is appropriate or not.

The passive form of giving can be observed in behaviour where the child is forced to stay a child due to the parent's disturbing patterns of interaction. We recognise this passive mode when it is expressed in extreme forms of dependence on the parent(s), which eventually leads to stagnation in development. According to Nagy, this is one of the worst forms of parentification because it demands permanent availability. The problem, thus, is that the giving of the child is not recognised appropriately. Parents do everything they can to keep the child under parenting control, within the confines of the so-called safety-nest syndrome. The implication is that their child(ren) should have few friendships and should always be available to the parents. The further implication is that coming of age will start late. The latter makes it difficult for them to take up their own responsibilities. This is the reason why individuation is retarded.

The consequences of parentification can arise lifelong in situations where tension grows in relationships. It is conceivable that different forms of ethical entanglements and severe expressions of disturbance are repeated in partner relationships.

In work situations, we see people walking away from meetings when the tension builds up (crawling between the curtains). Someone else will draw attention to him/herself and even try to deflect the tension towards themselves.

Another example is the so-called *spoiled child*. This deviation is not always easy to recognise because it seems as if the child is quite satisfied with what he/she has received. However, the undergirding problem is that the child is, in a very subtle way, used to reassure parents that they are good parents. So, the parents do not *take* from the child in an appropriate way. Vice versa, they rob the child of the opportunity to *give* to the parents in an appropriate way. What parents try to do is to prevent the child from becoming disappointed.

Unfortunately, they do not adequately address what the child really needs. It is a very disturbing mode of parentification because this child has not learned to tolerate and receive a strict *no*. Furthermore, the child does not learn how to deal with disappointments nor to accept them as part of daily living.

A child can go far in his/her attempt to please parents. They can even start to sacrifice themselves in order to give parents what they cannot realise or achieve for themselves.

They will even exceed their normal abilities and stretch themselves in order to compensate for the missed opportunities of the parents. The alarming fact is that in order to get high marks (the pleasing syndrome), they will put in a lot of effort to meet the expectations of their parents. The irony is, they feel in fact pressurised to maintain the pretence of being *perfect children*. This image of the perfect child can easily turn into a negative image when a child is no longer capable of compulsive giving. When the child starts to discover his/her own limitations, the dynamics of giving and receiving can contribute to negative consequences for processes of individuation. The dynamics could then turn into scapegoating with labels such as the spoiled or unsuccessful child (*the child as failure*).

In *scapegoating* the child is forced to take over the guilt resulting from the tension between the parents or friction within the family system (false guilt). The further implication is that the child has to sacrifice him/herself and could even be viewed as a culprit by other family members regarding wrongdoings. It is then not merely the child who has to sacrifice him/herself. He/she also becomes a victim and is sacrificed by the family (Michielsen 1998:104). The further impact of scapegoating is that one person within the family system (in this case the accused child) must carry the burden in order to distract attention from any other member. The child becomes a kind of substitute and must carry the shortcomings of the other. Parents then tend to blame the improper behaviour of the child as the main cause for their marriage problems. However, the irony is that while the child does everything to keep them together, this child is, in the eyes of the parents and other family members, the one who is blamed for the tension and thus the guilty one. The child as scapegoat becomes excluded from the inner circle of the family system. To use very harsh terminology, the child becomes 'excommunicated' from the intimate space of the family dynamics.

The sexually abused child: Violating the borders

A special form of parentification deserves attention, namely child abuse, particularly the phenomenon of sexual abuse that can happen between (grand) parents and (grand)children.

In sexual abuse, the asymmetry that is necessary for reliability and safety is violated in favour of very dubious and even selfish needs (often the need to exercise authoritarian power, to control, to dominate) of a (grand) parent, uncle, brother or sister. The implication is that important generational stratifications become disturbed and even violated. As far as parents and children are concerned, the interests of a child are paramount and should enjoy preference. Especially when their vulnerability is at stake, it should be possible for children to count on the reliability of a parent.

A child can be so loyal to a parent due to parentification that he/she even wants to compensate for deficits of that parent through sexual abuse. He/she can even try to defuse the tension in the parent relationship. The limits of *giving* appropriately by the child and of *taking* appropriately by the parent have been exceeded and become violated. In sexual abuse, the child is forced to bear an unbearable burden for the sake of others. In addition, there is a burden that all kinds of sexual misbehaviour should remain secret at all cost, with the further tragic consequence that secrecy depends largely on the child's responsibility to stay quiet.

Furthermore, a child rarely gets credit for the aspect of being the giving child in situations of abuse. Rather, the term *self-denying sacrifice* is appropriate here. It seems that the parent involved in sexual abuse, as well as his/her partner, are both virtually blind to injustice. For years, out of loyalty, young children (including adult children) can remain silent about sexual abuse. The long-term consequences can indeed be devastating. The effort to trust the reliable quality of relationships that abused children have to endure prevents them from engaging in healthy sexual relationships later in adult life.

There are situations in which the abused child is given a preferential position within a family as a bribe to the imposed silence. It is not uncommon for a child that when this obscured intimacy is terminated, the special position of the parent (despite the deep violation of trustworthiness), is missed by the child The further irony is that the abused child experiences him/herself as actually being guilty in cases where the parent is punished for the misdeed of sexual abuse. A further possible consequence is that loyalty to that parent must eventually become invisible.

The devastating question is now: Where to start when the balance of giving and receiving between people is disturbed? Where should one start when the dynamics come to a standstill and the relationships have been violated and destroyed?

4.5   The healing space of fairness

One of the most important lessons that has been learned is a comment from Hanneke Meulink-Korf long ago: It is quite remarkable that Nagy does not see parentification directly as pathology but as a disturbance on the balance of give and take; as an opportunity for growth and healing. That underlines the importance of taking great care and paying attention to this kind of disturbance. Nagy does not render only parentification but all forms of disturbances on the balance, as not being primarily and necessarily pathological. His constructive approach to all of these kinds of disturbances is the following: No label, no diagnosis, no full stop; they are merely commas on the way to a new story. On the contrary, his plea is rather for care and attention to the balance of give and take. This now requires a dialogical attitude because balancing within the dynamic of giving and receiving is always, due to multi-partiality, about the fair balancing of several people simultaneously. It requires interventions of the caregiver to journey with the client from a monologue about his/her own position, to dialoguing with all parties involved. To be able to see how someone is connected to third parties engaged (the other as third factor), as well as the challenge to deal with what has already been given and received in those balances concerning care and responsibility, requires a lot of trust from a client.

Patience is needed to instil confidence so that the person who comes to ask for help gains confidence to speak about what has been given and received, and whether it has been fair or not. On the part of the counsellor/pastor, recognition for what the client has given and received is a first condition before starting with relational interventions. Acknowledgment of the counsellor/pastor will only work if it is not exercised as a mere therapeutic intervention. Nagy opposes artificial methods and step-by-step plans of how to manage the situation. Recognition is evoked by a genuine ethical concern on the part of the caregiver for what has really been contributed, and what has been suffered due to a lack of reliability. To articulate all these issues that play a decisive role in the dynamic of giving and receiving, and to display genuine compassion and appropriate recognition, can indeed create a constructive opening for the client to recognise his/her contribution as an investment to the quality of the relationship. As it were, meaning is returned to the client. In this way, an almost forgotten memory of earlier reliability (which can increase the view of self-worth) is established.

Where confidence in self-esteem grows, space is created to see what others have done to contribute to the dynamic of giving and receiving within intersubjectivity. It also brings about an acute awareness of what has been neglected, and it creates the opportunity to discover how destructive the connections have been. A further advantage is that own deficits can be brought to light. It even reveals how third parties have been affected.

The healing of fairness within the dynamics of relationships and familial interaction requires a dialogical focus from the counsellor/pastor. What is most needed is an *attitude and approach of multi-partiality*. Besides the challenge to reckon with the client's assets and deficits, multi-partiality should simultaneously consider alternately what other stakeholders have invested in the dynamics of intersubjectivity (see chapter 6). However, in order to promote healing, it takes real patience and timing because resistance to a third party's contribution can be persistent.

Towards authentic subjectivity

Care for and attention to how everyone is involved in giving and receiving is fundamentally based upon loyalty and is geared for trust. Trust is needed for maintaining the intersubjective space of dialogue. If, for whatever reason, there is no confidence, the road to dialogue becomes difficult indeed.

Nagy describes three aspects that make an important contribution to the quality of mutual trust namely, *polarisation (differentiation)*, the polarities: *symmetry versus asymmetry*, and *multi-directed partiality*. They determine the interplay between subjectivity and intersubjectivity in dialoguing encounters. They determine processes of growth towards maturity. In this process, dialogue plays a pivotal role and is basic in providing the impetus for new constructive movements that can promote the balance of giving and receiving. Where that happens, hope for the future arises.

CHAPTER 5

Towards mature dialoguing: The basic aspects of timing and asymmetry

Encouraging encounters are not merely about dialoguing. They surpass the parameters of just keeping the relational dynamics going. Conversation and communication within the space of interaction and ethics imply more than merely the event of encounter so that the movement between the *I* and the *Other/other* becomes stagnated within the flow of mutuality and reciprocity. Dialogue within encouraging encounters is focused on growth, namely the growth of the individual and everybody involved; its aim is self-development and personal maturity.

The interplay between subjectivity and intersubjectivity has two goals in common (a) individuation as self-development (differentiation) and the cultivation of maturity as directed by a stance of responsible personhood and an internalised ethical sense of fairness and justice (trustworthiness and loyalty), and (b) to keep intersubjective transactions open in view of coming generations and the establishment of time as diachronic; timing as susceptible for the not yet of a Kairos moment. In this sense, timing and dialoguing promote human growth and the anticipation of newness and significant future modes of humane and fair interactions (*futurum*). In fact, timing and dialoguing should prevent the fixation of schemata of interpretation and the objectification of being.

5.1   *On becoming mature: Growing into adulthood*

We allow every human child the opportunity to grow up in a safe and healthy environment. This environment operates like a huge safety-net of reliable connections determined by trustworthy human beings. A network of loyal relationships functions like a breeding-ground wherein it is possible to flourish as a human being. It provides opportunities to grow into a sense of responsibility regarding the promotion of human well-being, sound relationships and the development of a healthy self-esteem. It is indeed a challenge to create such a network of reliable relationships in order to develop a mature stance and a sound sense of autonomy within the different demands stemming from this relational network. It still requires confidence to be able to move autonomously between the different relationships without losing sight of disposing fairness to the other and to oneself.

Trust is a keyword in order to move independently, with freedom and obligation, within this relational networking. The latter is necessary in creating and fostering an intersubjective space for authentic dialoguing. Nagy and Krasner describe three aspects of the dialogue (*polarisation/differentiation*, *symmetry versus asymmetry*, and *multi-directed partiality*) that contribute to mature individuation and, thus, promote the maintenance of close relationships. Close relationships are formed by kinship and/or the level of significant emotional need-satisfaction. According to Boszormenyi-Nagy and Krasner (1994:93), dialogue is at the core of relational reality. In fact, dialogue becomes the decisive context for the formation of mature, personal individuation (the process of *becoming mature*).

These three aspects provide fundamental guidelines for self-correcting resources. They point to missed opportunities for dialogue and provide directives for helpful interventions. They function as sources that stimulate creativity in the dynamic space of proximity and distance between partners, (grand) parents and children. As said, this is the reason why Boszormenyi and Krasner formulate very clearly and for good reason that fairness in dialoguing is at the heart of relational reality; it forms the condition for development into adulthood. This growth process indicates a time span for learning. One of the important conditions is that this learning process should be open-ended and not be pre-determined by fixed categories about individuation. In terms of a relational and ethical perspective, a human being is never a static entity, en bloc. As human beings, we are not enclosed monades, and therefore the quality of the time within which we exist, is never the same.

Dialogue within the framework of relational ethics furthermore implies that change is always possible. In fact, we as human beings are always in becoming. As subjects within intersubjectivity our existence is never complete. After all, authentic dialoguing teaches that the time before dialoguing is not the same as the time afterwards. On the contrary, dialogue constantly changes the quality of time and in this sense, penetrates all forms of temporality. It perforates the sequence of past, present and future.

5.2 Dialoguing time: The diachronic dimension

The quality and fairness of close relationships depend on dialogue. Dialogue depends on the authenticity of real human encounters (Buber). Each encounter has the capacity to heal the relationship. One can therefore dare to say that: 'Healing within and through human encounters' reshapes timing and renews time. How? By trustworthiness, trust and reliability. However, the healing capacity and power of trustworthiness can also be disturbed and damaged. But unfortunately, damaged trust cannot be restored. It can be healed, though, by new modes of encounters and the establishment of new forms of trust. But these new modes and forms will always look different than before. Renewed trust and confidence are the stepping stones to true dialogue.

Fair memory

Trust and reliability require a fair memory. One must remember the moment in time when one has encountered a trustworthy person, someone whom one could have trusted wholeheartedly. One should also remember these encounters wherein you displayed trust towards someone else; someone for whom you were trustworthy. This is what fair memory is about. A fair memory is about recognition of the person who contributed to the value of authentic human encounters; a person who displayed the kindness of giving.

Remembering does not mean to leave the past behind. Remembering is much more about the art of revisiting that kind of image that presented the true happenstances of the past. The Hebrew word for memory, *zachar*, has a unique meaning. *Zachar* is a Hebrew word from the Old Testament meaning to remember, recall, or call to mind. For example, when God remembers a human being, He visits these images that visualises his promise to man. In the same way it is fair to remember these moments of trust and reliability. To revisit these moments creates constructive merit that concretely journeys through time. By remembering them, they contribute to the opening up of possible and eventual true future modes of encounters.

Remembering true exemplifications of confidence creates a future inclusive view that incorporates the next generation. "When we say that the next generation (partly) lives in the time of the previous generation or the next, we use a specific concept of 'time'. Time is not an abstractum" (Meulink-Korf & Van Rhijn 2002:103vv; 2016:68).

Qualification of time: The diachronic dimension

Stories of trust tell about the quality and value of the time that has been. 'Time' is about more than chronological clock time or the days and years appearing on a calendar. Time as an existential event is intrinsically about a qualitative perspective on the significance of being. *Time is about qualitative time within the quantification of time (quantitative time)*. A qualitative interpretation tells about 'filled time' as part of our human endeavour to live a meaningful life. In this sense, one has to admit that the dynamics of giving and receiving helps to understand that the link between subjectivity and intersubjectivity plays a decisive role in processes of qualification. It is in this sense that one has to conclude and say that *the qualification of time is about ethically qualified time*.

In processes of qualification, memory plays a decisive role. Remembering time is in terms of an ethical qualification, reassessing moments of mutual trust. *In this sense time is diachronic*. One, thus, starts to reflect on encounters that promoted trust and presented reliability and trustworthiness. It recalls people who helped to instil new images of trust. It also revisits these moments that helped people to regain their trust in life. Recalling all these moments and encounters have a transcendent effect. In fact, they help to create time as a qualitative entity. And the opportunities to do this reside in the *present, in the actuality of now*.

Leon Wieseltier is a journalist who, when his father died, wanted to pray *kaddish* according to Jewish custom. *Kaddish* is about an ancient Jewish prayer sequence regularly recited in the synagogue service, including thanksgiving and praise, and concluding with a prayer for universal peace. That should be done on the Sabbath every week during worship. Kaddish is therefore valid and still an obligation for devoted Jews up to now. This always requires at least ten Jewish men (*minjan*). Wieseltier wrote a book about his journey to 'remember' and tried to honour his father in this way. At the end we read:

"Transcendence is not only achieved through mystical visions. It comes about through ordinary thoughts. Get a thought and you have detached yourself from the limitations of yourself and you thus embark on your way of becoming a pilgrim" (Wieseltier, 2000:601). This phrase could be captured within the following slogan: 'Get a thought and you become a pilgrim.' Being loyal to trust is a mandate; it transforms you into a pilgrim, always journeying and on the go (*homo viator*). Becoming a pilgrim does not mean to achieve a goal and to prove something. For a pilgrim, the goal is to be en route. In this present (as expression of qualitative time), an appeal is made to develop new modes of responsibility; it summons one to become reliable for anyone.

Seen in this way, the moment of dialogue is not only a relational event in the reality of lived life. Dialogue sets the parameters for a developmental approach to daily existence and being. In this sense, it immediately triggers *processes of becoming and growth*; it sets the contours for proceeding with life's journey. The present of significant encounters presents the *futurum*, thus the reason why the qualification of time by means of trustworthy dialoguing, transforms time into diachronic time; *dialoguing time is diachronic*.

On the one hand, our move towards the future is irreversible and chrono-logical over time. This kind of quantification is expressed in phrases like: 'Tomorrow, within the next a year, I will ...' On the other hand, we anticipate a future that surpasses the logic of time and the predictability of future events in terms of forecasts. Time therefore becomes perforated by the not yet of incalculability and the trusting of faithful expectations.

Confidence and trust inspire, namely, that we are on our way to a mea-ningful future wherein one anticipates significant modes of human encounters (*they are in becoming and not yet*). By expecting new trust and modes of hoping, the anticipation is already involved in processes of becoming. Future time becomes, in this sense, an ingredient of the reality of the present while it overarches both what had been (past tense) and what is happening now (present tense) but also what is in becoming (future as adventus). In fact, we start to anticipate, from the future back into the present, significant representations of what eventually will become. One partakes in the becoming of the future (*l'avenir*). This does not imply forecasting or predicting. *It is about the awe of vivid expectations!* We start to live according to the trust that is already within us. With this remark we are already toying with the character of pastoral thinking, that is, to live in the qualitative tension between already and not yet. So, after all, in this way God is in Himself in becoming in the sense that He is approaching us from the future into our present, a present that is already transformed by a not yet that is coming to us in the mode of an eschaton – '*the futuring God*'.

On dealing with a twofold future

In French, there are two words for future, *future* and *l'avenir*. On YouTube the French philosopher Jacques Derrida (1930-2004) has a short video clip. It reads as follows: "*In general, I try and distinguish between what one calls the future and 'l'avenir' [the 'to come']. The future is that which – tomorrow, later, next century – will be. There is a future which is predictable, programmed, scheduled, foreseeable. But there is a future, l'avenir (to come) which refers to someone who comes, whose arrival is totally unexpected. For me, that is the real future, that which is totally unpredictable. The Other who comes without my being able to anticipate their arrival. So, if there is a real future, beyond the other known future, it is l'avenir in that it is the coming of the Other when I am completely unable to foresee their arrival*" (Derrida 2019 Online).

The video clip underlines the fact that time cannot really be grasped and calculated. There is 'more' in time than we can observe by our senses, and it is precisely here where a diachronic understanding of time comes into play. We insist therefore that the time of dialogue is diachronic, creating new time in the unpredictable process of hoping; it is decisive in our anticipation of new modes of trusting (the quest for new confidence). Perhaps, they might be on the way already. One never knows!

We have argued that authentic dialogue is closely connected to a diachronic understanding of time. The following question has now to be addressed: What are all the hampering factors that cripple dialoguing and hinder groping for establishing authentic modes of dialoguing?

5.3 Three aspects of dialogue in the thinking of Nagy and Krasner

Every person will come across obstacles that have hindered and actively still hamper the path to maturing in relationships. Obstacles hamper the establishment of close relationships. Unfortunately, in all four of the dimensions (lenses) as mentioned by Nagy, obstacles will appear. They could be related to facts of life, memories regarding painful events or cases where someone has been humiliated. They reveal discrepancies and ruptures in established forms of trust, irrespective of the source. The fact is that a rupture offends one and causes the grieving of a human soul. Ruptures reveal our vulnerability. They can appear very suddenly, unintentionally and unpredictably. However, they cripple our ability to trust others and even ourselves. The sad thing is that they prevent our reaching out to the other so that one becomes quite blindfolded. They do not only cripple us but also prevent one from giving thorough attention to the other. In order to really connect to the other, the challenge for pastors and helpers is to probe into the realm of another human being's pain and grief. At the same time, we have to visit and assess our own reaction in order to understand our personal forms of resistance that can hamper the establishment of authentic dialogue.

Nagy and Krasner describe three aspects of dialogue that act as *self-correcting resources* in processes of human interaction (Boszormenyi-Nagy & Krasner 1994:93). Cognition of these aspects would be most helpful to detect and enhance everyone's position (subjectivity) in the networking of intersubjective relationship. In this chapter, I shall describe two aspects, namely, *polarisation* and *symmetry versus asymmetry*. The third aspect is about *multi-directed partiality* and will be dealt with in chapter 6. The latter plays a key role in a dialogical, intergenerational approach. The challenge in this third aspect is how to deal with many people simultaneously.

We now turn to the first two.

The first aspect: Polarisation and differentiation

One has to accept the fact that people are, existentially speaking, intrinsically different. A close relationship endures these differences, even tolerates them. It is precisely these differences, being different from the other, that provide the raw material for enriching relationships. That sounds positive but it is not easy, because to tolerate and use the differences appropriately requires enough mutual trust, and, perhaps even more, to see them as a source of enrichment. Without trust, differences give rise to suspicion, distrust and become blamed for the source of conflict.

In the writing of their book *Between give and take* (1986), Nagy and Krasner refer to the existential difference between people. They call it *polarisation*. Nowadays we prefer to speak of differentiation, and we know that Nagy later also preferred this concept. Polarisation has taken on the meaning of struggle and opposition that elicits removal, precisely because of differences. From a dialectical point of view, differentiation better indicates the recognition of differences. Differentiation does more justice to the existential uniqueness of everybody else. Recognition of differentiation arises from mutual respect. One can clearly experience differentiation when a fair distance is maintained in proximity. Vice versa, it is paramount to maintain a fair proximity in distance. This kind of exercising an attitude of fairness should be performed in such a way that spontaneity in relationships is not violated at all.

Not being the same, namely, being different from the other, recalls the first two people presented to us in the Bible. Adam (Hebrew for human) is initially alone next to all the animals that go two by two. In Genesis 2:18, God proclaimed that it is not good for man to be alone. God said that he will make a "helper suitable for Adam" (NIV).

The Hebrew word *kenegdô*/ כְּנֶגְדּוֹ in Genesis 2:18-20 is difficult to translate. In fact, *ezer kenegdô* does not mean 'a helper subordinate to him'. The Hebrew word *ezer* is a combination of two roots: *'-z-r*, meaning 'to rescue, to save', and *g-z-r*, meaning 'to be strong'. Furthermore, the concept captures the ambiguity and multifacetedness of two different entities. Help in the text indicates the other as an opposite (*ezer kenegdo*) with a unique identity. Opposite, being distinct (*kenegdo*), even has a connection with the same stem that means to tell (*telling*); an entity that can tell me something. This connection helps one to understand why the concept 'suitable helper' can become very confusing when it leaves the impression of a kind of subordination. The latter then ignores the meaning of a sound differentiation that is necessary for not being alone and becoming a captive of loneliness. And that is exactly the intention of God: Somebody as an opposite who can address the other and can start a narrative, promoting authentic dialoguing. Somebody who has something different to say than the other and who can, thus, contribute to the significance of the dialogue. It calls into being somebody who can make an appeal on one's accountability and responsibility but, at the same time, one becomes responsible and invited to become a narrator as well. The helping indicates in this sense somebody who can pull one out of one's sterile isolation. In fact, God created a helper in order to proceed from a deadly monologue into a vivid dialogue.

Furthermore, one has not to deal lightly with the meaning of *helper*. When this kind of invitational helper (essentially different from Adam) is missing, our being human could become deprived from the opportunity to be saved from devastating, inhumane isolation. We then miss the opportunity to be helped and supported to contribute to our humaneness and intersubjectivity. The Hebrew language has captured the very subtle, but indeed complex difference, in an excellent way. They both become *isj* and *isja* (there is correspondence) but thanks be to God, essentially different as well.

The burning question is now: How should one live meaningfully and fruitfully within these differences?

Under the aspect of differentiation, Nagy and Krasner describe two resources. This core differentiation helps to incorporate differences as part of establishing meaningful lifestyles. The two resources are self-delineation and self-worth.

The self here has nothing to do with emphasising the attention to the individual self and the urge for self-maintenance at the cost of somebody else. It does not refer to the basic plea for individual human rights, especially the right to be oneself (self-expression). It is precisely not about the latter. Differentiation requires being able to fairly define both the other/others and oneself. The implication is not to focus narrowly on choices that will merely benefit oneself at the expense of somebody else. It is also not about excessive attempts to promote the other/others at the expense of oneself. In every relationship, it always boils down to groping for fairness in order to maintain that unique balance of giving and receiving. *Self-delineation and self-worth are self-correcting resources, in the attempt to adjust and to promote fairness and justice in relationships.* And that always requires a different consideration because the people with whom we are related are unique and the situation and the time wherein we exist are always in flux and therefore different.

Self-delineation and self-validation

To attend to oneself and to set necessary boundaries are, for anyone, a huge challenge in processes of developing into maturity. Therefore, it is not for nothing that Nagy and Krasner discuss these aspects of *self-correcting* resources so extensively. It requires personal practice and a sound insight in self-correcting measurements in order to apply fair demarcation within the balancing dynamics of giving and receiving. It is indeed a very delicate process and not so obvious to know exactly how much one should invest and where to cut on contributions.

When one works together with people, it is so difficult to know how to be available in a fair way for the other and to know what to invest in the dynamics. It is a tricky endeavour because one does not want to disturb the process of balancing in an excluding manner. One does not intend in any way to be negative. One wants to do good in order to promote the concerns of the other. One also wants to develop a mature stance to the process of balancing. Sometimes one is driven by a voice from past experience that compels one to be *more available* for the other. It even puts the obligation on oneself to take up a responsibility that could cause unfair effects. It then so happens that one puts *more stress* on oneself and becomes emotionally drained and exhausted. By doing this we run the risk of robbing the other of the opportunity to respond in a mature and responsible way. Nagy calls this tendency to over-invest in caring and responsible actions, *overgiving*. If the tendency to overact in order to compensate (danger of *overgiving*), due to the fear of doing less, lasts for a longer period of time, and people cannot limit themselves, we see them drop out from what they have previously enjoyed working on or contributing to. We also recognise this danger with volunteers, precisely due to good intentions that are supposed to give them meaning. The difficulty to demarcate leads to *burnout* for many people and is, therefore, indeed a threat for pastors! One becomes spiritually affected and intoxicated, and eventually compassion fatigue sets in.

The tendency to give inappropriately has to do with injustice within the reciprocity of giving and taking. When someone has received little or no recognition for acquired earnings (entitlement), this could be interpreted as unfair in the light of the quest for justice. For some people it seems to be a solution to give extra (*overgiving*) in order to get that recognition after all. However, at a certain point, more giving teaches us that even despite *overgiving*, our giving is *never enough*. This leads to recurring disappointing experiences with others. Unfortunately, trust becomes damaged every time. A discouraging experience can simply instil the idea that, instead of an understanding *that my giving was not good enough*, it grows into the impression *that in my very being, I am not good enough*.

In personal and working relationships, we do see the consequences in people who are at the forefront of organising and who have difficulty saying 'no'. We see the ethical lack of self-worth in behaviour that reflects inferiority. Uncertainty about one's own personal significance is hidden in many variations. The fact is that a low self-esteem impedes authentic dialoguing and hampers the fostering of reliable encounters.

In terms of the previous outline, it was necessary to highlight the first aspect of Nagy (polarisation and differentiation) in order to better understand self-correcting resources. It also helps one to understand the importance of self-worth and to develop a balanced and realistic self-esteem in processes of dialoguing and intersubjective communication. One needs to discover one's own unique identity in the establishment of sound maturity. It is inevitably the case that somewhere between birth and death, one should become aware of one's unique meaning and value (*self-validation*). Our sense of meaning and self-worth becomes visible in relationships. Very specifically, it is tested in events regarding the merit of giving and receiving (*entitlement*). In reliable relationships, a person learns to define his/her unique self. It also helps to establish one's unique sense of being different than others and its impact on self-worth as a safe and secure source in processes of self-validation. In this regard, the pastor and caregiver can become most helpful in gaining an eye for what has been given and received. They can use this insight to help the person (client) to explore new avenues in establishing self-confidence within the dynamic of relationships.

Self-delineation and self-value are, as it were, two identical twin aspects that help towards fostering authentic dialogue. In this way, both a sound self-understanding and an insight in the unique identity of the other, can benefit and enhance the development of a mature and responsible attitude towards difficult challenges in life. One should also realise that every relationship is unique. Balancing in giving and receiving is, therefore, unpredictable. It cannot be managed in terms of general, prescriptive rules and regulations.

Self-delineation: Healthy entitlement and demarcation

When someone lacks self-respect, it is difficult to protect and demarcate the vulnerable self. That is specifically the case when someone, or even a group of people, suffers from inferiority. The real danger lurks that someone from the outside starts to exploit the vulnerable person and takes advantage of the delicate situation. It can then happen that the other enters the private me-space of the sufferer and causes a lot of damage to self-worth. One can compare this personal exploitation with the saying: He/she is like a bull in a china shop. In a very careless way, the other damages the brittle self-image of the sufferer and then departs afterwards without taking care of the devastating consequences. The person suffering from inferiority will experience his/her personal pain as a characteristic that cannot be overcome anymore. In the long run, the person will start to withdraw from all normal forms of communication. When healthy entitlement is lacking, there is little skill and inner capacity in protecting borders. The person becomes a captive of inner fear for him/herself so that it is virtually impossible to challenge the person to draw a straight line and to decide to defend him/herself over against the inflictions of the other. Due to anxiety and the fear for hurt, the person withdraws even more. For children and adults with a lack of self-confidence, it becomes very difficult to bounce back. The door is then wide open to humiliation, abuse and exploitation.

Healthy demarcation considers the self-delineation of the other. A healthy relationship counts on the appropriate delineation of both partners. When one becomes indifferent to the other or even acts in a sluggish way, one develops a careless attitude that is not willing to take into account the otherness of the other. Insensitivity and a nonchalant approach contribute to the devaluation and abuse of the other. Nagy is not afraid to use the word *exploitation* for this kind of insensitivity and lack of compassion. Within the terminology of Martin Buber, the relationship is now exposed to an I-it devaluation with less opportunity for the promotion of a dignified I-Thou.

Self-delimitation is enhanced by seeking moments of merit, that is, to start reflecting on the question to whom one has given credit within the networking dynamics of intersubjectivity. Recognition and acknowledge-ment of constructive giving enhance the capacity of self-healing. It is there-fore important for caregivers and pastoral helpers to focus on encouraging messages. In this way, caregivers can create costly spaces for the promotion of an inner sense of well-being. Barbara Krasner calls these moments of inner self-disclosure, the holy ground of new creation and reconnection. *"In those instances in which epiphany, awe, and grace are known and received, they are palpable confirmations of healing through meeting. Therapists, of course, are never entitled to impose their will on people who come to them in search of succour and confirmation. But therapists are entitled to witness to the holy ground of creation and connection"* (Krasner & Joyce 1995:216). With 'holy' is then meant a kind of sanctification of being (*qadosj*); concrete trust has been transformed into a gesture of true sanctification within the moment of intersubjective connection between me and the other, that is, the concrete manifestation of a reliable and trustworthy encounter; an indication of relational trust within the timespan of life to be set aside in order to be recalled as being costly and gratuitous indeed. With this grounded experience is meant not something that one can possess like property. With 'ground' is meant a basic life experience that founds moments of true giving and receiving; 'ground' as a living space where credit and deficits are given and received. In this sense, it was indeed a brilliant remark by Krasner, namely, that the pastor acts like a 'witness' to the holy ground of creation and connection. Albeit, after all, the real and authentic ethical recognition comes from the one to whom has been given!

Self-validation (empowerment)

In addition to self-definition, self-validation is another resource for establishing reliable and dialogical relationships. Self-esteem allows one to discover freedom within the relationship without fear of losing oneself or becoming detached from the other. It teaches one to listen to the conditions of the other without giving up one's own position. The empowerment of self-esteem arises where insight is gained due to earned trust (merit) resulting from the balance of giving and receiving, from given care and responsibility. Through care and responsibility, not only psychological needs are satisfied (second dimension), but also ethical merit is increased (fourth dimension).

Self-validation offers that freedom to become a more responsible (mature) partner due to legitimate merit. A mature attitude considers the credits and deficits that support relational integrity. Then, there are no improper expectations or requirements at stake anymore. Working towards more fairness in recognising everyone's significant self-worth (despite all the differences that exist) is not only important in family relationships but can also be very helpful when one is exposed to differences in groups and cultural diversity, even when those differences in history have become a bone of contention. It can even create an important moment to pause in order to transfer the account of inferiority to third parties (a rotating slate). After all, one has to accept the fact that in order to live a significant life, one has to understand that living with dignity and self-worth implies to always face differences and view them as opportunities for growing into maturity.

The second aspect: The advantage of symmetry and asymmetry

Symmetry and asymmetry help one to gain insight regarding the importance of appropriate proximity and appropriate distance in intersubjective networking. In order to assess the value and quality of dialogue, one has to develop respect for the appropriateness and correct proportions of balancing. The criterion is everyone's responsibility and respect for what occurs on the balancing edge of give and take. In making a fair assessment, one has to reckon with the fact that responsibility for appropriate distance and proximity is not always the same for everyone: Relationships are asymmetrical and symmetrical.

Intergenerational relationships (vertical) are existentially asymmetrical. Children can never repay parents in the same way for what they invested in their lives. During childhood, the contribution of parental giving in terms of quantity and quality is very different from that of children.

The relationship between parents and children can never become symmetrical. *Children must be able to count on the guarantee that their needs and interests should take precedence.* That explains the indebtedness of children regarding care and concern for their parents. On the notion of asymmetry, Meulink-Korf and Van Rhijn quote Emmanuel Levinas when it comes to the question where (in different positions) 'moral consciousness' resides. The child can never bear the responsibility of a parent.

Parent and child never coincide. This disproportion (the asymmetry) (Nagy, 1995) between the Other and the I, is exactly what moral consciousness is about. The moral consciousness is not about an experience of values, but of appropriate access (or contact possibility) (Nagy, 1995) to the realm of what one can call 'being outside us'. With the latter is meant notably the Other/other (Levinas 1969:29). Levinas here indicates the transcending moment when it starts to dawn on a human being (Meulink-Korf & Van Rhijn 2002:140; 2016:95).

In asymmetrical relationships, the movement of give and take is always in a moving balance and the needle of the scale is never exactly centred. Asymmetry helps us to realise that we are not the same, we are all different. In fact, radical sameness has never been the case. Even in future we will always be different and unique human beings. That underlines the importance of differentiation. Without the phenomenon of difference, even the account of history would have become a fake. *Asymmetry is not about a difference in power but about a difference in authority and the expression of awe.* So, there is no place for hierarchy here. It is about the maintenance of a safe ethical order. It does not rehearse about the attitude of someone who knows exactly what balancing entails. What it indeed reveals is how responsibility for beneficial safety is displayed and exemplified. "The tendency to overlook hidden asymmetries in an apparently symmetrical relationship, is often the cause of relational confusion and despair" (Nagy and Krasner 1968:81). This requires observance of the correct distance and proximity so that everyone's safety is guaranteed and the vulnerability of one and the other is not endangered or exploited in any way. Respect for asymmetry contributes to the prevention of narrowing or exceeding the boundaries of the other. What should be maintained and promoted is a safe space in which the other can make him/herself visible.

It can be helpful for parents to indicate the importance of asymmetry. To take cognisance of asymmetry is in the interest of the child. And the latter should always take precedence. A child must be able to always count on parental reliability. Even adult children still benefit from parents who respect the ethical space of asymmetry. This does not alter the fact that precisely as the needs of parents increase, the asymmetry in the dynamics of balancing could become reversed. Furthermore, children have every right and are obliged to take appropriate care of their parents. Not as a repayment due to the obligation of indebtedness but simply because it is an existential right to give.

Because of the asymmetry, the relationship between parents and children is never the same and should not be compared to connections with friends (general friendship). That is not to say that there can be no established forms of friendship, especially with reference to sport or hobbies or cultural interests. In general, the relationship between friends is symmetrical. The relationships between sisters and brothers, friends, partners, colleagues, and so on, are to a large extent symmetrical. Not as equals but symmetrically in the sense that the dynamics of balancing takes place according to the regularity of giving and taking. According to Nagy, these aspects of dialogue belong to the fourth dimension, namely, that of relational ethics. However, in the case of brothers and sisters there is a viable factor due to the intersubjective dynamics in intergenerational connections. Asymmetry amongst siblings becomes apparent when one of them is more vulnerable and in need of more care. There is more about sibling relationships in chapter 6.

In symmetrical relationships there is always a certain tension between the interests of one and the other because interests are different and variable.

Rights to give and receive equally should always be maintained. People have the right to expect it, to ask for it, even though all needs cannot be satisfied simultaneously. With only two in a close relationship, the dialogue can continue for a long time according to a certain balance. However, as soon as a third party appears, choices have to be made in weighing up needs and interests. This is also applicable between partners. Conflicts of interest are inevitable.

In symmetrical relationships, there may be a need for *temporary asymmetry*. Especially in cases where a professional person recommends it for the sake of the well-being of both parties involved. The necessary distance in proximity is then also not based on power, but on awe and respect. This is extremely important in cases where a person's health could become threatened as, for example, in the current global corona pandemic of the Covid-19 virus. Think of doctors, teachers, nurses but also pastors, where asymmetry is temporarily necessary!

> A pastor married for 25 years decided to give a party to his family and invited his entire church council. The company was cheerful, ate, drank and danced. Even the minister joined them. After the party, he said: Something had changed. Afterwards it was difficult to restore the asymmetry between the minister and the church council. A female deacon claimed the right to close friendship due to the tango with the minister.

The core issue at stake in the balancing dynamic of symmetry-asymmetry, is the quest for justice and the fact that human beings are summoned to act in a fair way. The more there is a tendency to ignore intergenerational asymmetric liabilities, the more it avenges in generational symmetrical relationships and becomes a source of confusion and disappointment (Nagy and Krasner 1986:91). Intergenerationally, parents and children have different choices to make in the quality of giving and taking that would have been the case in symmetrical relationships.

In Philippians 2:2-5, it is about one's own interests but, at the same time, to display concern for the needs and interests of the other. It is indeed difficult to constantly detect boundaries. Delineation is a dynamic process so that one has to reframe precious demarcations often. "Therefore if you have any encouragement from being united with Christ, if any comfort from his love, if any common sharing in the Spirit, if any tenderness and compassion, then make my joy complete by being like-minded, having the same love, being one in spirit and of one mind. Do nothing out of selfish ambition or vain conceit. Rather, in humility value others above yourselves, not looking to your own interests but each of you to the interests of the others. In your relationships with one another, have the same mindset as Christ Jesus" (NIV).

Meulink-Korf and Van Rhijn write: "It is difficult to understand ourselves as being ripped, detached from the very beginning from our natural environment that inevitably follows its own course. Being detached one becomes engaged in a long process of learning. In fact, one has to realise that one has become somehow an heir and partake in these learning curves. The engagement is often fragmentary, but not necessarily ineffective. The whole process is not about a 'theological system', but an exercise in practical, painful wisdom, that is, an irreducible sense of responsibility for the other person, the neighbour" (Meulink-Korf & Van Rhijn 2002:141; 2016:95).

The third aspect: Multi-directed partiality

Multi-directed partiality seeks to give confidence so that every vote is guaranteed in the ledger of credits and deficits. This third aspect of dialogue is the main key of the contextually oriented caregiver and pastor. It requires an attitude that at a glance immediately takes into account all those involved, both those who have died, as well as current people and future generations. It seeks to give confidence so that every vote is guaranteed in the ledger of credits and deficits. Multi-directed partiality is focused on fairness in the promotion of justice. Its aim is to address cases of injustice in relational networking. This attitude offers great opportunities for self-correcting resources that reveal mutual trust and fairness that were previously invisible (see chapter 6).

It is now paramount to come back to the importance of asymmetry in relationships. In this regard, a Biblical text on the rape of Tamar by her half-brother Amnon serves as example of what the consequences could be when asymmetry becomes disturbed and violated. The text also gives insight into the fact that David, as father of his children, was not wholeheartedly committed to the cause of justice in the asymmetry between parent and child.

5.4   2 Samuel 13:1-22: The case of disturbed asymmetry

King David had several sons and daughters. Amnon and Tamar were half-brother and half-sister. The text reveals how boundaries of demarcation are subtly stretched within the dynamics of relationships.

For example, when we closely follow the root text, we see how suggestive changes in names could be used to manipulate different positions. This game play can be very subtle and happens unnoticed. It shows how an almost inconspicuous mode of transgression takes place in preparation for a rape. In order to cover up for the transgression, smokescreens are used to disguise the injustice.

Asymmetry, as revealed in the story of the rape of Tamar, does not tell about the role of respect and awe (fourth dimension) and its impact on asymmetry but about power and powerlessness (third dimension). It shows how step by step, the destructive downward movement becomes more and more threatening.

All too often, the subtle signs of violated asymmetry are only recognised by third parties afterwards. This text calls for caution and concern for appropriate distance and proximity.

Violated asymmetry (sexual seduction): Amnon – Tamar

¹Some time passed. David's son Absalom had a beautiful sister whose name was Tamar; and David's son Amnon fell in love with her. ²Amnon was so tormented that he made himself ill because of his sister Tamar, for she was a virgin and it seemed impossible to Amnon to do anything to her. ³But Amnon had a friend whose name was Jonadab, the son of David's brother Shimeah; and Jonadab was a very crafty man. ⁴He said to him,

"O son of the king, why are you so haggard morning after morning? Will you not tell me?"

Amnon said to him,

"I love Tamar, my brother Absalom's sister."

⁵Jonadab said to him,

"Lie down on your bed, and pretend to be ill; and when your father comes to see you, say to him,

'Let my sister Tamar come and give me something to eat, and prepare the food in my sight, so that I may see it and eat it from her hand.'"

[6]So Amnon lay down, and pretended to be ill; and when the king came to see him, Amnon said to the king,

"Please let my sister Tamar come and make a couple of cakes in my sight, so that I may eat from her hand."

[7]Then David sent home to Tamar, saying,

"Go to your brother Amnon's house, and prepare food for him."

[8]So Tamar went to her brother Amnon's house, where he was lying down. She took dough, kneaded it, made cakes in his sight, and baked the cakes. [9]Then she took the pan and set them out before him, but he refused to eat. Amnon said,

"Send out everyone from me."

So everyone went out from him. [10]Then Amnon said to Tamar,

"Bring the food into the chamber, so that I may eat from your hand."

So Tamar took the cakes she had made, and brought them into the chamber to Amnon her brother. [11]But when she brought them near him to eat, he took hold of her, and said to her,

"Come, lie with me, my sister."

[12]She answered him,

"No, my brother, do not force me; for such a thing is not done in Israel; do not do anything so vile! [13]As for me, where could I carry my shame? And as for you, you would be as one of the scoundrels in Israel. Now therefore, I beg you, speak to the king; for he will not withhold me from you."

[14]But he would not listen to her; and being stronger than she, he forced her and lay with her. [15]Then Amnon was seized with a very great loathing for her; indeed, his loathing was even greater than the lust he had felt for her. Amnon said to her,

"Get out!"

[16]But she said to him,

> "No, my brother; for this wrong in sending me away is greater than the other that you did to me."

But he would not listen to her. ¹⁷He called the young man who served him and said,

> "Put this woman out of my presence, and bolt the door after her."

¹⁸Now she was wearing a long robe with sleeves; for this is how the virgin daughters of the king were clothed in earlier times. So, his servant put her out, and bolted the door after her. ¹⁹But Tamar put ashes on her head and tore the long robe that she was wearing; she put her hand on her head, and went away, crying aloud as she went. ²⁰Her brother Absalom said to her,

> "Has Amnon your brother been with you? Be quiet for now, my sister; he is your brother; do not take this to heart."

So Tamar remained, a desolate woman, in her brother Absalom's house.

> ²¹When King David heard of all these things, he became very angry, but he would not punish his son Amnon, because he loved him, for he was his firstborn. ²²But Absalom spoke to Amnon neither good nor bad; for Absalom hated Amnon, because he had raped his sister Tamar.

This history of Amnon and Tamar begins with, "*Hereafter*, it so happened." This 'hereafter' is quite remarkable. By this style of giving an account on events, the authors of the Bible tried to link the sequences of following events to previous happenstances. The reference is to the account on the cunning way in which King David took Bathsheba, the wife of Uriah. To get rid of Uriah, David wrote a letter to Joab: "Put Uriah in the front line where the fighting is fiercest. Then withdraw from him so that he will be struck down and die" (2 Sam 11:14). David could then take advantage of the situation. It will give him the possibility to take Bathsheba as his wife. However, what David did was evil in the sight of God. The Lord sent Nathan the prophet to David. Nathan pointed out the wrongdoing of David and said: "Why did you despise the word of the Lord by doing what is evil in his eyes? You struck down Uriah the Hittite with the sword and took his wife to be your own. You killed him with the sword of the Ammonites." Hereafter followed the verdict: "Now therefore the sword will never depart from your house" (2 Sam 12: 9-10).

David acknowledges his guilt. The firstborn son of David and Bathsheba was stillborn. David now comforts Bathsheba with the promise of another child. He went to her and lay with her. So, she gave birth to a son and they called him Solomon. The child should then serve as a kind of 'comfort child'.

These painful and emotional events of guilt resonate in the following chapter on Tamar's rape.

What mainly lingers is that sentence of the prophet Nathan: Evil will rise from your own home.

> It is important to emphasise that I worked from the Hebrew root text which shows a different meaning in terms of how the words were compiled and arranged, thus, the difference when compared with most of the other translations. This has been done on purpose in order to clarify how the names and relationships change subtly. The nuances will be indicated in italics in the text below.

Amnon, son of David, fell in love with Tamar, the beautiful sister of Absalom son of David. He made himself sick (sickness is reciprocal, it is grammatically a *hitpael*). Tamar was a virgin and it seemed impossible for Amnon to do anything to her. So far there is still nothing wrong with Amnon's crush.

> Those who were still virgins were given extra protection in those days, so approaching without permission was not done (Bab. Talmud; text Avot rabbi Natan). Since the rape of Jacob's daughter, Dina, there have been strict laws for punishment for rape.

Now Amnon had a good friend, son of a brother of David and therefore a cousin, whose name was Jonadab. He was known as a wise man. He then asked Amnon "Why do you, the king's son, look so haggard morning after morning?" (2 Sam 13:4). (Very interesting, the same word is used for the lean cows in Joseph's dream, Genesis 41:19). He asks him to be open about what bothers him. Amnon confesses his love for Tamar but now call her Absalom's sister, which insinuates more distance and makes asymmetry more symmetrical. (Tamar is now shifted from 'half-sister' to 'my sister' and eventually to '*Absalom's sister*'). It shows the objectification in distance which creates space for crossing the boundaries of intimacy in a very shrewd and easy way.

Then suddenly the name of Jonadav changes to *Jehonadav*. I have not found any commentary that gives meaning to this nuance, but it is not for nothing that it is written as later Amnon's name will also change. Anyway, he advises Amnon to stay ill until his *father David* comes to see him. When he arrives, Amnon can ask him to send Tamar to make some special bread for him as a meal. The word used for meal turns up here six times, but from now on *without the reference to bread*. And so, David came to Amnon.

Now the reference to David as 'father' has changed from 'father' to *King David*. Amnon asks him to bring his sister, but he does not ask to make bread, as Jehonadav suggested! He merely asks to make two *levav* (from *lev*/heart). *Lev* is used to indicate the place of emotion. So, we decided to translate *lev* with cake shaped like hearts (heart-cakes). This he wants to eat from Tamar's hand to make the distinction clearer between 'bread as a general meal' and this very special kind of cake as related to the expression of emotion. In addition to the game with the names, there is also now a shift in what needs to be prepared. An erotic aspect now creeps in unnoticed (heart-cake).

The question arises if whether David, as father and king, could not decipher the double message lurking in the symbol of the heart-cakes. At the very least, it insinuates sexual seduction. Or does he put it very conveniently aside? His own escapade with Uriah and Bathsheba is yet to be remembered, including the warning of the prophet Nathan that evil will rise from his own home. However, without any comment, David himself sends Tamar to Amnon's house to make a meal. The narrator then uses a sequence of verbs for all the actions she needs to make the heart-cakes (take, knead, make, bake, take, put down). This takes the momentum out of the story and condenses the tension, like a bated breath.

The moment that Tamar comes to Amnon with the pan, he refuses to eat and sends everyone away. He is alone in the room with Tamar. Only the storyteller is a witness. With two attempts, Amnon orders Tamar to lie with him and calls her '*my sister*' again. Then she speaks prophetic words "such a wicked thing should not be done in Israel!" And "don't humiliate me my brother". She warns him that he will be one of the greatest wicked fools in Israel. However, Amnon doesn't listen to her words. He then raped her.

After this humiliation, Amnon hated her with intense hatred. In fact, he hated her more than he had loved her. Amnon then told her to get up and get out. He not only sent her away but, at the same time, robbed her of a decent future. Not only literally, as she will no longer have a husband and therefore no children who will take care of her in future. But also, relationally she has become excluded, thrown back on herself, within the deep and lonely space of rejection. Tamar exercised the signs of grief: The tearing of her ornamented robe and ashes on her head, the signs of mourning. She put her hand on her head and went away, weeping aloud as she went.

Her real brother Absalom talked to her and said: "Has that Amnon (*Aminon*) your brother been with you?" Here again that small shift in the name, now possibly indicating derogatory. This brother commanded Tamar to keep silent about the matter (imperatively) because Amnon was her *brother*! Afterwards, Tamar continues to live in the house of *her brother* Absalom.

And what about David as father? Not a word from the father at all. There is a word from King David. He is furious about these things. But despite his anger, he does nothing to do justice to Tamar.

Surprisingly, Absalom never said a word to Amnon, either good or bad. Nevertheless, he hated Amnon because he had disgraced his sister Tamar. After two years Absalom acted. He ordered his men to strike Amnon down and kill him (2 Sam 13:28). It was the messenger Jonadab who brought David the message that Amnon was dead. Jonadab explained that this has been Absalom's expressed intention ever since the day that Amnon raped his sister Tamar (2 Sam 13:32). After these events Absalom fled and was on the run for three years.

When Absalom returned home, it is mentioned that three sons and a daughter were born to him. The names of the sons were not mentioned. Nevertheless, the name of the daughter was mentioned. She was called Tamar and became a beautiful woman as in the case of his sister (2 Sam 14:27). The account is impressive and could be rendered as an expression of loyalty!

Asymmetry between parent and child

Between parents and children, parents should safeguard the asymmetry in the relationship. A child must be able to count on that, even older children. David does not vouch for his daughter Tamar. This does not only apply merely to the David-Tamar relationship. The relational ethics between the father and other children (Amnon and Absalom) are also disrupted. Instead of the father (David), Absalom stepped in and did blame his brother. He did that deputy for Tamar (substitutionary). He then claimed the life of Amnon.

This is how the revolving slate rolls on from one generation to the next and becomes connected to the warning of the prophet that it could not be prevented anymore that evil will never return from the home of David. It is exactly how Nathan warned David: "The sword shall never depart from your house" (2 Sam 12:10). Although the relationship between brother and sister is symmetrical, every relationship requires careful asymmetry. When an appropriate distance and proximity should be maintained in the determination of positions in familial systems, asymmetry is fundamental. Very specifically, in cases where it is quite clear that inappropriate distance and proximity had been crossed and relationships become exposed to brute violence. Amnon brutally occupies that space by degrading Tamar on becoming a mere object. This has permanently disrupted the mutual balance in the relationship.

Exodus 20:14: The plea for loyal partnership in congeniality and kinship

Marc Ouaknin writes in his book on the Ten Commandments about disturbing the obligation of kinship (Ouaknin 2001). He explains the seriousness of this in an explanation of the seventh commandment: "You will not commit adultery," לא תנאף.

In Jewish exegesis, the seventh command should be rendered as a critical part of all ten and should therefore be read simultaneously with verse one: "I am the Lord your God, who brought you out of Egypt, out of the land of slavery". And immediately follows in the same breath: "You shall not commit adultery." In other words, I have delivered you and, therefore, you (second person singular) will keep the command and exemplify it in terms of the quality of that freedom and what it entails within relationships. That puts adultery in the light of a mandate – a command that should be taken seriously indeed.

This seventh pronouncement is preceded by: "You shall not kill." Murder is violence and happens where the address resonating from this word-text is ignored. Hannah Arendt aptly captured the meaning of the text when she said: Where the other is not respected as unique, violence arises and that is murder. Murder is total objectification of the other, and the same applies to adultery. Murder and adultery are closely linked to one another. In fact, they follow each other in the line of commandments. The history of David and Bathsheba precedes the murder of Uriah and repeats itself in adultery between Amnon and Tamar and so the wrongdoing continues emanating into the murder of Amnon.

> Adultery, *na'af*, means adultery, especially in the sexual area. Israel itself at that time had little polygamy compared to other nations. Most relationships were monogamous. Sexual relations with another woman were forbidden and even more prohibited when this woman was married. Where a married man committed adultery with an unmarried woman, the latter lost her virginity and so diminished her dowry value accordingly. This is not an absolute ban on divorce, because it was well known in those days that divorce did take place. For example, when a letter for divorce was officially issued (see Moses in this regard), this kind of arbitration letter did provide for the material care for the woman as well as her children. So, regulations were in place to safeguard the vulnerable position of neglected women and children.

According to Ouaknin, in Rabbinic doctrine, the imperative in the command 'You shall no commit adultery' is broader than mere sexual abuse between a man and a woman (Ouaknin 2001:139). The seventh word is a valid imperative for all societies. It demands the trustworthiness of partners, especially for children who are at issue when sexuality is at stake. It is a commandment for relational delineation when somebody is inappropriately manipulated for the sake of someone's own need and selfish desires without regard and respect for the other person and all others involved. Their boundaries of kinship are harmed. The context which should have functioned as a kind of guarantee and *safety net* is unfortunately no longer reliable. In fact, adultery cannot anymore guarantee the future of each other and the children born out of that relationship.

Sexual border crossing often results in divorce. Families are falling apart and with that, intergenerational relationships start to disintegrate. Family stories about merit and deficit are less openly discussed. One should reckon with the ethical value of relationships because loyalty is at stake. However, in cases of final separation, files about the transfer of legacies become deleted in the family memory and are lost. Final separation impacts on stories about where the child and his family originated from, about the joy at birth, or how grandparents managed to survive, and which values were important in a family. After all, every child has every right to ask questions about "where do I come from?" With a view to the future, a child needs the stories of reliability in which the words and accounts about kinship can be heard as basis for themselves to also act in future in a fair and reliable way within the networking of intersubjectivity.

These are decisive words and categories that Nagy and Krasner used to describe these aspects of dialogue that foster authenticity, reliability and trust-worthiness in the balancing of giving and receiving. In fact, there are indeed many. Due to their importance, they will be listed here again: Differentiation, self-definition, self-demarcation, self-worth, symmetry versus asymmetry. Albeit, the intriguing question is: Where to start as a social worker or pastor in the complex situation of families where mutual trust is broken? The third aspect of an attitude of *multi-directed partiality* will help us to hear and see those different people at the same time and start to do them justice. It is an attitude that goes beyond professionalism; it becomes an attitude to life; a mode of being; the how of relating in intersubjectivity. This caring and sensitive attitude seems to be the beginning of all contextual wisdom. But without the hitherto described insight into authentic dialogue and reliable encounters, we cannot learn the dialogical directedness and value of this attitude.

CHAPTER 6

Multi-directed partiality: The quest for inclusiveness

It has become clear that in the focus of dialogue and human encounters the concern for the authenticity of the human I is pivotal, which explains the emphasis on individuation, self-worth and development into maturity. But at the same time, there is the concern for promoting humanness and fostering fairness in the creating of free spaces for taking care of the interest and significance of the other. Both are decisive for establishing authentic dialoguing. At stake in networking is ethics; that is, the attempt to build trust and maintain justice. This aim is never static, and in fact it is unpredictable.

Networking revolves around the art of fair balancing and trustworthiness. Therefore, two decisive factors in the dynamic movement of intersubjective encountering are: (a) reciprocity within the dynamics of giving-and-receiving and (b) the concern for the apparent paradoxical tension between symmetry and asymmetry. They do determine processes of balancing in human interaction.

But now the burning question: Why this appealing emphasis on fair balancing?

The answer to the above is because the scope and landscape of fair balancing is determined by the concern and care for the other/others. Networking in a relational ethic presupposes simultaneously intersubjectivity with many others. Due to diachronic timing and the stretching from past into the present and forwards into the future of coming generations, the concern for many others is always at stake. The implication and challenge in helping and caregiving are to deal with all the others at the same time. In caregiving, the focus in healing and human well-being cannot be narrowed to selfish needs. It should simultaneously always focus on the interests and contributions of all others. That is why the focus in this chapter is on inclusivity within the approach of multi-directed partiality; the third aspect of dialogue which Nagy describes.

6.1   The crucial role of multi-partiality: Towards a core strategy of inclusivity in dialoguing

According to Nagy, this third aspect in dialogue, namely multi-directed partiality, can be called the *core strategy* in authentic dialoguing. Core strategy is about a professional attitude that also includes a method. This multilateral attitude is based on reciprocity in relationships (Boszormenyi-Nagy & Krasner 1994:93-120). Furthermore, the aim of this method is to detect reliable resources in order to make the mutual movement of giving and receiving visible to all others. This core strategy wants to recognise fairness. Its aim is to give credit and acknowledgement when trustworthiness and loyalty have been established. The realisation of fairness creates space for authentic dialoguing. To make the giving and receiving of everyone visible, trust is needed regarding the ability, skilfulness, and trustworthiness of the pastor and counsellor. Trust is created when it is experienced that the pastor and counsellor do not exclude anyone. When everyone involved is treated in a fair way, and alternately recognised and considered, relational ethics becomes visible. And when the other matters, the *I* (individual) also matters, because in this core strategy the focus is multifaceted.

To be able to work from a dialogical orientation and to take several people, at the same time, into consideration, an attitude of multi-directed partiality is paramount. This focus requires the ethical involvement of every person as he/she is embedded in his/her versatile relational world. This endeavour of multi-calculation and multi-acknowledgement (*to always reckon with*) is applicable to both intergenerational as generational relationships. It encompasses a concern for someone who is present, but even those who are absent. The approach is all-inclusive and, thus, includes deceased persons and unborn offspring. In the context of close familial networking, the ethical involvement of third parties could furthermore encompass all role models such as teachers or girlfriends. In fact, everyone who has ever been involved in the dynamic movement due to the balancing momentum of giving and receiving, as well as everyone who can still contribute in future, should be acknowledged and included.

Because attitude is crucial, we emphasise again: Dialogically oriented pastoral care does not focus exclusively on a problem or pathology. It even does not seek instant diagnoses and quick answers. The attitude of multi-directed partiality requires from the pastor to orient him/herself to someone's diverse relational resources. In this endeavour, caregivers should reckon with the underlying structure of *existential giving and receiving* within the relational dynamic of intersubjectivity. It is fair to give the various voices acknowledgement for their counting input regarding credit and deficits. The implication thereof is to always be sensitive to the life history and relationships at stake in that specific context. Obviously, not everyone in a family agrees on everything at the same time, because everyone is making their own ethical weighting of the ledger. In the ledgers, one can detect different balances regarding the value of life, as well as the quality of intergenerational and generational reciprocity. In that ledger (ledger of merits and credits) everyone's contribution to humanity and reliability is recorded. But also, the shortcomings of others and injuries inflicted to and by others, as mentioned and assessed in the ledger, are notified.

The pastor and helper as caregivers: The decisive role of attitude (habitus)

As it were, multi-directed partiality requires a multiform of attitudes and a flexible disposition, that is, to take turns 'behind the seat' of everyone involved, dealing and understanding everyone's assets and shortcomings. However, this kind of flexibility is not so simple because focusing on the other does not imply a neutral stance from the side of the caregiver. Where necessary, it requires, temporarily, a disposition of partiality. To merely ignore acts of injustice but at the same time not to acknowledge what has been done right, should not be appropriate. That is the reason why flexibility often asks from the caregiver to become biased when focusing on the position of the other/others.

The role of the caregiver is indeed complex because, in helping, one has to deal with one's own preferences as well. In pastoral engagements and interventions there is always the danger of objectification. Therefore, from caregivers and helpers are required self-insight and self-knowledge; that is, the maturity and sensitivity to suspend and/or put aside prejudices that could have an objectifying effect temporarily. Only then can people, despite all their differences, become visible to each other as a person and subject. In this way, a compassionate space is created wherein it is possible for people to discover that this attitude of the helper/caregiver contributes to establishing confidence. It creates space for the arising of new connections; it kindles hope for the starting of genuine dialogue. The point is it takes patience to do justice to everyone in their versatility.

How prejudices can get in our way of being multi-partial is clear from the very familiar parable of *the prodigal son*. This inscription is not in the text and is added later by the translators. However, the problem now is that it leaves the impression that we already know in advance who is lost in this parable. This impression is further reinforced by this late inscription. The further problem with this inscription is that the heading creates a kind of skewed presupposition that points in the direction of sheer moralism. A preferred heading should rather be *A father had got two sons*. Well, that already implies a difficult choice.

6.2   *Luke 15:11-31: A father had got two sons*

[11]Then Jesus said:

"There was a man who had two sons. [12]The younger of them said to his father:

"'Father, give me the share of the property that will belong to me.'

"So he divided his property between them.

[13]"A few days later the younger son gathered all he had and travelled to a distant country, and there he squandered his property in dissolute living. [14]When he had spent everything, a severe famine took place throughout that country, and he began to be in need.

[15]"So he went and hired himself out to one of the citizens of that country, who sent him to his fields to feed the pigs. [16]He would gladly have filled himself with the pods that the pigs were eating; and no one gave him anything. [17]But when he came to himself, he said,

'How many of my father's hired hands have bread enough and to spare, but here I am dying of hunger!

[18]I will get up and go to my father, and I will say to him:

> "Father, I have sinned against heaven and before you; [19]I am no longer worthy to be called your son; treat me like one of your hired hands.'"

[20]"So he set off and went to his father. But while he was still far off, his father saw him and was filled with compassion; he ran and put his arms around him and kissed him. [21]Then the son said to him:

> 'Father, I have sinned against heaven and before you; I am no longer worthy to be called your son.'

[22]"But the father said to his slaves:

> 'Quickly, bring out a robe – the best one – and put it on him; put a ring on his finger and sandals on his feet. [23]And get the fatted calf and kill it, and let us eat and celebrate; [24]for this son of mine was dead and is alive again; he was lost and is found!'

"And they began to celebrate.

[25]"Now his elder son was in the field; and when he came and approached the house, he heard music and dancing. [26]He called one of the slaves and asked what was going on. [27]He replied:

> 'Your brother has come, and your father has killed the fatted calf, because he has got him back safe and sound.'

[28]"Then he became angry and refused to go in. His father came out and began to plead with him. [29]But he answered his father:

> 'Listen! For all these years I have been working like a slave for you, and I have never disobeyed your command; yet you have never given me even a young goat so that I might celebrate with my friends. [30]But when this son of yours came back, who has devoured your property with prostitutes, you killed the fatted calf for him!'

[31]"Then the father said to him:

'Son, you are always with me, and all that is mine is yours. [32]But we had to celebrate and rejoice, because this brother of yours was dead and has come to life; he was lost and has been found.'"

The preceding events: The muttering of Pharisees and teachers

For Jesus, a parable is not like a bolt from the blue, entering the text like a helicopter. Parables are connected to preceding events and, thus, function within a learning curve. They are connected to problematic issues and questions in order to become, so to speak, 'educational' for the readers and hearers. Luke 14 captures the preceding events. It refers to muttering Pharisees and teachers. They used to criticise Jesus constantly. Their main objection was that he welcomed sinners and tax collectors, ate with them and healed on the Sabbath (Luke 15:1-3). They thought they need to sharpen what is good and bad, to differentiate between who is good and bad, who is a sinner and who is not. But by telling them this parable, Jesus started to demythologise those images. He answered them with three successive parables that have more or less the same structure. The parable of 'a father had got two sons' is the last in the series of three.

The three parables start the same: There was 'someone'. This person could in fact be anyone, 'just any human being'. Furthermore, these parables have the same theme: Losing (the pain of loss), getting lost and being found. In the first two, there is an account of lost possessions: a sheep and lost money. There is also the mentioning of joy about what has been lost and been found. Very noteworthy is the fact that Jesus adds in both of the first two, that this joy will also be in heaven: "I tell you that in the same way there will be more rejoicing in heaven over one sinner who repents; rejoicing in the presence of the angels of God" (Luke 15:7; 10). At the end of the first two parables, Jesus still addresses the Pharisees and scribes.

The third parable about the father and the two sons is not about lost property but about a human being who has been lost. At the end of that parable there is a celebration, but only on earth, not in heaven. There is a father on earth who is happy about the return of his son. It is quite remarkable that in this parable Jesus does not rehearse about a sinner who has returned. He is not coming back to the categorisation of human beings as merely sinners. He is also not addressing the Pharisees and scribes, and with that Jesus leaves the end wide open, beyond categorisation and discrimination, open for everyone's own interpretation.

The parable: The fair father with two sons

The parable starts with a quite general remark: "There was a man who *had* two sons." It reads as if one does not receive sons, you just get them. But in terms of the Bible, life is a precious gift. The youngest asks for a share (*ousia*) of a property (*bios*) that is due to him, which is usually part of the estate. *Bios* means life. What he asks for is a share that rightfully is his due. He does not ask everything from the father, it is merely about a part (*a share of the property*). There is not written 'no inheritance' or 'no legacy' which is often interpreted moralistically. Just because he demands part of the property and does not claim a full inheritance does not mean that the father has nothing left.

> I once heard a sermon about this parable in which the preacher told the congregation that the son has in fact signed a kind of death certificate, issued prematurely because he dared to claim the inheritance before the father has actually died. With this kind of meaning, interpretation and morality become hand-in-glove. This is an example of unfair partiality that is likely to be taken over by members of the church through a sermon.

One needs now to be very careful indeed to not run the risk of portraying the son in a better light than how the account depicts him. He did not *ask* for a share but according to Jesus, he *commanded* his father: Give me! Jesus put an imperative in his tone. Then the father gave both the youngest son and the oldest son the share that is due to them.

Surprisingly, I never learned at Sunday school that the eldest son also got his share. However, within a close reading, it turns out that this father acted in a very fair and just way.

> According to the stipulation of the Tanakh, if it were an inheritance, the eldest son would have to receive a double share under the *bechor*-rule (first-born right), which stipulates that the

firstborn of a father or mother will receive a double portion of the inheritance.

Soon thereafter, the youngest decided to withdraw from the family and to redeem his part after which he took all he had and set off for a distant country where he squandered his wealth in wild living. Literally it says he *scattered* everything. Jesus mentioned here that his life was in a devastating condition, namely, beyond help, irretrievable and totally lost (*asotos*, a hapax that only appears once in the Bible). In the original Greek the word for 'prodigal' is ἄσωτος (*asotos*) meaning the one who cannot be saved, not the one who returns or the wastefully extravagant. *Asotos* is a many layered word. It could also mean dissolutely, profligately. The important point is that ἄσωτος (*asotos*) does not refer to a kind of judgement. One should rather say that it indicates a kind of concern. As a narrator Jesus elaborated that there was hunger and a severe famine in a country far away.

The words 'lost', 'dissolutely', 'profligately', 'far away' and 'hunger' reinforce the fact of how this son has been thrown back on himself. So, he went and hired himself out to a citizen of that country, who sent him to his fields to feed pigs. He longed to fill his stomach with the pods that the pigs were eating, but no one gave him anything. It is also to be noted that the son did not *take* or *usurp* anything.

When he came to his senses, he decided to rise and get up (*anastasis*; in Greek ἀνάστασις; a raising up, rising as from a seat; a rising from the dead). So, he said: "I will set out and go back to my father". His going back is like a turnaround, turn-about. The motivation to get up is his hunger. This decision is a monological one, all taken on his own and not about a kind of sacred conversion. In the words of the philosopher Ludwig Feuerbach (1850) (Online 2020): "A human being exists according to who he/she is and according to what he/she eats" (*Der Mensch ist was er ist, und isst*; Ludwig Feuerbach (1804-1872). The son decided to confess to his father: "I have sinned against heaven and against you."

The father-son relationship is still in proportion: The father has remained merely father to him. He also rendered himself as no longer worthy to be called son of his father. His wish was to be made like one of his hired men. He rose up and went to his father. While he was still a long way off, his father saw him.

The father did not ask any questions. Noteworthy is the fact that he met him and was totally overwhelmed by pity.

> The Greek word for inwardly compassion is *splangnizomai*, which corresponds to the Hebrew word for compassion and inner pity. The meaning is closely related to *rachamim* = uterus; the lap as the protective place and space for the becoming and caring of life. No one has more beautifully depicted this maternal place and intimate embracement with the father in the parable, than Rembrandt van Rijn in his etchings and painting: The head of the son on the lap of the father.

The son literally repeated to the father what he initially intended: He acknowledges his blame (guilt) and claims to be unworthy as a son. The father did not seem to hear this. In fact, the father ran to his son, threw his arms around him and kissed him. The father immediately turned to his servants and said: "Quick! Bring the best robe and put it on him. Put a ring on his finger and sandals on his feet. Bring the fattened calf and kill it. Let us have a feast and celebrate" (Luke 15:22-23). And then follows the remarkable motivation: "For this son of mine was dead and is alive again; he was lost and is found".

How beautifully this would have ended the parable with a very romantic resonance: And they lived together happily afterwards. But Jesus adds a twist to the rehearsal of the events. There is an unexpected third who suddenly turned up and voiced what bothered him. One should not forget that the father had two sons. The other is not skipped by Jesus. He was busy in the field. When he came near to the house, he heard music and dancing. People were celebrating. But why? So, he called one of the servants and asked what was going on. In the reply, he heard about 'your brother' and 'your father'. In fact, the fattened calf had been slaughtered. But suddenly the eldest froze, he became motionless. He did not want to move at all. It could be the case that he deliberately did not want to enter his father's house. It could also be that he '*could not*' come in. The '*could not*' should perhaps be put into brackets: (*could not*). It is therefore perhaps better to keep it this way because this bracketing points to a hesitation. In fact, one is cautious not to fill in exactly what or who made him distance himself from the festive mode in his father's house. It also remains an open question why he did not opt for applying the principle of multi-partiality?

He did not want to approach anyone. He became angry and refused to come nearer even though his father approached him. He responded with a complaint: "Look! All these years I have been slaving for you and never disobeyed your orders. Yet you never gave me even a young goat so I could celebrate with my friends." And now the distancing reproach: "When this *son of yours* who has squandered your property with prostitutes…" *His brother* became suddenly *son of yours*.

This son distanced himself from the familial connection and put himself outside the relationship. He objectified and detached himself from his brother by means of a very one-sided assumption and perspective that put the brother in an even worse light. *This son* became objectified into '*that son of yours*' who devoured his life with whores/prostitutes. It is noteworthy that Jesus added the word '*whores/prostitutes*' here and put it in the mouth of the elder son. With this addition, the following question surfaces: Did Jesus want to indicate how quickly a moralistic interpretation disqualifies the history of the other? Was this verdict made based on what we did not know? Was this conviction regarding being a sinner quickly formulated due to a moralistic presupposition? However, this kind of speculation distracts the reader from a closer reading in terms of Jesus' response and a possible hidden kind of multi-directed partiality.

It is indeed an amazing sharp remark and critical interpolation what Jesus initiated here. Jesus himself left open the judgment about the two sons. He quickly displayed that the father also lovingly supported the eldest son, and so bracketed an unfair and judgemental reproach. In a most tender and compassionate way the father said: "My child." The eldest is invited into the space of a pitiful father. "Child, you are always with me, and everything I have is yours" (Luke 15:31). Then follows the urgent plea of the father to celebrate and be glad, because this brother of yours was dead and is alive again; he was lost and is found again.

And with this very costly phrase '*was found*', Jesus closed the narrative. Nothing is mentioned about any celebration in heaven. The fest is now here on earth amongst fallible human beings. Indeed, merry making is here on earth.

Jesus then left open how things went afterwards between the brothers and the father. In doing so, Jesus left unanswered the question to the Pharisees and the scribes in order to reflect on the puzzle of who is now rightly identified as 'good' or 'bad' in this third parable. Jesus pointed neither to the oldest, nor the youngest son, nor the father. At stake, is not judgement anymore. In the parable Jesus displays a liberating perspective, namely when one does not approach the predicament and fallibility of our being human with a judgemental attitude but with a pitiful heart, as in the case of the embracing encounter between father and 'guilty son', then one starts to calculate life no longer in terms of 'good' or 'bad' but as personal. We become reframed as '*mine*', even the so-called '*lost sons*' and '*lost daughters*' are drawn into the comfort of 'everything I have is yours'; *receiving* and *finding* reframes life into during festivity; blaming merely brings about exclusiveness and detachment. Multi-partiality is an invitation to inclusivity.

6.3   *Multi-directed partiality: A framework for inclusivity*

The basic stance in caregiving and helping is multi-directed partiality. One even dares to say that almost always multi-directed partiality is at stake in healing endeavours and caring interventions. In literature on helping and caring, there are other supplementary concepts that help to understand the dynamics of multi-directed partiality, such as inclusivity and alignment (directional). They help to underline the meaning of multi-directed partiality with a view to uniqueness. Inclusivity in a professional attitude becomes visible when everyone's right to have a voice is monitored step by step. No one is left out when it comes to weighting fairness. Everyone's assets (credits, merits) and shortcomings (failures) may come to light and the impact thereof on third parties.

Inclusive multi-directed partiality requires a pastor or caregiver to be aware of how each person is affected by their interventions. Questions, proposals, acknowledgements always influence more than one person. Sometimes the impact is afterwards. Different parties involved are each entitled to be approached with respect and compassion. Inclusivity encompasses how people are spoken about, irrespective of whether they are present or not. This means that the pastor's multi-directed partiality never ends. It always remains an issue and *stays to the point*.

This attitude of inclusive, multi-directed partiality is important not only when obstacles and schisms in families and partner relationships are involved.

It underpins many forms of professionality. It thus contributes to skilfulness in dealing with conflicts within churches, communities, companies and any organisation.

The multidirectional attitude in partiality emphasises the alternately addressed focus of the partiality. This offers an opening to everyone's acquired rights, indebtedness and obligations. The further advantage is that this approach also sheds light on how events have different meanings for different people at the same time. It also reveals what each person has invested or what it has cost them; it highlights the concrete mutual responsibility of partners in a relationship, including those who will be involved furthermore. By partiality, Nagy means that helpers and caregivers become sequentially, possibly for a short time, an ally (partner) of every member of the client's relational network, which always consists of at least three persons, of which the client is one (Boszormenyi-Nagy & Krasner, 1994:348). This biased option (multi-directed partiality) is not about justified prejudice or favouritism; that is, to side with one person at the expense of somebody else. That is not even the case when someone has been wronged. This skill of becoming a temporary ally is not about appreciation or approval at all. Even with good intentions, gestures of subtle confirmation do not contribute to any form of solution. In fact, it has no real value for the healing of relationships. It also does not contribute to the promotion of relational ethics. With compliments, a person is not released from his or her own quiver of self-justification, mischief and retribution (Michielsen 1998:31).

Multifaceted or multi-directed partiality is about engagement with everyone involved. The choice of the order of first attention depends on the different circumstances of people and especially on their vulnerability at that time. When you see Nagy at work (there are still recordings available) you see that the most vulnerable person is given priority by him. Sometimes these 'aligned persons' are young people, but they can also be one of the parents. It can even include members of the next generation. The choice of the order creates dilemmas indeed and is not excluded from any form of risk. One should, therefore, always take into consideration that multi-directed partiality can only be partially achieved. Limitations in this approach are obvious.

The discussion of the value and advantages of this approach in helping and caregiving engagements was necessary in order to provide a framework for what inclusivity in therapeutic interventions entails. It highlighted the multi-dimensionality of pastoral skillfulness. With this brief interlude, we can now return to the parable of the father with his two sons.

The multilateral dimension in the parable

There is a much-read book by Henri Nouwen about this parable: *The return of the prodigal son* (*Eindelijk thuis*). Nouwen had a strong desire to see and study Rembrandt's painting up close. In order to study this painting, he travelled to the *Hermitage Museum* in Saint Petersburg. Fortunately, he was given the opportunity to silently contemplate the painting for several days. He chose varying positions to focus on the different characters and eventually to identify with them in turn. There were indeed many nuances: Nouwen as the 'prodigal son', as the 'eldest son', as the 'father'. What impressed Nouwen was how the lap of the father, as depicted by Rembrandt, offered perspectives on God's boundless compassion. It is indeed true that alternate identification is not the same as multilateral and multi-directed partiality. Identification seeks to be or to act like the other and is not focused on mutual relationships. That explains the importance of reflecting on a multi-directed perspective when studying the painting.

When looking at the parable with a multifaceted attitude, the focus is more on the dynamics of interrelational interaction as it took place between the three characters in the parable. Also important are the different reactions and responses of the three within this encountering space. The intention is not to unravel the parable therapeutically. However, it does raise interesting ethical relational questions that are worth highlighting.

It is already clear that the oldest son is the most vulnerable. He had withdrawn from the relationship and became detached from both the brother and the father. His brother had become 'that son of yours'. He no longer pronounces the word 'brother' nor 'father'. The connection became broken and lost. Within a multilateral assessment, questions could be posed regarding the validity of his stance and reasons for his choice. For the time being, answers would be premature.

For the pastor, appropriate questions would be: Who or what made him unable to relate constructively? Or: What did he need to be able to recognise his family members as 'father' and 'brother' again? These kinds of questions could help to suspend or refrain from judging this son. This is what a multi-directed perspective teaches and is about. Furthermore, a multi-directed approach helps to keep the familial connections and sense of belonging intact. And at least, such an approach cannot cause further harm to the already brittle connections.

One could imagine what would happen in a family within the setting of a father with two such different sons. It could perhaps be that the concern will turn to the eldest brother regarding the impact of the youngest brother's departure on him. Did he miss him and was the house a deserted space without him? Perhaps, he also wanted to quit and get away as soon as possible? The remark on squandering his property with prostitutes does not sound merely like a reproach. In the blame echoed the notion of destructive merit. Even the right to take revenge; there is an account to be settled. One can even detect some kind of evil lurking in the very hurtful remark. The point is, at this moment there no longer exists trust.

Imagine a family in our current setting where one must face the triadic dynamic between a father and two sons. The multilateral question emerges, namely, whether the father missed his youngest son. If indeed, how did he respond to the loss? Immediately, there is another question surfacing: Did the father adequately give the eldest son credit for the way he continued to fulfil all his obligations at home? One could read in the later remark of the father, namely, that *he was always with him*, a kind of acknowledgement. However, that was not be compared with the pity he bestowed to the youngest son after his return. It is quite clear that the remark that *everything the father possesses belongs to the eldest*, did not appease him and motivate him to take part in the festivities. Within the detail of the account, and the eventual loss of trust, one could start toying with the question: What would have happened if the principle of multi-directed partiality was applied to the complexity of this triadic dynamics? What could have been the impact of this approach on the attitude of the eldest son? Could new forms of trusting have perhaps been established?

Loyalty in diverse settings: The father with two different sons

The following intriguing question should be posed here: How does one manage to stay loyal to several children simultaneously? How does one cope as a parent in such a diverse setting?

Let's go back to the parable. The father displayed deep joy when the youngest return back home. But does this spontaneous expression of joy imply that he was less loyal to the eldest? In the words of Henri Nouwen, the question could be posed in another way: What would '*boundless mercy*' entail when it becomes applicable to the eldest son? All these questions are very relevant to every parent. Another question should be addressed, namely how do siblings respond when one is favoured over against the others? The basic stance and conviction are that multi-directed partiality can make a remarkable contribution to the intersubjective dynamics of the family system, as well as to the quality of their mutual interaction.

6.4 Siblings: The mutual interaction between brothers and sisters

The way in which the communication between the two brothers has abruptly been ended discloses the complexity of sibling relationships. From a contextual perspective, Leen Hermkens gave extensive attention to this complexity in her research on sibling interaction (Hermkens 1998:157-179). Through her research, all these very powerful factors that determine the development of a sense of belonging between brothers and sisters, were identified. She also probed into these resources that can promote sibling connectivity. Probing into the reality of sibling relationships, it became clear that a lot of irritation and friction could develop, ending into detachment and estrangement. In single parent families, the interaction and connections become even more complex and, unfortunately, in our current society that is a growing tendency.

In most of the generational connections (horizontal dimension) a choice is possible. However, in sibling connections it is different. In fact, one cannot make a choice of who is your brother or your sister, or not. In this matter, one has really no choice. Their being together is a given and existential fact in terms of familial interaction. When compared with other symmetrical relationships, the connection between siblings cannot easily be broken. Between brothers and sisters, also between half-brothers and half-sisters, there exists a mutual interconnectivity that could be called loyalty.

Furthermore, the relationship between siblings is not purely dyadic. Always existent is a third intergenerational factor, namely, parents and grandparents. In terms of relational ethics, the account on family interaction makes it clear how difficult it is to keep the balance between giving and receiving intact. The characteristics of familial relationships are shaped by birth, mutual care and the kind of contributions each one deposits into the relational networking.

In line with Nagy's thinking, Hermkens also reasons that familial connections are ontic and an existential given that must be dealt with. The concern to give to parents in terms of what they need is stronger than in the case between brothers and sisters. Vertical loyalty, therefore, receives more attention than in the case of horizontal loyalty. That what is given to parents or what parents give to their children, is quite different from giving and receiving in sibling interaction. One also has to reckon with the fact that sibling-parent connections are triadic and thus unique: mother-father-child. That explains the complexity of the balancing dynamic. The way in which loyalty is displayed can cause severe conflict between family members. In the event of giving more, or less, this unbalance can be interpreted by family members differently. It could be interpreted as favouritism which eventually becomes the cause of fierce mutual competition. When one of the parents dies, this kind of disturbance in the balancing dynamic can become critical.

Hermkens' research identified how psychological differences such as ego-strength, coping mechanisms and emotional or mental preparedness, impact on the giving-receiving dynamic in different ways. The readiness to display mutual care and acceptance of one another is dependent on the quality and mode of different parenting styles and familial traditions (the culture of a family). Within extended families, the well-being of the group is a priority. In this way children learn to earn merit in a very constructive way. It helps them to discover their sense of self-worth. On the other side, the structure of the large and extended family can also become a hampering factor in processes of self-individuation. When the message is continually received, 'but this is our custom', a healthy self-demarcation could be retarded.

It was a very long tradition to evaluate children in terms of the position they take in the series and sequence of the family line. An example is the classic typology of the eldest, then the middle child and thereafter the youngest. The supposition was that the eldest was the one who was the most exposed to a strict upbringing. He/she would therefore develop a more refined conscience than the youngest. According to this theory, the youngest will be more moderate and flexible, less dogmatic and more popular with peers than the eldest. They will be more prepared to take risks. Their social skills will also be more developed so that it will be easier for them to perform in group dynamics. One must admit that these kinds of categorisation often coincide with reality. However, there lurks a kind of Darwinist anthropology behind this kind of typology. It assumes that, through competition and power struggles, people should gain an advantaged position in conquering scarce resources (particularly in getting parental love). Normally that will occur at the disadvantage of other sisters and brothers. Nothing is then mentioned about relational-ethical consequences. Fortunately, this kind of anthropological perspective has become outdated (Hermkens 1998:163).

Relational ethics teach that every child experiences the relationship with parents, brothers and sisters differently. The balance between giving and receiving for one person in the family will be coloured differently than the needs and abilities of the other. Within the dynamic tension and challenges of differentiation, a child learns to develop an own unique perception of self-worth. He/she also develops skills for self-demarcation. In this way the child becomes a mature participant within the dialogical playfield of familial interaction. When the balance becomes unfair within the triadic processes of interaction between parents and children, it has an immediate impact on the mutuality of sibling interaction. Sibling interaction can thus be retarded and harmed. In this process, Hermkens refers to the very strong impact of parental judgements and verdicts. It influences opinions regarding who in the family is good and who is the so-called *black sheep*, who is favoured and who is always pointing the finger at the other as being the guilty one.

The following example illustrates the harming effect on Simon, being the middle child between three brothers and the youngest (his sister). He lived all on his own. He died quite unexpectedly at the age of 43. The memorial service was prepared by the minister, the eldest brother and his sister. There was no contact with the youngest brother whatsoever. The minister asked about the absent brother. They said that as a child he sometimes took some money, secretly. When that happened, they were taken out of bed early in the morning and placed in the kitchen in order of age. Then the mother asked if the culprit could step forward. Nobody reported and she asked the father to give Simon a hiding. It was accepted that he was obviously the culprit. They took it for granted because he was the smartest. A few years ago, when the mother died, it was revealed that Simon was not the cunning thief, but the youngest of the brothers, who was now in fact absent. When it became clear, he never dared to meet Simon again. He also never wanted to be associated with his mother or father anymore. The preacher asked who in the family has been most affected by these situations. The brother and sister hesitated: Was it Simon or the youngest brother? He suggested that they have a conversation with this brother about how the parents' input has confused the relationships. It could then be that perhaps he might be convinced to partake in Simon's funeral.

In families with an unambiguous biological origin, brothers and sisters must deal with several ledgers. In fact, there are at least four intergenerational ledgers: Two on the father's side, two on the mother's side, and the generational ledgers from the current family. In children who have been adopted, the ledgers become more complicated. There are the ledgers of the biological parents as well as the ledgers of the adoptive family. The consequences are carried along and affect development into maturity during adulthood. The impact of just deeds or unjust events is also different for every brother or sister. The question regarding what is fair and reasonable in the balance between siblings requires a multi-directed partial approach. It helps one to discover the multilateral ethical and existential balance between them. At the same time, one must reckon with the dyadic and triadic complexity of this existential balance (Meulink-Korf & Van Rhijn 1997:99). The triangle is simultaneously about the question of what happens between two people and how it influences one another, as well as the impact of the possible third factor.

Every child and every generation must find their own way in integrating both family legacies and social legacies (stemming from tribes or other connections). In that sense, every human child has a mandate to reduce the burdens of the previous generation and to preserve and/or strengthen the benefits. This is even more complex for children who have been adopted and/or children who do not know who their biological father or mother is.

When a child has a physical and or mental disability, it colours every experience in the family dynamics. The care and responsibility for that brother or sister, and for the parents, can be a heavy burden indeed. The further problem is that it can rob one of the freedoms to take care of one's own life. Children see clearly what a child with a disability demands from parents. The point is that they should always be ready to side with him and to step into the breach on his/her behalf. Obviously, this burden and responsibility should be determined by loyalty. In addition, the indebtedness to the disabled brother or sister can have a hindering effect on one's own development. Herein family members must make their own decision regarding the impact on behaviour and attitude. In the making of fundamental choices, considerations can have a polarising effect.

Within these very complex networking dynamics, the pastor, trained in multi-directed partiality, will be able to reveal and address the different balances of everyone involved. Here it is pivotal to identify forms of giving and receiving and then to bring them into discussion. It is, thus, important to give credit to every person's contribution to the dynamics of giving-and-receiving, and to publicly address the value thereof. Openness and trust within family relationships make space for a dialogue about what is more or even less appropriate within everyone's choice. It is in this context that Meulink-Korf and Van Rhijn have described the skills applicable to support a dialogical-directed attitude.

6.5   Some basic skills contributing to a professional stance

In pastoral caregiving and counselling every conversation and encounter is unique, new and unrepeatable. One does not work with a kind of fixed pre-knowledge about the person. Even the context of that person is an uncharted field. Within the first meeting and encounter, the other is approached with what Meulink-Korf and Van Rhijn (2002:185; 2016:117) call: *The wisdom of uncertainty*. This uncertainty requires openness and suspension of prejudices.

Within the first meeting and session it is quite natural that the caregiver or counsellor will toy with the question: "What is going on here between people?" This wondering is not about curiosity but is aimed at trying to understand what is occurring between these people in terms of possible transactions and the dynamics of balancing. Within the dynamics of not-knowing, multi-directed partiality requires a very specific disposition based on a principle of trust. A very specific disposition is about the skill of being constantly aware of asymmetry. It is important to maintain this disposition throughout sessions and meetings. It is also decisive to maintain a kind of distance so that one does not become too emotionally involved.

From the side of the caregiver, distancing asks for prudence to include people in this relationally and ethically oriented method. One must know that this method has its own language and asks other types of questions than in the case of just general conversations and talking. Initially, it is difficult for both clients and caregivers to understand that this help is not always about the rationality of logical questions. From the outset, questions will be less individual and more relational.

One of the first conditions is to help the client to understand not to fall back on images that reduce the interaction to merely a subject-object interplay. The pastor is challenged to assist the client in this regard so that he/she can understand what exactly the point of departure for the interactional dialogue is about. In this regard, it is pivotal for pastoral caregivers and helpers not to apply the rules of a generalised morality in order to translate the character of the relationship.

Basically, a dialogically (contextually) oriented attitude starts not with general rules but with the how (mode), where (place and space) and when (timing) wherein each person finds him/herself within the reciprocal dynamics of a relationship. The direction of the conversation is to always move from the particular to the more general framework and problematic field and context. One then starts to probe regarding what is going on within this very reciprocal space of interaction. One has to detect what kind of indebtedness is at stake and what forms of earned merit have been established. It is indeed important to understand what and how much they already have invested in the relationship or perhaps in the so-called third party. It could be that latent forms of trust lurk underneath the surface and should become addressed openly and revealingly. Asymmetry in the client/pastor disposition helps to monitor the context and not allow it to become one-sided. Furthermore, appropriate distance warns one not to probe too deeply in a client's destructive forms of entitlement.

The wisdom of uncertainty' promotes the establishment of a culture of professionality. Professional experience helps, for example, to detect the impact of loyalty on relational dynamics as well as possible forms of conflict that accompany the complexity of dialoguing. In any case, all these factors should be openly addressed and discussed with all people involved. The focus is indeed heuristic. It is decisive to describe how the different parties are positioned in terms of each person's subjectivity and exactly how all these factors impact on intersubjectivity. The undergirding presupposition is then that intersubjectivity should never derail into an *entre-deux* (an insertion or something placed between two things that can have a bonding effect). Connectivity always implies the third factor or third party that also contributes to the dynamic character of intersubjectivity. Due to this third factor it becomes obvious that new questions should be posed when probing the quality of the relational interaction.

Conversational and communication skills also include that counsellors and pastors should hear the client's version without quickly filling in personal feelings and opinions, or even projecting their own shortcomings. This requires constant awareness that every intervention has consequences for all present, but also for non-present participants. Such a mode of close listening can be most helpful when choices have to be made regarding appropriate questioning, as well as to decide where the focus is in prioritising the urgency of needs, and whether the questions will be helpful at all for the fostering of interconnectivity. It is always important to reckon with an appropriate distance in order to prevent becoming prey to possible inappropriate forms of empathy. That is because the display of empathy, despite its value, could easily lead to an emotional kind of blindness for the phenomenon of asymmetry in therapeutic positioning. If this happens, caregivers run the risk of gradually assuming the role of the better parent, partner, son or daughter.

Nagy and Krasner write as follows: "Rogers thought that therapists owed their clients substitutive parenting … In our view, however, it is questionable to presume that helpers are privy to such vast supplies or reserves of empathic giving, nurturing attitudes and offerings" (Boszormenyi-Nagy & Krasner 1986:380). The basic skill for authentic dialoguing and counselling in pastoral caregiving is not to depart from one's own framework of reference and presuppositions about skilful counselling. Pastoral counselling is about the art of how to dwell with the other without dominating the process with own convictions because the movement is always from oneself into the direction of the disposition of the other.

Skilfulness within the profession of caregiving's first requirement is *self-insight*, that is, to be critically aware of one's own, personal levels of irritation and allergic predispositions. When one is not able to visit these personal predispositions, one's skilfulness is hampered, and perhaps no longer contributing to the well-being of the other. One becomes a victim of one's own vulnerability as connected to different emotions and physical ailments. The problem then is that it becomes virtually impossible to attend to the ethical balance and the multi-relationality of the other and his/her system of intersubjective networking. It is indeed a real unique skill of how to bracket one's own personal shortcomings in order to provide a sustainable form of caring and helping.

Connecting listening and speech

A conversation is mainly about listening, specifically listening to signals that tell more about a person's relational ethical reality. Connecting listening is about the art of how to focus on the other's devotion to his/her connectedness to a basic constellation of ethically based directions, and how they relate to appropriate verbalising and articulation. Listening as appropriate articulation in processes of verbalising, and the act of creating language for authentic modes of speech in conversations, is so to speak: *To listen into speech*.

A focused mode of listening is based on trust in order to invite the other to disclose his/her more inner world of personal experiences to the helper or caregiver. The previously discussed four dimensions in chapter 5 are most helpful in order to detect more structure and order in relational dynamics. Their aim is to prevent an instant approach in counselling that tends to ignore the ethical dynamic in processes of balancing. All four dimensions are operating within balancing. Connecting listening helps to assess how fair and just the life of the person in need was up to that stage in his/her life. It is interested in exemplifications of trustworthiness and loyalty. The further advantage is that connecting listening becomes heuristic; that is, to sojourn with the other in the search for the renewal of existing relationships.

Dialogical listening turns into dialogical speaking. The core of this mode of speech is 'connecting together'. Connecting speech seeks where the different persons could have trusted each other and how the connection between persons can be made visible. An important aspect of connecting speech is to be vigilant about how not to make people disloyal among themselves (Van Rhijn & Meulink-Korf 2002:202-206; 2016:139-140). That happens when we go along with the reproaches that people make to each other. And sometimes that happens without us being aware of this pitfall.

> A pastor visited a young couple who wanted to have their first child baptised. He was at the point to ask them what or who gave them the desire to baptise the child (the instigating factor). It soon

became clear that these parents had been arguing more recently. The man said he was annoyed because his wife always went to her mother to clean up her house. Her mother was an alcoholic and the man absolutely did not want his child to meet her. So, he banned his wife from taking the baby to her mother. The woman squealed: "It's my baby and it's my mother, too." The pastor wanted to appease and said: "How sorry for your mother to drink too much!" Then the woman got up and screamed: "You too! You are all the same! It is about my mom and I want to take care of her too. Furthermore, it is my sincere wish that she should usher the baby to the baptismal font!"

This is an example of what non-connecting listening and connecting speech is about. The pastor seems to want to respond empathically with the remark 'how bad', but in fact, the pastor was communicating on a deeper level of being, a judgmental attitude. He did not reckon with the fact that connecting speech should be careful not to promote disloyalty. His professional introduction of an empathetic response makes the woman disloyal to her mother. It also made both husband and the pastor suspicious and caused further detachment. Connecting in this situation is more likely to identify common concerns, but each in a different way.

Connecting speech should have focused more on intergenerational connections in caregiving. Both partners then could have discovered the value of intergenerational caring: One to the previous and the other to the next generation, which is not to say that both do not have eyes for the mother as well as for the child. However, pivotal was to find language for everyone's unique care and to acknowledge that special need. It could also have contributed to finding ways to safeguard intersubjectivity and fair balancing between the parents. In this safe space, it would then have been possible for both to become engaged in authentic dialoguing in order to act fairly and promote justice to one another. That is the reason why it will be important to come back to the advantage of bracketing presuppositions and judgmental approaches. In this regard, texts from the Bible provide appealing examples to illustrate the value of authentic listening and connecting speech within intersubjective dynamics and processes of balancing.

Suspension of judgement

When Jesus started to speak about 'the suspension of judgement' he did so in terms of images rendered from a pastoral context (Van Doorn 2007:113-128). The parable of the man who planted a fig tree followed immediately after the mentioning of the Galileans whose blood Pilate had mixed with their sacrifices (Luke 13:1). Jesus then raised the intriguing question: "Do you think that these Galileans were worse sinners than all the other Galileans because they suffered this way?" After this question he proceeded to the following question about the eighteen who died when the tower of Siloam fell on them. In both cases the question about guilt followed. "Do you think they were more guilty than all the others living in Jerusalem?" (Luke 13:5). All these questions were about guilt, judgement, being judged and eventually about the causality between death due to the supposed connection to being guilty or not.

Hereafter followed the parable (Luke 13:6-9):

> [6]"A man had a fig tree planted in his vineyard; and he came looking for fruit on it and found none. [7]So he said to the gardener,
>> 'See here! For three years I have come looking for fruit on this fig tree, and still I find none. Cut it down! Why should it be wasting the soil?'
>
> [8]"He replied,
>> 'Sir, let it alone for one more year, until I dig around it and put manure on it. [9]If it bears fruit next year, well and good; but if not, you can cut it down.'"

Jesus told the parable due to the possible presupposed causal connection between death and guilt. At stake is the question about the suspension of judgement. In a nutshell: Someone owns a vineyard and has planted a fig tree in it. The owner has been coming to look for fruit on this fig tree for three years and had not found any during this period. Then followed an absolute judgment: Cut it down! A devastating judgement indeed.

Jesus referred to the period of three years when he addressed the Rabbi. But quite remarkable, he was not doing this for nothing. Besides the symbolic reference to number three, there is an interesting reference in the margin of the Nestle-Aland *Novum Testamentum Graece*: Leviticus 19:23 et seq. The passage is about rules of life, but then suddenly an interlude on dealing with fruit trees turns up. Besides various rules about life, verse 23 refers to the planting of fruit trees. For three years its fruit should be considered as forbidden; it must not be eaten. Then follows a summoning: In the fourth year, all its fruit would be holy and should be viewed as an offering of praise to the Lord. But in the fifth year one had been allowed to eat its fruit. Then followed an important statement: "In this way your harvest will be increased. I am the Lord your God" (Lev 19:25). Based on this rule, it seems that the owner in this parable might have been premature with his order for destruction. Yet, Jesus let him say to the gardener: Cut it down! The reason seems to be quite reasonable because why should one destroy the earth and make it useless. The owner, thus, made use of the rule of causality. What is indeed useless gives the right to be condemned and should be removed. If Jesus did not continue with this parable, it would have left the impression that the question about the reason for the death of the Galileans, and the eighteen of Siloam who died when the tower fell on them, could be now explained in a very reasonable way: They were of no use anymore. What a radical condemnation would that have been! The further implication would then be that grace and mercy are also useless and meaningless when faced by fate and the irreversibility of causality.

Jesus portrays a different outcome than the total rejection with which the owner makes his judgment. Jesus puts a comma behind the account on the two devastating events. His approach is not about a final full stop, so, immediately the story continues.

The gardener, he who was employed by the owner and works in the vineyard and takes care of the fig tree planted there, turns out to have a totally different approach than the owner. After receiving the command from the owner to cut the tree down, he responded with a very astonishing imperative: "Sir, leave it alone for one more year!" Literally in the Greek the imperative to leave the fig tree alone means: Release, make free! It is not without reason that Jesus used the words 'release, let go' (aphiēmi ἀφίημι), the same word that we know for 'forgive'. Jesus reverses in his resemblance with 'release, let go, forgive' the previous judgement of the owner with an expressiveness that goes beyond logic and all rules of morality.

In the figure of the gardener, Jesus points to a judgement that is merciful. And this connection between judgement and mercy makes justice visible and audible. This kind of compassionate judgement transcends the causal regularity as often reflected in deterministic guilt-sin connections. Here, it is perhaps important to compare this parable with the previously discussed parable of the father with his two sons. With the verdict *"leave it alone for one more year"* the judgement is suspended, and, thus, postponed. Immediately chronological time is transposed into diachronic time but, at the same time, linked with the Kairos of prophetic time! The suggestion to dig around and to fertilise (another year option) is a sound indication and illustration of connecting speech!

With suspension is not meant delay or cancellation. It is indeed not about that kind of sluggish passivity: 'Well, let us see, and, let it be'. Suspension of judgement is not about an act of carelessness as if it does not matter how one acts. It is not about the everything-is-okay stance that projects a cool attitude as if human acts are neutral. The gardener does not represent a don't care stance. On the contrary, he exemplifies how an investment of solicitous care can make a difference to the quality of the soil and the growth of the fig tree. A time to fertilise is in fact about the demonstration of prophetic time. In this very courageous demonstration, future time is being pulled into the events of present time; it opens space for concrete actions of caring solidarity.

When we turn to the further developments after one year, the challenging question will be: "But if there are no figs, no fruit at all, what then?" Then comes the great surprise when Jesus said: Then the tree needs to be cut out! It is not in the job description of the gardener to cut the tree down in cases where it does not produce fruit. It is the task of the owner to make a final assessment and to give the command to cut it down.

Luke 13:9 brings the parable to an end. But this ending presents a kind of closure on the attempt to explain death by means of the devastating causality: Death-guilt (the full stop approach). However, the latter is more about the challenge to really deal with the endeavour of bouncing back in life; that is, to link death to the comma of 'fertilising' life, until … This 'until' does not wave in nothingness but brings the intriguing questions back to the comma of personal responsibility, namely the lightness of being guided by the light of the gracious gift of time. *For one more year* corresponds with the tone of 'amazing grace'!

Patience: Ethics in action!

The plea 'for-one-more-year' is contra the logic of time; it transcends the normal calculation of farming as an agricultural endeavour. In the parable, time is stretched beyond the scientific approach of the owner whose concern is production and profit. In this stretching of time, one of the most 'beautiful characteristics' of God is displayed. Ethics becomes supplemented by the aesthetics of long-suffering: To endure with patience. The parable, thus, illustrates the beauty of God's patience.

Long-suffering or patience, in Hebrew *arach*, and in Greek *makrothymos* (μακροθύμως, with forbearance, patiently; used in Acts 26:3: "I beg you to listen to me patiently" is indeed a many layered concept with delicate nuances. In both the Hebrew and Greek, the meaning indicates: To make longer/become long, stretch, out of breath, wrath or time. It is translated with patience. One of the interesting aspects in the parable of the fig tree is the stretching of time; that is, to make time longer in order to suspend judgement.

When it comes to interpersonal relationship, patience is an ethical act that uses time by moving away from what must be done immediately. Time becomes an ally (Van Rhijn & Meulink-Korf 2002:237; see chapter 6; 2016:163). Immediateness is released; life is not anymore 'instant'. Time is released for reflection in which distance arises from the events that determined the relationship up to then. In all dimensions of existence, the flexibility of time creates the necessary detachment that is pivotal for the solitude of patience. It is as if all movement in time becomes illuminated by the light of ethics. When it is possible to release the urgent demands of time, one's eyes start to '*see*' the '*unseen*' beyond all logic while the awe of expectation discloses a future that is approaching us. In this sense, ethics is supplemented by aesthetics – the beauty of forbearance and patience. A new perspective with unknown initiative suddenly lies ahead. One can suddenly start to add: Unknown, unparalleled, unprecedented, unheard-of, untold, not dreamt of. Why? Because hope starts to set in. It is also possible that conflicting and mutually exclusive interests come to light that require care and attention. There is suddenly time available to dig around and to start fertilising life. Taking a Kit-Kat break can be fair, or even cause long-suffering. Nevertheless, the new ethics of patience beautifies human existence.

Moratorium: The necessary luxury of compassionate pausing

Nagy refers to the necessity of a moratorium. The latter implies more than merely the pause of not achieving. It is deliberately about a chosen strategy in consultation between care provider and client to temporarily take no action. In everyday life, a moratorium is known as a legal term when a (temporary) suspension of payment is decided upon. In contextual thinking, a moratorium refers to a decision of a person to temporarily not take any relational action. A moratorium is then applicable when clients must deal with difficulties concerning certain events in disturbed relationships. It indicates a deliberate break in which refraining from actions, agreements and conversations contributes to the dynamics of balancing in order to create space for healing and significant recovery of intersubjective networking within the reciprocal interaction of all parties involved. After all, there is a limit to the ability of waiting patiently in order to be able to assess the quality of responses. Even to make sure that the other will eventually act appropriately. Suspension of action has a temporary effect, as in the parable above: The fertilising and recovery impact of 'for-one-more-year'. The latter does not mean adjustment or unlimited postponement. Nor is it a matter of acquiescence in the sometimes seemingly unchanging sequence of events or the absolute, irreversibility of timing.

The limitation in waiting and endurance is determined by an ethical interest, for example, when it can no longer be tolerated that someone else is victimised. An ethical intervention becomes decisive. A decision to use time is always ethical in nature due to the concern for the other person's vulnerability. The pastor can help to interpret the temporary pause for solitary silence in the relationship, and to start using it as an exemplification of concern not to further deteriorate the relationship. It is not about sheer indifference or revenge, but rather about non-indifference, that decides to let go of the urge to make contact immediately. In this way, the other remains respected as a subject even in the temporary distance created by a moratorium. This fruitful distance can thus be called *the luxury of compassionate pausing*. This stance is indeed necessary because it can, thus, happen that a way back to the healing of distrust becomes impossible and a decision has to be taken to unfortunately end the relationship.

Liturgy and multi-directed partiality

The liturgy in worship refers to people belonging to the church, as well as to outsiders, strangers and the so-called socially outcasts. In liturgy, all kinds of people should be addressed in prayers, songs, lectures, sacraments and actions. A multi-directed focus requires the pastor to be attentive and careful about the value of an inclusive approach. The point to be grasped is that no one should be left out. This could happen easily when we exclusively praise the mothers of children as special on Mother's Day. Women who for whatever reason have not delivered children are excluded from that recognition. The same principle is applicable to celebrations on Father's Day.

Attention to inclusivity, the inclusive multilateral orientation, can be expressed in such language as 'anyone who opts like a father or mother in displaying care to all others'. It recognises everyone who is in any way involved with children. This involvement does not prescribe that one has to literally become a parent. Everyone can take up responsibility for all other children, especially for neglected children. The impression can easily be created during the blessing at the baptismal font when the minister starts to focus on the infant, that others become excluded. The impression could then be that all other unbaptised children are excluded from the blessing. It could specifically happen in the performing of liturgical acts such as prayers, choices for hymns, and how texts are exegetically interpreted and explained. Therefore, pastors and preachers should be sensitive to inclusive language in order to alternatively encompass all within the compassionate space of liturgical events.

The following case about the renewal of marriage vows illustrates the core of the argument about inclusivity in the performing of church liturgy.

> In a very special worship service, married couples were given the opportunity to renew their marriage vows. Twelve couples stood hand-in-hand in front of the pulpit. The congregation responded with songs of praise. The minister thanked them for their willingness to commit themselves for the upkeep of their vows and input to enrich their marriage relationship. He stretched his hands over them and blessed them. In the back row was a man whose wife had left him a year ago for a new partner. He later told the minister that he had never felt so lonely and desperate in leaving the church service.

Professionality operates not within the restrictions of predetermined regulations. In this regard, *the wisdom of uncertainty* is a huge source for persisting in a multi-directed and inclusive approach. Anyone who is aware of this unique uncertainty should be better equipped to care for people despite conflicting differences. They should also be able to apply the principle of dialogical focussing to the enhancement and promotion of more meaningful interaction within mutual conversations. In the parable of *a father who had two sons*, we have seen something of the advantage of replacing a judgemental approach by the waiting of compassionately being there for them. This kind of gracious generosity is also applicable in parental interaction. The flipside of this approach is now about the question of whether children can honour their parents and display respect in turn.

The fifth command in Exodus 20:12 reads: "Honour your father and your mother." Obviously, the way in which each child is going to respond to the word 'honour' will be differently indeed. To see and recognise the importance of each person's unique contribution requires without any doubt a multi-directed approach. The constructive impact of the command to honour your father and your mother is so pivotal that it requires a separate chapter.

CHAPTER 7

Relational ethics in "Honour your father and your mother"

The commandment to honour one's parents immediately puts the whole discussion on dialogue and encounter within the familial paradigm. Encounter is not about meeting the other merely in the present, it is not about a consultation with an expert. Encounter is embedded in processes. And these processes surpass the professionality of counselling rooms. Encounter is about journeying with the Other/other; it is about processes of life and relational interaction. What this commandment adds to the meaning of encounter is that meeting the Other/other is an ethical event that links past generations as well as future generations into a networking whole wherein familial connections are pivotal in terms of establishing healing, helping and care. Dialoguing is indeed intergenerational.

7.1   To honour: Obedience, obligation or ethical concern?

One could perhaps argue that the notion of "honour your mother and your father" is the most popular and well-known commandment of all. Even people who were not brought up in the Christian tradition echo this alignment as a refrain. The obligations in this commandment resonate often in one's mind for the rest of one's life.

Unfortunately, in many of the more conservative Christian circles, this commandment has been emphasised in such a way that it sounds like a dictatorial order in which reasonableness is sometimes hard to trace back. This is quite sad, because the commandment offers perspectives on the enrichment of daily encounters in life. It also gives insight into the prospect of what an intergenerational dialogue entails. In fact, within this context the command articulates the multilateral dimension of real dialoguing.

The intention in a dialogical focus in pastoral caregiving is to assist people to link with all others, and to become mutually connected within local contexts despite differences and cultural diversity. This is specifically the case when the relationships between parents and children were disturbed and damaged due to many reasons. For example, loss of asymmetry between parents and children can lead to a disruption of trust and mutual reliability. It is important to emphasise that this asymmetric parent-child relationship is aimed at respect and assurance. The implication is that the interests of the child should take precedence over those of the parent. Asymmetry is not about a one-sided power play. It is definitely not about the exercising of parental power over children.

One should acknowledge that the fifth commandment about the honouring of one's father and mother was too often used as a phrase to display dominionship and authoritative power. By referring to this commandment, parents have unilaterally obliged children to obey it. The long-term impact on the lives of children could be devastating indeed. Even into old age, children have sometimes forced themselves to give credit and display respect. The problem then develops that one honours them in a very one-sided way which does not even corresponds with their current life circumstances.

This fifth commandment can play a very constructive role in family pastoral care. It could even make a substantial contribution to the conversation and communication between parents and children. The discovery that 'honour' in the Bible does not mean a demoted form of 'obedience' could be most helpful. Furthermore, when one discovers that the first part of the commandment does not function on its own but is in the second part connected to an enriching promise, the fifth commandment becomes a blessing in disguise. In fact, it becomes fascinating material for an intergenerational dialogue. This fifth word is intended to establish a bridging function in the intergenerational transfer and transactions between parents and children. Parents and children are both involved in intergenerational transactions regarding giving and receiving.

For the sake of contributing to the value of family care, a discovery of the fairness of this fifth commandment could make a huge contribution to the understanding of what a multi-directed perspective in pastoral caregiving to families entails. One can even dare to say that both caregivers and families should rediscover the value of the perspectives comprehended in the fifth commandment. That has led to the decision that a discussion on the interplay between command and blessing and its contribution to the dynamic of giving and receiving cannot be omitted from this book.

Towards the interpretation of the commandment

It could happen that when you approach someone with the question to how they would respond to the obligation to honour their father and mother, you will often get a negative response. For many, this challenge is rather scary and oppressing. The commandment seems, for young children and adolescents, very authoritative as an appeal that compels one into an obedient obligation. To honour parents is in many cases a heavy burden that hampers the free space of reciprocity. Unfortunately, what is heard is only the first part of the command. What follows the comma becomes irrelevant. For many it is unknown territory. The focus is in a very negative way on the demand to 'honour'. With this focus the significance of the pronouncement becomes disconnected from the familial framework and forced to stand on its own. Even parents and grandparents interpret the meaning of 'honouring' quite arbitrarily. It is unfortunate that until this very day, the requirement to 'obey' has become moulded into a very prescriptive mode which eventually becomes associated and synonymous with 'honouring'. Unfortunately, this narrowing of the commandment ignores its broad meaning, which could have contributed to a constructive conversation between parents and children. These could be conversations about kinship in which the assets and shortcomings from the family memory could have been discussed. For example, it could be fruitful discussions about how to preserve the good in the family ledger and transfer possible advantages to the familial dynamics for the sake and well-being of the next generation.

It should never be forgotten that the fifth commandment is meant to inspire family members. It could promote a dialectical vision on the relationship between parents-children and grandparents-grandchildren. This option puts our discussion in the centre of the discourse on the value of relational ethics as presented by Nagy, namely the advantages of an intergenerational dialogue for sound familial interaction.

The astonishing exclamation: Pastor, it cannot be true!

During 2005, I had the opportunity to become involved in Bible studies for churches about the fifth commandment. I partook because I was busy with a research project on how different cultural communities deal with the notion of loyalty. I was specifically interested in the question of how loyalty impacts the praxis of the honouring of parents as well as vice versa.

Due to the cultural diversity in South Africa, it was indeed a question of how to address people in the research project. Personally, I have a deep resistance to address people in terms of their skin colour. Unfortunately, many divisions in South Africa are determined by colour of your skin which refers to *the dilemma of pigmentocracy*. To a large extent pigmentocracy determines one's history; that is, the history of one's parents and ancestors. It also determines wealth and human well-being. Well-being is closely related to safety and human health. In order to deal with all these issues with dignity and respect, I am forced to refer to categories of pigmentocracy without necessarily auditing these categories.

In order to illustrate how loyalty impacts the praxis of the honouring of parents as well as vice versa, I will refer to two case studies.

(a) I was guest in a congregation of the *Uniting Reformed Church in Southern Africa* (in Afrikaans: VGKSA). Most of the members were 'coloured people'. The communities they represented were not that rich. Most of the congregants were in fact poor. At the evening session approximately forty people attended. In the back row sat eight young teenage girls. They were all expecting babies. They were compelled to partake in at least six sessions about faith issues and general education. If they persist and complete the course, they could get permission to let their babies be baptised. For me it was quite extraordinary to become aware of their presence at the back of the church. It was obvious that they did not pay much attention and formed a kind of 'mutual alliance'.

> Within many coloured communities more than half of very young girls expecting a child, do not align to a specific partner. One can estimate that 50% of the male partners are not permanently dedicated to the expecting girlfriend. In this sense, one can call them 'absent fathers'. The implication is that they are not really involved

in the well-being and day-to-day struggles of these expecting mothers. The problem is indeed very complex. Their absence should not always be interpreted in terms of sheer irresponsibility. Van Onselen (1976) wrote: "In South Africa and the region, the structural separation of men from children and families is a result of a combination of colonisation and urbanisation. These factors have radically transformed family arrangements and roles over the course of the 20th century." During all these years the problem accelerated. The phenomenon of non-engagement is not in all cases related to irresponsible behaviour and a non-willingness to care for the child. Many factors do play a role like unemployment, substance abuse, alcoholism and travelling long distances to jobs. There are a lot of research projects being launched to attend to the problem of the 'non-engaged father' in these communities. There are also many subsidiary helping programmes and resources in place to address the problem. "While this problem is often raised as an issue of concern, little is known about the reasons why so many fathers disengage from their children's lives. Moreover, research in this field has largely failed to present the voices of absent fathers themselves in order to capture their perspectives on fathering" (*So we are ATM fathers; A study of absent fathers in Johannesburg, South Africa* 2013). In this study, the principle of multi-directed partiality can be detected. It does not only address the problem of the 'absent, non-engaged father' but also gives attention to many organisations involved in helping and caregiving.

Back to the sessions of the Bible study. After an introduction on the fifth commandment, I started with an exposition on the concept of 'honouring' and explained that there is not written '*obedience*' as translated in many Bibles for children. I was explaining that honour means something that weighs quite heavy, something that becomes a priority, when a guy in the front row rose. He reacted quite strongly and exclaimed very loudly: "Pastor, I am sorry, but this can't be true! Just look, what will happen when one is not obedient!" He turned around and pointed to the girls in the back pew. One of them was his daughter. He was quite adamant and said that if she were obedient, she would not have become pregnant and exposed to her very devastating condition. Immediately the other members of the congregation confirmed that. I was deeply moved by the reaction of this father. This father responded literally from a disposition of a deep ethical concern (brokenness), but also due to loyalty. In the very brief phrase of 'it cannot be the case' echoed the pain of parental powerlessness. One senses in his exclamation a kind of helplessness, even a mode of despondency. But one also hears a yearning and longing for how to contribute qualitatively to a better future for his children and grandchildren. Simultaneously, in my mind there was the question of what the immediate impact of his very bold statement on the girls in the back pew could be. Due to the alliance of her friends, I did not have the opportunity to meet with the daughter of this father in private afterwards. My question stayed unanswered.

(b) The following evening, I was a guest of a group of young people, mainly students and graduates. Once a week they came together to meet for Bible studies, led by a preacher. All were white youth. I also dealt with the fifth commandment. I tried to explain the literal meaning of honour as connected to the Hebrew notion of כָּבֹד (kâbôd): 'Something weighing heavy, giving weight'. They listened attentively, even kept quite quiet. We continued with the explanation of weighting heavily. I connected this metaphor to explain that honouring is about a kind of giving weight (acknowledgement) to the position of a parent, a kind of priority that weighs heavy on one's concern for the well-being of the parent as response to the care they displayed through all the years; a kind of acknowledgement regarding what they invested, the food they provided, the safety they guaranteed, even a response to the fact that a child was conceived by parents and one's being is a result of their intimate relationship. This explanation brought about a vivid discussion. It soon became clear that not all contributions from parents are necessarily worth weighting and that there are also shortcomings, painful at times. However, there is always a lot to acknowledge that being a child of your parent (sense of belonging) is valuable and worth to recall and to remember. These people in their twenties and thirties then completed questionnaires regarding their parents' merit. The questions focused on their legacy: For what has been learned from them; for support that has been received; the dedication of the parents and their commitment to issues concerning the ultimate in life. We spoke on mutuality and reciprocity. Inevitably, we addressed issues like indebtedness due to the challenge to take them seriously, giving weight to them, acknowledging their contribution to the family ledger and processes of balancing (giving-and-receiving). Even the question of how to give them credit after their death received attention.

At the evening session, one of the participants, a man in his early thirties, did not participate in the conversation. In fact, he remained aloof. Afterwards he asked for a moment to meet personally for a conversation. He talked about the great difficulty of how to honour his parents and his obligations towards the family business, because in his family, 'honouring' was deemed as blind obedience to the interests of his parents. It was quite difficult for him to figure out what his role should be. Since the farm is part of the family ledger and has belonged to the family for five generations, it was difficult for him to decide what his place in the intergenerational link should be. He shared how he declined to become heir to the family business and his intention to study in a totally different field. His parents blamed him. Not always openly but indirectly he could pick up their reproach. That was the reason for him for staying away from home for long periods. Through this conversation, he started to pick up traces of merit. For the first time he discovered the very fact of his existence of being their child. His eyes were opened for the fact of how he was financially supported by them during his studies. He admitted that the evening session confused him. He also said that he was considering about going home the coming weekend. He even became curious to find out more about his father's wishes and reasons for becoming a farmer himself.

The two case studies are examples of how this commandment can be interpreted differently with different possibilities of how to put them into practice. It is therefore understandable why the commandment to honour your father and mother, and the link to the blessing that one might live long in the land the Lord your God will give you, should deserve thorough attention.

I will start with an exposition of the Ten Commandments as a whole unit within the context of Exodus 20. The structure and composition of the account and dialogue illuminate the fact that God spoke and dictated all these words.

7.2 *Exodus 20:1-17*

¹Then God spoke all these words:

²"I am the LORD your God, who brought you out of the land of Egypt, out of the house of slavery; ³you shall have no other gods before me.

⁴"You shall not make for yourself an idol, whether in the form of anything that is in heaven above, or that is on the earth beneath, or that is in the water under the earth. ⁵You shall not bow down to them or worship them; for I the LORD your God am a jealous God, punishing children for the iniquity of parents, to the third and the fourth generation of those who reject me, ⁶but showing steadfast love to the thousandth generation of those who love me and keep my commandments.

⁷"You shall not make wrongful use of the name of the LORD your God, for the LORD will not acquit anyone who misuses his name.

⁸"Remember the sabbath day, and keep it holy. ⁹Six days you shall labour and do all your work. ¹⁰But the seventh day is a sabbath to the LORD your God; you shall not do any work – you, your son or your daughter, your male or female slave, your livestock, or the alien resident in your towns. ¹¹For in six days the LORD made heaven and earth, the sea, and all that is in them, but rested the seventh day; therefore the LORD blessed the sabbath day and consecrated it.

¹²"Honour your father and your mother, so that your days may be long in the land that the LORD your God is giving you.

¹³"You shall not murder.

¹⁴"You shall not commit adultery.

¹⁵"You shall not steal.

¹⁶"You shall not bear false witness against your neighbour.

¹⁷"You shall not covet your neighbour's house; you shall not covet your neighbour's wife, or male or female slave, or ox, or donkey, or anything that belongs to your neighbour."

The words of the Decalogue: Ten wording directives for meaningful living

From the beginning I started speaking about the 'ten words' and not about 'ten commandments'. We tried to keep in step with the grain of the original text. Literally it says, 'ten words': "And God spoke all these words." They are the *debarim* and not fixed commandments. Due to Greek, we became used to the translation of these ten words as the Decalogue.

Debarim and *decalogue* refer respectively to *dabar* and *logos*. We then understand *debarim* in the sense of a process of verbing; that is, word as an act; a word that is at the same time acting out, demonstrating, exhibiting. One can thus say that the Decalogue is about the wording of life events directing human existence into the *logos* (purposefulness, sense of calling, destiny) of significant being and fair coexistence.

The imperative tone

All ten words start with an imperative, which entails Biblically speaking, more than a fixed commandment. An imperative wants to be understood as mobile, impelling human beings to respond in an appropriate way. But even then, the process of wording implies more than merely significant mobility. Wording captures the essence of our being human and thus becomes the grammar of a language that articulates destiny in such a way that it changes time. As language of transformed time, time becomes diachronically open for the surprise of the not yet. But even this dynamic of the renewal of time is narrowing the meaning of wording to a large extent. Because when God starts to pronounce life in terms of an imperative, righteousness is at stake. Wording can therefore not be merely a fixed and blunt command. The imperative mode is about a calling, opening the eyes of the hearer to start to understand what is the destiny and meaning of processes of change. Wording as transforming is about an urgent appeal to turn around; it is about a new orientation and disposition. A good illustration is the calling of Abram in Genesis 12:1: Leave and go!

Rosenstock-Huessy wrote about the function of an imperative which differs from merely making a general statement like the rehearsal of an event. For example: I walk; you walk; it is yet raining. This general statement provides no appealing perspective on meaningful orientation in life. It says nothing about how life should be lived. Authentic human living starts with an imperative and clearly reveals what is required from one to live in a significant way (Rosenstock-Huessy 1963:884). The imperative transforms the *I* of an individual into the relational dynamics of 'you'; the you as shaped by the other/others within the interactional dynamics of intersubjectivity. An appealing imperative is about a wording that addresses one in such a way that it requires an answer. In this way, the imperative always displays a hopeful perspective on righteousness; a righteousness that invites the future (*futurum*) into the actuality of now (the present time of actual, human existence).

The wording in the ten directives for life should be heard and interpreted as vivid invitations to depart from previous modes of being into a fascinating new start. One then enters the open-endedness of time. That is the reason why all ten words are vital ingredients of the liberating space of unique human freedom. The introductory remark of "I am the Lord your God, who brought you out of Egypt, out of the land of slavery" creates a space for significant responsibility and the making of meaningful choices. With this very profound introduction, the framework and tone are set for entering the stage of life.

God addresses one in the second person singular: 'You'. It is in this very personal address that the ten wording directives penetrate the networking web of our daily existence as it evolves around the presence of God's being there for us. This is how these ten words have been passed down to us. They enter our life as personal claims, namely, what is required right now from all human beings irrespective of race, gender or culture. But there is a warning in the processes of wording as well. As in the case of Abram, one needs to be prepared to take a risk. One needs to be willing to embark on a journey without a map or compass or GPS towards the uncharted space of the promised land.

Arranging and grouping the ten words

We are going to follow the Jewish division of the ten words. This alignment is the oldest version and should receive prior attention above other arrangements. One table contains the first five words, that is, the wording wherein the name of God occurs. The second table also has five words, but it does not contain the name of God. The first table is about the relationship between God and human beings while the second table is about the mutual relationship amongst fellow human beings. The fifth word is exactly in the transitional place where the first table hinges into the second table. It is inserted within an in-between space like a bridge linking the first section to the second section and directly to the following directive: "You shall not murder (kill)". This in-between place already says something about the key role of relationships between grandparents, parents and children.

The whole composition of the ten words is based on the introductory remark: "I am the Lord your God, who brought you out of Egypt." With this remark we are back to the most basic phrase in the existence of God's chosen people, namely the *exodus* and the refrain of 'freedom'. All the imperatives emanate from this liberating perspective: 'I am liberated and, thus, free!' All ten words evolve around this concept. Therefore, it dictates the meaning of both the first and the second table. In fact, the whole composition and arrangement flow like an avalanche from the interplay: *I am your God – you are free.* The further implication is that due to this combination, no command can ever imply new forms of slavery. The point is: God has set me free and, thus, introduced the new 'concrete humanism' based on divine righteousness: Free human beings existing in the presence of the '*exodus-ing* God'.

Besides two pronouncements (Remember the Sabbath; Honour your father and mother), all the other words are composed on the rhythm of a negative: You shall not. This 'not' (לֹא) is like the middle C in the tune of the commandments. The negative sharpens the undergirding positive in all ten alignments: Life as exhibition of the freedom granted by the Exodus-God.

The fact that the fourth and fifth word do not start with לֹא is, as exception, not out of step with the rhythm. The composition here helps to understand that the fourth word (remember) and fifth word (honour) are interconnected. This coherence is strengthened by a grammatical construction that is not present in the others, namely an imperative in the form of an *infinitivus absolutus*. This connection between the fourth and fifth wording events cannot be separated from the dynamic moments of 'remembering' and 'keeping' (verse 8). The combination remembering-keeping (commemorating) is quite remarkable because in this vivid connection past, present and future are pulled together.

Marc-Alain Quaknin writes about commemoration as 'remembering your future'. He founds this dynamic meaning on the pronouncements of Rabbi Rasji: "Dwell or orient yourself in the remembering of the Sabbath," and in doing so, "continue remembering the Sabbath constantly." The imperative mode used here concerns the future. In fact, the commemoration of the past cannot dictate anymore. At stake, now is the present and the future (Quaknin 1999:87). Remembering and commemorating the Sabbath keep the perspective of the future alive. By means of remembering and commemorating, one becomes engaged in a dynamic that bypasses the present due to the urgent pressure to grant meaning to the becoming of life, and to all future generations that will enter the present of human existence. In this dynamic momentum, parents and children are becoming dialectically interconnected.

On the diachronic of commemoration and the coming future, a brief excursion is quite insightful. Bernard of Clairvaux (1090-1153), was the leader of the Cistercians and founded many monasteries based on the ideal of poverty. He believed that the abbeys should be established in 'uncultivated land', where the creation of God was not yet complete. He aptly called those abbeys '*memoriae futurorem*': memorials of the future (Duby 1979).

Differences between the Exodus account and the Deuteronomy text

In the book of Deuteronomy, more words are used for the ten words compared to Exodus. This is no coincidence; it is also significant for the transfer from parents to children. In Deuteronomy, the fourth wording is not only focused on the creation as work of God. In this account the focus moves from creation to sanctification and justification within the ethical framework of the command; that is, the perspective of righteousness: "Remember that you were slaves in Egypt and that the Lord your God brought you out of there, with a mighty and an outstretched hand" (Deut 5:15). The liberation is quite inclusive. Everything in the household is now included, children, servants, animals, all of them should rest. The Deuteronomy text repeats three times "As the Lord your God has commanded you" (see both the fourth and the fifth command). In this way the coherence between the fourth and the fifth command (wording) is strengthened and emphasised. The appeal is therefore to be rendered as quite urgent. In the fourth command, the imperative is enforced by "So that you may live long and that it may go well with you in the land your God is giving you."

The following question arises: What is the basic reason for the differences between Exodus and Deuteronomy?

In Exodus the ten words were given three months after the departure from Egypt. They were given to a group of people who could be identified as *the first desert generation*. Their being slaves in Egypt is still very fresh and vibrant in their memory. At Mount Sinai, God promised his people that when they adhere to the stipulations of the covenant, they will indeed be the property of God. The people sanctified themselves for three days and on the morning of the third day they trembled because of the thunders. Moses then went up the mountain where God spoke the ten words (Ex 19-20).

And now the difference between the two texts. Deuteronomy is about the *second desert generation*. After all, the first generation was afraid to enter the promised land. Their fear of the giants in the land was greater than their confidence in the God of the covenant. They were sent into the desert for the second time, for forty years, for another generation. For a second time Moses had to pronounce the ten words, but now with some additions. The second generation should not repeat such a display of unfaithfulness as in the case of the first generation. Thus, the reason for sharpening the principle of justice as established by Moses the first time when he had spoken these words. We are dealing here with a distinction between generations within a definite timespan. It is not just about repetition of two texts. Each generation has a different responsibility regarding transgressions of a previous generation. They are, therefore, challenged to deal with the legacy of the previous generation's mistakes in order to adhere to the obligation within their own unique context. The legacy should be purified while the new generation should return to a more constructive attitude. This concern for a next generation resonates along throughout the Deuteronomy account: Please attend anew; do it: "For the sake of your own well-being as well as for the welfare of the children after you" (Deut 4:40, 5:29, 12:25, 28).

Explaining the significance of the different words in the texts

To honour

Respect is not part of our DNA. It will be difficult to detect and examine respect and honouring under a microscope. It is not an article one can buy in a shop. It is not a complete fact (*fait complete*). There is no fixed stipulation for respect. Honouring is about what occurs between people regarding the mutuality and reciprocity of giving and receiving. In reality, honouring is, as a verb, an exemplification of the relational and ethical quality of intersubjective networking. In honouring, one acknowledges the heaviness of giving as an exponent of graciously living. Honouring, thus, becomes a factuality of life. The question is then not about the '*what*' of the giving, but *the fact of giving itself* (the existential event of unconditional sharing).

Honouring comes from the Hebrew כָּבֹד (*kâbôd*) which is translated into English as 'glory'. It has the root meaning of 'weight' or 'heaviness' (properly). This offers a clue that glory has to do with weight, and this is confirmed by a passage such as 2 Corinthians 4:17, which speaks of the "weight of glory". The grammatical form used in the text (which is quite rare) is from the *pi'el*, meaning to honour and to validate (sensibility). Regularly when words are used in the *pi'el*, the consonants can take on an opposite meaning. In this case, it is the same. The implication is that meaning can point into the direction of becoming insensitive; that is, to 'desensitise'. That is fascinating because the two different meanings can both be applicable, and therefore they sometimes overlap. It is not one or the other, but one and the other, both together.

In the first Testament, the positive meaning of honouring as 'giving weight to' is quite common. It then refers to honouring the Lord. The meaning of insensibility is used when people have trouble when conditions became too heavy to bear at all. This was, for example, the case during the plague of the locusts in Egypt (Ex 10). With the first five plagues it was Pharaoh himself who hardened his heart. With the following five plagues, it was the Lord who hardened the heart of Pharaoh (Ex 7:13, 22; 8:15; 9:7) (Sacks 2019:59). The Book of Job also refers to the heart that is becoming too heavy. (Job 33:7: "Nor should my hand be heavy upon you"). In addition to the meaning of 'honour', כָּבֹד (*kâbôd*) also has the meaning of the liver, which is not surprising when we consider that the liver is the heaviest organ in the body. From these examples, it appears that with 'honouring' we have to think in the direction of 'giving weight' or, in a dialogical way: To acknowledge, namely, in the sense of putting a lot of emphasis (giving weight to) on the balancing momentum of giving and taking (to render this balancing of being of uttermost importance; it could not be ignored or denied, therefore: *nota bene*, NB – mark well). In this sense, כָּבֹד (*kâbôd*) attains the meaning of an ethical obligation and does not merely refer to a decent form of respecting. Honouring renders in fact a more concrete contribution than only to act in a decent way.

> One of the students in South Africa recognises the difference in translation in his own Xhosa language. In the 1975 Bible translation, honouring is translated with *beka*, which means 'honouring as giving weight'. In the 1996 translation, honour is translated with *hlonipha* which only means respect. He believes this is a toning down of the meaning of 'honour'.

It becomes clear that when one refers to the obligation to honour one's father and mother, the link with the fourth alignment cannot be negated. Honouring and remembering are supplementary to each other. 'Commemorating and remembering' sound like a mandate that should be handed over to the next generation; a mandate transferred from parents (inclusive, everyone as potential parent) to children. And this mandate is regulated by righteousness and freedom. Parents are, thus, carriers of a mandate. Honouring is, therefore, indissolubly connected to this mandate. To honour is not only a given endeavour to children. It starts in fact with what parents have given to them. The respect and validation are not products of parental mindfulness. Neither is it a binding obligation due to traditions or customs. Respect and validation, the same as in the case of honouring and commemoration, originate from the first wording alignment based on a founding principle, a theological statement: "I am the Lord your God, who brought you out of Egypt, out of the land of slavery" (Ex 20:2).

The fourth word asks to remember, not to be a slave and not to become enslaved again; to treat the stranger within your portal and public space in the same way as God cared for you. That is a legacy that should be kept intact to be transferred to the next generation. It should, thus, be taught to them in all forms of education. This challenge renders from parents, elderly and educators, the art of verbal articulation in order to translate the significance of commemorating and remembering into language that is meaningful to a younger generation during conversations and moments of dialoguing. The challenge is about the skill of how to let them discover in the transferral of the mandate, a sense of becoming authentic subjects (individuation).

In the mandate, the fourth and fifth word become interconnected. Where parents and children learn this perspective mutually together, the notion of 'honouring your parents' proceeds into intergenerational sequences, from parents to children to grandchildren to … Seen in this way, honouring is infinitely more nuanced than the projected blind obedience in children's Bibles. This perspective helps one to understand better why the father in the Bible study session was so adamant about the pregnancy of his daughter. When he stood up and revealed his resistance and protest, it was about obedience to the legacy of a mandate. He sees himself as a carrier of a divine mandate. This was his understanding of how to exemplify obedience to the word. For him, in his heuristic attempt to act in obedience, he developed this perspective. It was his internalisation of the mandate in order to do justice to his children and descendants. In this sense, he desperately needs acknowledgement. He acted responsibly and with sanctified dignity.

The previous outline brings us back to the notion of obedience. It only appears once in the Tanakh. The imperative to listen appears often. But interestingly, 'listening' is seldom used in combination with parents (fathers, mothers). One should listen to God, not so much to parents. In the case of parents, the mandate is about honouring. And honouring is about a different category than listening.

> It is indeed a burning question why in the tradition, the inter-
> pretation of 'honouring' as blind obedience became established
> in parental guidance. But even more intriguing, why is it that this
> very blunt view on obedience became transferred to government
> and church? Eventually, obedience to parents became replaced
> by authoritative institutions like state and religious communities.
> It became a fixed moralistic interpretation that should slavishly
> be followed. In World War II this mechanistic subjection to
> authoritative institutions became so mandatory for Christians
> and institutional theology, that it caused even obedience to the
> German occupation.

So 'honour' is not a claim to repeat or copy parents, not in appearance, in behaviour, or any other form of parenting demands. After all, every human child is unique, and, as such, has his/her own ability and responsibility to make a constructive contribution to life and a meaningful future. Personal contributions are unique and never the same as one's parents. Human existence is never obvious. Our being human is authentic, irreplaceable and unrepeatable. If that was not the case, there was no reason for our being human and the striving towards meaningful existence. This is how Martin Buber wrote in his book: *De weg van de mens* (*The way of man*). Honouring requires acknowledgement for what has been given to you. Honouring is thus unlimited and abundant. It continues until the death of one's parents or oneself.

In the Rabbinic tradition, many reactions to the fifth command are well known. Here follows an example:

> One day, a teacher gathered all his students around him and urged them to also ask questions and criticise. The students said to him, "Master, your behaviour amazes us. You never act like your father and your master we knew before he had chosen you as successor. How do you feel about his legacy? What about your display of loyalty?". The Rabbi took a serious look at his students and replied: "It is very simple, there is no more faithful son than me! In everything I do, I act exactly in the same way that my father did before me. He never imitated anyone. Well, neither do I" (Ouaknin 2001:113).

In Judaism, 'honouring parents' implies an obligation for children to display a year of mourning after their death. They have then the obligation to say *kaddish*, weekly prayers for the deceased, after they have passed away. This applies to all other family members for thirty days.

Rabbi Tarfon had an old mother, and every time she wanted to get into bed, he sat on his knees. So, she could use him to climb into her bed. And every time she wanted to get out of her bed, they repeated the ritual. One day he praised himself for this in a teaching and learning session. His colleagues replied to him, "You haven't even gotten half of the honour you owe her" (Ouaknin, 2001:102). Honouring yourself is not honouring your parents.

Your father and your mother

'Father' and 'mother' in Hebrew do not refer merely to one's biological parents. They refer to a very broad spectrum of different nuances. For father also applies: grandfather, father of the tribe (ancestor, patriarch), protector, counsellor. In many cases 'father' is an honorary title for a teacher, prophet or priest. The following also applies to mother: ancestress, progenitress, matriarch, stepmother, grandmother, aunt, counsellor, midwife. In a nutshell, everyone who acts like a father and mother to the child deserves to be honoured. And that is biblically speaking beyond the boundaries of purely biological relationships. Within the notion of the extended family in many African cultures, this very broad and inclusive meaning of 'father' and 'mother' is quite common. The view is that the intimate space of familial connections and the trustworthiness of family cohesion are, according to African spirituality, the best place to grow up. Within the view of the extended family there is the saying: *It takes a village to raise a child*. Within the tribal system, there is always a mother or father available. The brothers of the father are also fathers, and the sisters of the mother, also mothers. Within the intimate circle of kinship, the ancestors are reckoned as important factors of familial cohesion and interaction. The imperative to honour is comprehensive and includes all the mentioned categories. One has to reckon them all as part of the relational community (Gathogo 2008:5). Honouring is not about veneration or worshipping. According to Velapi Mhkize, honouring ancestors is definitely not about worshipping them. In fact, in the honouring of the ancestors, it is not the ancestors themselves who are honoured, but the spirit in which they existed. In this way, every human being is part of an intergenerational chain. If necessary, the whole series of ancestors could be consulted, going back seven generations. In African thinking, there is a view that after the seventh generation, we can no longer distinguish between history and myth (JM Coetzee in *Dagboek van een slecht jaar*, 2007:9).

According to Genesis 2:24, a man will leave his father and mother in order to be united with his wife, forming an own unique community with all the demands and responsibilities attached to taking care of one's family. This shift into the direction of one's own family does not imply honouring one's parents less. In contrary, according to Exodus 21:15 and Leviticus 20:9, very strict punishments were in place when parents were neglected and cursed. "If anyone curses his father or mother, he must be put to death"

(Lev 20:9). In ancient Israel, familial structures were imperative in order to survive. The familial structures helped to establish close kinship connections (Jagersma & Vervenne 1992:186). The 'nation' consisted of interconnected families (extended family circles) under the leadership of parents opting as genealogical units (family trees), while at the same time functioning as backbone for the whole history of Israel. In order to belong to nation and kin, personal commitment, responsibility and, simultaneously, collective responsibilities are required.

Moses addressed his people as a group called by the Lord to become the *qahal Jahwê* – gathered to become a nation. But this totality is focused on the person as subject as well. That is the reason why the words of Moses seem to flow seamlessly over into the pronouncement of 'you' (Sacks 2016:108). This underscores the question of answering personally to the imperative that is being put to everyone for the sake of the community, even when it comes to honouring the parents' legacy. No one can do it for you, in your place. This also applies to everyone currently living in a very individualised society. After all, every society asks for contributions to the cohesion and well-being of the greater whole.

In a family with several children, every 'father-mother-child' triad is coloured differently. Each child will contribute and respond to the challenge and structuring of 'honouring' differently. A child will inevitably honour the mother quite differently than in the case of the father-child interaction. This will also differ from the responses of the other siblings. The dynamics of relational ethics is, within intersubjectivity, differentiated and therefore open to diversity. In this sense, 'to honour' is a differentiated phenomenon but still vital ingredient of the personal interaction between parents and children within the balancing dynamic of 'giving and taking' (Van Doorn & Meulink-Korf, 2009:7-9). The differentiation implies that there cannot be general criteria available to assess appropriate abilities and hampering disabilities in the process of honouring parents. It is indeed difficult to measure different levels of every person's reliability. A general presupposition loses sight of the special differentiation that is necessary to foster authentic dialoguing between grandparents, parents and children.

Often it is difficult for children of divorced parents to find a fair balance in how to give respect and weight to each parent in a way that is just to them.

There is even more conflicting interest existent in newly formed families. The display of loyalty and invisible loyalty has a major impact in how this new structuring will become deployed (see chapter 3).

As the Lord your God has commanded you

Deuteronomy 5:16 adds to the imperative of honouring: "As the Lord your God has commanded you." This *as* refers to God but is simultaneously directed to the individual person as well. Commanding here has the meaning of commissioning. The word 'command' occurs first in the Tanakh in Genesis 2:16. It refers to the prohibition regarding one tree in the middle of the garden that Adam and Eve were not allowed to eat from. There was a clear restriction on the eating of the fruit of this tree.

Not everything that belongs to man is everyone's property and can be appropriated. There are indeed certain limitations and restrictions in place. In Deuteronomy, these commands are considerably more common than in Exodus. This difference in emphasis has to do with the exposure of that 'second desert generation' to the predicaments and requirements of their context. The latter shapes abilities and impacts on the character of the demands applicable in that specific setting.

So that your days may be long

'So that' brings about a sudden unexpected change in the whole sequence of wording regarding the ten alignments following the event of the exodus: "The Lord who brought them out of Egypt, out of the land of slavery". This directive of a significant *so that* is quite new. The commanding tone of 'honour' is rendered as a purposeful direction and motivational perspective: "So that you may live long in the land the Lord your God is giving you." This new connection to the obligation of honouring is not about causality. *One has to note that there is not written 'because'.* Thanks to God, there is no causal link between honouring and a quantitative approach: Calculating in terms of 'more or less' and the extending days in terms of numbers and a promised new calendar. 'To extend' is grammatically in the *hi'fil* which indicates that you are not the subject enabled to prolong your days yourself. The second part of the fifth word is not about a promise regarding the achievement of a reward to be paid on a very specific day in future. The second part as connected to the first (honouring) confirms the honouring as a *blessing*.

Tradition has created the idea that if you do not honour your parents, your life would become shortened quantitively. Unfortunately, with such a scenario the character of the blessing is missed totally. "The idiom 'that your days may be long …' which is found chiefly in Deuteronomy, not only envisages a chronological extension of time, but points to the rich blessing of the society which is in harmony with the divine order" (Childs 1991:419).

Days here is not quantitative but refers to diachronic, qualitative time. In Genesis 1:1-5 God called out, pronouncing to the light: 'Day' (the renaming of light). This is not merely about a chronological time span. Over against darkness, God pronounced 'night'. The impression now is that one needs to start counting time in terms of the twenty-four-hour classification of time in terms of clock time.

However, God counts differently. When God called 'let there be light', He reframed light by calling it 'day'. And He called it 'day one'. God only counted the day as a day when there is light. That is how it was said: "And there was evening, and there was morning – day one." It is now suddenly about a prophetic counting of the days. It announces that the night has passed into life and light is shining again illuminating everything – it penetrates the threat of darkness. This happpenstance within the brightness of light is then called 'day'. This shining brilliancy redefines our chronological counting of days.

'Honouring' and 'the extending of days', do not indicate an increase or extension in terms of quantitative time. They are about a qualification of time in terms of the enrichment and signification of time. Time is no longer to be qualified in terms of darkness and disasters. Darkness in Hebrew thinking is not nothingness. It refers to substance, namely that which can rob human beings from their significance and dignity due to destructive (evil) forces that are constantly threatening the whole of the cosmos. Darkness is some-*thing*. In this way, the creative event of bringing about light deconstructed the chaos of emptiness, nothingness and darkness (*Tohu wa-bohu*). *Tohu wa-bohu* (תֹהוּ וָבֹהוּ), is a Biblical Hebrew phrase found in the Genesis creation narrative (Genesis 1:2). The two Hebrew words are properly segolates, spelled *tohuw* and *bohuw*. The Hebrew *tohuw* is a many layered concept referring to inter alia waste (trash), desert; emptiness, vanity; nothingness. It indicates void emptiness. Albeit, the point is that the qualification by light brings about a total new perception of threatening forces that could destroy any form of order and a sense of meaning and purposefulness. Therefore, one could dare to assert that even the current force of the corona-pandemic could be penetrated by the light of gracious reinterpretation. Covid-19 therefore can be reframed from sheer anguish (the threat and destruction of death and dying) into hopeful reorientation and fair justice (the opportunity of reframing a crisis into significant change).

> For example, a Rabbi once asked his students, "How do you know when the night is over, and the day begins?" Someone said: "That's when you can differentiate a dog from a sheep." "No," said the rabbi. Another responded and asked: "Is it when from afar you can distinguish a date tree from a fig tree?" "No," said the Rabbi, "The night has come to an end when you can face the visage the person you meet and start to recognise in the countenance the feature of your brother or sister. Until then the night will be with us."

"And that it may go well…"

This too is an addition in Deuteronomy when compared to the version of the Ten Commandments in Exodus. The combination of 'going well' with 'that' is very specifically attached to the Deuteronomy text. Within context of the second desert generation, the focus is much more on the individual and how relationships will impact on the following future generation and offspring. This focus on the coming generation (the unborn offspring) is also empha-sised by Nagy. In his contact and conversations with families, he focused on the most vulnerable. That explains his attention to the younger generation. They are the people who still need to journey through life so that their future well-being is totally dependent on the quality of current relationships and the making of appropriates and reliable choices.

It is indeed a question: What is meant by 'well' in well-being?

'Well' as connected to 'good' in the language of the Tanakh is *tov*, טוֹב. God is summoning human beings and the whole of creation (cosmos) to the well-being of *tov* (יִיטַב; *yi·tav*). In fact, in Genesis 21:9 it is written that after the creation (*bârâ*, בָּרָא) of land, God saw that it was *good*. With creation (*bârâ*, בָּרָא), is not meant to just make or to shape in general (handcrafting). Creation is about separation, to divide, to tear apart. God is ordering the *Tohu wa-bohu* (תֹהוּ וָבֹהוּ (Gen 1:2) in a new way. God has set the brute mass apart by dispersing it; He separated in the sense of summoning (creation as word-event) into being, into light. In this way a differentiation between light and darkness took place. Darkness received a different place, separated from the space of light. This event of separating is called by God: *Tov*. This pronouncement was repeated with the separation of land and sea. The creation is all about *tov*. And with the creation of man and his/her position in the middle of the cosmos, God said: "It was very good!" (Gen 1:30). The *tov* is now repeated: *Tov, tov*.

The point of the argument is, that to honour one's parent, is *tov*. Parent-child interconnectedness is now displayed within the illuminating space of God's light. Honouring a parent or grandparent by children offers a new perspective on a humane space for significant living, created by God; that is, a life that is extracted from chaos. 'That it may go well' is not an abstract fact, but a concrete event that reframes life as an event of receiving; well-being as a gracious gift of extreme enjoyment, soulful validation.

In the land your God is giving you

What exactly is meant by 'land'? Literally the reference is to *adama*; it means red soil or reddish powder/dust. It is used to indicate the substance which God used in the creation of Adam, the first human being; the red soil which had been used for the formation of man (human being). "The Lord God formed the man (הָאָדָם; *ha·'a·dam*) from the dust (עָפָר; *a·far*) of the ground (הָאֲדָמָה; it is not yet *ha eretz* (אֶרֶץ)," as the promised land for Israel, or a nation. What is at stake is life in relationship with others, indicating responsibility on the given *adamah*. In a strict sense, one never possesses *adama*. One receives *adama* and in this sense, one enters *adama*. On this soil, one never erects partitions that set off and keep the other out. Land that God gives is not a land that can be claimed, or which is subject to rights, or which may be appropriated. It is not the land that belongs to Mr X or Mrs Y. It becomes difficult to realise when 'land that God gives' is identified with land that has been owned by Mr X or Mrs Y for generations (entitlement), despite legal claims due to tradition and loyalty. Levinas puts it this way: "*Adama* is the literal teaching of the Bible, in which the earth is not an individual property, but belongs to God" (Levinas 1987:48).

Adama is the carrier, the ground for human welfare on which man is called to be human: To become a humane creature living in dignity together with the other. Marianne Storm, therefore, reasons that soil/ground is ethical and relational; ground as an assignment where the tight grip on yourself is given up, where a trust in God or another person grows and envelops (Storm 2006:4). Ground then indicates a place and qualitative space where the *I* is dethroned in order to develop into maturity and humanity; to dwell meaningfully on ground as a relational entity where justice in relationships is being shaped and enfleshed. Especially, the formation of ethical relationships. Buber translates *adama* with: *Boden der Heiligung* (ground that is sanctified). And in this way, the earth is transformed by the fifth word as place and space for getting rid of 'one's shoes' (ownership), because one is exposed to the sanctification of the whole of the cosmos – holy ground for dignifying human existence in co-humanity.

According to Genesis 2:7: "The Lord God formed the man from the dust of the ground." 'Formed' refers to the work of a potter, shaping clay to become a piece of art and worthy object. Like pottery, human beings are frail and vulnerable, exposed to both 'good' and 'evil'. It is exactly this very frail human being who has to live peacefully in coexistence with fellow human beings. But this living in peace is not without sweat and toil. One is exposed to suffering, whether this 'ground' (*adama*) is a plot in downtown or a far remote place in the desert. This plot should be where *adama* becomes qualified by *eretz* (אֶרֶץ).

Those who know themselves being called to exist within the parameters of *adama*, always remain in service of a way of life in which humanity shapes and transforms soil into holy spaces for humane encounters. Man is in this sense, always a subjected being, ('subjectus/subjecta'), subjected to a calling that coincides with the challenge to become stewards of the earth, and to establish justice in the formation of ethical based relationships.

Martin Buber maintains that *adama* directs the way which human beings have to journey in order to experience fulfilment in life. "There is something very precious that can only be found in one, single place on earth. It is about a great treasure. The latter one can call *fulfilment of existence*. And the place where this treasure can be found is right there, firmly where one is standing right now" (Buber, *De weg van de mens – The way of man*).

It is expressed emphatically that 'the Lord, your God, *gave* that ground to you'. 'Giving' is a participatory asset and receiving action (*participium activum*), which means that it is a continuing action, expressing one's concern for God, continuing from the past, to the present into the future. It does not say that God *will and shall give*. The ground does not come as a reward ever at the end of life. It is not about a dividend in the form of a few extra days; a kind of bonus because one has served and honoured one's parents in an excellent way. To dwell on the land (*adama*) is materialised in the form of a blessing. And the intention of this blessing is to build a bridge to the second table. Bridging is echoing a transfer from serving the Lord into acknowledging the other as fellow human being. And immediately, the second table starts with the imperative: "You shall not murder" (Deut 5:17). You! second person singular. Do not kill; nothing at all! Therefore, that fifth word about honouring the parents and the ground that God has given. It thus serves as a springboard, as a place of transition, into meaningful living, displaying righteousness within the networking of intersubjectivity. Or as a student aptly remarked: "When one reads the fifth word in this way, it becomes a bridge to the humanisation of life. It envelops into a responsibility through which you act as steward (guarantor) of the ground that the Lord, your God, has given you and by which you should honour your parents."

7.3   *The dilemma of decision-making (the choice)*

Staying true to the assignment to honour the father and mother implies difficult choices. The making of difficult decisions comes into play when you want to honour your parents but simultaneously have to stay loyal to a third party. An example is when Jonathan was challenged with the choice to remain faithful to his friend David, against the wishes of his father Saul. But then also, despite his choice for David, he still must continue with honouring his father.

In 1 Samuel 20:1 we read how David fled from Naboth at Rama and went to Jonathan. He asked him: "What have I done? What is my crime? How have I wronged your father, that he is trying to take my life?" Jonathan could not believe David: "Look my father doesn't do anything, great or small, without confiding in me. Why should he hide this from me? It's not so" (verse 2). David suspected that due to the very close relationship between him and Jonathan, Saul did not share all his plans with his son. Together the two decided to test how valid was Saul's wrath regarding David's position in the kingdom.

David suggests not to show up at mealtime the next day. He will hide in the field with Jonathan's approval. Then, when Saul asks about David's absence, Jonathan will let David know his response through a thoughtful plan that will use the distance of arrows to express the magnitude of the danger from Saul's wrath. Jonathan swears to David to really communicate the results so that he can leave in peace. "May the Lord be with you as He has been with my father" (1 Sam 20:13). This blessing beautifully displays Jonathan's double loyalty (to both his father Saul and to his friend David).

Everything went as they agreed. Saul became so angry with David's absence and Jonathan's affection for David. He ordered Jonathan to bring David to kill him. Saul's wrath was so intense that he even hurled his spear at his own son. Then Jonathan knew for sure that his father's intention is to kill David. Immediately, he communicated this message to David by means of the arrows. Then both friends realised that the time of saying goodbye had come. They made a covenant and David left.

What deserves to be noted is how Jonathan managed to maintain the loyalty to David but, at the same time, must continue honouring his father. Jonathan disobeyed his father's command to bring David to him so that he could be killed. In his choice, he had to deal with a double kind of loyalty. He did not betray his father. He merely disobeyed the unjust command of his father to bring David so that he can kill him. The alignment to honour the parents does not require that parents be blindly obeyed. In a most magnificent way Jonathan gave credit to his father's legacy by honouring him with the following blessing which referred to a prior blessing bestowed onto his father by the Lord: "The Lord may be with you, as He has been with my father" (1 Sam 20:13).

The sequence of alignments: From the fourth to the fifth to the sixth wording

One should deal with the close connections between the different alignments. They are interconnected. Every parent should take up the responsibility to commemorate what is written in the fourth word so that it could always be remembered to keep the Sabbath holy. This important message should be transferred to the next generation. On their part, every child is summoned to honour his/her parent as well as every person who opted in the capacity of being a parent. One has to keep in mind that honouring does not require blind obedience. On the contrary, each generation is not called to repeat and imitate how the previous generation lived and acted. It is rather about a calling to sanctify the land/soil that 'the Lord your God gave to you as token of his gratuitous blessing'.

When children honour parents due to a sound sense of freedom and respectful indebtedness, they become themselves a blessing resulting from an acknowledgement of God's gift to them. That means to consider, assess and weigh the heritage, legacies and stories that have been received from parents and grandparents. How to pass on the inheritance, the legacies and the stories, the benefits and the burdens in a constructive way to the next generation, can become tough indeed. This challenge sometimes impels one to make difficult and often awkward choices, though!

In fact, every one of us comes across them day by day within the happenstances of life. Each of us exists within an in-between space and place wherein a transition to a next generation occurs constantly. The burning questions to face are: How do we pass on what we have heard, seen and learned to the next generation? How can we get entangled when we are compelled to make different, often awkward, choices for the sake of a better world? How does our loyalty sometimes become a stumbling block and get in the way of establishing sound relationships? To whom our loyalty weighs more? Is the preponderance more in the direction of the previous or the next generation? How does the balancing of giving and receiving relate to honouring the reasonableness of parents? These questions give an indication of how difficult it is to balance legacies within the ethical and relational challenge of establishing loyalty in intergenerational dialoguing. The next chapter will deal with 'legacies and loyalty'.

CHAPTER 8

Legacy: The ethical imperative in multi-directed partiality

Nagy means by legacy, the ethical imperative to the current generation, namely, to discern what in life should contribute to the meaningful survival of the next generation and their offspring This discernment is exercised within an acute awareness of the legacy of past generations. In other words, the narrative regarding the freedom of entitlement in the history of a family is an important resource for providing security for the carer or parent. The legacy can also serve as an example of how the obligation of the ethical imperative exemplifies what counts in life and what will be meaningful for next, coming generations.

Legacy is not about an obligation to repeat past mistakes. It is about the obligation to free offspring from violating habits, harmful traditions and inappropriate legacies (delegations) inherited from previous generations. Safeguarding, and to act as guarantor for the other, should be rendered as a kind of relational, ethical resource (legacy). It should thus be passed on to the coming generations.

8.1 Receiving and the passing on of legacies: The intergenerational thoroughfare passage

Parents and children each have, in their own capacity, the duty to pass on what has been received from previous generations. They function as thoroughfare between different generations. Everyone receives unsolicited material and immaterial inheritances. Material inheritances include money and goods, genetic traits and land. The intangible legacy contains family stories that tell of struggle and bravery, pride, guilt and shame; ideas of what is just and what is not; collected wisdom from ancestors and mothers. Achievements from previous generations are partly passed on to the next generation. It is fun when it is about family games, habits and rituals. It gets more complicated when the recurring family stories are about how cultural differences to be dealt with, and how one, as representative of the next generation, is different in terms of custom, style and context. This also applies to how form and content is given to religion and spirituality (religious rituals). The first instalment of incitement is initially given to a person. One receives the family traditions, customs and genetic material wrapped up as a personal inheritance. Rabbi Jonathan Sacks writes: "Everybody is struggling with meaning of life and concerns about the world we leave behind. We must not only talk about our passions but also about wisdom out of different traditions as they are handed over in love and respect from generation to generation" (Sacks 2005:15; 2016:25).

Intergenerational patterns

All these family legacies shape intergenerational patterns. For Nagy, what we are presented with is more than merely an 'inheritance'. He calls it 'legacy' (bequest) and thus expresses that for each generation the question arises of what they want to pass on from that legacy and how they do it: At stake, is the choice that is made at the 'place of transition' – thoroughfare passage. A choice that for the rest of one's life always returns and should always be assessed anew. Again and again the question arises because the realities and context of one's living conditions are in flux and thus always subjected to change.

Receiving a legacy means being vested with a responsibility to weigh to what extent legacies are constructive, beneficial or not. The challenge at this checkpoint is to weigh whether the balances and deficits are fair to be lived with, and whether they could be passed on to the present and future generations. The shift from the previous generation to the next generation is like a roof tile construction where the credit, merit and trust are like the adhesive, binding everything together (Meulink-Korf & Van Rhijn 2002:103; 2016:68). In other words, reliability is the continuity that binds together. Positive legacies are a bond between families and generations. These are the stories that are passed on at family gatherings, and where the protagonists are depicted with humour, or at least, put into a milder framework. Valuable memories are shared at this conjunction. They connect and strengthen loyalty between the different generations, like a biography that will be read in the future as part of the whole of the familial tradition.

Like a mandate

Legacy is in fact multi-lateral and in the plural because it has to reckon with the fact that every person could be linked to at least four families. In a legacy many bequests come into play. So, legacies are not just about what is received, they call for an obligation on *how* to pass it on. The challenge is how to deal with differences. In this sense, every legacy is in fact a *mandate*, a commission. Legacies are embedded in a relational reality. It is therefore obvious that we are part of this networking reality. Legacies do not merely determine human behaviour in the present, but also the future. In this way we partake in the future of coming generations.

Legacies are relational because the judgment about the fairness of how we pass on legacies is not weighed up by an objective external body. It is the future generations who will judge our choices. And the criterium will be how we have preserved and invested in humanity for their sake and how we have left the earth to them as safely as possible. At stake are their welfare and well-being and the preservation of the earth.

The fact that we are accountable for this is testament to an intrinsic tribunal that wants to do justice and calculates who comes after us (Meulink-Korf & Van Rhijn 2002:71; 2016:49). There is no obvious obligation to repeat what has been established and exemplified by parents and grandparents, nor can it be required to remain faithful to legacies that are not equitable. Each person is personally responsible for carefully sifting out his/her legacies, weighing them in terms of fairness and making choices that contribute to justice for the present and future generations. Although customs and traditions can be very valuable, they cannot be intended as guiding voices and normative determinants that could eventually hinder a relational reality and counterpunch human development. Where that steering is a factor that takes over personal responsibility, legacy has become a delegate, a prescribing rule that impedes healthy autonomy.

Delegate: When legacies become compellable and enforceable

Nagy refers to delegates when the voices and legacies of grandparents/parents compel and obstruct a free choice. There are many discrepancies and deviations (fault lines) in every family and every community due to blind obedience to delegates. In cases of enforcement, it is usually about the demanding, scolding and authoritative finger of the 'ought to be', pointing to a very demanding 'you must and should'! This compelling tone obstructs fairness in balancing and enforces unfree loyalty.

> A thirty-year-old woman complained: "When my parents come to stay and I pray to God differently than my parents, it always ends in arguments after dinner. I don't believe the same way my parents do and when they leave, I am left with a feeling of not doing well enough. I feel a kind of failure. I then start to wrestle with the very burning question: To whom am I disloyal when my image of God changes, and I am frank about it? To God, to my parents or to my children?"

Children can become entangled in conflicting loyalties due to compelling delegates. It can feel like betrayal when one starts to interpret these legacies as enforced delegates, as prescriptions for personal responsibility and thus as necessary for individuation and appropriate autonomy. It could indeed be very encouraging for parents to see that a child with a different perspective and decisiveness is reliable and is investing in a more prosperous and significant future. This can even be regarded as a refund for their previous care and parental responsibility.

Multi-directed partiality in the passing on of legacies in decision-making: On being partial for coming generations

We live between generations, the so-called in-between of a generational gap. On the one hand, we want to be loyal to the previous generation. On the other hand, we want to be loyal to the next generation as well. But in the meantime, we cannot neglect our obligation to bestow justice to the current generation. With all due respect to the previous generation, our main critic is the next generation.

After all, they deserve solidarity, although they cannot yet answer and respond. Their response is still not-yet. To maintain fairness in solidarity requires an attitude of multi-directed partiality, even knowing that at this stage there can be no kind of reciprocity. And yet, despite the factuality of a not-yet, they are still making an appeal to the present generation. They hold them accountable in the mode of an ethical imperative, entering the present from a not-yet, but becoming future. The claim applies to 'me' personally, I am liable for life. I am personally asked to make choices and compelled to answer: '*Respondeo etsi mutabor*' (I answer even if I have to change, Rosenstock-Huessy 2003). Meulink-Korf and Van Rhijn write: "Or is it just human that the future of others still has priority, also, precisely, the future of those who not-yet cannot claim for themselves? That a future takes precedence in which the individual no longer belongs and partakes, a future for the vulnerable?"(Meulink-Korf & Van Rhijn 2002:61; 2016:39). Every time an individual makes a more constructive contribution to the well-being of those who come after, thereby letting go or withholding what is destructive, the quality of life changes at that moment. Making effective decisions requires a certain awareness of decisiveness in the balance of give and take (receive) between generations. Being part of that co-responsibility for the future, frees us from the idea that we live purely between birth and death, that our life is purely ours. Not everyone is aware of that extension of life, prolonging into the invisibility of an unforeseen future.

> I try to learn the French language. I like it indeed, but to be honest, I am predominantly motivated by my bilingual grandson. He has a French father and a Dutch mother. I would like to share some future with him. During one of the lessons, the word 'future' came into play and was discussed. A lady said she has nothing in common anymore with that word. She is now quite old (71) and there remains for her only one day at a time, and that is 'now'. Her motto is: Live today and that's it, because with death everything is over. I tried to say something in my best French, something like "our biography doesn't end with our biology". In fact, we can still contribute to the future by investing into our grandchildren. Firmly she said, "*Moi, je n'ai pas un futur!*" (I, I have no future!). But that, to my mind, is indeed very unfortunate and sad for her.

Transgenerational solidarity

Legacies oblige one to make informed choices, always asking whether the welfare of others is served. This includes questions about pollution of the earth, depletion of raw materials, questions about the effects of globalisation on local communities and life at grass roots level – glocalisation. (Glocalisation is a combination of the words 'globalisation' and 'localisation'; the term is used to describe a product or service that is developed and distributed globally but is also adjusted to accommodate the user or consumer in a local market and cultural setting). The Covid-19 pandemic also questions how carefully and selectively we transmit life compared to how we received it. It poses new questions about connectedness between nations, and the gap between rich and poor that still has to do with forms of racism and colonial thinking. It is a constructive obligation and healthy policy to break with self-evident customs and traditions where necessary. Such intergenerational breaks and socially detachments are not new. As long as there are generations, there has been discontinuity in continuity and will be in future.

In this sense, I recall how Moses did not ask of the different generations in the desert for blind obedience, but for a new responsibility, for the sake of 'the children after you' (offspring) with which he also envisages the unborn children (Deut 5:3). Because of the obligatory commitment to the next generation, Nagy speaks of *transgenerational solidarity*. Here, solidarity is used and not loyalty, because it also considers those who do not belong to family or the same generation. This transgenerational solidarity is an extension of the family ledger in which the balance of assets and liabilities are entered. Transgenerational solidarity is a claim to pass on legacies in a way wherein fairness and justice are the criterion. It is good to know that Nagy was personally very concerned about the neglect of the consequences of the environmental crisis. The concern for a next generation is embedded in the multi-directed partial attitude because it calculates with several generations at the same time, including the not-yet visible next generation.

In an article on transgenerational solidarity, Nagy states that every person is a link in the chain of survival in terms of promoting this human kind of solidarity (Nagy 1987:292, 308). There is a capacity for evolutionary progress in every human being. When that ability is ignored or bypassed, instead of progress, a retreating movement of confidence results in destructive consequences. Nagy calls this retreating movement *entropy*, which shows increasing disintegration and simplification. (In nature we know entropy as a retreat, for example the rolling up of young leaves that have yet to unfold;

lack of order or predictability; gradual decline into disorder. Entropy is also a measure of the number of possible arrangements the atoms in a system can have. In this sense, entropy is a measure of uncertainty or randomness).

Nagy has a self-invented word for what prevents relapse and stimulates the process of folding open: *negentropic*. (In information theory and statistics, negentropy is used as a measure of distance to normality. Negentropy is reverse entropy. It means things becoming more in order. By 'order' is meant organisation, structure and function; the opposite of randomness or chaos). Unfolding requires trust and dialogue, and that is what Nagy's thinking is all about and that certainly applies when it comes to the next generation.

Anyone who works with families recognises the importance of making the mandate of transgenerational solidarity clear as a debt to the next generation. Relational ethics, that balance of appropriate and equitable giving and receiving, is thus guaranteed to benefit the intergenerational movement. Aspects to be able to make those choices are: An autonomous individuation that is acquired based on self-worth and self-validation through mutual recognition of merit. This requires insight into responsibility for the other and from the other, both interpersonal and transgenerational! Where this is in motion, a basis for dialogue is created.

Everyone is liable within the parameters of their intrinsic tribunal as prevention for survival. From a constructive, forward-thinking (negentropic) orientation, man is a rebuttal to withdrawing into what we now see in nations. For example, in many forms of conservative backlashes, the blunt Trumpism of 'America first', radical groups and gangsterisms. In this increasingly automated world, we have become more and more anonymous and it has become more difficult to know ourselves as personally liable. The development of George Orwell's *'big brother is watching you'* via cameras and mobile phones certainly does not help to signify human behaviour and interpret it for development of self-worth.

The question arises: How can relational ethics stimulate family interconnectedness and promote the building of personal constructive merit? After all, this is necessary to be able to carry responsibly a mandate for a more just future. Nagy's article published in 1987, is unprecedentedly topical: "Humanity faces a new historic reality of possible self-imposed extinction, and no informed human being can ignore its threat without committing a serious, almost pathological denial. The prospects of this reality threaten our own lives and, even more likely, our children's lives" (Nagy 1987:296).

It has been more than thirty years since Nagy wrote these sentences. How impressive it is more than ever! The processes towards a new reality certainly contribute to more humanity. However, what we see above all, is a continuing disintegration of reliability in human relations and political relations. The urgent question that remains is whether the consequences for the future will not be too much for those who are young and yet to come. May we, the older generation, expect them to be responsible in our place? Perhaps, is that not a brutal form of parentification!

The intriguing triadic position: The intergenerational thoroughfare

In terms of the intergenerational dynamic, the current generation is called to operate in the in-between space between past and present. This conjunction can be called an intergenerational thoroughfare; the current generation functions intergenerationally as transfer point (see chapter 7: Honour your father and your mother). It is they who pass the relay baton of the ledger to the next generation with the benefits and deficits of the past included. Those who do not have children are also covered by this mandate and cannot escape the responsibility of passing on legacies to the next generation, including weighing up what contributes to their well-being and what does not. Whether we have children or not, everyone lives between generations and operates in that place, at the same time, as heir and testator. This is undeniably a triadic position in which the not-yet, unborn generation (although literally still silent), is already in becoming; the yet crying 'third'. In this sense, they are making an appeal on our liability (Meulink-Korf & Van Rhijn 2002:95, 2016:62).

We are not only connected to the previous and coming generations, but as individuals, we are also part of the current generation, but not on our own. We are always relationally and ethically linked to one another. The relationship is asymmetrical because the interests of the next generation take precedence over those of the previous generation. Everyone is within one's own capacity, generationally structured and linked. And as such, one has the unique opportunity to choose how and what to pass on or edit. In everyone's past there are events that evoke pride and shame and guilt. And in-between, there are many intriguing ethical entanglements as well.

8.2　The impact of loyalty

Loyalty as stumbling block

Every generation has the freedom to sort out what is just and fair and what is not. The challenge is about a reassessment regarding the ethical value and impact of legacies. The choice implies, inter alia, to try to bend, reframe or stop the ongoing destructive bills (revolving slate). The choices we make may be at odds with how our grandparents made and applied them within the context of networking. This can create a crisis, because legacies are all about that strange irrevocable bond called loyalty. Loyalty is dynamic because it is there for both those who come after us and those who have gone before us and passed away. But loyalty is also embedded in complexity and often paradoxical discrepancies. Loyalty can get in the way of freely choosing how to strain legacies. Loyalty can hinder us from being critical about how our parents lived life and the choices they made. This can create tension if we do not want to be part of the choices that parents have made or repeat ethical commitments, convictions and traditions. Some of this became clear during the lectures of third year students of theology at Stellenbosch, South Africa in 2015.

These students from the Stellenbosch University were active during the national student uprisings in 2015. The reason for the resistance was the threatening increase in tuition fees. The strike was widely held amongst the 30 000 students residing in the university town of Stellenbosch. One Thursday morning we were forced to face an empty lecture hall. Outside, young people (mostly students) from all cultures were united, dancing and singing. The irony is that the day before, the topic during the lectures was: 'How to deal with legacies in your family'. The lectures also dealt with legacies containing ideologies and often skewed policies about life, for example, the consequences of apartheid. The students felt that they were not concerned with discussing this topic within their current setting. Their response was not ignorance but rather the need to reveal an urge to articulate current attempts to express identity: '*You know, we are free borns!*'

Within their context, the slogan '*We are free borns*', does not express sheer indifference. Rather, there is a desire to set the heavy burden of the past aside for the time being. However, that desire is not a license to leave legacies carelessly behind. It is not about blunt insensitivity. It is merely about the reframing of legacies. Their response is about an inability to interpret legacies at that stage in a dialogical perspective; to deal with legacies from the hermeneutics of relational ethics, namely, legacies as related to fairness and reasonableness. Loyalty to a previous generation will remind them inevitably and continuously where they are coming from, and what the legacy of the struggle was about. However, commemorating previous events should not always be a heavy burden making them captives of the past. Instead of merely carrying burdens, their striving is to pass on the legacies of the past, reframed by a new perspective so that coming generations will benefit from the way they have dealt with their legacy (bequest) within their own framework of comprehension.

We discover a certain tension between legacies (bequests) and loyalty. Loyalty to the previous generation (parents and grandparents) can be mandatory and become an obstacle to making free choices about how to display responsibility. Loyalty sometimes seems to ask for blind obedience in order to repeat, in a very fair way, the context at that time and how it was shaped by different circumstances than in the present. We often see that families and communities (including religious and ethnic communities) operate in a more or less closed circuit where rules are clearly prescribed and passed on. The more conservative the rules, the tighter the borders are defended and guarded. To deviate from the previous tradition is blamed as treason.

Now that the world has moved into the technological revolution of digitalisation, the influence of globalisation cannot be ignored at all. Currently it becomes more important for young people to express themselves within the language and terminology of their own unique context. The choices they are going to make will differ from the customs and paradigmatic frameworks of the family system they are stemming from. The same goes for religious communities and tribes. But how do you communicate these kinds of deviations when you still want to honour your parents and other loved ones from whom you have learned how to cope with the happenstances of life? Because you do not want to be disloyal and cause harm to their legacy, loyalty becomes a very complex phenomenon. Loyalty and legacy then tend to lead to friction and cause some tension in the familial transactions, which affects the relationships of whom it concerns. From a relational ethical point of view: Subjectivity comes under pressure and simultaneously the dynamic of reciprocity in intersubjective dialoguing.

The dilemma of decision-making: The making of hard choices

Religious communities, groups operating in very specific political conventions, are often shaped by a strong desire to combat for a more just world, even when it is difficult to foresee what exactly the outcome will be. In the case of ethnic groups, the order and conventions of the group should simultaneously be maintained and respected. Most of times, they are regarded as fair and should always be upheld. The further problem is that these conventions usually represent traditions, stretching over several generations including ancestors. People initially join groups with good intentions. But unfortunately, it is inevitably the case that traditions, rituals, rules and agreements grow and change over time. It is indeed true that they capture valuable insight gathered over many years and reflect the struggle of previous generations of how to survive and cope with painful life events. It is therefore quite understandable that, when people are subjected to radical changes and drastic new forms of cultural and political transformation, they tend to stay loyal but often in a very reactive way. Meanwhile, new habits and possibilities that are different are pouring in. Loyalty and solidarity are put under huge pressure. We see this, for example, in church communities where secularisation and globalisation have unmasked rituals and confessions that have attained the status of sacral rites and are viewed as self-evident. As a counter-reaction, we see amongst elderly the tendency to retreat into defence mechanisms that represent a more conservative stance. This kind of regressive defence mode causes a dilemma due to a conflict of interests. For young people, decision-making becomes extremely difficult because they want to share life experiences stemming from a different context than the traditional framework of the family or community convention. However, they still want to remain loyal to parents and the values of their own community. That is why we have the phenomenon of *conflicting interests and conflicting loyalties.*

How to freely enjoy self-confidence as expressed in new friendships and peer groups inevitably brings about a conflict of loyalty. The fact is that in their own circles, the new kind of conventions often contributes to a beneficial sense of well-being. The dilemma now is how to foster these new forms of self-validation but simultaneously not to cause conflict with the customs of the family or to obstruct the culture of origin. Without any doubt, hard choices have to be made by them. Young people, more than older people, cannot avoid making choices that are not in line with family traditions. Conflicting loyalties due to different legacies representing tradition, rituals and customs re-emerge at every '*life event*'. It becomes pinching when imposed rules and habits exceed the parameters of lived subjectivity. The demand for new commitments is then becoming stronger than relational bondages representing previous connections. Choices then risk becoming relational fractions that can run right through families.

We recognise the dilemma of legacies and loyalty in South Africa, specifically during elections and political campaigns. Within the framework of familial connections, and the legacy of 'the struggle', there is an unspoken requirement to remain loyal to the ANC. In the meantime, the younger generation would like to make a different political choice, and in many instances for good reason. From a historical perspective, historical accounts narrate on how countless people had been left with a very painful dilemma. For example, a Jewish man in Amsterdam told how, five years after World War II, his employer forced him to work with a nice colleague who was from Germany. Years later, he could become suffocated when he was in one room with him. The murder of many of his family members became a distancing factor between them. He could not restrain himself from seeing this man as a co-bearer and historical representative of injustice. Mediation efforts did not lead to the establishment of a better and healthy relationship. He disclosed the pain in his heart: "How can I be more loyal to this benevolent man than to my family who was murdered!" Eventually he resigned himself. It has been a painful memory all through his life, simultaneously mixed with a sense of guilt towards that colleague who was indeed a very fine gentleman.

Legacies within diverse cultural settings: The dilemma and tension of conflicting loyalties

Learning to live together within different cultures and clashing historical realities creates dilemmas where conflicting loyalties are inevitable. These dilemmas are but part of the reality of intersubjective interaction and the mutuality of coexistence within different cultural settings. Loyalties contradict each other when *it seems* that, if we choose one before the other, we are against the other. But, due to multi-directed partiality, that is not necessarily the case. Siding with the one does not necessarily imply rejecting the other. And yet, it can feel like betrayal to the culture we did not choose at that stage. It requires a process of trust to openly make choices. It creates, without any doubt, tension because when we make fundamental choices and simultaneously want to apply the principle of fairness and justice, decision-making can become tough indeed. The different loyalty to parents, grandparents, and communities requires boldness of speech and fair decision-making. For example, in traditional African cultures, the following firm principle prevails: 'We and the land are one; our mutual sense of belonging is all-inclusive, incorporating space, place, land and soil'.

To a large extent the African worldview is holistic and all-inclusive. In this cosmology and anthropology, space and place are determinants of communal identity. In many of the local communities, the space and place of 'kraal' is of great importance. 'Kraal' refers to the encirclement of small indigenous communities fenced in to live together. But at the same time, 'kraal' is an indication of both communality and centrifugal forces of interaction and vital decision-making. In many African spiritualities and cultures, 'kraal' is a communal meeting place right in the centre as a physical place – a kind of communal court. There is the hearth as a place of meeting where public discussions take place. It is here where the spirits of ancestors are consulted, and elders of the tribe meet to discuss communal issues and make important decisions. Kraal is thus, for the tribe or clan, a sacred place and space. There it is determined who or what is the cause of evil, what is needed to clear guilt from the community, and which rituals are necessary and applicable to maintain justice and fair balance.

During the time of colonisation and later the application of the apartheid policy, many inhabitants of small villages in the rural areas were forced to leave their 'land' in order to work in the cities and mining industries. Due to urbanisation and the need for employment, the movement was from rural areas into the outskirts of the cities. However, in the *townships* around Cape Town (approximately three million inhabitants) there is no original 'kraal' anymore. Communal life is disturbed, and traditions have become disrupted. Furthermore, it was virtually impossible to maintain the custom of meeting together in order to discuss communal issues and to address questions about evil and guilt. In this sense, a cultural secularisation took place, contributing to the loss of '*safety nets*' (a relational network; communal encirclement), the loss of a sense of belonging and interconnectedness. The careful screening of legacies came under great pressure. Sometimes there seems to be no choice. And if there is one, it remains a dilemma as illustrated in the following case:

> A thirty-year-old man said: "I feel pressurised to live between different time frames. In connections to my family, time means: A relationship with livestock, cattle, farmlands, sacred land, family and ancestors. Outside the parameters of close family connections, time is filled with money making in order to afford a house, a car, studies, going out. In the intimate circle and interior of my personal family life, I am indispensable as a father for the hard work, care for the livestock and still to function as leader. It is also my duty to reckon with the role of ancestors, as well as for the legacies of previous generations. We cannot survive without these cultural obligations. In our social environment and in our house where the children grow up, my wife opts as the leader in raising the children. She drives the car better than I do, while I am responsible for making coffee and hanging out the laundry when she is at work. I still have to learn that time spent with my family is also about living within the in-between space of intergenerational interaction. Yet, I'm not sure how to manage. On the one hand, I need to be loyal to previous generations (the familial legacies), but on the other hand, I need to be loyal to the coming generation as well. I realise that it is important for my children how I deal with their interests right now. But that makes me insecure about my family connectedness and obligations."

From this case study we learn how the tension between heir and testator creates the dilemma of conflicting interests and the difficulty to apply the principle of loyalty. Familial and intergenerational tensions are inevitable. They are always existent and put one before difficult choices that require consideration for what is fair and what not, concerning the well-being of the next generation. The tension boils down to personal responsibility and not becoming disloyal to the legacies of previous generations. The balance between personal freedom and the obligation to legacy is a tricky game and cannot take place without investment of time, the making of difficult choices and the quality of personal input.

The quest for new modes of loyalty

Horrifying and painful experiences inflicted on 'our' family can demand a total blindfolded mode of loyalty, as for example, in many conflicting political and historical settings. That holds true whether that is about a Jewish man in his relationship to German people, or due to the ideology of apartheid and its impact on the disposition of black people in their daily connections and interactions with white people. Another painful example is Christians executed by Boko Haram in Nigeria and how it impacts on interfaith connections between Muslims and Christians. If one really intends to start with new campaigns for the establishment of a new, fairer, just world order, the forming of new forms of interrelation loyalty is quite complex. The question then is how to deal with previous modes of loyalty to past generations, including the legacy of those who passed away or were hurt, but then simultaneously to become engaged in a constructive manner to address the quest for new modes of loyalty. This challenge is indeed difficult.

For pastors and counsellors, multi-directed partiality is becoming paramount and decisive. After all, when someone with his/her legacy is merely unilaterally loyal, there is always the risk that the shortcomings and wrongdoings of the past will be shared and presented in the mode of obsessive retributive revenge. The risk is then quite possible that the bill is passed on to innocent third parties. Multi-directed partiality is a core attitude because, as a pastor and counsellor, one cannot become a victim of someone else's one-sided prejudice. That is not fair to either the client or the so-called perpetrator. That would inevitably make someone disloyal.

Loyalty requires that we take seriously the interests of the family or community in which we grow up and that we also try to address the concerns of those who need help. One really has to meet the need for help and support as far as possible. In these cases, the expression of true loyalty becomes really tested, even in cases of destructive legacies. It does require groping for dialogue between generations, groping for new trust and confirmation of the value of close relationships. For the pastor and counsellor, it is all about connecting listening and speaking. There are always ways to conceive in which, even in seemingly disloyal decisions, loyalty can become visible anew and affinity can be reconfirmed. Perhaps precisely by taking responsibility for new choices, even if that carries a risk of causing changes in relationships. However, loyalty needs to be promoted and extended forward. We are heirs and testators of the future.

This also applied to Gideon, son of Joash the Abiezrite. God bestowed him with a mandate to destroy his father's idols. The people of Israel have become entangled in the nets of idol-worshipping. Gideon stands between generations. It is moving how, in this brief, rather unobtrusive Bible story, loyalty between father and son continues to move back and forth in a very respectful and dignified way.

8.3   The purification of legacies: Judges 6:25-32

Gideon is ordered by God to destroy the legacies of his father Joash. He certainly does not do that impulsively. A lot precedes his purifying campaigns. To begin with, we are first told that the sons of Israel committed evil in the sight of the Lord. The people have waged wars, been defeated, and strange customs penetrated their religious devotions and worshipping. During the reign of Joshua, he did a lot to reinstate the Yahweh cult in Israel. But after he died and the previous generation who knew him passed away, a generation arose that neither knew something about the transformations of Joshua, nor of the rituals in worshipping God and what he did for them (Judges 2:10). A wind of change swept through the country. Thus, the following warning: "I am the Lord your God; do not worship the Gods of the Amorites, in whose land you live. But you have not listened to me" (Judges 6:10). Unfortunately, the children of Israel started to worship foreign deities: Baal and Ashera.

It was believed that whoever worshiped Baal as a god should become blessed with fertility, including the fruits of the land. No wonder, that in times of famine, much was sacrificed to Baal in the hope of rain. Fertility from idols was also important for women who, for whatever reason, sometimes stayed in the Baal temples for a while with the expectation of being able to conceive.

In times of crisis, children were even sacrificed to Baal in hopes of good will. This was an abhorrence in the eyes of God. In terms of the Yahweh cult, there were very strict orders and regulations concerning worshipping of Baal. Ashera was represented with a pillar or erected pole, especially in Canaanite regions, symbolising a mother goddess.

Ashera appears 40 times in the Bible, always as a forbidden idol and often mentioned in the same breath with Baal, almost like a 'couple'. In ancient

Bible translations, such as the Dutch translation (the '*Statenvertaling*' – State translation), the feminine aspect of Ashera is left unidentified by translating it into more masculine terminology, namely, as a 'horrible forest god.'

God forbade the worship of idols because it was believed that productive power could then be transferred to natural and material objects, granting promises regarding numerical success like material gifts from nature, fruits, animals and children. Promises included rain, harvest, productivity, fertility and even miraculous healing. Biblically, this detracts from confidence and trust in the God of Israel whose power does not reside in the blind and destructive forces of nature. His power is described as relational: Mercy and justice for those living in injustice. God is angry with the addiction to such powers, viewed as sheer idolatry. He started to punish the people due to their lack of responsibility to their religious legacy by putting the promised land and worship cult in the hands of looters and other peoples who humiliated and exploited them.

Despite severe punishments, the Israelite people remained stubbornly dependent on Baal and other deities. Finally, God handed them over to the Midianites, a people supported by Amalek. The Amalek-people had a negative charge and association against them. This we gather from the Exodus and desert tradition. They were specialists in exercising surprise attacks on the people of Israel. The strategy was to attack from the back of the procession where the most vulnerable were located. The crops on the land were destroyed by the Midianites, so that there was no longer a daily portion of food for the Israelites. Hunger became a daily threat. As often is the case, hunger becomes the reason to turn to God, screaming and pleading for help. And it is right here, at this stage, that Gideon enters the stage of Israel's weal and woe.

The calling of Gideon

Eventually the Israelites cried to the Lord because of Midian. The Lord then sent a prophet to tell them that although he had snatched them from the power of Egypt, and from the hand of all the oppressors of Israel, they did not listen to the voice of the Lord (Judges 6:7-10). An angel of the Lord came and sat down under the oak in Ophrah where Gideon, the son of Joash, was threshing wheat in a winepress to keep it from the Midianites. The angel approached Gideon and confirmed that the Lord is with him, calling him a mighty warrior. However, Gideon doubted due to everything that had happened to them.

He started to negotiate and said: "If now I have found favour in your eyes, give me a sign that it is really you talking to me" (Judges 7:17). He then went in and prepared a young goat, and from an ephah of flour, he made bread without yeast and offered it to the angel under the oak. With the tip of the staff that was in his hand, the angel touched the meat and the unleavened bread. Immediately fire flared from the rock, consuming the meat and the bread. Thereafter, the angel disappeared. Within an exclamation, he faced the angel of the Lord. The Lord then said to him: "Peace! Do not be afraid. You are not going to die" (Judges 6:23). Gideon built an altar and called it: "The Lord is Peace." He was then ready to face the Lord in order to hear what his calling was about.

Judges 6:25-32

25That night the LORD said to him,

> "Take your father's bull, the second bull seven years old, and pull down the altar of Baal that belongs to your father, and cut down the sacred pole that is beside it; and build an altar to the LORD your God on the top of the stronghold here, in proper order; then take the second bull, and offer it as a burnt offering with the wood of the sacred pole that you shall cut down."

27So Gideon took ten of his servants, and did as the LORD had told him; but because he was too afraid of his family and the townspeople to do it by day, he did it by night. Gideon destroyed the Altar of Baal.

28When the townspeople rose early in the morning, the altar of Baal was broken down, and the sacred pole beside it was cut down, and the second bull was offered on the altar that had been built. 29So they said to one another,

> "Who has done this?"

After searching and inquiring, they were told,

> "Gideon son of Joash did it."

30Then the townspeople said to Joash,

> "Bring out your son, so that he may die, for he has pulled down the altar of Baal and cut down the sacred pole beside it."

[31]But Joash said to all who were arrayed against him,

"Will you contend for Baal? Or will you defend his cause? Whoever contends for him shall be put to death by morning. If he is a god, let him contend for himself, because his altar has been pulled down."

[32]Therefore on that day Gideon was called Jerubbaal, that is to say,

"Let Baal contend against him,"

because he pulled down his altar.

Conjugation of verbs: The reframing and narrating of time – 'a time as new'

From generation to generation, Israel had worshipped foreign gods, always mentioning Baal and Ashera. Idolatry became a custom and ongoing religious legacy in Israel. After Gideon had built his altar, 'The Lord is peace', God spoke to him during the night and ordered him to destroy his father's idols. Twice it is clearly stated that it concerns matters of 'his father', the generation before Gideon. The summoning came to him in the mode of three imperatives: Take! Tear down! Cut down! It is striking that the assignment to build a new altar was suddenly not set in the mode of an imperative but is written in a *futurum*: "Then you have to build." This difference in conjugation of time seems inconspicuous, but it is quite significant. In the grammar, the turn of time points to a 'time as new' that did not exist before. Grammar can be ethical as well. It does not consist merely of written characters. Conjunctions can write new history and call time into being.

Space for justice: On the top of a stronghold

Gideon was summoned to build the altar "on top of the walled fortress/stronghold". It literally refers to a fortress. Fortress is a common word in the Bible, often also used for God. Psalm 27:1 says: "The Lord is the stronghold of my life" (צוּר, flint, rock, fortress, cliff; מִשְׂגָּב, high place, fortress, protection, stronghold, refuge). It means more than just a military castle, citadel or fortress, as often translated. The concept entails more than merely being a strong building (stronghold). It has also an ethical meaning as space for righteousness: A place of refuge, *safe house*. It is the place where the poor (*anavim*) feel safe and be protected. Therefore, when Gideon destroyed the idols and built the altar on top of the mountain, this restored place became a safe space, a haven, a place of refuge safeguarded by God as the One and only.

To make the movement from imperative to *futurum* plausible and, thus, create a new time frame, Gideon took ten men from his servants. In this context, the number ten is not insignificant. Ten is the number of adult men required to celebrate a Jewish prayer service up to this day. Ten men are a *minjan*. (In Judaism, a minyan (Hebrew: מִנְיָן \ מניין *minyán [min'jan]*.,pl. מניינים \ מִנְיָנִים *minyanim*, is the quorum of ten Jewish adults required for certain religious obligations). The Talmud, Megillah 23b says when ten Jews come together, God is in their midst. When Abraham summoned God not to destroy Sodom and Gomorrah, ten righteous men were enough for God: "I will not destroy her for the sake of ten" (Gen 18:32).

According to Luke 17, there were ten leprous men who were healed by Jesus. One came back to give thanks! We could thus say that Gideon and his ten men are going to celebrate and worship; acting out their confidence and trusting as an exemplification of religious dedication and pious worshipping.

The way through the night until dawn: The next morning

Apparently, Gideon was afraid to be seen during the day by those who belonged to his father's house and by the men of the city. He therefore exercised the destruction of all the places of worshipping idols during the night. He destroyed the altar of Baal, and with the slaughtering of the second cow, he made an offering on the new altar on the top of the mountain.

When the night was over and it dawned, the city woke up. When the men of the city saw what happened, and knew it was Gideon who was responsible for the destruction, they 'straightened their shoulders' and headed straight for Joash, the father (literally it said that the shoulders of the men were strong). They demanded from Joash: "Bring out your son, so that he may die, for he has pulled down the altar of Baal and cut down the sacred pole beside it."

At that moment, something very dear and special happened. After Gideon first vouched for his father by purging his inheritance from idols, the father, in turn, was now responsible for the son as being threatened by the inhabitants of the city. That exemplification of trustworthy reciprocity between father and son is moving indeed. First it is Gideon, who albeit on behalf of God, put an end to the father's slavish dedication to idolatry, and then, without a word of protest, the father took the place again to vouch for his son, literally substituting the place of his son. This act is liberating and life-giving, opening up a new future for all involved. This son will not die but live! The legacies have been sifted out and the asymmetry between the two generations has been restored – a new beginning dawned.

8.4   The revolving slate

One must face the following reality in life: We cannot smooth out all wrinkles in human existence. We are frail human beings exposed to failure, wrong-doing, shortcoming, injustice and irresponsible behaviour. Therefore, the following intriguing question stands: What is going to happen when legacies cannot be purified or restored? When deficit, damage and guilt cannot be rectified or stopped and become unintentionally being transferred from one generation to another? Nagy calls this predicament a *revolving slate*. He borrowed this concept from economy and the judicial regulations for law and order (judicature). He refers to 'mutual accounts' and 'rotating account' which are recorded in a so-called 'ledger'.

What Nagy had in mind is the fact that the generational account can become quite 'heavy' and the receiving person overburdened, even be blamed for issues that one is not responsible for. And so, a revolving slate becomes established; that is, a new victim is established because a person with an unpaid debt transfers the 'guilt' and hurt to another relation, other than the one where the debt has been caused. The slate causes a kind of 'displaced retribution'. In intergenerational terminology, the 'revolving slate' implies that the children inherit an account about something that was unsettled between the parents and their ancestors. The outstanding guilt of pre-generations becomes the responsibility of possible 'innocent children'.

The revolving slate is about more than an ongoing alcohol addiction transferred from one generation to the next. Eventually it takes on the form of a kind of *self-fulfilling prophecy*. The latter sketches a quite bleak situation and would without any doubt be a hopeless prospect. Nagy was sensitive to the ethical consequences of shortcomings and unsettled conflict of parents on the self-esteem of children. When parents and bystanders do not see and recognise that a situation is endangering and hampering the self-confidence of a child, they themselves carry the outstanding bill (deficit) with all its consequences and thus contribute to the burden of the intergenerational account. In this way, entitlement becomes a harming factor. It becomes a kind of indictment and invoice to be settled. This credit account often has a destructive effect: A kind of built-up right to take over the deficit as claim that eventually needs to be settled – *destructive entitlement*. The implication is that the innocent other creates a bill to be attended to (destructive entitlement) and thus the need of vindication and retribution. It becomes an entitlement that a child receives, unsolicited, an injustice that can turn into a retributive right with which the deficit is recovered from innocent third parties. Due to 'destructive entitlement', the motivation of children to obtain fair and constructive modes of justice becomes impaired and could eventually be obstructed. This personal obstruction contributes to distrust and split loyalties. Eventually, the latter can curb further constructive development (adulthood). It could even damage the so-called third factor in intergenerational relationships: the justice of the human order. When the latter is violated due to a massive distrust in the relational reality, the eventual innocent third factor is grieved and deeply wounded. In fact, it even puts the unknown future about a humane society at risk. In this sense, destructive justice influences personal life, where it causes internalised damage. The account is usually declared to innocent third parties and to a next generation. And so, a *revolving slate* is established.

History shows that children who suffered parental injustice eventually take this legacy over in the mode of a claim and obligation. We see an example in Europe where in the 1960/1970s many guest workers were brought in from Turkey and North African countries to commit themselves to the reconstruction. They worked hard, long days, many hours and thus contributed to the economy. In time, their families also came to live here. They gathered in close communities and formed neighbourhoods. This first generation has made a major contribution to the prosperity of the Netherlands. Unfortunately, the balance of what has been given, and what has been received, was not reciprocal. The unbalance created a generational predicament in the form of a shortcoming. The children of these immigrant workers stand between two cultures and have difficulty knowing which country they belong to: That of the country of origin of the parents or that of the new country. They are often stigmatised as foreigners even though they were born here in the Netherlands.

During the economic crisis, a guest worker was fired. In this way, the legacy of the youngsters became destructed and negative, including crippled family honour, disadvantage in income and education. They had to take responsibility for these negative consequences resulting in what can be called a 'destructive right'. In this way, the second generation was placed in a negative light. Eventually destructive rights became translated into protests, riots and crime, which, in turn, call for legal processes and punishment like imprisonment. The question is whether it would be helpful to see and acknowledge that this revenge and anger is a form of setting right the wrongdoing inflicted to their parents. They want to 'pay back' (in the place of their parents) by acting due to the negative impact on parental legacies. This phenomenon of 'paying back' (substitutionary responsibility) which one can call *vicarious parental giving*.

Loyalty to the previous generation was also visible in the student uprisings during 2015 in Stellenbosch. The revolts threatened to get out of hand for a moment. An unexpected lecture was introduced by Prof Dr Pumla Gobodo-Madikizela (Research Chair in Studies in Historical Trauma and Transformation at Stellenbosch University). In the morning before the lecture started, she had conversations with student leaders. The phenomenon of the revolving slate could be traced back in those conversations. In her lecture, Prof Gobodo addressed the phenomenon of repetition of trauma in children of parents who were forced to live in irregular locations (townships). The repetition of that trauma then functioned as a destructive right. She used an example from that morning's conversation with the students.

A black student told the group how confusing it was for him to live in a house with others (students' dormitories) during his studies and to have the luxury of showers and toilets in the passageway. When he spent the weekend with his parents in the township and saw how his old mother had to walk many metres to a dirty toilet at night, he was troubled with anger and shame. His troubled response was due to what had been lacking her all her life and which still had not changed. Prof Gobodo explained that for this student, pars pro toto (a part or aspect of something taken as representative of the whole), the trauma of the parents was still an open wound. The pain and anger due to the poverty of the parents, which was still the same, bothered him. It journeyed with him and became a heavy burden as an unpaid bill. This revolving slate does have implications on self-esteem. It can very unexpectedly become displayed in actions of retaliatory revenge (out of loyalty) as transferred and presented to third parties. The trauma of the parents appeals to children to give (paying back) vicariously in the form of anger and resistance. According to Prof Gobodo the student rebellion created an opportunity for the students to claim payment of that bill, inherited from the destructed legacy; the rebellion as exponent of destructive entitlement. This made it clear that the student uprisings narrated a multidimensional, and, above all, an ethical relational story.

What about guilt accompanying the legacy?

The question that remains to be answered is the following: What happens when there is guilt attached to the legacy due to injustice, but no justice has been done yet to address that debt? How does this deficit or shortcoming accompany the transfer of the legacy to a next generation? Does the liability in these cases pass from parent to child? In this regard, the notion of the 'sins of the fathers' in the Bible can be informative indeed.

8.5   'Sins of the fathers': Exodus 34:4-7

In pastoral conversations, Bible verses occasionally emerge, raising questions about how God punishes children for 'the sins of the fathers'. An example of this is found in Exodus 34:4-7. Here we read that Moses had to chisel out the two stone tables for the second time. Moses went up Mount Sinai early in the morning. Then the Lord came down in a cloud as if eternity passed by. Moses then addressed God, the One and only. He made use of the text in Exodus 20:4-5. But interesting, he did not repeat the text literally. He reframed the text within a more compassionate perspective: "*The Lord, the Lord, the compassionate and gracious God, slow to anger, abounding in love and faithfulness, maintaining love to thousands, and forgiving wickedness, rebellion and sin. Yet he does not leave the guilty unpunished; he punishes the children and their children for the sin of the fathers to the third and fourth generation*" (Ex 34:6-7).

Moses uses all the words he could find to name God's attributes. This is the God who he learned to rely on during the long journey with those unruly and stubborn people through the desert. All those words precede the saying that God visits the iniquity of the fathers to a third and fourth generation. But what about the second generation?

What is striking is that the second generation is missing here, which could perhaps at that time just be the addressed generation in the desert. Just as we are the ones addressed, being the current intermediate generation. The statement about visiting the next generations sounds harsh and judgmental at first hearing. However, the down-to-earth reality teaches us that the burden and consequence of injustice do indeed leave a trace that impacts future generations. Inevitably, future generations have to deal with the challenge of how to detect a constructive path in life, facing the debris that parents have left behind or caused.

The visiting of God (*paqad*) has indeed a negative and positive meaning: To punish, to call to account and to pay attention, to care about, to care for someone's fate. The sequences do not refer to the fatal necessity of a causal link. God merely calls human beings to accountability, that is, to care for the third and fourth generations. And here, I would like to emphasise that it does not say that God will punish children for the injustices of previous generations. It should therefore be repeatedly and emphatically stated: There is no causal link!

God visits the children with his compassion in addressing the failure of parents, confronting them and challenging them to restore the good, so that the next generation will suffer less from it. Each generation is thus given an assignment, a chance to settle outstanding accounts of the parents, and not to fall into the same trap, repeating previous mistakes without being timely warned.

What is comforting in this text is that there is a limitation: Up to the third and fourth generation, the rebuke is coming to an end. This warning and summoning to act in a more responsible way is now further highlighted by Moses in terms of what preceded the rebuke: A movement of grace that continues infinitely into thousands of generations, at least two thousand generations. The calculation is in the plural and that is an indication of amazing grace – "Showing love to a thousand (generations) of those who love me and keep my commandments" (Ex 20:6).

In Ezekiel, God seems to put an end to this idea about the third and fourth generation: "The fathers eat sour grapes and the children's teeth are set on edge. As surely as I live, declares the Sovereign Lord, you will no longer quote this proverb in Israel" (Ezekiel 18:2-3). Sons and daughters will not die because of the sin of the fathers and mothers! It is for your own account (Van Rhijn & Meulink-Korf 1997:16).

On evil, guilt and forgiveness

The verdict uttered by Meulink-Korf and Van Rhijn seems quite a harsh judgment: "It is for your own account." In doing so, they follow Buber's vision that guilt cannot remain unaffected and cannot be settled by anyone other than the person who caused it. There can be no forgiveness in the sense of just washing away debt. Their pronouncement has everything to do with personal liability and accountability.

Unsolicited, every person has to deal with debt that is passed on from generation to generation. We all run into it from time to time. The worldwide shock caused by the Covid-19 crisis has sharply reminded us of the debt that weighs on everybody, that is, how we created and contributed to a world in which this explosion was possible.

The question arises of how we pass on evil and injustice, how we relate to it personally. And at the same time, how we relate to debt and guilt that cling to it. Guilt always has relational consequences. Guilt lies between people and first belongs to the person who caused it. It cannot be undone by third parties. The complexity of guilt and forgiveness requires attention and there is much to be reflected upon from a relational and ethical point of view.

However, even before we speak on guilt and forgiveness, in the next chapter we will consider and reflect on the acts that precede guilt: Injustice and evil done to others. How we as pastor and counsellor can help perpetrator(s) and victim(s) depends in part on how we relate to evil and to those who cause it. And sometimes, we ourselves are deeply involved as well. We cannot exonerate ourselves.

CHAPTER 9

Injustice and evil: The interplay between perpetrator and victim

While writing this book, the undergirding question surfaced: How can authentic dialogue provide a structure for communication and a framework for humane guiding in pastoral care and counselling? One of the major challenges is the overcoming of personal resistances and prejudices that have the potential to objectify the other person as well as ourselves. Objectifying the other prevents the heuristic search for dialogue and the focus on subjectivity and intersubjectivity. It is inevitably the case that everyone can become exposed to objectification. It can happen to us all. It is conceivable that we have a one-sided bias for persons who have wronged, disrupted or damaged someone's existence and obstructed the other's quest for humane treatment and trustworthy encounters. One can even respond with heavy resistance, up to rejection. The real challenge in humane caring starts with this resistance by exceeding prejudices. Thus, the burning question: How does one respond to relationships tending to become biased? The question is important because the challenge in authentic dialoguing and humane encounters is to always instil justice to all others, to apply a multi-directed approach whether the other is perpetrator or victim. After all, you are neighbour to all human beings, whether friend or foe!

At stake in authentic dialoguing is the establishment of fair and trustworthy relationships. Relationships are ethically based. That is why we have the emphasis on an unbiased habitus of caregiving stewardship and service.

9.1   Relating to the Other/others: The art of caring and helping

Jonathan Sacks wrote about helping the enemy, quoting Deuteronomy 22:4: "If you see your brother's donkey or his ox fallen on the road, do not ignore it. Help him to get it to its feet" (Deut 22:4). The explanation of this verse in the Talmud continues: "If [the animal of] a friend is to be unloaded and the animal of the enemy is to be loaded, then you must first help your enemy – to suppress bad inclinations" (Bava Metsia 32b). The Torah does not teach: "Love your enemies." The Torah teaches: "Help them!" (Sacks 2019:158-159).

The realm of presencing in pastoral caregiving: *Coram Deo*

Conversations about perpetrators, guilt and forgiveness are recurring themes in helping and caregiving. In human encounters, one inevitably needs to face both 'good' (trustworthy) and 'bad' (untrustworthy) people; one has to meet perpetrator(s) as well as victim(s). As already argued, multi-directed partiality is inclusive. In helping and caring, the challenge is to be with 'them', where they are; experiencing and sensing them within space and place; living in coexistence together and meeting them irrespective of who they are, always willing to be present and available. That is indeed the case in all forms of helping, caring, counselling and ministering. Specifically, in the pastoral ministry, our being there for them operates on the basis of the principle of living '*coram Deo*' – an acute awareness of the presence of God, facing the Lord. We stand there together with the other, irrespective of the question of whether the other is our enemy or opposition. We stand before God, regardless of one's wrongdoing, irrespective whether we are 'good' or 'bad'. Thus, the very challenging question: How to remain faithful to the recognition of the other as a unique subject when injustice and guilt are at stake? The art of caring and helping is the almost impossible skill of discovering the other as person, unique subject, and humane being; that is, to probe behind the vulgar behaviour of the 'monster', the vulnerable and frail human being.

From a dialogical point of view, in caregiving we should become aligned with the principle of multi-directed partiality in order to enhance the quality of the relational interaction between people. The quest for balancing and the search for a middle position are indeed challenging and difficult. It is in this respect that a dualistic view of good and evil becomes a huge obstruction. From the perspective of the extremes (either or), it is virtually impossible to relate both to the perpetrator and the victim, maintaining the approach of multi-directed partiality in caregiving. Motivation and support are most needed in order to act more dialectically. According to Nagy: "… the dialectical approach defines the individual as partner to a dialogue, that is, in a dynamic exchange with his/her counterpart: The other or non-self" (Nagy and Spark 1973:19). The other as the opposite, that is the challenge in guiding the perpetrator on the basis of the prospect that he/she is subject and not demeaning object.

Basic vital existential questions

When we need to face the magnitude of evil, we are suddenly overwhelmed with questions regarding the ultimate in life. How can we as a subject approach the other person, despite his/her malice? How can we see and recognise the other as a subject? What helps us not to fall into the trap of objectification, and thereby place evil outside us? Does the perpetrator need our attention and care as well, or should the transgressor be left in the lurch and become excluded from the relational and mutual dynamics?

There are the following recurring questions that have echoed through all the ages regarding the character of forgiveness and guilt. From the side of the victim: If I forgive, does it mean that I undo the other person's guilt? And, if I cannot forgive the perpetrator, I feel guilty. But how on earth is that possible? From the side of the perpetrator: I have asked for forgiveness, but the victim refuses, what can I do?

In the pastoral ministry, these questions become even more difficult when the God-question is posed. Suddenly caregivers have to deal with the theological legacies of evil, guilt and forgiveness. Comments such as: "You must always be able to forgive everything because Jesus says so and demands it from Christians." But is that really the case? Or: "Because God forgives man, shouldn't we always forgive everything and everyone?" But is that indeed the case and the demand of the gospel? Is it indeed true that violated human relationships are suddenly restored and become reciprocal merely on demand by a voice from the outside so that conflicting human beings are miraculously reconciled into trusting relationships? Confusion about evil, guilt and forgiveness can keep people immensely busy and become an obstacle to finding new confidence and establishing trustworthy interaction.

Answers to questions about guilt and forgiveness are never instant and readily available. They always require careful weighing, some kind of wrestling and torment. Debt and forgiveness can never be generalised and should never become detached from the very specific person and context; it always depends on unique people within the circumstances of a very special event. It tells about specific people. Guilt is always relational-ethical; it concerns the perpetrator, but simultaneously always affects several other people involved as well. It concerns at least victim(s) and perpetrator(s) and all others related to them. The structure of groping for dialogue certainly appeals to one to operate within the confines of multi-directed partiality, especially when one must deal with the complexity of biased transactions in relational networking.

Establishing a relationship of trust requires approaching, seeing and hearing the other/others as unique subjects. At the same time, one needs to become aware of the ethical challenge, namely, to take up responsibility for the relationship and to act in a fair and trustworthy manner. Guiding people in the precarious processes of injustice, guilt and forgiveness requires personal preparation and unconditional dedication. This kind of preparation needs what one can call in a very witty way: Attention to the *hygiene of caregiving*; it means paying attention to how to relate in a fair way to evil and dealing with the intriguing question of who caused it. That preliminary work is now under discussion. The next chapter will take a detailed look at guilt and forgiveness.

Towards a dialectical attitude

Appropriate multi-directed partiality is about a dynamic position. Within the dynamics of fair balancing, it is centrifugal, taking a middle-position. This attitude always approaches the ethical concerns of right and wrong, the complexity of perpetrator and victim, from a dialectical perspective. An inclusive approach cannot operate within the opposing and extreme position of either/or. Furthermore, for multi-directed partiality, a position in the middle does not mean neutrality, but the flexibility of alternating partiality. "The dialectical resolution is never a bland, grey compromise between black and white, it is living with live opposites" (Nagy and Spark 1973:19).

A dialectical attitude can be delicate and inconvenient indeed, because it implies involvement as well as the challenge to simultaneously deal with contradictions. If one does not become aware of all the complexities, one easily falls prey to the trap to put evil outside oneself, acting as if evil is not being part of one's own relational reality. One cannot distance oneself from evil.

Keeping at a distance happens, for example, when evil is connected to past experiences by putting the blame solely on the other. This is been done frequently by pointing to them as the guilty ones, as being essentially evil, bad perpetrators. In this way, we keep our distance from evil and people who wronged, while exonerating ourselves. But by doing this, we jeopardise the quality of the relationship. In fact, we violate the ethical quality of the relationship because we resist taking responsibility for evil, nor for guilt, neither for reparation, nor forgiveness. Thus, the intriguing question for the caregiver: How can we relate dialectically to good and evil at the same time without distancing ourselves from the ethos of sincerity and trustworthiness? Before we get to an answer to these questions, we have to delve even deeper into the trap of allocating evil a place outside the realm of personal responsibility.

The ethical predicament: If we can only name 'evil'!

According to the Biblical account, it seems that from the beginning of creation, human beings found it extremely difficult to relate to 'good' and 'evil' in a fair and responsible way. The tendency is to always see evil as principle or substance exterior to the essence of our being human. To objectify evil as a metaphysical reality is to complicate ethics. The more evil becomes externalised to the realm of fatal causality, the more irrational presuppositions will be created, and the impression will be strengthened that the interplay between prosperity/welfare and adversity/misfortune is determined by the a priori of fixed regularities outside the realm of personal responsibility.

What we experience is that when evil becomes objectified, there are many attempts to qualify and name the external realm of mischief: the serpent, the devil, the evil, the evil spirit, the Baal, the witch. These are identified as the causative agents of evil. When evil is defined and identified by one denominator, it becomes so easy to act in a very passive and ignorant way; we then start to tune in with Doris Day: "Que sera, sera, whatever will be, will be." And when we are faced with this very mechanistic regularity of fate, we introduce God as a *deus ex machina'* (a god introduced by means of a crane in ancient Greek and Roman drama to decide the final outcome).

In the Christian tradition, God is often designated as the cause of misfortune, sickness and death. As if we think we can detect exactly how God rules life. In this way, God also becomes an object to be manipulated by sheer prescriptions in terms of selfish need-satisfaction. It is then very easy to just ignore the fact that God made himself known as a merciful and caring entity (subject) who enters into a relationship with human beings on the basis of a covenantal promise that he will always be there where we are; the ontology of being-with (him being a unique subject). By the attempt to determine a causal factor for the happenstances of life and the cause of history, we start to abdicate from humane responsibilities. When evil is placed outside of man (God, idol, witch), it seems as if it is not our responsibility anymore. This happens in explanatory theories based on mechanistic causality as indication (rational, positivistic explanation) of the disruption of existence in history. It is then so easy to point the finger to violent blacks, smugly whites, nationalistic reactionists.

Within religious paradigms, the culprits are then: Muslims, Christians, Jews as the source of evil. Or in times of the corona crisis: The 5G cellphone towers as original cause in the spreading of Covid-19. We argue: If only evil has a name, it becomes manageable and so we can excuse ourselves. But when it comes to dialogue, we have time and again argued that authentic dialogue is not established within the fixed stipulations of prescriptive principles, mechanistic systems or static rules.

If one really wants to opt as a compassionate caregiver, and to develop a helping ability in the guiding of people according to the principle of multi-directed partiality, this is not possible when evil is located in a metaphysical realm outside man. Martin Buber lectures on that impossibility. He was careful enough not to choose between the extremes of either or, the good or the bad person, goodness or evil. He rather opted for the middle, centrifugal position.

9.2　Martin Buber: The middle position between good and evil

Martin Buber does not locate evil outside man, but places man him/herself in the middle position between good and evil. In his book *Martin Buber: The life of dialogue*, Maurice Friedman did some extensive research on the philosophical and theological lectures of Buber, including the question regarding the place and position of good and evil in human existence (Friedman 1955).

For Buber, evil is not merely a matter of conscience. Nor are good and evil dualistically located over against one other. Buber opted for a middle position. He wanted to avoid giving evil an absolute power as some kind of blind fate, dictating the trajectories of our being human. We should relate personally to both evil and good because it is precisely in this kind of existential repositioning that new opportunities are created for the making of responsible decisions in our way to liberation and a significant future. For Buber, the focus on the future is vital and decisive so that evil and guilt cannot automatically be passed to future generations.

Reaching out wholeheartedly

By the notion of *with all your heart* (wholeheartedly), one detects the close connection between Nagy and Martin Buber in their sincere concern for the next generation. According to Buber, it is crucial for man to always attend to personal self-development and how to maintain a balanced and healthy lifestyle. One needs always to be engaged in the praxis of daily happenstances in life. And this endeavour entails much more than just relating to good or evil. It takes practice to keep asking questions about how to serve life with an *undivided heart* (Deut 6:4); a heart that is not bound by false pretences, a heart that does not waver between two often opposing polarities. And this endeavour is never finished but is an ongoing challenge.

An undivided heart, focusing on liberation and justice, cannot develop in an atmosphere of utter contradictions such as a choice between good and evil, hope or despair, strength or destruction. Focusing on the good things in life can be merely realised in an atmosphere wherein different aspects of existence are both recognised and receive significant attention. This requires the boldness to recognise the ambivalence that exists in all life endeavours: Good and evil, meaning and hopelessness, boldness and vulnerability. This kind of realism must reckon with the fact that to deal with ambivalence and the many paradoxes in life implies a willingness and commitment to a lifelong learning process (Friedman 1955:21). Human beings are in desperate need to seek direction in life skills; that is, how to deal with all bipolarities simultaneously. For Buber, this means not to attend merely to the human and existential dimensions of life. To cope with life is a religious endeavour as well. At stake is what God requires in order to deal with the demands of relational networking. Furthermore, in line with this, the question also applies to every person of how to address dialectical issues regarding nature, conservation and occurrences within the happenstances of life. Our disposition should therefore be all inclusive and multi-dimensional.

Withdrawal: The selfish monologue within the guilt of missed opportunities

When human beings withdraw and ignore the realm of relational networking, the fatal consequence is that one becomes disconnected from his/her own unique destiny and sense for purposefulness. After all, according to Buber, every human being is irreplaceable and therefore unique. Everybody is challenged to make a unique contribution to life. "It is everyone's duty in Israel to know and to remember that our capacity is unique in this world. We are irreplaceable. Never there has been on earth a human being with the same abilities and characteristics. If we were replaceable and only a reproduction of previous species, we have become indeed redundant and not necessary; every human endeavour is then in vain. However, every single person is a new appearance on earth and his/her task is to perfect his/her aptitude in this world" (Buber 1964:19). When human beings separate themselves from relationships, from the interplay: Man and fellow human beings; our being human and our relationship to this word/nature and the whole of cosmos; to great or small devastating disasters, we start to separate ourselves from our unique calling and vocation in life. We, thus, withdraw from the quest for human well-being and the promotion of general welfare and universal wholeness. This tendency increases as we become encapsulated within the confines of a private and incurvated monologue. The chance of dialogue is thus lost. And that threatens the future. Buber constantly emphasises that whoever withdraws from the relationship becomes guilty of staying within the limited confines of our self, the solipsism of incurvature. *Original guilt consists in remaining with oneself*" (Friedman 1955:117). Being self-centred, no decision has been made in terms of relating to good and evil, nor to deal with guilt, nor to the person concerned (the possible victim).

To relate means to reckon with evil and to find a form of how to exemplify good, how to do justice to irreversible injustice committed to the other/others. Relationships ask to find a way to invest justice into the realm of injustice, to confront evil with good, with reaching out despite the atrocious impact of evil on human dignity. Those forms become public when victims start to relate to evil by doing good (the investment of love to fellow human beings). The following example illustrates this reaching out.

Connecting to evil by doing good

It so happened on the 27th of January 2020 in Amsterdam. It was *National Memorial Day* in the Netherlands because it was 75 years ago that the Auschwitz extermination camp had been liberated by the Russians. By mentioning Auschwitz, all other extermination camps are mentioned at the same time, where Jews, Gypsies, homosexuals, disabled people have been murdered. It concerns more than six million unique human children. In the Netherlands, 102 000 Jewish people were taken to the camps in wagons for animals via the Westerbork transit camp. Someone there had written their names by hand on a list for transportation, one by one. Now after 75 years, all those names and ages of the 102 000 people taken away and murdered were publicly pronounced at the Westerbork camp. This continued day and night for five days. More than 800 volunteers called the names at the top of their voices.

Eva Weil spoke at the Auschwitz monument in Amsterdam on that day. As a three-year-old girl with her parents in Westerbork, she was on the tip to become transported. Fortunately, liberation came in time for them. Still, now in old age, she gives informative lectures at schools to make young people aware and to sensitise them that this destruction must not be forgotten – never again. She talks to young people about the future and how to prevent this inhumanity from repeating itself. Nowadays she does that together with the granddaughter of Albert Gemmeker. He was the German commander who entered 80 000 names by hand in Westerbork. The granddaughter of this commander wants to constructively use the evil of her grandfather for promoting a more just world. Even though Eva Weil was actually a victim and her comrade the perpetrator's granddaughter, they work together in the midst of the extremes. In this way they relate to evil and good.

'To relate to evil and good' is an appeal to reframe that which is bad and gruesome, to restructure it and to do justice to those suffered due to inflicted injustice. This also applies to those who suffered to discriminatory violence and became humiliated. In this attitude, inhumane acts are not left behind to be buried in the graveyard of the past. They are bent constructively as benevolent investments to the next generation, the offspring. According to Buber, the art of relating resides in self-sacrifice, not to be personally self-centred anymore. Taking a position in the middle requires critical reflection, considering choices, and the making of decisions. Every day one should start anew, again and again. After all, relating to evil and good is of significance not only in the great inhuman disasters of history as in the shared examples. Every day, time and again, it confronts one with the whirlpool of deliberate, interpersonal offenses and failures despite good intentions.

Indecision: A whirlpool next to an abyss

Friedman points out that, for Buber, indecision is the first step to evil: "He portrays the first of these stages, decisionlessness, through an interpretation of the myths of Adam and Eve, Cain and the Flood. When Adam and Eve take the fruit, they do not make a decision between good and evil but rather imagine possibilities of action and then act almost without knowing it, sunk in a 'strange, dreamlike kind of contemplation'. Cain, similarly, does not decide to kill Abel – he does not even know what death and killing are. Rather he intensifies and confirms his indecision. 'In the vortex of indecision … at the point of greatest provocation and least resistance', he strikes out" (Friedman 1955:118).

For Buber, indecision exposes human beings at point zero; the most vulnerable position in one's existence. It is then virtually impossible to make an informed decision because the ability to resist evil is at point zero. In the confusion of indecision (Buber calls it vortex – whirlwind), man acts irresponsibly and foolishly. "In no other area of human experience it is more difficult to preserve the attitude of the 'narrow ridge' than in one's encounter with evil, yet here too the metaphor of the 'narrow ridge' expresses the central quality of Buber's thought" (Friedman1955:9). "Although many significant changes occur in Buber's thought during the fifty years of his productivity, it is in this middle position between the unreality and the radical reality of evil that we shall always find him" (Friedman 1955:23).

So, people always find themselves in the middle position, always facing the discomfort of an ambivalent attitude that never disappears completely. This middle position, thus, always requires unique considerations. When we realise the challenges related to this middle position, it becomes clear that it is a dynamic, active place that compels one to take action and to move forward. Indeed, a very complex position in which we cannot quickly judge evil and injustice. But, unfortunately at the same time, one is challenged to form an opinion about it and to become related as well. The predicament of this position is that one cannot calculate the amount of guilt prematurely. This inability makes it extremely difficult to gain insight into the complexity of forgiveness. It is about that narrow ledge above the abyss of nothingness, where one is challenged to relate in a humane and significant way; where one is forced to make choices that are fair and reliable for everyone involved, even for offspring, the so-called future generation.

Tendency to good and tendency to evil

Martin Buber was brought up within a Jewish background. He studied both Hasidic and Rabbinic traditions. It is therefore understandable that his mindset and reflection were shaped by the Hebrew framework of reflection and conceptualisations from the Old Testament. Within this paradigmatic background, both good and evil tendencies are viewed as inextricably linked to our being human. Both good and evil urges are part of every human child. That man has received both is based on a striking grammatical spelling in Hebrew in Genesis 2:7.

God forms man (used as an inclusive category) from red soil (the dust of the earth). "The Lord God formed the man (הָאָדָם; ha·'a·dam) from the dust (עָפָר; a·far) of the ground (הָאֲדָמָה; ha·'a·da·mah)" (Gen 2:7). For formation (*wajitser* – pottery) there is a double *jod* which is attributed to both inclinations; *yetzer ha-ṭov* and *jetser ha ra*. Adam, man, was formed by God, by making use of earthen elements (red soil) which included both good and evil inclinations (*yetzer ha-ṭov* – the good impulse and *yetzer hara* (Hebrew: יֵצֶר הָרַע – the congenital inclination to do evil). *Yetzer ha-ṭov* (יֵצֶר הַטּוֹב), the good inclination, refers to the potential within us to do the right thing. In Jewish thinking, this good inclination (impulse, plan) is closely related to the creation narrative in Genesis, where it is indicated that when the Lord created the heavens, earth, all living creatures and breathed his life-giving breath (spirit) (נֶפֶשׁ *nép-eš*) into man, he proclaimed it all to be very good (*tov me'od* – טוֹב מְאֹד). God breathes his life-giving breath, *nefesh chaja*, so that man can distinguish and thus learn to relate to both. This explanation does not recognise evil as an anonymous force that has power as a blind fate outside of man or has power over man. It is like a process in which the movement constantly goes back and forth between the different inclinations and options when human beings have to make important decisions in terms of the planning of their life schedule. In this regard, Buber refers to the metaphor of 'the narrow ridge' where it points to the fact that man eventually lets good impulses (inclinations) prevail over evil tendencies. This bipolar dynamic is not about a dualistic polarity but indicates a dialectical attitude in the recognition of evil and good when dealing with the complexities of life-giving forces (see the link with life-giving spirit – נֶפֶשׁ *nép-eš*).

Buber is not alone in a dialectical attitude to evil and good. In the last century, dictated by two world wars, philosophers and theologians searched for informative theories (often explanatory theses) and models of how to relate to evil without losing sight of the good in creation as well. It is especially the German theologian Karl Barth (1886-1968), who has elaborated the relation to evil in *Kirchliche Dogmatik* (*Church Dogmatics*) (KD III, 3 par 50).

9.3 Karl Barth: The speechlessness of naming evil (Das Nichtige – *sheer nothingness*)

Barth discerns evil from good, transcending the boundaries of a dualistic view when it comes to a dialectical approach. According to him, there is no name available to name 'raw evil', because the magnitude of evil is not merely about the negative, like destruction and annihilation. It is also not about the absence of God's righteousness. In fact, raw evil is related to sheer nothingness (*Das Nichtige*). Nothingness is simply *that which is not* belonging to the humane creation of God. But it is, in the cosmic realm, a real entity as well. Not naming it, or to refer to evil as a non-substantial factor of opposition and resistance, constantly threatening and corrupting human existence, are indications that evil is principally non-comprehensive and undefinable. Yet, Barth believes, not naming the extreme evil at all would be more unjust because those who suffer from it would be left unarticulated in injustice. The nearest indication of evil is that it belongs to the shadow side of God's creation. However, Barth perceives evil in its full seriousness as 'the object of unqualified fear and loathing' which 'takes the forms of sin and pain, suffering and death.'

Due to the very precarious, dubious position of evil in creation (that which *is-not* but indeed exists), the only way to talk about evil is in the language of dialectics. Within the realm of creation, there exist light and dark, land and water. There is, in other words, a negative side as well, but then always dialectically connected to a positive side. There is not only a *Yes* but also a *No*; not only a height but also an abyss; not only clarity but also obscurity; not only growth but also decay; not only opulence but also indigence; not merely beauty but also ashes; not only beginning but also end. This shadow-side is, however, as much a part of the perfection of creation as the positive side. To equate it with evil as *nothingness* is no less than blasphemy. So, creation is not merely filled with good, it also includes the dark side. Those are the negative aspects in existence such as suffering, illness, death. These also belong to God's good creation, which is comforting and shows that God also relates to man in the shadow side of his/her daily existence.

God called out to the light, 'day'. Against the shadow side, God called 'night'. The good and the dark side are like day and night in our existence; they alternate in which the discontinuity and continuity of existence are exposed. Life is about living the ambivalence, paradox and dubious side of daily existence. God operates within this dialectical movement and bestows his mercy despite the threatening side of nothingness.

The further implication of Barth's view on the displacement and inexpressible position of evil in creation is that naming evil in terms of a 'shadow side', and the connection with 'night', is not enough. *There is an evil that cannot fit into this schema of categorisation.* It is too gruesome and unjust because there are no words to describe it. We know of such great evil in both personal life and historical events. There is such a magnitude of injustice in experiences of life that there is in fact no language to describe its connection to God and his creation. At the same time, not naming it becomes even more unjust. It cannot be overlooked, because then those who suffered and are still suffering are overlooked, they are then labelled as the nameless ones in history.

Horrific evil happens and belongs to existence. But how do you call it when it does not deserve a name, and it is so alien to the good in creation? "This evil is so horrible to God that it should never and never at all be mentioned, nor mixed in one breath with something that occurs in, or stems from, the good of creation" (Van Doorn 2003:140). For that evil, Barth came up with the non-translatable word *das Nichtige*. Our predicament is that sheer nothingness points in the direction of absolute meaninglessness. And such a category resides outside and beyond any system of God's pronouncement, and is thus incomprehensible but must be named yet, bringing one to the brink of human articulations as well. However, besides this predicament, every person has still to relate to it. After all, it is also our responsibility!

We cannot ignore our obligation; we just have to relate to it. The same responsibility applies equally to man as cause of this evil, contributing to the magnitude of injustice. Clearly, Barth will not, and will never, put the cause of this evil before God. We must keep away from causal interpretations with God as the source. What stands out is Barth's dialectic approach, namely, that both the good and the dark side belong to God's creation. The implication thereof is that we need to live within this dialectic by means of the contra of justice and good. In this dialectic dynamic, man is called to relate to the worst forms of evil. This is our vocation and responsibility. That requires an attitude of reflection, an approach of decision-making, choices, wisdom of life, so that, as we learned from Buber, we move away from indecision as an exponent of evil.

In Friedman's work on the notion of indecision, we came across a biblical version, used by Martin Buber. Buber detected how indecision played tricks on Adam and Eve when they stood before 'the tree of the knowledge of good and evil'; that one tree in the garden from which the fruits should not be eaten, and yet, we read that they approached the tree. The same phenomenon of indecision played a role in the story of Cain when he murdered his brother Abel.

Both these two cases are quite decisive in terms of our argument that, due to the ethical character of relational networking, evil should be addressed. Thorough attention should be given to these texts due to the impact of indecision on the endeavour of fairness in human encounters. But also, and that could be quite decisive for pastoral caregiving, to discover how God relates to people involved in evil as well as to the guilt of fallible human beings.

9.4   On being human: The interplay man-woman within the framework of the knowledge of good and evil (Genesis 2–3)

With reference to Genesis and the creation narrative, Adam started to name the animals two by two. He gave names to all the livestock but suddenly discovered that he was alone without a partner. The Lord God then said that it is not good for the man to be alone and decided to make a 'helper' suitable for him; 'a help as an opposite'. Adam called her Eve, the living one (Gen 2:23).

In chapter 1 it was explained that 'helper' is not about a help that fits seamlessly with the human being (Adam). It rather points to differences between man and fellow human beings. In fact, that was the case from the beginning. Eva is 'an opposite', one who, in her gaze, observes; Eva becomes a figure inviting Adam to recognise and acknowledge her. The point is, from now on, man (inclusive category) has to live within the factuality of differences and diversity.

The tree of life: The knowing of good and evil

Suddenly, for the first time, the notion of evil (*ra*) turns up in the Bible (Gen 2:15). One tree has been planted in that garden, which bears knowledge of good and evil, including its fruits. The tree stands there as an upright sign, as a *corpus alienum* within the space of human freedom. God brought about an order within this space of human freedom; a kind of stipulation, directive and form of restriction, and thereby imposes a rule for what is not allowed within the freedom of creation. It turns out to be a disturbance, because the tree of knowledge of good and evil points to desire that arises from the start as an upwelling urge; the urge of grasping, and, thus taking in the fruit of knowledge about good and evil. And that is exactly what God has set a limit to. Man cannot know everything about right and wrong; it cannot be understood thoroughly. Not even to be grasped by force.

With this tree God has planted the everlasting question in the middle of life, namely, how to relate to good and evil within a clear restriction: Not to know it fully. It is impressive that the first human couple (pars pro toto) could not resist this temptation. It does not matter here whether it was the male or female who trespassed first, ignoring the limitation. Both made no deliberate choice to protect this director of knowledge. Both were not really committed to adhere to the restriction. In fact, both denied the limit that had been set and the assignment to relate to it appropriately. Both ended up in indecision. According to Sacks: "Man's first impulse is denial." Exoneration and scapegoating took over. The male started to blame the female, in turn, the female pointed to the snake in order to blame the serpent (Sacks 2016:161).

This is our predicament and short-sightedness: Guilt always resides in the other person, preferably outside us. Simultaneously the tendency is to separate evil from good. It is so easy to just make evil an object. By doing this, man places him/herself outside the possibility to relate to it. In turn, the implication is that man, thus, makes him/herself into a mere object, incapable of autonomy and acting from the confines of personal and authentic subjectivity. Sacks borrowed the following quote from Jean-Paul Sartre: "The self-deception that we are not subjects but objects manipulated by forces over which we have no control" (Sacks 2016:161). For Buber, Adam and Eve acted here not in freedom but based on indecision. In this way, they took the fruit from the solipsistic perspective of 'I am on my own', an isolated monad. In other words, choosing for themselves as an act of selfish maintenance. And that is beyond the parameters of a dialectical attitude.

The narrow ledge of discomfort

To exist as fellow human beings in coexistence is not easy and does not come automatically. Buber underlines the fact that it requires practice to live together with fellow human beings; that is, the art not to live in an atmosphere of mutually exclusive opposites, one opposing the other. To keep moving and not to dwell on the extremes requires constant probing and searching, considering and reappraising. This is the dynamic in the dialectic between good and evil, between hope and despair, between tenderness and violence, and ultimately, between life and death. And sometimes that ledge is narrow and uncomfortable: *The narrow ridge* (Friedman 1955:17, 113, 126). And yet, man is called to endure ambivalence and to persist living in an incessant dialectical movement. Living together is a matter of constant weighing of, oscillating between seeking justice while confronting evil, especially in the engagement with those who cause evil and injustice. And most importantly, do not overlook yourself!

After the wrongdoing, God judged Adam and Eve. They were severely rebuked. So, God punished both as well as the snake. In future, their way across the earth will be a way of pain and toil. The predicament right now is that they possess knowledge concerning good and evil. There is no way back, they cannot reset time. As punishment, God sent them out of the garden of freedom. But then divine mercy interfered: They will not go naked through the world, not uncovered (Gen 3:21).

God clothed them with animal skin garments, fitting seamlessly. It is like receiving a second skin, preventing them from shame; the humiliation of facing the world in the nakedness of shame with all the trouble they will have to face while journeying through this world; existing within the parameters of the curse that now bedecked the earth. They are like skirts pointing forward to Joseph's garment (Gen 37:3), and Aaron's priestly garment (Ex 28:4). This was a wonderfully comforting sign of God's mercy despite his judgment of man becoming a captive of his/her ambivalence and indecision. From the so-called 'fall' of Adam and Eve, this broad and general judgment from God will echo all through our human existence, in all circumstances throughout the ages. This will be exemplified in the Cain narrative, in his indecision, and the murdering of his brother.

9.5   God within the realm of human coexistence: Human beings living together (the God-Cain-Abel triadic)

After the topic 'man and his wife', the theme 'man and his brother' follows. The book of Genesis reveals the contours of how human beings in their struggle to live together as brother/sister; narrating how difficult it is to live in coexistence with fellow human beings and to create one community. The struggle it will bring about is revealed in the different family stories. So, we will continue with this theme until the last chapter of the book of Genesis.

Only after Jacob's death does *man* (furthermore indicating a comprehensive understanding of our being human without any reference to gender-based differentiations) and his family become a people – a kind of 'nation' called the people of the Lord. According to Genesis, the birth of relational and communal life is not described in terms of moralistic laws. God holds man personally accountable for his/her choices. There are two options: life or death (Deut 30:19-20). The claim is an appeal not to shudder in indecision when making fundamental decisions regarding the promotion of humane coexistence. And indecision, Buber teaches, is the beginning of evil. We see it in Cain's murder of his brother Abel.

Cain is the man of the earth, agriculture, and Abel is the shepherd, the livestock. They are two brothers, existentially totally different. These are actual differences in terms of sheer factuality, merely for the time being, but Cain could not tolerate the differences and became a victim of deadly rivalry. In this story too, God revealed how he relates to those who have committed evil.

Genesis 4:1-17

> [1]Now the man knew his wife Eve, and she conceived and bore Cain, saying,
>> "I have produced a man with the help of the LORD."

²Next, she bore his brother Abel. Now Abel was a keeper of sheep, and Cain a tiller of the ground. ³In the course of time Cain brought to the LORD an offering of the fruit of the ground, ⁴and Abel for his part brought of the firstlings of his flock, their fat portions. And the LORD had regard for Abel and his offering, ⁵but for Cain and his offering he had no regard. So Cain was very angry, and his countenance fell. ⁶The LORD said to Cain,

> "Why are you angry, and why has your countenance fallen? ⁷If you do well, will you not be accepted. And if you do not do well, sin is lurking at the door; its desire is for you, but you must master it."

⁸Cain said to his brother Abel,

> "Let us go out to the field."

And when they were in the field, Cain rose up against his brother Abel, and killed him. ⁹Then the LORD said to Cain,

> "Where is your brother Abel?"

He said,

> "I do not know; am I my brother's keeper?"

¹⁰And the LORD said,

> "What have you done? Listen; your brother's blood is crying out to me from the ground! ¹¹And now you are cursed from the ground, which has opened its mouth to receive your brother's blood from your hand. ¹²When you till the ground, it will no longer yield to you its strength; you will be a fugitive and a wanderer on the earth."

¹³Cain said to the LORD,

> "My punishment is greater than I can bear! ¹⁴Today you have driven me away from the soil, and I shall be hidden from your face; I shall be a fugitive and a wanderer on the earth, and anyone who meets me may kill me."

¹⁵Then the LORD said to him,

> "Not so! Whoever kills Cain will suffer a sevenfold vengeance."

And the LORD put a mark on Cain, so that no one who came upon him would kill him. ¹⁶Then Cain went away from the presence of the LORD, and settled in the land of Nod, east of Eden. [17]Cain knew his wife, and she conceived and bore Enoch; and he built a city, and named it Enoch after his son Enoch.

Eve gives birth twice

The Genesis 4 narrative immediately starts with the narrative on pregnancy and birth. After the climax of intercourse – they became one flesh. According to chapter 3, Adam made a mess, in chapter 4, Adam made love. But now verse 1 makes a quite remarkable announcement. Eve gave birth to a 'man', the reference is gender based: male. Eva said: "With the help of the Lord I have brought forth (*cana*, קנה *qnh*) a *man*." And his name will be Cain. Acquiring קנה in the text has a positive meaning: To acquire as to buy, to buy off (ransom), to deliver (Ex 15:16; Ps 78:54).

Eve gave birth a second time after Cain. Now she gave birth to a son and a *brother*. This is expressly stated: "She gave birth to his brother." His name is Abel. That this child is a brother is emphasised because it is repeated seven times in the narrative. It is the same with the name of Abel. And this is important because, according to the Bible, the number seven indicates fullness, sufficiency. Abel's name means: In vain/meaningless, vapour, light as a feather. And this is how the book of Ecclesiastes starts: Everything is in vain (everything is like '*abel; hă-ḇêl*, הֶבֶל). Life is framed by vanity, everything vanishes. In the name of Cain's brother, Abel, it is as if this naming already indicates the vanishing of life.

In the order of their existence, Abel, the youngest, is mentioned first. Abel becomes a shepherd and Cain as a servant of the red soil (*adama*), a man of the earth; the red ground from which man is formed, the land where man is called to serve and to take care of the Garden of Eden (Gen 2). Cain appears to be deeply connected to it: Five times the notion of *adama* returned, connected to his name!

It is quite strange that preference for the second son, more than the first, is a theme in the book of Genesis. In the Biblical tradition, the firstborn is the *bechor* (בכור) and has the birth right. In Genesis there is always a reversal in who the *bechor* (firstborn) is and we see a preference for the second: Cain/Abel, Ishmael/Isaac and

Esau/Jacob and Perez/Zerach, Manasseh and Ephraim. God's preference for the second has nothing to do with privileges but is focused on the notion of election which determines an existential vocation and destiny. Election refers to responsibility and the latter determines everything that lives on earth, even the being of coming, future generations. It emphasises that in the order of God, there is no natural system as a natural succession. In this order, the preferential ḥēsēd of God prevails.

The gift of bread and the gift of flesh

Abel kept flocks and Cain worked the soil. Cain brought some of the fruit of the soil (a gift of bread) as an offering (gift); Abel brought fat portions from some of the firstborn of his flock. The Lord looked on Abel and his offering (gift, *mincha*), but on Cain and his offering he did not pay attention. The text clearly states 'gift', and not 'sacrifice' which is often translated as such and which is given a sacral touch that can quickly be interpreted moralistically. Due to the connection between offering/sacrifice and the ritual of worship, the impression could be that Cain's sacrifice would be of less quality. That is not in the text. That is about sheer interpretation. Both brothers offered a *gift*. The text is not about a qualitative difference but about disposition and dedication.

God saw Abel and did not look at Cain. Cain received no attention. He turned to Abel, the man who is thin with lightness and exposed to vanity. God did not 'see' (accept) Cain neither his gift. For Cain, this was so confusing that he became angry and his face was downcast.

The shattering of visage: 'Cain's face fell to the earth'

God saw that Cain's face (*panim* פאנים, face, person, presence) fell, his face shattered so that his whole being became downcasted (Gen 4:5). Face appears five times in this text, as much as the *adama*. *Panim* is more than the face that can be seen; it is about the true face (visage, make up as indication of true disposition) that hides behind someone's facial appearance. It expresses the entire human being in his/her availability to hear and be heard.

Whoever shows his face, is willing to answer the Other/other with *Hinéni* (Here I am). In terms of Levinas' emphasis on visage as a sign of authentic human encounters, face is about the unmasking of true intention. Facing a human being coincides with the quest and source for authentic humanity, founded in the prior of a face-to-face encounter (visage) and directed by the principle of *l'un-pour-l'autre* (one-for-the-other). And answering is exactly about *l'un-pour-l'autre* (one-for-the-other), encountering within the space of brotherhood and sisterhood. *Panim* is never singular in the Bible. Man is always a human being within fellowship with the Other/other (with fellow human beings). Facing the other is never in the singular, in encounters there are always more faces at stake – a multitude of faces. Without the other, man has no face, there is no *panim* to be seen. Without visage, face vanishes. Martin Buber says about the fall of Cain's face that, in fact, he turned away from the relationship, and without true relationship, he hit the bottom line of human existence, vanishing into the nothingness of red dust. In other words: He turned away from the 'I-Thou' dynamics and became degraded and objectified within the fixity of 'I-it'. And with that, every dialogue vanishes like a mirage, and hope for a better future disappears into the nothingness of futility.

Cain separated himself from God and his brother. What immediately became noticeable was that God did not separate himself from Cain. He addressed him with a surprising question: "What made your face becoming downcast? Isn't it true that whoever does good brightens the face, lifting it up?" (*nasa*, lifting, lifting up, pushing upwards, carrying away – 'he raised', נשא). *Nasa* is also used for forgiveness. A sincere and soul revealing question from God to this man probed into the fabric of our very being human. Probing into the how of being is such an intensely relational question. It reveals the sincere divine involvement of God with the predicament of our being human. According to God, there is no reason to hang your head and become downcast. "There is no cause for it; you have only to do well and then you will be able to stand firmly on your feet, with upright stature" (Casuto 1998:212).

The question of 'losing one's face' is the question about an invitation to come in touch with the basic features of our being human, namely the quest for subjectivity, the art of decision-making and the graceful opportunity of choosing. The direction of God's wisdom is: Whoever does not do good and whose face does not open, easily falls prey to sin and deceitful passion. The evil inclination becomes a wild untamed gallop not controlled by the rein of good inclination

A challenging gap in the text

A transition then followed. Cain spoke to his brother. The different versions of the text clearly indicate that it is not quite clear what the text wants to narrate. In the middle of the verse is a *pisqa*, a gap, a space. It is to be questioned whether Cain would have said directly to Abel: "Let's go out to the field." There is no object behind: "And he said … *wajomer*". There is an empty space like in poetry! Is this the threatening space of the introductory preface, the confusing whirlpool of indecision? Other text versions have filled in the space: Cain said to his brother: "Let's go to the (open) field". Casuto opts for the following translation: "And said … And when they were in the field …" (Casuto 1998:213-214). There in the field, they were like brothers among themselves, without witnesses. Except for God, and the storyteller(s) who knew what God said.

And so, it happened

Wajehie, and so it happened: Something that had never happened before, something new. Cain stood up to his brother and killed him. For the first time, there is a reference to death; violence and murder entered the scenario of our being human. No one saw how it happened. There was no witness at all. And yet, God responded with a confrontational question: "Where is your brother, Abel?" Your brother, of course!

With all the violence in history, that rhetorical question continues up to this day. Where is your brother, your sister? A direct claim, the question applies to everyone, to you personally. And so, one can continue, filling in the names of men, women and children, the names of all those marginalised people who disappeared from our radar screen and WhatsApp, the faceless voices behind Facebook. But why is that? It happened because our face became downcast instead of doing the right thing and standing up straight. At stake here is the question of responsibility for the brother, the sister, the fellow human being, for each other. The question that not only asks who the other person is for you, but first and foremost, who you have been for the other person.

The question to the brother is a radicalisation of the question of God to his parents in Genesis 3:8: "Where are you?" And now in the case of murder: "Where is your brother?" Cain said: "I don't know." After the manslaughter, there is the denial, the lie. Cain's answer is staggering: "Am I my brother's keeper?" It is not only a denial of his personal responsibility, but of '*l'autre, c'est mon affaire*' ('The other is my concern'). Man denies his claim, and thus, his guilt by putting evil outside himself. An absolute indifference, he makes no difference between the enemy and his brother's life, he makes no difference between life and death, not even the extremes concern him. In this regard, Levinas writes: "The personal responsibility that one person has to another is such that God cannot abolish them." In the Rabbinic commentary on the dialogue between God and Cain, his answer: "Am I my brother's keeper?" is indicated as being more devasting and vulgar than impudence. It is posed by someone who has no sense of human solidarity and who (like many philosophers) thinks that everyone exists for themselves and that everything is allowed. And a page further: "The sin committed against God falls under divine forgiveness. However, the sin that offends man is not God's business" (Levinas 1987:45-46).

Then the Lord said: "What have you done? Listen! Your brother's blood cries out to me from the ground" (Gen 4:10). God heard a voice that called, that screamed forth from the *adama*, streams of blood (plural) pouring down from your brother. That multiple blood fused, every drop counted and added to the avalanche of streaming blood. The only address where the call of that multiple blood was heard was within God himself. The scream of man reaching heaven came from a brutal act of committed violence, reflected in a dark pool of bloodshed. It echoes through all the ages so that God hears lament until this hour (Ouaknin 2001:65). Ouaknin thus refers to the comfort of a God who, even today, hears the cry of the multiple blood that flows from murder and violence all over the world.

Cain will no longer experience the power of his *adama*. Previously, the serpent and the *adama* had been cursed due to the excessive desire of Adam and his wife and their denial of guilt (Gen 3). But now, in the case of Cain, man is cursed. Cain was driven away from the *adama*, wandering over the earth without direction (*erèts*). The worst thing happened to him. He became separated from the face (*panim*) of the *adama*.

A sign of life for Cain!

In the negative question, "Am I my brother's keeper?" lurked shrewd denial. But on a more fundamental level, Cain acknowledged his crime. The denial was in fact a kind of acknowledgment. His guilt was too big for him to carry and so he was hiding from God's face. Actually, he was repeating what happened before with Adam and Eve. He even feared to be killed himself.

From now on, Cain's total existence would become exposed to vulnerability. But God heard him and promised to care for him with merciful compassion. After receiving the news of the curse, Cain responded: "My punishment is more that I can bear" (Gen 4:13). But God said to him: "Not so" (Gen 4:15). The intention of punishment and retribution was not to destroy and kill Cain. Therefore, God put a mark on Cain so that no one who found him could kill him. In fact, God made a very strong statement to safeguard Cain's life: "If anyone kills Cain, he will suffer vengeance seven times over" (Gen 4:15). "Even in the dark hour after he has become guilty against his brother, man is not abandoned to the force of chaos. God himself seeks him out, and even when he comes to call him account. His coming is salvation" (Buber 1952:56).

In this sign, God and Cain remain connected. God did not move away and became detached. God stayed true in his faithfulness to this frail human being. From now on, God no longer spoke directly to Cain again. There is no indication of further conversations. The only further reference to Cain was in the third person and quite formal. We only find matter-of-fact information regarding his marriage, family building projects and offspring so that a certain distance was maintained.

Cain departed from the face of the Lord. East of Eden he had intercourse with his wife (he acknowledged her). She became pregnant and gave birth to a son. And there is posterity for Adam and Eve. After the murder, well … posterity … reopening to the future. Who would have thought about such a benevolent outcome? Cain built a city – a community, and gave the city the name of his son: Enoch (the devotee).

God and Cain after the murder

Despite the brutal act of murder, God maintained a relationship with Cain. In God's care to Cain we can see that his judgment is not equal to the eastern laws of revenge: An eye for an eye, a tooth for a tooth. God heard Cain and promised him that violence would not destroy and kill him. He will bear a sign that anyone who dared to kill him will be avenged sevenfold. It is the first time that God installed a sign (*ot*), a mark of protection. The sign will be a memorial and at the same time a protest against blood feud.

The sign confirms God's steadfast love and covenantal faithfulness. There are many examples of this kind of confirmation by means of a sign. In Deuteronomy 6:8, 11:18, it is about the *shema* as a sign on the hand and forehead. This sign is about a short prayer, a kind of licensing on the event of journeying with the Lord by means of the GPS-directive of his command; a kind of commitment to love God with an undivided heart. In Exodus 13:9, 16, they are Matzahs as the sign of God's merciful passing by during the Passover night. In Genesis 9:12-13, 17 the rainbow is placed as a sign, with which God reminds himself of the covenant with the people! These signs keep telling us about the faithfulness of God: "He who does not let go of what his hand started."

Cain was the first in the Bible to bear this sign of God's faithfulness as a mark in a more personal capacity. In the Rabbinic commentaries, a multitude of guesses were mentioned in order to detect what the sign would have looked like. In fact, the entire alphabet was brought into discussion in order to decipher the meaning of the mark. There is also a difference of opinion about the location of the sign, the forehead, the hand, or the heart. However, what is worth recognising is that God remains dialectically related to those guilty of evil. The person who has done wrong is not condemned completely and forever to remain a captive of irreversible transgressions. Being guilty is not about a total lockdown. God created a new opening. It is not the first time that we have seen this attitude of God. After all, it started with Adam and Eve, after eating the forbidden fruit of the tree and hiding in the garden as a withdrawal from an intimate relationship with God. And now it happened again with Cain. It is a recurring rhythm in the long lines from Genesis to the sealed grave of the buried Christ. Suddenly, the impossibility of an absolute imprisonment behind a large and heavy stone slab became an astonishingly opened, unlocked grave – the resurrection of Jesus the Messiah. The sting of death, the stench of decay, the shame and guilt of judgment on fallible, perishing human beings are transformed into the fragrance of life, shining forth from the sign of the resurrected Christ; the sting of death (cross) had been transformed into the victory of life (resurrection). The mark is reframed by the aroma of life as revealed in mortal bodies. Therefore, despite the convulsion of death in mortal bodies, life is at work within a *futurum*.

These stories about the attitude of God's caring concern are teaching lessons to all human beings about how to relate to the earth (*adama*), to those who have done evil and are guilty and despairing victims. We are therefore called to take the middle position towards perpetrator and victim and all others concerned.

9.6 Our vocation to the earth (adama)

The story of Cain's failure and transgression is not merely tragic. It also has something endearing, Cain's deep connection with the *adama*, the earth, the dust of red soil. Marianne Storm has studied, in a challenging book, the meaning of life on the face (*panim*) of the earth, the *adama* (Storm 2006). Life on the face of the earth is a new form of language in which the earth itself is becoming a subject. It displays an intimate connection between our being human and the earth. As such, man and earth connect relationally within a very intimate mode of stewardship. "The *adama* can produce crops and as a field she can withhold her yield from humans. The *adama* who is cursed due to man's gruesome abuse, produces only thorn and thistle (Gen 3:17-18), and to the man who killed his brother, the field yields nothing" (Gen 4:12) (Storm 2006:48).

From the beginning (Gen 2:6), *adama* has been relationally determined in a triadic relationship with God as initiator, man and his fellow human beings (the people of God – nation) as stewards, and the earth as common ground for human settlement (the cosmic dimension). To talk about the *adama* is for man to be aware that life is inclusive, and as human beings we are called to be available through and for the other. That availability is because of the appeal of the other/others to our creatureliness and intersubjective relationality as determined by the ethics of responsibility. That availability is due to the appeal by the other regarding human accountability. With that call, the human *I* is dethroned, and the autonomy of man is reframed in a new light. Therefore we receive the call to exceed the limitations of exclusive self-maintenance. A responsibility that is not tangible but that arises as being authorised by the other, *l'autre, c'est mon affaire* (the other is my concern) (Levinas). How inspiring and challenging it can be to feel and talk about the earth as a gift, to approach it as a subject, within the networking dynamic of intersubjectivity, and to hear the call that emanates from the whole of creation.

The *adama* is not a ground for taking root and settling and possessing. She is there to relate to it, as a person, as a subject. Storm concludes in her research concerning the difference between land and ground/soil (respectively *erèts* and *adama*) that *erèts* is about a givenness (it has been given to man as a gift). *Erèts* should still become *adama*; soil that needs to be reworked by Adam in the light of his commitment to serve the earth (*avodat* – the toil of work as service). This is the only way to make ground a safe space of home. That remains true and a vital challenge, wherever, whenever, worldwide, and in all time: *Ha olam*. The tragedy of Cain is that the earth is no longer home to him, he will wander through life estranged from the earth as a place for established settlement by means of stewardship and responsible being-with the other.

A plea for justice

Serving the earth, human stewardship is all about *justice*, the ethics of reliable accountability and fair responsibility. In terms of this ethical qualification, the earth remains the space of everlasting personal responsibility towards the other/others as well as to oneself. To become engaged with evil is in fact a plea for 'justice' between people, no matter the conditions, context and happenstances of life. That plea does not make forgiveness of guilt easier at all. However, it does make it more possible and feasible to take care of. Buber points out that it takes a process of repentance and reliability to gain confidence. It is about trust that was not there before and that arises from a process of authentic dialogue.

Forgiveness is a verb, a process in which the grammar of the verb moves from *praesens* to *futurum*. Martin Buber has described this existential route. We will continue with the explanation of that in the next chapter. Then we will also discover that Nagy prefers not to speak of forgiveness. He introduces the concept of exoneration. The latter applies mainly to intergenerational processes.

Within the context of this chapter, remembering the words of Martin Luther King is quite appropriate because they are an appeal not to blame, but to embark on a road that opens up new avenues for future peaceful coexistence. King said these words in Washington in his famous speech *I had a dream* on the 28th of August 1963. He challenged human beings to specifically place evil in the middle, not to shift it to the periphery of life so that human beings could exonerate themselves by starting to forget. On the contrary, we should continuously be related to the gruesome and destructive consequences of evil and its effect on human dignity and the maintenance of human rights.

> But there is something that I must say to my people, who stand on the warm threshold which leads into the palace of justice: In the process of gaining our rightful place, we must not be guilty of wrongful deeds. Let us not seek to satisfy our thirst for freedom by drinking from the cup of bitterness and hatred. We must forever conduct our struggle on the high plane of dignity and discipline. We must not allow our creative protest to degenerate into physical violence. Again, and again, we must rise to the majestic heights of meeting physical force with soul force.

CHAPTER 10

Reframing time: Guilt, forgiveness, exoneration

We need to take the very timely warning of Martin Luther King extremely seriously, namely, that we must not allow our creative protest to degenerate into physical violence. Entering the dialectical space between our good and evil tendency, multi-directed partiality has to explore avenues that can reframe the future into new opportunities to promote justice, fairness and trustworthiness. We are challenged not to merely 'restore' time but to 'renew' time. This endeavour implies that guilt should become reframed into a total new paradigm. Thus, the burning question: How is this possible without degenerating into the cul de sac of revenge and dread? How do we supersede the deadlock of guilt as final penalty without any option for the renewal of the relational networking, the application of relational ethics and the establishing of constructive connections for safeguarding a meaningful future for coming generations?

It is in this context that the notions of guilt, forgiveness and exoneration should be reassessed. Are guilt, forgiveness and exoneration merely attempts to turn a blind eye to irresponsible behaviour, the evil of ignorance and the violence of destructing the principle of *l'autre, c'est mon affaire* – the other is my concern?

10.1 Guilt and forgiveness within the confines of a judicial process

In the balancing of giving and receiving, there are many variables in terms of how people deal with factors violating the order of justice. When it comes to relational ethics, the intention is not to merely safeguard fairness and trustworthiness. Due to mistrust, injustice, hurting and human shortcomings, the balance time and again becomes disturbed by conflicting needs and loyalties. This brings us to the question of restoring the balance and to work towards healing and a new framework for human well-being. And it is right here that the notions of guilt and forgiveness come into play and need thorough critical reflection.

Guilt is a category sui generis. One could argue that guilt is a structure of our being in this world. As an existential category, even an ontic feature of our being human, guilt concerns everyone. Everyone is in debt; no-one is not guilty. Forgiveness concerns every human being. No-one wants to be cut off for good from the dynamics of intersubjectivity and relational networking. According to Martin Buber, one is guilty when the human order of existence is violated and damaged.

Guilt is related to the quality of choices regarding irresponsible actions, negligence of sound ethical directives, carelessness including what has been omitted. I am guilty when I deprive the other person of the justice of his/ her existence. That wide range of injustice includes physical violence up to manslaughter, spiritual violence that belittles, subtle comments, gossip. Blame is on the one who causes the injustice; the one who acts in an unreliable way. Guilt, therefore, always comes into being within relational interaction and the dynamics of intersubjectivity. Guilt is always relational because it affects one or more people. The question of forgiveness cannot therefore be a monological movement, but rather a search for the trust of the other person and, therefore, for groping for dialogue.

Following Buber, Meulink-Korf and Van Rhijn, we will reason that the beginning of the process of forgiveness starts with the following questions: How does the debtor relate personally to the debt? How does the perpetrator as a subject realise what the guilt caused by him or her, looks like? How did all the wrongdoings affect and damage the existence of the other/others? All these questions point to the fact that guilt, the acknowledgement of guilt and forgiveness are not about instant solutions but are embedded in complex processes, and therefore require personal insight, critical analyses, as well as practice to recognise them as ethical related issues and judicial in character.

Nagy introduces a new concept when it comes to blaming and the attribution of debt: *exonerating*. He refers to the possibility of relieving the burden of guilt on the basis of right and reasonable circumstances. As a family therapist, he sees exoneration in the intergenerational relationships as a constructive act when parents' guilt can be nuanced fairly and no longer must be charged in full. To lighten the weight of guilt also asks for a relational-ethical process.

Nagy emphatically distinguishes exoneration from forgiveness. He clearly opts for exoneration due to his fear that forgiveness is too closely associated with a general romantic understanding of generosity. Exoneration is definitely not about a cheap compromise. Exoneration should be linked to both accountability and retribution. That underlines the importance of introducing a juridical term. With the concept 'exoneration', Nagy appears to be seeking conditions which can transform fatal intergenerational transmissions. Exoneration functions within the relational ethics of the ledger. It should be linked to fairness and loyalty in order to contribute to renewed relationship and the possibility of transformation; that is, the making of a total new start.

Guilt and forgiveness: A recurring theme

In pastoral care and counselling, questions about guilt and forgiveness are a recurring theme. It is a complicated theme because guilt is seldom un-ambiguous. Forgiveness cannot seem to come about outside of the ethical conscience and sense of responsibility of both the victim and perpetrator. In connection with this theme, there are recognisable questions: What or who makes someone guilty? Who will suffer with the perpetrator due to his/her irresponsible behaviour? Who will suffer with the victim? What, if the perpe-trator does not confess guilt? Can a reimbursement be made? If that is not possible, is there a right to retaliation? Does a victim always remain a victim? These questions make it clear that we cannot answer the questions about guilt and forgiveness with general answers. After all, they always concern specific people: Both perpetrator and victim; all people are included. Guilt and forgiveness are complicated because injustice affects every person differently.

The relational complexity requires a pastor and counsellor to delve into the versatility and multi-dimensionality of human relationships and the dynamics of intersubjectivity. Insight is needed to relate dialectically to the processes of guilt and forgiveness. Following Nagy, Meulink-Korf and Van Rhijn, we are also directed by Martin Buber's thinking on the interplay between guilt and forgiveness. We will certainly return to the somewhat unusual but liberating concept of Nagy on exoneration, namely forgiveness as process, because it shows that debt does not necessarily have to be carried along as a heavy burden for future generations.

10.2 *The place of guilt in processes of healing and human well-being*

History has taught that guilt caused by human violence cannot be reversed. Our thoughts quickly turn to major disasters such as racism, genocides, the Holocaust, Apartheid. But not being able to undo guilt also involves crimes committed in the small, unobtrusive happenstances of everyday life; thefts, sexual abuse, aggression. The point is that guilt cannot simply be ignored or erased either. The human mind and body bear the scars from generation to generation. We see this in perpetrators of injustice and their families, and we also see it in those who have been damaged and hurt by it. These scars go with a legacy, sometimes not overtly unnoticed, but it can become destructively anchored.

When guilt remains unspoken and unaffected, the destructive trail deepens. Guilt dislocates and cannot remain unseen and untouched. It should be revisited and addressed exactly at the point where the hurt originated and the wrongdoing occurred. Guilt concerns the guilty one and should be traced down to the culprit where it belongs. Without acknowledging guilt, a victim is left in the lurch and eventually becomes a victim of his/her own contrition and pangs. It may give the impression that the guilt is shifting from perpetrator towards the victim, because the person hurt becomes involved as if he/she is instrumental to the harmful event. The place of the wrongdoing and guilt is with the perpetrator. If guilt is outstanding and nothing has been done about recognition and responsibility for the person, people or group concerned, no forgiveness can be asked. Eventually the victim becomes locked down in his/her predicament and that is unfair and unacceptable. Right at the beginning of this discussion on guilt, it should be made crystal clear that no victim should get the impression that the attention for the perpetrator leaves the people who bear the consequences unseen and in the lurch. Talking about forgiveness and reconciliation too soon does not make the world more just. And that is what it's all about.

That does not mean that a victim does not have to relate to the act or perpetrator and is forced to forget everything. The challenge to relate to guilt is complex, both for the victim and the perpetrator. The endeavour of relating to guilt requires, to a large extent, to be responsible for guilt as well as for forgiveness. Because at stake, in both cases, is the ethics of relational fairness/ righteousness and thus the commitment to the upkeeping of justice within the realm of intersubjectivity; that is, how to live in a humane and responsible way with the other/others. Neither the perpetrator nor the victim could be released from that responsibility and try to escape accountability.

The dehumanisation of guilt

With the dehumanisation of guilt is meant attempts to ignore, to deny or to withdraw from guilt. It also refers to attempts to get rid of guilt in terms of instant solutions and artificial acts: *the Pontius Pilate syndrome of washing the hands*. The dehumanisation of guilt includes, furthermore, acts of detachment like just washing away the stains of guilt or smoothing out the wrinkles of guilt, rinsing guilt, hiding behind rituals, forced forgiveness under duress.

Over centuries, the Christian tradition of faith has introduced various forms and rituals that would make it possible to undo guilt. For example, at the time of Martin Luther, guilt could be bought off through a ritual or indulgence in various forms. To this day, confessions of guilt can be whispered in the confessional without the victim taking part or even become addressed in his/her possible contribution to the wrongdoings. In this way, the guilt of the victim is unaddressed.

In the pastoral ministry, theological presuppositions sometimes sound like compelling morals. Rules that speak on behalf of the Bible are introduced: 'Well, this is our obligation to always forgive'; 'forgiving is our professional job'; '*actually*, we don't have a choice in this matter'. That '*actually*' sounds like a voice that should trigger my conscience and make an appeal to the victim without taking into consideration the pain and hurt inflicted by the wrongdoing. In the meantime, the victim must come to terms with the impact of personal woundedness on his/her sense of dignity. And worst of all, this kind of appeal to automatise forgiveness like a spiritual mechanism becomes identified with the 'will of God' or with the very pious notion of 'the example set by Jesus Christ, Superstar'.

With that alleged demand for forgiveness, tradition has too often over-looked what has really been suffered. The automatisation of forgiveness prevented caregivers and ministers from really dealing with the reality and contextual complexity. Often the impression has been left by tradition that the ability to forgive the perpetrator seems to be a greater act of faith (a kind of religious achievement) than the willingness of the perpetrator to acknowledge his/her guilt. How many men and women have been doomed to this piety of silence contributing to a negative morality of muteness!

All talk *about* guilt and forgiveness, all rituals, and prescribed, liturgical prayers and confessional rituals, do not necessarily change the position of the victim in his/her quest for justice. With instant forgiveness, the injustice inflicted on the sufferer and wounded person become camouflaged. Without any doubt, liturgical formulae and collective confessions of guilt can touch and encourage us. The advantage is that people become aware that they are at least connected to each other due to the fellow and mutual interaction of believers (*koinonia*) as well as a heightened sense of communion with God. But meanwhile, and this is quite unfortunate, formulae carry the risk of skipping the predicament of the other/others who suffer. Furthermore, a communal and a group's sense of guilt are not yet necessarily and honestly connected to the actual consequences of what that guilt entails for the victim. This means that public acknowledgment of guilt and doing justice to those who have been offended by injustice are only possible in a personal capacity: *I am guilty!* Guilt is not a feeling, not even in the liturgy, it is existential.

With this exposition, it seems that forgiveness and true acknowledgement of guilt are virtually impossible for fallible and deceivable human beings! It is perhaps possible that one should acknowledge that true forgiveness is a divine challenge and does not reside in the capacity of emotional human beings. However, forgiveness and reconciliation are fundamentally focused on justice and without recognition and repayment of guilt and fair retribution, no justice has been done. Eventually, innocent third parties then must bear the destructive burdens (both on the side of the victim and the perpetrator).

Careful insight and sensitivity are required of those who work in pastoral care and counselling. How can we best guide those entrusted to us, and who have put their trust in us, regarding their questions of guilt and their struggles to forgive in order to come to terms with the pain of hurt? How can we assist both perpetrator and victim in their quest for a fair and reasonable settlement of the inflicted trouble between them?

Pumla Gobodo-Madikizela pleads for reciprocity when she writes: "Victims need to a large extent forgiveness. This need should be assessed as part of the process of becoming a whole person. Simultaneously it disempowers the perpetrator in the sense that it deprives the perpetrator of the power to destroy or spare him/herself. This is part of the process of regaining self-confidence and becoming empowered again. By responding to the perpetrator's repentance with empathy and forgiveness, many victims regain the sense that they are morally important again" (Gobodo-Madikizela 2003:158). Now empathy is not yet a relief from guilt, but it can be an impulse to see and to discover the subjectivity of the other.

To be able to provide reliable guidance on guilt and forgiveness, we cannot ignore the awareness of our own experiences of guilt; that is, a personal awareness that knows about being guilty and sometimes being a victim as well. It is the other, perpetrator and victim, who remind me of my subjectivity, and, therefore of my responsibility. Therefore, dealing with guilt and being prepared to forgive are inevitably a never-ending, personal learning curve.

Guilt: An existential and relational phenomenon

Anyone who damages the existential human rights of a human being, and by doing this, neglects a basic right to exist, is to be blamed. Such a person is guilty in terms of violating the human dignity of the person concerned (Meulink-Korf & Van Rhijn 2002:147; 2016:100). Martin Buber puts it this way: "Guilt arises in the order of being when this order of human existence is violated due to the unjust exploitation of one person by another" (Buber 1957, Guilt and guilt feelings). Following Buber, Nagy also reasons that concrete guilt, inextricably, means indebtedness due to an existential embeddedness in the relational reality of daily living.

So, concrete guilt is not an abstract concept; it is not driven in the last instance by merely the fleeting and capricious experience of feelings (the affective dimension). In the first place, existential guilt is not about psychological phenomena such as fear of punishment or loss of love, as frequently argued by Sigmund Freud. Existential guilt can always be traced back to concrete acts of injustice and an acute consciousness of refraining from what should have been done in order to promote justice in very precarious settings. It concerns renouncing solidarity and neglecting compassion. Those who renounce compassion and withdraw from solidarity distance themselves from the reciprocity of a relationship and leave the other in the lurch. Even if we do not know about guilt caused by irresponsible behaviour, we are automatically engaged in a whole invisible network of others who were affected by my wrongdoing. It is often the case that one is not even aware of this invisible and silent audience and the multiple ripple effect of guilt.

A guilty party is responsible for his/her own fault. For both Buber and Nagy, existential guilt cannot be reimbursed by a third party. A ritual cannot erase guilt externalised from the personal framework of the victim's sense of responsibility. According to Buber, that is even the case with divine forgiveness. God does not forgive in an abstract metaphysical space. Forgiveness and guilt are focused on an awareness of true subjectivity. Within the mutuality of reciprocity and interrelation interaction between fellow human beings, it is only the perpetrator him/herself who can address personal guilt properly. Outstanding guilt cannot be forgiven by anyone other than the victim him/herself. No God, no minister, no judge, no guru, no king can grant forgiveness outside the parameters of personal accountability. Likewise, no one else can ask for forgiveness other than the perpetrator him/herself. Were it true, forgiveness would take the form of a metaphysically inspired omnipotence and that would exceed the boundaries of our being human; the interplay forgiveness-guilt would then become an inhumane business.

No one has any knowledge or information about what happens to guilt and forgiveness between God and man. That falls under the intimacy of the 'strange acquittal' (Meulink-Korf & Van Rhijn, 2002:59, 2016:38). That relational acquittal between God and that unique person takes place in a very sacred space. No human being can penetrate this space by means of rational speculation or positivistic analyses. That divine acquittal, however, does not discharge the responsibility for justice and righteousness between people. Rather, divine acquittal is a commandment for the reality of life lived. We should appeal to grope for dialogue where new confidence arises so that justice can be instilled.

This also affects society and its institutions. With regard to these social institutions, Gobodo-Madikizela focuses on the importance of personal acknowledgement as the first condition for a significant starting point for discussions on guilt resolution: "The question is no longer whether victims can forgive the perpetrators of their wrongdoing, but whether we can create conditions in all our institutions in which alternatives could be discussed in a frank and unbiased way. As far as the Holocaust is concerned, there is sometimes more emphasis on commemoration than on dialogue, while the dialogue is of great importance if my honest intention is that victims should live together with the perpetrators again, creating a coherent society wherein people of different cultures can live in harmony with themselves and all others. Of course, dialogue cannot solve all the problems of a society that has suffered massive violence. But opportunities can be created to broaden justice through telling, acknowledging and recording" (Gobodo-Madikizela 2003:146).

Neglected guilt

Guilt that remains neglected (untouched and unaffected) shifts as a negative relational legacy on the balance of give and take. In this sense, guilt becomes bequeathed. The victim's acquired, destructed right is often transferred openly, or concealed, to his/her nearest fellow human being, including his/her next of kin (*revolving slate*). It is often unpaid bills and unaddressed issues that hinder the progress and envelopment of reliable relationships in life. At the most unexpected moments, this can be claimed as overdue guilt. Neglected guilt can emerge and become visible as an avenging right (retributive justice) that is passed on to innocent third parties.

For Nagy, guilt resides in the fourth dimension of relational ethics, always in conjunction with all other dimensions of his view on the dynamics of intersubjectivity. Nagy prefers to speak of 'indebtedness' rather than pure guilt. 'Being indebted' exposes more directly the relational character of guilt because existential guilt is about 'being indebted (accountable) to … someone.' At the same time, this formulation says something about the complexity of guilt, specifically about the perpetrator's relationship to guilt. It addresses the fact that in the perpetrator's response, he/she cannot ignore the complex situation of the victim. Therefore, the culprit (the guilty one) is challenged to do something about his/her guilt. This implies to become engaged in an intensive revealing process wherein guilt cannot become neglected. On the contrary, the debtor has to start facing his/her guilt personally. For Nagy, this realisation is about an intrinsic tribunal in which the victim, and what has been suffered, becomes the perpetrator's conscience, creating a screaming voice that calls for retribution.

Forgiveness and reconciliation are often too big words, too comprehensive, too general in common language, to capture the magnitude of inhumane woundedness. Without perpetrators having insight into what they have done to people in their personal life or to society at large, these words become inappropriate to address the pain of the victim. Even though sincere and good intentions are sought to find new avenues for reconciliation, the reconciliatory process must face, time and again, disillusionment and disappointment. What is the reason? The options for building trust stand against the shipwreck of distrust and unaddressed woundedness.

Prof Christo Thesnaar (Department of Practical Theology, Faculty of Theology, Stellenbosch University) did some thorough research in his doctoral dissertation regarding the interplay between reconciliation, guilt and forgiveness (Thesnaar 2001). He served in the *Truth and Reconciliation Commission* in their attempt to create a forum where both victim and perpetrator could meet and share their painful stories without fear of prosecution. It was clearly pointed out that the unwillingness to acknowledge guilt, and the lack of fair retribution since the magnitude of guilt became too painful and massive, created stumbling blocks and made authentic dialogue virtually impossible.

To illustrate the impact of a sense of guilt on the transgressor (perpetrator), the author Antjie Krog (1998:46) referred to an anonymous letter by an Afrikaans-speaking, white South African, received by Archbishop Tutu during the second week of the trials. The letter had been disclosed and read to the audience. It read as follows:

> Then I started crying for what happened, even though I can't change anything about it. Then I started looking into myself to understand how it was possible that no one simply not knew and recognised what was going on! How on earth was it possible at all that so few tried to do anything about the demeaning situation? How was it possible that most of times I was merely a spectator, watching from the comfort zone of my private pavilion? Then I started to wonder and wrestle with the question: How is it possible to live with that guilt and shame from within the interior of my most intimate subjectivity and very being? I do not know what

to say; I do not know what to do; how to respond and to act. I apologise to you about my ignorance, inability to articulate my anguish and remorse. I am sorry for all the pain and the sadness I inflicted. I am not saying that very easily, due to external pressure. I say this with a wounded and broken heart, with tears in my eyes … (Thesnaar 2001).

Focusing on dialogue and new trust requires serious questions about guilt and forgiveness. Wisdom and patience are most needed in pastoral guidance, helping and caregiving. In his thinking, Martin Buber reflected on guilt and forgiveness. As a Jewish person, he was the victim of the brutal murder of many of his family members. His house and books, and some of his writings, were destroyed during *Kristallnacht* on the 9th of November 1938.

To his mind, there is a guilt that cannot be forgiven. And yet he realised that one must start to restructure one's life; one needs to take up responsibility anew. To become engaged in new forms of dialogue between people, hope becomes rekindled again. In the year of the *Kristallnacht,* he was appointed in Jerusalem, Palestine (at that time under British rule but later becoming the state of Israel). His emigration and becoming a citizen of Israel, and his thinking about guilt and indebtedness, are all part and parcel of his paradigmatic background at that time. It is also noteworthy that Buber was always prepared to advocate for one Arab-Jewish state. He mastered the art of transcending destructive revenge and sought, in the complexity of his context, for new righteous modes of significant coexistence.

10.3 Guilt and forgiveness in the thinking of Martin Buber

In his article 'Guilt and guilt feelings', Buber carefully explains how the questions surrounding the possibility of guilt and forgiveness are not about a once off solution. Both are embedded in an enveloping process (Buber 1957). This process is not merely about a personal, intrapsychic event, in relation to the self. The process of envelopment is also about an encirclement of the two concepts, analysing all the issues attached to both guilt and forgiveness, weighing them, discussing all the aspects critically within an honest dialogue. The point is, it asks dialogue, a kind of dialectic movement within reciprocal encounters, wherein both victim and perpetrator are willing to face one another. One has to become related to guilt; the issue at stake should be debated by both sides; it is a question for both debtor and victim.

For Buber, guilt is existential. Because when "someone violates the order of the human world, whose basic framework and paradigm are recognised as that of one's own and as valid for all human existence", thus, the reason why guilt can be classified as existential. Guilt feelings and actual guilt are not necessarily the same. There is an important distinction: Guilt resides in *being*, and in this sense, it is ontic. Guilt feelings reside in the affective dimension of the human soul, and in this sense, it is psychic. For Nagy, there is also a distinction. Guilt is concrete and existential and relational. Guilt feelings can be reduced to neurotic traits from a conflicting stream of thoughts; it is about an intrapsychic event that does not always have to be relational-ethical (Michielsen 1998:78).

According to Nagy, this neurotic feeling of guilt belongs to the second dimension, the psychological dimension; that is, how a person responds to the factuality of historical events and interprets them; how a person responds to needs, behaviour, emotional urges and observes the impact of life events on human existence, because all these phenomena determine individual behaviour. That is the reason why neurotic guilt feelings deserve expert psychological and perhaps psychiatric treatment. At the same time, it touches the fourth dimension because neurotic guilt is allied with loyalty and based on it. For Buber, neurotic feelings of guilt always affect the existential realm of being due to either a loss of trust between people, hampering factors during adolescence or earlier exposure to destructive violence.

The turning point: Repentance

Buber argues that a person can refuse to accept the consequences of his/her guilt and not hear the call to restore confidence. For Buber, to embark on the road to restoring confidence and trust, the Jewish concept of repentance (to turn around and to return) (*teshuva*; Hebrew: תשובה) is necessary, which means a reversal to good. Turning over to the good is only possible through penance and repentance, letting the good tension prevail over the bad (Van Rhijn & Meulink-Korf 1997:432). In this process of turning around, the pastor or counsellor can only guide someone towards repentance. Willingness cannot be forced externally. Whoever has caused evil must turn away from the abyss of his/her own soul by free will. Only in this space of self-confrontation and critical self-reflection the other person's call could be heard properly and answered appropriately (*respondeo ergo sum*). This is where the willingness to take responsibility for being guilty and authentic guilt arises. According to Buber's reflection, this requires a route of critical self-enlightenment in order to embark on a process of repentance and acknowledgment of guilt. That is not the end of the turnaround: Recognition requires restitution in order to make the guilt bearable for the victim.

For real forgiveness to take place, Buber is convinced that reconciliation is decisive. Reconciliation should occur on three levels: (a) The judicial level of justice and legal law; (b) conscience and personal responsibility, and (c) faith, the spiritual and religious dimension. In the legal field (a) there is room for acknowledgment and punishment in court. This takes place in accordance with the laws of society. With reference to the religious and spiritual dimension of faith (c), one needs spiritual directors/coaches, pastoral counsellors or clergy/ministers where confession, repentance and penance could take place, and the relationship between the guilty one and God and all others concerned can be addressed. But the turning point of real repentance (on the level of authentic being) as a commitment to reconciliation, takes place within the conscience combined by a true sense of personal responsibility (b).

Our conscience

According to Buber, for guidance and counselling, one needs to consult the therapist. It should be noted that in Buber's time, there was still a great distinction between the spiritual director and the therapist. In our day, many pastors are professionally trained to operate as responsible counsellors.

That does not alter the fact that the third way of faith should certainly not be skipped! On the contrary, a pastor disposes of the language and vocabulary to assist man to face God. But this route is not necessarily the real reconciliation required by the victim. For Buber, this route implies a willingness to go to trial all the way through conscience.

The conscience is for Buber (1983:222) the ability to make a radical distinction between reasonable and unreasonable issues and events regarding past, present and future behaviour. It takes three phases to proceed from conscientious awareness to the phase of healing. It is important to reckon with three phases. However, they should not be treated as a step-by-step manual to be followed according to a fixed plan. The starting point is in fact the turning point where one must become reconnected to oneself. It is called *self-illumination/enlightenment*. To embark on this first route of repentance does not imply to slavishly follow imposed commands, prohibitions and restrictions that determine the direction for a continuous conscientiousness, stemming from tradition, cultural or social conventions and customs. On the contrary, the condition for self-insight and self-enlightenment implies detachment and distancing from the compulsion of strict stipulations.

In general, rules and laws depart from objective facts (sheer factuality), while self-reflection discovers the *I* as a subject. This discovery helps one to start thinking in terms of intersubjectivity. Regarding self-enlightenment, Buber refers to *the soul-searching endeavour probing into the inclinations of the heart by focussing the conscientious spotlight of honest self-confrontation on the unfathomable depths of guilt. This inner search discovers a guilt that reaches deeper than merely touching the violation of taboo's, habits or guilt feelings.* It is by looking into this existential and ontic realm that we encounter the shudder of the magnitude of our own existential guilt as manifested there. Guilt is then exposed together with all its startling connections. It awakens an awareness of one's own reality and dispositional make-up. Staring into this realm of self-exposure impels one to acknowledge and articulate this soulful experience in terms of a very raw, but very authentic confession: *I DID IT*, I am the guilty one! This confession of one's own reality opens up new avenues for radical reform, change and attaining a new attitude.

The deepest word in conscience is the wording and pronouncement: Here I am, *Hinéni*. This acknowledgement paves the way for proceeding to the second stage. This stage implies to hold on to the confession. It requires a willingness to persist in the realisation of real guilt and to be connected to those who suffer under the wrongdoings of the past, leading onto penitence! Acknowledgement and confession are not easy. In fact, they can become an even unbearable burden as the realisation dawns that with the confession of guilt, the ledger is not closed. Being guilty further implies that the indebtedness travels along through the whole lifespan of that person. It is by continuous persistence that the will grows to actually do something very concretely with the guilt. With the pronouncement: I am guilty, one takes the first step into the direction of contributing to real healing!

In the third stage of conscientiousness, Buber uses the word reconciliation. The latter comes into play when the ability becomes visible to contribute substantially to the restoration of the damaged order of being. This can be done in various ways. But the first movement should be in the direction of the person(s) concerned, to whom you owe. In addition to the victim (not instead of), and within an active commitment to the world, a wider scope regarding the display of indebtedness becomes feasible and could be realised. Wounds can be healed in countless other places, other than where they were struck. But the victim's guilt is a first inevitable course. According to Buber, only when reconciliation becomes a real option in the third phase of the process of conscientiousness, can one start talking about real forgiveness.

A master's student in South Africa argues that restoring confidence in the relationship is out of the question. "*You never arrive!*" In fact, you can never get to the place where the wounds were inflicted, where it all happened and started. During apartheid there was no real relationship between white, brown and black people in the sense of being responsible for each other. Since there was no confidence, we cannot speak of restoring confidence in the relationship. According to her, a transformation is needed on the way of coming to grips with conscience. With this remark she finds herself on the borderline of the second phase moving into the third phase. She is challenged within this tension of how to transit from perseverance in the sense of the realisation of guilt into the willingness to take concrete steps to make compensation for the outstanding indebtedness, to make good for guilt. And that was the constructive contribution of the Truth and Reconciliation Commission: It created a forum to articulate guilt properly. It also provided an opportunity to recognise and acknowledge the devastating and inhumane consequences of injustice captured by personal stories and confessions of debtors. But the process has often got astray and to a certain extent stuck to the first phase of personal acknowledgement: 'I did it.' Not everyone was prepared to proceed from perseverance and transformation to real compensation. In this way, anger and the plea and deep yearning for retribution and revenge remained echoing through all the painful stories.

Together with Buber, we discovered that forgiveness is a legal process that not only seeks repayment of what has been suffered, but also requires more personal insight to turn around, to change and transform relationships. Turnaround, conversion, as the willingness and ability to work towards responsibility for what is at issue in our immediate environment concerning the violation of human rights and human dignity, including taking into account the future of who is still to come, underlines a concrete fact in processes of relational healing, namely, that compensation and retribution do not suffice. More is at stake: The radical conversion to the ethics of fair and reliable acts of responsible engagement.

Van Rhijn and Meulink-Korf (1997:280; 2019:276) wrote as follows: "The individual is impeached and challenged as a single." In doing so, they emphasise once again the importance of being a subject; only this subject, and no other, can make a unique contribution to new configurations of justice within the dynamics of relational networking. The victim is also challenged to reach out from his/her vulnerability to the need of the other/others and not to withhold a gesture of establishing real forms of justice.

The route from guilt to forgiveness requires a procedure. It requires insight, recognition and willingness to become reliable. In the Bible, we also come across forgiveness as a course of justice in the history of Joseph and his brothers (the others). It tells about the long journey that the children of Jacob/ Israel took to become one community. Everything comes into play: The long waiting for the brothers to recognise evil, the feeling of Joseph for reliability and trustworthiness (*chēsēd*), including recognition and acknowledgement. Now that we know Buber's plea for the course of justice, we recognise this desperate need for the configuration of justice in the weal and woe of the brothers, which preceded the request for forgiveness. We, therefore, turn to the story of Joseph.

10.4 Joseph among his brothers

In Genesis 37–50 we read the long story about Joseph and his eleven brothers. They are all sons of Jacob, son of Isaac, son of Abraham. Jacob's two youngest children are the children of his most beloved wife Rachel. She died when Benjamin, the youngest, was born. Jacob loved Rachel dearly. It so happened that Joseph and Benjamin became the preferred children. Moreover, when Joseph received a multi-coloured cloak from his father Jacob, the whole sibling network became infected by jealousy and destructive prejudice amongst the ten older brothers.

Joseph reinforced this annoyance by talking about his dreams in which his older brothers had to bow down before him. Literally it says that the ten "hate him and are no longer able to speak to him in peace (*shalom*)" (Gen 37:4). And yet, Jacob sent his son Joseph to his brothers who were far in the fields of Shechem. Very noteworthy, he sent Joseph to pose specifically the question regarding their *shalom*. This did not seem very proper for the brothers and raised a big question: Why? What made their father send this kind of message of peace? This is indeed a quite logical and understandable question. However, the answer to this question we do not find in the Bible and have to leave it open, unanswered.

It must be a dramatic moment when the brothers saw Joseph approaching. No one wrote more moving about that moment than the writer Thomas Mann in his trilogy *Josef and his brothers*; he wrote about the bewilderment, the long-held rage that focused on Joseph (Mann 1997). Right there, on the spot, the ten brothers decided to kill Joseph. That decision created disagreement amongst them because Ruben, the eldest, proposed that it was better to throw him in a cistern rather than to kill him. Ruben wanted to bring this brother back to his father (Gen 37:22). However, they threw Joseph into the cistern, where he survived and did not die. For the time being, the brothers could relax and eat together in peace.

When a caravan passed by towards Egypt, the brothers sold Joseph to the Midianite merchants (Ishmaelites). The only one who objected was Ruben, the eldest. On Joseph's cloak, the brothers left traces of blood from a goat to give Father Jacob the impression that Joseph was killed by a ferocious animal. Jacob recognised Joseph's cloak, saw the blood and wept, grieving and mourning the death of his beloved son. He refused to be comforted and prefered to grow old with a broken heart. "In mourning will I go down to the grave to my son" (Gen 37:35).

Joseph in Egypt

In Egypt, Joseph entered the service of Potiphar, soon becoming the commander-in-chief of the Pharaoh of Egypt. Potiphar trusted Joseph. Until what happened? Until the wife of Potiphar entered the stage. She cunningly projected her own sexual desire on Joseph and said: "Come to bed with me" (Gen 38:7). Joseph refused. When she wanted to force him to sleep with her, he ran out of the house, leaving his cloak behind. By using his cloak, she insinuated that Joseph was guilty of adultery. So, Joseph ended up in prison.

Again, it was a dream that helped him on his way, a dream about an imminent famine. Miraculously, he was released from prison to work constructively and help fill the barns of Egypt with abundant grain. Thus, in the period of hunger, there will be abundance. There is so much abundance that anyone who suffered from this hunger across the borders of Egypt could come to fill sacks of grain, encountering Joseph who took care of the project and eventually became viceroy (governor of the land). Thus, Egypt became 'saved' and enriched by Joseph's constructive engagement with the predicament of the suffering people of Egypt.

The ten older brothers also ended up in Egypt, the abundant country, because of hunger. And now we have the irony. When Joseph's brothers arrived, they bowed down to him. Just as forecasted by his dream! Joseph immediately recognised them, but also became aware of the empty space of Benjamin, his full brother. This son Jacob kept with him (Gen 42:4). The brothers did not recognise Joseph. Joseph accused them of being spies. They totally denied the accusation and informed him about their family in Canaan. They referred to the youngest who was with his father while the other became lost. He decided to test them and requested to see that one brother (Gen 42:15 et seq). He put them all in custody for three days. What he wanted to do, was to test them regarding trustworthiness and loyalty (hēsēd). He did it by putting silver cups and money in the sacks of wheat, while keeping Simeon in captivity. Reuben offered his two sons as substitutes, and Judah offered himself as surety (he learned about surety in Genesis 38; see chapter 4). Again and again, the brothers proved to be reliable while in the meantime they wondered more and more whether all this had to do with the injustice they inflicted on Joseph. They became aware of their guilt. Struck by conscience their hearts sank and they turned to each other, trembling and said: "What is this that God has done to us?" In fact, their courage (lev = heart) faded away (Gen 42:28). So, with anguish in their heart, they returned to Jacob.

Again, hunger forced them to return to Egypt, and despite Jacob's broken heart, they now took Benjamin with them. When Joseph saw him, he was deeply moved but did not reveal himself yet. For another time, Joseph tested them on trustworthiness (hēsēd). This time the silver had been put into Benjamin's sack! When that was discovered, and they were brought before Joseph again, he threatened them by not letting Benjamin going back to Jacob.

But then Judah stepped forward and pleaded on behalf of his father Jacob. He said that when they would not bring Benjamin back to his father, he would eventually die: "Your servants will bring the grey head of our father down to the grave in sorrow" (Gen 44:31).

All together back in Egypt

At this moment in the narrative, there is a total turnaround. Judah's plea revealed their most inner inclinations. "Please let your servant remain here as my Lord's slave in place of the boy, and let the boy return with his brothers. How can I go back to my father if the boy is not with me?" (Gen 44:33-34). They moved from indebtedness to retribution and compensation, from achievement to sacrifice; to pay back the ledger by means of substitution.

At this moment Joseph could no longer control himself and maintain an aloof attitude. He started to weep so loudly that the Egyptians heard him (Gen 45:2; 14-15). He wept at two occasions and later for the third time. Joseph summoned them to come and live in the land of Goshen. He further commanded them to bring his father Jacob and all their families to settle down in the best of the land of Egypt.

When Jacob came to the end of his life, he blessed all the sons, one by one, after which he said in a very concrete way: "He drew his feet up into the bed, breathed his last and was gathered to his people" (Gen 49:33). After a long period of mourning, the brothers brought Jacob's body back to Canaan. They marched in a long procession and buried him in the cave of Machpelah, the resting place of Abraham (Gen 50:1-13).

And only then, when Father Jacob was dead and buried, when the brothers were back in the land of Egypt, the conscientious threat of their guilt regarding the injustice inflicted to Joseph, surfaced: "What if Joseph holds a grudge against us and pays us back for all the wrongs, we did to him?" (Gen 50:15). So, they sent word to Joseph, saying, "We ask you to forgive your brothers their sins and the wrongs we committed in treating you so badly." Quite remarkable, it is not directly the fear that drove them to ask for forgiveness, but their indebtedness to their father. Therefore, they decided to ask Joseph for forgiveness by making use of the words and instructions of their Father Jacob (Gen 50:16-17). What a long way to journey from acknowledging guilt, groping for reliability, willingness to atone, up to the plea for forgiveness!

The moving plea for forgiveness: Genesis 50:15-21

The biblical text:

> ¹⁵Realizing that their father was dead, Joseph's brothers said,
>> "What if Joseph still bears a grudge against us and pays us back in full for all the wrong that we did to him?"
>
> ¹⁶So they approached Joseph, saying,
>> "Your father gave this instruction before he died,
>>> ¹⁷'Say to Joseph: I beg you, forgive the crime of your brothers and the wrong they did in harming you.'
>>
>> Now therefore please forgive the crime of the servants of the God of your father."
>
> Joseph wept when they spoke to him. ¹⁸Then his brothers also wept, fell down before him, and said,
>> "We are here as your slaves."
>
> ¹⁹But Joseph said to them,
>> "Do not be afraid! Am I in the place of God? ²⁰Even though you intended to do harm to me, God intended it for good, in order to preserve a numerous people, as he is doing today. ²¹So have no fear; I myself will provide for you and your little ones."
>
> In this way he reassured them, speaking kindly to them.

Forgiveness: Weakness under cowardice

The encounter between Joseph and his brothers unfolds like a film. You see the image in front of you: Ten brothers groping for confidence and not knowing how to start. They shuffle and look for a start to speak, how to address Joseph. See how they are still hiding behind the father. He is introduced as 'the unsuspected third person' to speak for them. Thus, it becomes an intergenerational dialogue about death! The dialogical arrangement of the text clearly shows these direct and indirect dialogues infiltrating the whole family system and intergenerational interaction.

And then the very moving moment of disclosure. It is as if the whole drama proceeds to the dénouement. This moving moment started when the brothers saw that their father was dead. '*Seeing*' is remarkable because Jacob's funeral in his own country had been quite an undertaking. Seeing here must mean 'insight'; a kind of gaze that pierces through the veil of pretention. They started to consult and contemplate amongst one another fearing that Joseph would accuse them due to their indebtedness and evil inflicted on Joseph. So, they wrestled with the painful question: "What if Joseph holds a grudge against us and pays us back for all the wrongs, we did to him?' (Gen 50:15).

The brothers lined up for Joseph. Most texts here write that they 'approached' Joseph. But literally it was written as a command: ṣiw-wāh (a word that has been grammatically amplified [pi'el] with the meaning of a command, a direct order indicating to prepare for an assignment). According to the brothers, their father Jacob offered them that command (צִוָּה ṣiw-wāh). They began to speak to Joseph but not directly, not addressing him as a subject. They uttered the words in the name of their father: 'He would have told them'. However, this reference to Jacob and his ordering cannot be traced back as a written text in the entire Joseph story. Therefore, the following questions need to be posed to the brothers: Did they fear Joseph? Were they afraid that Joseph will take revenge and punish them? Did they merely fabricate the words of Jacob to use it a smokescreen to hide behind? Do they use their respect for Jacob as a shield? We do not know.

Whatever the intention with the reference to Jacob, their wording of fear and urge to meet with Joseph echoes a kind of acknowledging of guilt and insight in the evil inflicted on Joseph. It sounds like a direct confession for the first time. The evil they have done is in fact a 'violation of the law' (pesja). That is more than a crime. It is not simply the same as sin and guilt. In addition to injustice to a person, it also always involves a breach of the covenant of God and therefore a violation of a divine commandment. A breach of law implies a breach of confidence. Whoever commits a breach of law is no longer reliable to live within the space established by the covenant. The only way back will be insight and recognition, providing a significant route to recovery: "He who conceals his sins does not prosper, but whoever confesses and renounces them finds mercy" (Prov 28:13).

When we turn to the words of the father, the instruction should be read more as a request to address this violation of the law and the impact on the judicial framework than a confession. The father would have said: 'Lift up, give attention to the breach of law and the sin of the brothers.' Almost always this 'cancellation' or 'elevation', 'abolish', 'counteract' has been translated as 'forgiveness'. Literally there is an imperative of *nasja*: lifting, lifting up, carrying, relieving (*nasa* in Hebrew, depending on the spelling, can mean either 'he traveled', נסע, or 'he raised', נשא). Should we translate with 'forgive', then this should not have the meaning of undoing or washing away. The meaning rather indicates making space, making it lighter, making it portable. This *nasja* (lifting, do away with), we mainly encounter combined with sin, breach of law, guilt, prayer.

> In Greek, the verb *afièmi* is used for 'forgive', with the meaning of 'to let go, to lift up'. In Matthew 18:22-35, the question of forgiveness arises when Peter asks Jesus to forgive (let go) the sinner seven times. With this question Peter refers to the remark that Cain was avenged seven times and Lamech seventy-seven times (Gen 4:24). However, the point is that Jesus contrasts un-limited revenge, with unlimited forgiveness; to forgive in the sense of letting go. Forgiveness in the sense of 'to release' requires a different attitude than to let retribution continue. Nielsen writes in his commentary about the willingness for developing a disposi-tion of releasing the other from all forms of indebtedness: When that willingness disappears, one hits the bottom line; that is, the whole foundation for fellowship is taken away, the basic reason for maintaining interpersonal relationships in the congregation of the Lord, becomes disrupted (Nielsen 1973:126-127). In the text of Matthew, Jesus does not speak of forgiveness outright. It is more about return, giving back and to discharge somebody. Three times, the reference is to this act of returning and giving back, paying back, settling the account (*apodidōmi*, to deliver, to give away for one's own profit what is one's own, to sell; to give back, restore; to pay off, discharge what is due).

It is remarkable that the brothers in this pericope reframed the wording of their father in the mode of an imperative; they reframed the instruction of *nasja* into a command! And they made it even stronger by repeating the imperative: "Now please forgive the sins of the servants of the God of your father" (Gen 50:17). They emphasised the fact that Father Jacob's God, is also the God of Israel (see Genesis 32:28-29 where God gave Jacob the name Israel). In doing so, they indicate that they belong to the people of this God.

And then Joseph wept again. The surprising fact is that their words are no longer lip-service but have become enfleshed in an act (*debarim*). It is the third time that he wept (Gen 45:2, 14-15; 50:1). This crying is not due to self-pity but from a relational desire to become reconnected again. After these words, Joseph could no longer keep his distance and stay detached. Something new began. Levinas, the French philosopher, wrote about the meaning of Joseph's tears: *Vulnerability (weakness) deprived from cowardice is about the awakening of compassion.* It is about a human being becoming released from holding on to the pretence of being in control (Levinas 1990:33). The weakness/vulnerability without cowardice manifests itself in the reflection of the tears. Joseph has given up on life until then. He let go of the past for the sake of connection with his brothers (a relational connection). He let go of his reluctance to connect relationally. He let go and that is pre-eminently 'to lift, to carry' or to forgive. This release initiates an ethical movement that changes existence forever. Not simply. We know what preceded this process between Joseph and his brothers; this struggle to become reconnected again. In terms of Buber, this process is in fact a trial like in the court of consciousness.

The brothers were not yet experiencing the reversal into symmetry of reciprocity. Once again, they bowed asymmetrically deep, with their faces turned towards the earth. In fact, they offered themselves as Joseph's servants. But Joseph, in that moment, renounced power as viceroy to the brothers. They needed not to fear anymore. The point is, he did not think of himself as acting in the place of God. It was indeed God, who in his *hēsēd*, did not calculate in terms of revenge but, due to his mercy, turned the encounter into good. As a brother, Joseph was now able to provide for Jacob's people, the brothers and the children after them. Joseph deliberately said that he will provide, sustain them (אָנֹכִי אֲכַלְכֵּל אֶתְכָם). Within this framework, caring/providing/sustaining (*coel*) certainly has no authoritarian association here. Its meaning is more in the direction of 'keeping alive'. The special verb form only occurs in this magnificent narrative regarding the encounter between Joseph and his brothers (Gen 45:11, 47:12 and 50:21). The evil afflicted upon Joseph did not return in the boomerang of revenge. It did not continue in the form of a revolving slate.

The book of Genesis tells about the becoming of man, the effort to live as one community. Now there is one nation of Israel. Joseph will see three generations. His grandchildren will be born on his lap. He will stay with his people. When he faced his 'death bed', Joseph spoke of the God who will care and make them ascend to the land he had promised to give to Abraham, Isaac and Jacob. Joseph is embalmed by his brothers – and placed in a coffin – in Egypt! A new book could now be opened where the future will be determined by the phrase: From now on they will be called '*The people of Israel*' (*ha am*). A new king rose in Egypt. The Exodus of this people, from this country, is about to begin; a long journey before they will reach the promised land. And for two generations long, Joseph's bones (mummy) will be carried on a journey through the desert.

10.5 *Existential guilt and guilt feelings within the framework of exoneration: More than generosity (Nagy)*

Nagy takes existential guilt seriously and it is interwoven in his thinking and all his work. Guilt is related to his concepts: Loyalty, the balance of give and take, legacy, multi-directed partiality. For Nagy, *guilt* is non-transferable, it can never be reimbursed by anyone other than the one who is responsible for it. In line with Buber, *forgiveness* can also only be bestowed by the victim him/herself.

Existential guilt and feelings of guilt are distinguished but can become entangled. With that, Nagy leans on Buber. Feelings of guilt tell about an intrapsychic dynamic that is driven from elsewhere (Van Rhijn & Meulink-Korf 1997:324; 2019:308-312). Living with guilt feelings can become so confusing that it takes on neurotic traits. Neurotic guilt refers to a kind of unreal guilt in the sense that the impression of guilt is not in accordance with the actual event and the reality of the context. People suffer from guilt, which has a destructive effect on their own lives and that of others. That in turn, can present in existential guilt. It is up to the pastor and therapist to help reduce psychological guilt feelings and to connect these feelings to a real image of actual guilt. Reference to that guilt should not be a forced, artificial reproach, nor should it be a cheap and easy indemnification from being guilty.

Relational-ethical questioning helps to discover the difference. Questions regarding guilt and guilt feelings are in search for equity on the balance sheet of give and take. Careful weighing of the relational balance sheets is urgent with a view to their fairness and reasonableness. Guilt is always existentially and concretely reflected in existence, connected to the networking dynamics of relationships. It is even possible that guilt feelings can exist without existential guilt. It requires caution because having feelings of guilt can be a possibility of paying back for an alleged deficit, a motivation and a form of inappropriate giving. Guilt feelings that are not justified are sometimes used to claim victimhood. That is a form of objectifying the self. For caregivers, this requires a process of learning how to transpose oneself into the individualised space of subjectivity in order to discover the fairness of actual or not actual guilt. Ultimately, it leads to being able to attain appropriate responsibility in the relationship to the person(s) concerned. More than Buber, Nagy places emphasis on accountability and liability, owing and being obligated. Existential guilt almost always affects several people. Only everyone can determine what the consequences are for themselves and who belongs to them. A third party, no matter how trustworthy, cannot forgive the debtor for his/her debt, replacing the victim. Substitution would be an improper route to address the balances of give and take within the reciprocal dynamics between perpetrator(s) and victim(s).

In the same way as for Buber, existential debt is for Nagy guilt that is related to real life experiences of hurt and injustice. "Existential guilt is based on actual damaging righteousness of the human order" (Borzormenyi-Nagy & Krasner 1986:60; 1994:78). Existential guilt is *beyond psychology* and resides in the reality of being. Guilt as a culpability is the result of what has been done or failed to act according to normative directive of the *justice of the human order*. According to the ethics of relational interaction, one is obliged to the obligation of debt; that is, that which one owes the other and should be repaid. The measure of guilt does not reside in the question whether 'I feel guilty', but in the magnitude of the consequences for the other person, namely his/her suffering due to injustice.

As a family therapist, the focus in Nagy's approach is on that which is currently at stake between parents and children. The question is whether the intergenerational asymmetry of the relationship is safe and guarantees trust and reliability. The asymmetrical relationship is the basis for healthy reciprocal care, which includes irrevocably the mutual responsibility to attend to fair indebtedness.

Nagy's stance on forgiveness

For Nagy, the concept of forgiveness does not qualify as an appropriate category to translate relational-ethical language. There are several reasons, from which the most important is: "The act of forgiveness usually retains the assumption of guilt and extends the forgiver's generosity to the person who has injured him" (Boszormenyi-Nagy & Krasner 1986:416; 1994:478). It cannot be the case that guilt remains intact and unaffected. Guilt remains in the memory and goes as a reminder along to the future. By denying the relational seriousness and woundedness, the original guilt is further increased. In the case of a damaged relationship, it is for Nagy all about restoring human justice.

If the issues of hurt are not addressed properly, guilt travels along in the relationship. Nagy is also suspicious of ritual forgiveness, which is visible in religions when there is a liturgical act of forgiveness performed, or in the case of generalisations like the notion of collective forgiveness. That cannot take away the personal impact of relational guilt. It also runs the risk of skipping the concrete human being in his/her personal subjectivity. In this regard, Levinas argues that almighty forgiveness as exponent of the metaphysical understanding of divine grace is in fact inhumane, precisely because of the skipping and neglecting of the victim's autonomy (Van Rhijn & Meulink-Korf 1997:343; 2019:327). On the part of the victim, this happens when there is a case of forgiving too generously, too soon without appropriate insight into the complexity of guilt, and without being heard properly, and no acknowledgment that has been made. In effect, only the asymmetry between victim and perpetrator is increased, which can eventually become a reversal in the power play within the relational dynamic. It deprives the perpetrator of his/her responsibility and the opportunity to fair retribution which is in fact the accountability of the debtor.

Restoring justice is not about restoring a fixed order that was out there. Above all, to restore justice implies attending to a perspective based on newfound trust and the reframing of time which dawns upon the dynamic of intersubjectivity. The time there after can never be the same as the time before; there is a discontinuity, a breakthrough to timing as a new form of being. Future is unlocked and a different mode of the not-yet enters the realm of existential justice (Van Rhijn & Meulink-Korf 1997:341; 2019:235).

Nagy and Krasner address another possibility for the restoration of justice, which seems to reside mainly within the asymmetry as related to the intergenerational dynamics of familial relationships. In doing so, they seem to be mainly focused on how guilt is addressed in order to prevent destructive consequences for the next generation and possible damaging effects on the networking of future offspring.

Exoneration in the thinking of Nagy and Krasner

Nagy and Krasner introduced the concept of exoneration when it comes to guilt and indebtedness, and how to do justice to the relationship so that the balance sheet of giving and taking does not become stuck. To exonerate is a fairly unknown concept and unique in family therapy. It is originally a legal term, not so strange to Nagy because he grew up in a family of lawyers. The term occurs in business contracts that may include a clause describing liability for damage and shortage. In that clause, an exception can be made for full debt under certain conditions. Those conditions are described in the contract when circumstances are assessed fairly and liability is not fully charged. The term occurs in business contracts that may include a clause describing liability for damage and shortage. In that clause, an exception can be made for full debt under certain conditions. This is called an exoneration clause. Under this clause, the debtor is (partially) released from the burden of his/her debt.

Exoneration as relieving the debt of equity is an important possibility for Nagy within the dynamics of family relationships. Due to certain circumstances, the weight of guilt is fairly weighed and possibly charged less, which creates new space on the balance sheet of give and take. Nagy describes it as follows: "Exoneration is a process of lifting up the load of culpability off the shoulders of a given person whom heretofore we may have blamed" (Boszormenyi-Nagy & Krasner 1986:416, 1994:478). Exoneration is mainly an action from children to parent(s). "At the level of reasonableness and fairness, the creditor abdicates from his/her taking a position as a judge" (Van Rhijn & Meulink-Korf 1997:362; 2019:345). Even after the death of parents, an initiative can be taken to reassess guilt. This reassessment does not primarily say something about the parents' guilt, but about the indebtedness of children, owed to parents; that is, their responsibility to always act in a fair way. In this way, guilt is no longer a hindrance on the balance sheet of giving and receiving. It creates the opportunity for the earning of new forms of trust. Even the tendency to retaliate can now be abandoned. This certainly will serve the next generation. The merit of exoneration benefits the person who enters the process; it concerns the merit of reliability (constructive entitlement).

I remember a gentleman who had a rather negative criticism of his mother because, when he was still small, she was hardly ever at home when he came from school. In a way, it made him feel lonely and he struggled to establish long-term relationships. Many years later, he was still angry about it. He found it difficult to be there for her, now that his mother was suffering from dementia and became more dependent. In a pastoral conversation, he was advised to inquire from a sister of his mother whether she knew where his mother had always been. This aunt said that for many years, his mother stayed behind cleaning the school building to earn a small extra income. Since she did not want her son to be ashamed of her amongst his classmates for doing this kind of work, she never wanted to tell him. For the son, this conversation prompted a reappraisal and total reframing of the guilt he imputed to his mother. In this process of exoneration, the hope arises that the son would gain confidence to move openly on the balance of giving and receiving between him and his mother. It is important that he can now be responsible for owing her, and giving her the care she most needed. It thus became the expectation, that in this situation, the intergenerational asymmetry between mother and son will slowly become reversed. In the meantime, the fundamental asymmetry regarding mutual respect remains natural and will inevitably continue.

When parents are still alive and mentally healthy, it may happen that they can still dedicate themselves to fair and just acts towards their children. Thus, the asymmetrical relationship becomes authentic again and they, in turn, acquire merit. Exoneration is a risk in terms of the renewal of time. However, it reduces the chance that the outstanding bill becomes transferred to innocent third parties. For Nagy, this is all about justice. Reneé van Riessen writes that the fertile advantage of 'forgiven time' creates a different dynamic (Van Riessen 2019:75).

Exoneration is always triadic because it is a matter not only between children and parents, the next generation is also involved. After all, the revolving slate of retaliation and possible revenge no longer repeats itself. To be clear, exonerating is not an excuse, an emotional apology. It is about making the weight of existential debt lighter, according to justice and reasonability.

Parental guilt can be so great that a re-valuation cannot lighten the weight of guilt. Meulink-Korf and Van Rhijn refer to an example concerning the conflicting dilemma for children of Nazi parents who sympathised with Hitler (Boszormenyi-Nagy & Krasner 1986:181; 1994:212). This also applies to children of grandparents and parents who had had an active share in Apartheid and contributed to torture and exclusion. Parental guilt has an inhibitory effect. It is also related to shame. Their dilemma is how to be openly loyal to parents but, at the same time, to take fair responsibility for those who have been disadvantaged by them. "The legacy of ancestral shame and guilt requires redress and exoneration in so far as they are possible" (Boszormenyi-Nagy & Krasner 1986:182, 1994:213). The initiative for reparation (redress) must come from the parents. A child cannot repay their guilt.

Nagy is careful not to moralise and/or objectify guilt. About guilt, he remains, in principle, dialogically focused on the relational-ethical consequences of the violation. The consequences are addressed by weighing them relationally for possible retaliation, retaliation then not as revenge. For Nagy, retribution is relational. It concerns the question of who is accountable for guilt, whether retribution is fair and just, or not?

Right to retaliation

According to Nagy, retribution has several meanings. Meulink-Korf and Van Rhijn explain it extensively in *Appealing spaces* (Van Rhijn & Meulink-Korf 1998:304-328; 2019:292-312). Traditionally, retributive law has functioned as both rewarding and avenging law in society. Doing right was rewarded, doing wrong was punished. It was a clear legal order that ensured a reasonably healthy society. These regulations of the judicial order were usually dictated by a clear system and rules made by the state or by the power of the church, or by both. For example, a punishment for theft or murder could be a pilgrimage to a distant cathedral.

In the area where I grew up, in a water-rich delta area, several villages and cities have drowned in great floods. In the excavations in these drowned areas, thousands of small metal plates with the name of a cathedral have been found, sometimes more than 1 000 kilometres away, for example *Santiago de*

Compostella. These insignia tell about how around 1100 AD, the judicial and ecclesiastical power together organised guilt and punishment.

After the Enlightenment, the self-evident nature of this legal order disappeared. The church became less central and lost authority and power, making clarity about guilt and punishment more diffuse. This made it more difficult to recognise wisdom about guilt and punishment. Nagy writes: "To the extent that strict religious regulation of conduct diminishes in society, the question arises: What takes the place of belief in divine justice?" (Boszormenyi-Nagy & Spark 1973:72). Indeed, an intriguing question: What has taken its place? After all, a legal system without sanctions cannot exist. A certain amount of justice is needed in retaliation for the survival of those concerned, both for the victim and perpetrator. For Nagy, the aspect of 'justice for the sake of survival' applies in particular because of a fair reduction of the burden of that guilt for future generations. For him fairness is always connected to the regulative principle of multi-directed partiality. However, fairness does not mean that retaliation can be skipped. The point is that retaliation and retribution should always be directed by justice and fairness. Nagy opposes freedom as the escape route of always apologising and attempts to excuse oneself: *Tout comprendre c'est tout pardoner* (wanting to understand every-thing is having an excuse for everything). Real guilt includes actual sanctions, punishment, or penalty.

Nagy once referred to an event in which he was consulted in a prison for a woman who had murdered her child and was depressed (Dillen 2004:167) She felt guilty, but despite attempts from multiple psychological and psy-chiatric approaches to take away that guilt, her condition did not improve at all. That is how Nagy was consulted and approached for a counselling session. When he entered the room where she was waiting, the caregivers were watching on the other side of the one-sided, blinded window. She quickly said to Nagy: "I'm guilty for killing my child." Nagy immediately agreed to her guilt and confirmed her acknowledgement. The caregivers behind the window held their breath in shock. How dare one say such a thing? To their great surprise, a constructive conversation started between the woman and Nagy. She acknowledged her guilt because she felt recognised in her guilt. In fact, for blunt murder there is no excuse. Therefore, Buber clearly stated that real forgiveness starts with the very clear pronouncement and acknowledgement: I did it and no other!

Retributive and distributive justice

In addition to *retributive law*, Nagy also refers to *distributive law* (respectively *retributive and distributive justice*). In the literature we encounter some confusion when, in addition to *justice*, it is translated with *injustice* as well. When Nagy talks about justice, he means that righteousness is at stake and that this meaning must continually resonate very clearly. The term 'justice' is not used here as a philosophical abstraction or as a legal requirement. Relational justice, as we understand it, is rooted in trust and becomes liberated by truth (Krasner in Michielsen et al 1998:58-59). Catherine Ducommun-Nagy describes extensively both concepts, and the distinction between them, in her book *From invisible to liberating loyalty* (2008:73).

Distributive justice

We use distributive justice when we refer to that kind of justice in cases where damage or hurt has not been directly affected by another, like diseases, the pandemic of the corona virus, natural disasters like drought or flood, social injustice like racism and poverty, and war. These are events that offer one person opportunities for justice without being directly asked. Distributive justice can become complex indeed. Many questions could be raised without definite and direct answers. For example, the idea that the cake should be distributed fairly and voluntarily amongst all, but simultaneously there are differentiations in terms of those who perform more, and thus receive more. Or: Those who have less deserved to be favoured. In any case, the question of justice is at issue when it is decided who, unasked-for, will be given a share of adversity or prosperity and who will not. The concept of 'distributive justice' also reflects on how power is handled and who is responsible for its distribution. This can create a dialogue concerning what is fair and what is not, for whom it is more or less fair and how justice can still be done. What is not fair, but received by a person wholly at random, can be rendered as a distributive right. In other words: distributive injustice. In this case, it is not clear who caused the injustice or violation. The culprit is not accountable while the fact of the injustice continues to exist. Where often the reference is to 'pure bad luck', contextual theory refers to this kind of contradiction in justice as *distributive injustice*.

An example of *distributive justice/injustice* is the shooting down with a missile of the passenger plane MH-17 over the Ukraine in 2017. It was assessed as an act of war. This act killed 298 innocent people and caused indescribable suffering to all the next of kin. Despite the evidence, no acknowledgement of guilt took place. Nobody was prepared to take responsibility for this violent act. The trials started in March 2020, but the four accused never appeared. The recognition of this distributive injustice in terms of what had been suffered and is still to come has hitherto come from third parties. When this suffering and this effort are not rendered as sufficient, the injustice suffered by the victims becomes increased immensely.

Within families, distributive justice regarding what children received unsolicited as parents' burdens, is in fact distributive injustice. With long-term pampering and/or exploitation, parents let their own desires and interests take precedence over those of the child. The purpose of giving to the child is then merely meant to benefit the parents. The well-dressed child leaves the impression of having good parents. This, however, exceeds the child's autonomy and could be viewed as sheer exploitation, because it damages justice in a child's life. That is the reason why Nagy speaks in this case of distribution justice as distributive justice. Especially for a spoiled child, loyalty to the parent(s) is not about freedom, but an obligation that makes an open discussion virtually impossible.

Distributive justice is not the last word in the vocabulary of contextual therapy regarding the interplay between fairness-unfairness. More fundamental is the question of a dialogical approach in caregiving, thus the further necessary emphasis on multi-directed partiality. It is then about groping for relational openings, by those who acted under difficult circumstances in a very trustworthy and reliable manner. They are the people who offered sparks of hope. One can build on previous examples of reliability. They are in fact invitations to invest in new forms of trust; incentives to reinvest in new realisations of confidence. In this way, victims of distributive justice can gain more in terms of mutual interaction than merely becoming objectified into passive victims. Becoming merely a helpless victim is to be exposed to the loneliness of personal vulnerability; a victim role leaves someone alone in his/her vulnerability.

The question for the pastor and counsellor is how someone, despite injustice, learns to take responsibility for the fair balance of give and take in a constructive way. When that step cannot be taken, shortfalls can be wrongfully claimed from innocent third parties. Applying distributive justice runs the risk of switching to retaliatory justice as a revolving slate. And that causes guilt again.

Retributive justice

Retributive justice is at issue in the event of fair compensation for what the other person has done. Retributive justice applies to events that are the result of someone else's actions and where one or more culprit can be designated. This right is officially governed by legal rules in the interpretation of the law. Retaliation and retribution become involuntarily imposed as punishment or compensation. According to Nagy, this right to retaliation is significant in society to prevent disintegration.

Failure to recognise retributive justice manifests into destructive claims. This means that there is still a right to receive although nothing has been given. Michielsen writes in the explanatory notes to the contextual concepts: "... where someone does not receive what he/she is reasonably entitled to or where someone was not able to give or gave too much without receiving anything in return ... then retributive injustice is at stake" (Michielsen 1998:280). Michielsen points to retributive justice in the deficits on the balance of give and take. That is mainly and very specifically the case between generations; that is, there has been a shortage, trust and justice have been damaged, a child has not been able to give according to his/her own ability.

When parents demand too much from a child and cannot guarantee that this child will receive safe and fair treatment, because these parents have no other choice due to illness or war or other calamity from outside, then retributive justice comes into play. If this is not seen and recognised as an injustice in the life of not only the parents, but also in the life of this child, it will continue as a revolving slate in the form of retributive justice into subsequent generations. With reference to the intergenerational revolving slate, Ducommun-Nagy points out the importance of exoneration (2008:75). Parents may previously have to deal with injustices of which the shortages have not been seen and heard. Multi-directed partiality helps to make it possible to openly discuss how these unarticulated forms of wrongdoings affect justice and injustice on everyone's balance sheet of giving and receiving.

Other than distributive justice, retributive justice does operate with the notion of a guilty party. Sometimes the inflicted evil is openly visible and sometimes not. With sexual abuse, there can be a good reason for the victim to conceal this suffering by, for example, sparing the guilty parent or to keep the family together (parentification) This kind of hiding experienced hurt, could become a heavy burden indeed. With concealment the child causes him/herself new modes of suffering. Another victim could aggressively pass on the injustice to third parties. "Nagy emphasises that out of destructive justice, perpetrators often become blindfolded to the suffering they inflicted on others" (Dillen 2004:141).

Retributive justice often degenerates into destructive merit that calls for retribution. This is especially true in cases where there has been no possibility of 'speaking directly' or groping for dialogue. How retributive justice continues is recognisable in children where the lives of parents have been wronged in an unjust manner and now they want to claim that injustice substitutionary. One can hear this urge and desperate yearning in Palestinian youth, crying out for revenge over the humiliation of their parents. See how young people in South Africa are still destructive because injustice and humiliation of parents have not been concretely recognised and paid back. Nagy points out that attention for retributive justice, which should especially be guaranteed by the secular legal system, is unfortunately receiving less and less attention (Dillen 2004:141).

In *Between give and take*, Nagy and Krasner point out how retributive justice exists in children with a congenital defect or chronic illness, who in fact got it unsolicited (Boszormenyi-Nagy & Krasner 1986:388-389; 1994:445-446). No culprit can be identified. The child depends on third parties for help and assistance so that the retaliation cannot be recovered, responded to, or become projected towards someone or something else. That is already enough reason for destructive entitlement. A sick child has more to bear than the adult or parent because, already at a very early age, that child is responsible for necessary measurements that are not appropriate for his/her age. A great contribution from Nagy is that he gives attention not only to the bearer, but also to what it implies for the balance sheet of giving and receiving of all family members and relatives concerned. Retributive justice makes an appeal on all of them to help share the burdens proportionately, including the dependent child precisely because by giving and receiving, constructive merit is attained.

Hope on the renewal of time

The theme of guilt repeatedly confronts us with our mission in pastoral care and counselling. The importance of it requires carefulness because it always involves a next generation. We must relate to it because we are responsible for guiding the process. We are not responsible for the processes of forgiveness and/or exoneration ourselves. "No one can organise forgiveness or operationalise it in pastoral care or therapy. The work of forgiveness and exoneration is carried in all sobriety by the hope of renewal of time. But this stance implies a kind of hope that is not accompanied by illusion" (Van Rhijn & Meulink-Korf 1997:369). This hope is not a dream, not an abstraction that creates false expectations. It is about a renewal of lived time and anticipates the not yet of still outstanding time, which is viable due to the balance of giving and receiving. This mode of renewed timing occurs amid the most ordinary happenstances of daily living and that provides the most hopeful signs for investing fairness and justice in the here and now of *presencing*.

Towards a hopeful approach

Guilt, forgiveness, relieving the weight of guilt, these are intensive processes that cannot move without a real dialogue. Dialogue is the ontic function of creative hope within reliable intersubjectivity. Real dialogues overcome barriers and nurture trust between generations, relatives, partners, friends and colleagues. Trust is the breath in human existence.

With the experience and development of his contextual therapy, Nagy wanted to contribute to a more equitable justice within families. To this end, Buber's dialogical approach provides a positive perspective, especially where trust between people has been violated. Every person is woven into a relational-ethical context of sometimes more and sometimes less reliability. But every day there are sparks of reliability that spring up on all those dynamic balances of giving and receiving from people, contributing to the justice of the human order.

I want to conclude with one of the most beautiful biblical stories about suffering, repentance and regained confidence in the future. Thus, the encounter between a patient, listening God and a suffering human being deprived from all his crutches in life: The moving, but encouraging encounter between a caring God and a lamenting Job.

10.6 Encouraged to encounter: Job invites guests at the table!

The road to a new beginning requires courage to regain confidence in the brokenness of existence and to connect with the future. That is not possible without that unique network of relationships in which we connect every person. It is in the movements of giving and receiving that every human life is significant, whatever happens. In joy and joyful connection and when relationships break, even when disasters break out over life, the contribution of every person matters. But how does man keep perspective in uncertain times? As an invisible power, the Covid-19 virus threatens so many people's lives, both in terms of health and income, survival and security of bread, the questions of meaning arise all over the globe.

In the biblical story of the life of Job, we find all challenging aspects of lived life. Man's struggle to live meaningful even when everything is different; our human endeavour in order to keep an eye on the future; our struggle to become align with the Ultimate in life; all the existential endeavours that determine significant existence. For Job, all who belong to him, and to whom he belongs, are cut off from him by death and great disasters: his wife, his ten children, his fields, his cattle, his wealth, his health. He hit the bottom line of nothingness.

Job's story is still relevant today because it intrigues the questions about the justice of suffering. Friends come over to Job who, in long conversations, try to merge the bleak future of a human being on a rubbish dump with causative explanations for disasters and suffering. As often, voices of neighbours seek refuge in explanations of cause and effect. Job's patience is now being put to the test because he finds no answer in their good intentions.

But what about Job's God? Is God indifferent? The fact is, God kept quiet for quite a long time before a divine voice broke into the silencing space of human rubbish and sheer brokenness. And the voice of a listening God and a complaining human being met within the dialoguing encounter about the mystery of life and the fear of loss. God spoke to him from the thunderstorm, Job responded from the torment of anguish. God took Job, as it were, on a tour regarding the secrets of creation. And this is how the conversation between a divine Tour Guide and a heuristic human being started. In that journeying together, God brainstormed Job with dozens of questions pointing to a different order, one of which Job was totally ignorant. In opening those secrets, one thing became crystal clear: The ignorance of man to explain everything and to be able to understand everything. To discover this kind of 'sacred wisdom' is to make a detour around the cul de sac of human suffering. Perhaps, could it therefore be that even not-knowing is a mode of answering?

By showing Job the world beyond his scope of empirical observation, it appeared as if God is up to game play. However, it is not about game play but about the agony and ecstasy of our being human. God is indeed divinely serious because God addressed him as the Other. The intriguing questions and exposure to most fascinating cosmic sceneries made Job look up from his monologue about his own suffering. We usually say: It never rains but it pours. Suddenly all the soul-revealing questions poured upon Job, one after the other: Job, if *you* know how well life works, if you think you are wise and should be able to explain the reasons for your suffering and injustice, please be fair and answer me! Have you ever started the dawn of one morning in your life with an upcoming glow of red, yellow, indigo, greyish blue and gleaming silver? If you know so well, I beg you, please tell me? Have you ever undertaken a trip, touring the treasure rooms of hail? Can you show me the brightness of flashing lightning?

These are questions that put Job's wisdom about the cause of his decline into a new perspective. No, Job did not receive a rational answer from God to the why of suffering. Why not? Because God is not like some scientific researchers and academic professors with satisfying explanatory theories in order to achieve a degree on cosmic disclosures. On the contrary, with his questions, God removed Job from himself as the centre of the world amidst his suffering. By all these questions, we are ushered as frail human beings from the podium of a lecturing hall to the devastating space and place of global trash, sitting next to a desperate human being *in dust and ash*. Job discovered that his being is but a fragment of the bigger picture, one small piece within the cosmic puzzle of amazing mysteries. By becoming connected to a greatness and magnitude beyond his understanding, he discovered that he relates to a non-finite part of creation and cosmic expansion. His existence is more than the result of cause and effect, moving from one disaster to another. Despite sheer rubbish, trash, anguish and pain, there is a mystical connection (Levinas: 'metaphysical mystique'; *désir métaphysique*). In all of creation, there is an interconnectedness as cohesive factor that points, most of times in a very paradoxical way, to wholeness within brokenness.

Abel Herzberg wrote a play about Job in which the main character, Salomon Zeitscheck, struggles. He was a simple tailor before the *Second World War* and lost all his family members during the Nazi regime. He worries about guilt and punishment (the occupiers) and punishment without guilt (himself). He wrestled with causal quests. Solomon eventually learned to discover connectedness in faith, hope, and love: "There is a word in every word that belongs to the unspeakable; in every part there is a part of the indivisible whole, equal in every kiss, despite the shortness of life and the display of mortality. Everything who and what we are and what we do is but a fragment within the bigger picture of a cosmic whole" (Herzberg 1991).

Job recalled all his complaints, the suffering supersedes the paradigms of his limited mind: "Surely I spoke of things I did not understand, things too wonderful for me to know" (Job 42:3). Until then, the possible cause of all his suffering was outside of him, or perhaps only inside his psychic turmoil. Albeit, what would be the difference? It was impossible for him to differentiate clearly. The fact he had to face was: He was in a sackcloth and ashes. Until? Until God reframed Job's perception from a finite gaze into the brilliance of an infinite gaze. Job's turnaround followed, the magnitude of transformation, from frailty to wholeness. He started to take responsibility, moving his disposition from being merely a victim to promoting life by committing himself to the enrichment of life, together with the other/Other in cooperating coexistence.

It is quite amazing, suddenly before him is, so to speak, a set table. How touching and relational-ethically, imaginative, is this new vision! Before him is prosperity, receiving twice as much as he had before. His cup is running over. Job invited guests: All brothers and sisters and friends. And see where this table is bedecked: *On dust and ashes* (Job 42:6, 11). That requires turning around (*tesjoeva*)! The remains of the disasters are certainly still there. The scars are permanent. But Job is no longer overcome with it. It does not prevent him from living, sharing life relationally. He dwells in joy together with his loved ones at a table where he is sharing, distributing, giving!

The surprising thing is that Job's story does not end here. Job's life resumes, although the time after it is not quite the same as before. Job received back from God everything that was lost. Strikingly different: He received everything back, but twice! Double numbers of animals, sheep, camels, cattle, donkeys. Job also received seven new sons and three new daughters and hear how he named his three girls, fairy-tale names, they are so sweet to him: Pigeon, Cinnamon Blossom and Powder Box! How did he manage to fabricate and coin these extraordinary names and regain courage to face life anew? But beware, the story is not about a fairy tale! It is indeed true that Job received everything back, double, but remember, except the children! He lost ten children but now there are ten 'new children'. All together twenty. But how is such a calculation possible? Without any to-do, fuss or checking the number with a calculator, the ten dead children were counted wordlessly together with the ten living. The dead are not left behind in the graveyard of a past tense, they too remain part of the bigger picture, interconnected in the renewal of eschatological time.

That is what the arithmetic of amazing grace is about. "There is a word in every word that belongs to the realm of the unspeakable."

Whatever happens, do not sing 'Que sera, sera, whatever will be, will be', but: Set a table and share, reach out, give – abundantly!

Bibliography

Banon, D 1987. *La lecture infini*. Paris: Seouil.

Boszormenyi-Nagy, I & Spark, G 1973. *Invisible loyalties*. Hagerstown: Harper & Row.

Boszormenyi-Nagy, I & Krasner, B 1986. *Between give and take: A clinical guide to contextual therapy*. New York, NY: Brunner/Mazel.

Boszormenyi-Nagy, I & Krasner, B 1994. *Tussen geven en nemen: Over contextuele therapie*. Translator N Bakhuizen. Haarlem: De Toorts.

Boszormenyi-Nagy, I 1987. *Foundations of contextual therapy: Collected papers*. New York, NY: Brunner/Mazel.

Boszormenyi-Nagy, I 1995. Interview with Ivan Nagy, on 20 January 1995 (not published). The manuscript refers to the original English text. In the text there will be one citation from the Dutch text by authors. There is no hard copy, only field notes taken by the researchers. This text is differentiated from the 20/1/1992 text by its date: 20/1/1995.

Boszormenyi-Nagy, I 2000. *Grondbeginselen van de contextuele benadering*. Translator N Barkhuizen. Haarlem: De Toorts.

Brown, RE 1966. *The Gospel according to John I-X!! A new translation and commentary*. (Anchor Bible). New York, NY: Double Day.

Buber, M 1952. *At the turning: Three addresses on Judaism*. New York, NY: Farrar.

Buber, M 1957. Guilt and guilt feelings. *Psychiatry: Interpersonal and Biological Processes*, 20(2):114-129.

Buber, M 1964. *De weg van de mens*. Translator Louise de Moor. s'Gravenhage: Boucher.

Buber, M & Rosenzweig, F 1981. *Die fünf Bücher der Weising*. Heidelberg: Verlag Lambert Schneider.

Buber, M 1983. Schuld en schuldgevoelens. In M Buber, *Adam, waar ben je?* Translator T de Bruin. Hilversum: Folkertsmastichting voor Talmudica.

Buber, M 1990. Hope for this hour. In M Buber, *Pointing the way: Collected essays*. Translator MS Friedman. Amherst: Prometheus Books.

Burggraeve, R 2002. Violence and the vulnerable face of the other: The vision of Emmanuel Levinas on moral evil and our responsibility. *Journal of Social Philosophy*, 30(1):29-45.

Cassuto, U 1998. *A commentary on the Book of Genesis. Part one*. Jerusalem: Magnes Press, The Hebrew University.

Childs, BS 1991. *Exodus*. London: SCM.

Coetzee, JM 2007. *Dagboek van een slecht jaar*. Translator Peter Bergsma. Amsterdam: Cossee.

Colpaert, M 2007. *Tot waar beide zeeën samenkomen: Verbeelding, een sleutel tot intercultureel opvoeden*. Heverlee: Lannoo.

Den Dulk, M 1998. *Vijf kansen: Een theologie die begint bij Mozes*. Zoetermeer: Meinema.

Derrida, J. 2019. Jacques Derrida (1930-2004). https://www.youtube.com/watch?v=RgLDHbF3lr0). Accessed on 6 December 2019.

Deurloo, KA 1994. Studies in Deuteronomy. In F Garcia Martinez (ed.), *The one God and all Israel in its generation: Honour to CJ Labuschagne on the occasion of his 65th birthday*. (supplement to *Vetus Testamentum* 53). Leiden: Brill.

Dillen, A 2004. *Ongehoord vertrouwen: Ethische perspectieven vanuit het contextuele denken van Ivan Boszormenyi-Nagy*. Antwerpen: Garant.

Duby, G 1979. *Saint Bernard, l'art cistercien*. Paris: Flammarion.

Ducommun-Nagy, C 2008. *Van onzichtbare naar bevrijdende loyaliteit*. Translator M Michielsen. Leuven: Acco.

Feuerbach, L 2020. Feuerbach, Ludwig (1850). The natural sciences and the revolution (*Die Naturwissenschaft und die Revolution*), http://www.eoht.info/page/The+Natural+Sciences+and+the+Revolution. Accessed on 22 May 2020.

Friedman, M 1995. *Martin Buber: The life of dialogue*. Chicago, IL: The University of Chicago Press. Used edition from Religion Online, http://www.religion-online.org/cgi-bin/relsearchd.dll/showbook?item_id=459 (3 of 6). Accessed on 15 January 2019.

Gathogo, J 2008. Some expressions of African hospitality today. *Scriptura* 99:275-287.

Gobodo-Madikizela, P 2003. *Veroverde vergeving; Oog in oog met de killer Eugene de Kock*. Translator Meile Snijders. Amsterdam: Balans.

Hermkens, L 1998. Broers en zussen: Een dynamische balans. In M Michielsen et al (ed), *Leren over leven in loyaliteit: over contextuele hulpverlening*. Leuven: Acco, 157-179.

Herzberg, A 1991. *Drie rode rozen*. Amsterdam: Querido.

Jagersma, H & Vervenne, M 1992. *Inleiding in het Oude Testament*. Kampen: Kok.

Jagersma, H 1995. *Genesis, verklaring van de Hebreeuwse Bijbel*. Nijkerk: Callenbach.

Krasner, BR & Joyce, AJ 1995. Truth, trust and relationships: Healing interventions. In *Contextual Therapy*. New York, NY: Brunner & Mazel.

Krasner, B & Joyce, AJ 1998. Elementen van toegewijde verbintenis. In M Michielsen et al (ed), *Leren over leven in loyaliteit*. Translators A van Rhijn & H Meulink-Korf. Leuven: Acco, 51-80.

Krog, A 1998. *Country of my skull*. Cape Town: Penguin Random House.

Levinas, E 1969. *Het menselijk gelaat*. Translator Ad Peperzak. Baarn: Ambo.

Levinas, E 1990. *Humanisme van de andere mens*. Translated with notes by ATh Peperzak. Kampen: Kok Agora.

Levinas, E 1990. *Vier talmoedlessen*. Translator C Quené. Hilversum: Gooi en Sticht.

Mann, T 1997. *Joseph und seine Brüder*. Frankfurt am Main: Fischer Taschenbuch Verlag GmbH.

Meulink-Korf, H & Van Rhijn, A 2002. *De onvermoede derde: Inleiding in het contextueel pastoraat*. Zoetermeer: Meinema.

Meulink-Korf, H & Van Rhijn, A 2016. *The unexpected third: Contextual pastoral care, counselling and ministry: An introduction and reflection*. Translator N Visser. Wellington: Christelike Lektuurfonds.

Michielsen, M et al 1998. *Leren over leven in loyaliteit: Over contextuele hulpverlening*. Leuven: Acco.

Mkhize, VV 2009. *Umsamo: The new African business literacy*. Randburg: Knowress.

Naastepad, ThJ 2004. *Verborgen midden: 2 Samuël. Uitleg van de boeken Samuël, 2*. Kampen: Kok.

Nielsen, JT 1973. *Het Evangelie van Mattheus, Deel II*. (PNT) Nijkerk: Callenbach.

Nouwen, H 2009. *Eindelijk thuis*. Tielt: Lannoo.

Oosterhuis, H & Van Heusden, A 1999. *In den beginne: Het boek Genesis*. Amsterdam: Prometheus.

Ouaknin, MA 2001. *De tien geboden*. Translator MTh Kunstenaar. Amsterdam: Boom.

Rosenstock-Huessy, E 1950. *Der Atem des Geistes*. Frankfurt am Main: Verlag der Frankfurter Hefte.

Rosenstock-Huessy, E 1963. *Die Sprache des Menschengeschlechts: Eine leibhaftige Grammatik in vier Teilen*. Heidelberg: Schneider.

Rosenstock-Huessy, E 1996. *Ik ben een onzuivere denker.* Translator Ko Vos. Aalsmeer: Dabar-Luyten.

Rosenstock-Huessy, E 2003. *Het wonder van de taal.* Translator R Kooijman. Vught: Skandalon.

Rozenzweig, R 1987. *Solidarität mit den Leidenden im Judentum.* Berlin/New York, NY: De Gruyter.

Sacks, J 2005. *To heal a fractured world: The ethics of responsibility.* New York, NY: Random House.

Sacks, J 2016. *Een gebroken wereld heel maken: Verantwoordelijkheid leven in tijden van crisis.* Translator H van der Heiden. Vught: Skandalon.

Sacks, J 2019. *Exodus,* Translator K van Klaveren. Middelburg: Skandalon.

Storm, M 2006. *Adamah, levensgrond.* Delft: Eburon.

Thesnaar, CH 2001. Die proses van heling en versoening: 'n Pastoraal-hermeneutiese ondersoek van die dinamika tussen slagoffer en oortreder binne 'n post-WVK periode. Ongepubliseerde proefskrif ingelewer vir die graad Doktor in die Teologie aan die Universiteit Stellenbosch.

Thesnaar, CH 2019. A divine discomfort: A relational encounter with multi-generational and multi-layered trauma. Inaugural lecture delivered on 12 June 2019 at the Faculty of Theology, Stellenbosch University.

Tutu, D & Tutu, M 2014. *Het boek van vergeving: In vier stappen naar harmonie met onszelf en de ander.* Translator C van den Berg. Houten/Antwerpen: Het Spectrum.

Van Doorn, N 2003. De gave schepping en het rauwe kwaad. In Rens Kopmels & Ad van Nieuwpoort (eds), *Terug tot Barth! Elf theologen over de actuele betekenis van Karl Barth.* Delft: Eburon, 134-148.

Van Doorn, N 2007. Zegen mij met geduld. In M Thans (ed), *Uit betrouwbare bronnen.* Zoetermeer: Meinema, 113-128.

Van Doorn, N & Meulink-Korf H. 2009. Het vijfde woord in contextueel pastoraal perspectief. *Interpretatie,* 17(8):7-9.

Van Doorn, N 2016. Spreken is zilver, dialoog is goud: Profetisch spreken. *Vakblad voor Contextuele Hulpverlening,* 21(4):21-25.

Van Doorn , N 2019. Toedelend onrecht … wat bedoel je er mee? *Contextuele Berichten,* 24:14-18.

Van Onselen, C 1976. *Chibaro, African mine labor in Southern Rhodesia, 1910-1933.* London: Pluto.

Van Rhijn, MA & Meulink-Korf, JN 1997. *De context en de Ander: Nagy herlezen in het spoor van Levinas met het oog op pastoraat.* Zoetermeer: Boekencentrum.

Van Rhijn, MA & Meulink-Korf, JN 2019. *Appealing spaces, the ethics of humane networking: The interplay between justice and relational healing in caregiving.* Translator DJ Louw. Wellington: Bybelkor.

Van Riessen, R 2019. *Van zichzelf bevrijd: Levinas over transcendentie & nabijheid.* Amsterdam: Sjibbolet.

Verwoerd, W 2018. *Bloedbande: 'n Duister tuiskoms.* Kaapstad: Tafelberg.

Wieseltier, L 2000. *Kaddisj.* Translator Tinke Davids. Amsterdam: De bezige Bij.

NOTES

NOTES

NOTES

NOTES

NOTES

NOTES

NOTES

NOTES

NOTES

NOTES

CPSIA information can be obtained
at www.ICGtesting.com
Printed in the USA
BVHW051012241220
596449BV00008B/604

9 781776 160587